# STRUCTURED ASSEMBLER LANGUAGE FOR IBM MICROCOMPUTERS

Alton R. Kindred

HBJ

Harcourt Brace Jovanovich, Publishers
and its subsidiary, Academic Press
San Diego  New York  Chicago  Austin  Washington, D.C.
London  Sydney  Tokyo  Toronto

# PREFACE

Most students are first introduced to computer programming through high-level languages, such as BASIC, Pascal, or COBOL. These languages are designed to simplify the student's task of expressing a problem to be solved. Yet, these languages are far removed from the machine language in which the computer must be instructed to do its work. High-level languages commonly are used for most application programming. Thus, both in their academic work and subsequent jobs most students will be concerned primarily with high-level languages. So you might well ask, "Why study assembler language?"

## REASONS FOR STUDYING ASSEMBLER LANGUAGE

Assembler language provides a number of benefits to the student, regardless of the eventual language in which programming is actually done. In more than 25 years of teaching I have observed that those students who are familiar with assembler language learn other languages faster and perform far better than those who have not learned assembler. Some of these benefits include the following:

1. A knowledge of the internal functions of the machine that utilizes assembler language.
2. An awareness of alternate choices of instructions to accomplish various operations.
3. A better understanding of how the functions of high-level languages are converted to specific machine instructions.
4. An ability to write subprograms for special purposes not available in high-level languages.
5. A detailed understanding of address modification, register operations, and other functions common to many languages.
6. An ability to diagnose object code and analyze core dumps in debugging.
7. An ability to implement an understanding of the hardware features of one machine as a basis for studying the capabilities of other machines.

## FEATURES OF THIS TEXTBOOK

This book is aimed primarily at the college-level student. It meets most of the objectives of the CS 3 course in ACM Curriculum '78. However, its pace and abundant examples make it understandable to anyone familiar with one of the high-level languages, such as BASIC or Pascal. Access to a computer compatible with the IBM PC or PS/2 is important.

The book employs many techniques to design and write correct programs. Structured programming is demonstrated and practiced throughout. Initially, program design is shown in flowchart form, pseudocode, and assembler language. Later, the flowcharts are eliminated and pseudocode appears as comments in the assembler source statements.

Each type of program structure—sequence, repetition, and selection—is clearly identified by the use of names such as IF, THEN, ELSE, ENDIF, WHILE, WEND, REPEAT, and UNTIL. Consistent use of these names helps to ensure proper structure.

Programs begin with simple input/output operations involving character data and gradually move on to arithmetic, number conversions, binary arithmetic, address modification, and table handling. Later chapters deal with subprograms, advanced arithmetic operations, macro definitions, linking assembler language programs to other languages, and control of the video screen for monochrome and color adapters.

Data types and machine instructions are introduced only as needed and immediately utilized in examples and sample programs. Detailed summaries are presented in the appendices.

Instructions are included not only for the original 8088 processor but for the newer 80186, 80286, and 80386 processors.

## ORGANIZATION OF THE TEXTBOOK

I recommend that the 14 chapters in the book be studied in the sequence they are presented. However, certain chapters may be omitted or taken in a different sequence if desired.

Chapter 1 presents fundamental computer terminology, functions, and concepts and treats binary and hexadecimal arithmetic operations. It also introduces DEBUG as a tool for examining main storage and analyzing the execution of instructions.

Chapter 2 explains the roles of the assembler, linker, and EXE2BIN program and shows the differences between COM and EXE programs. It describes the organization and purpose of each program segment and explains the types of statements that appear in assembler language.

Chapter 3 presents both DOS and BIOS interrupts for input/output operations and for handling the screen display.

Chapter 4 introduces the structured programming conventions to be used with assembler language and shows how to implement the program logic through the use of conditional branching. Nested structures and compound conditions are included.

Chapter 5 covers arithmetic and logical operations and presents useful routines to convert data entered as characters from the keyboard to numeric form for internal operations. Then it shows how to convert binary numbers back to character form for display on the screen.

Chapter 6 discusses operation of the stack and both internal and external subroutines. A library of useful subroutines is created and placed in a library for use throughout the rest of the book.

Chapter 7 presents the different addressing modes and demonstrates address modification for processing strings and tables.

Chapter 8 covers advanced techniques for doing arithmetic on multiple words and converting long strings of digits from the keyboard into multiple words in storage. Binary-coded decimal operations are also presented.

Chapter 9 presents the string handling instructions with the direction flag and repeat prefixes. The sample program uses the bubble sort technique.

Chapter covers disk file operations using DOS interrupts. Data organization with structures and records is also presented.

Chapter 11 demonstrates macro definitions, repeat blocks, equates, and conditional assembly. A useful library of macros is furnished. The sample program presents the insertion sort technique.

Chapter 12 contains many advanced assembler control features and directives not treated elsewhere in the text. It also presents the new simplified segment definitions introduced with MASM 5.0 by Microsoft, Inc.

Chapter 13 shows how assembler language routines may be linked to other languages. Two programs are presented for each of four languages: Pascal, FORTRAN, BASIC, and C. Parameters are passed from the programs in each language to an assembler language routine, and results are returned to the calling program.

Chapter 14 covers BIOS interrupts that service the video display screen, as well as placement of data and attributes directly into video memory. Sample programs provide work with both monochrome and color/graphics adapters.

Appendices include answers to exercises; the complete list of ASCII codes; instruction summaries for the 8088, 80186, 80286, and 80386 processors; flag settings; all directives available in the MASM 5.0 assembler; reference information for EDLIN, DEBUG and DOS; and a glossary.

Each chapter contains a statement of objectives, numerous illustrations, and one or more complete illustrative programs. Each chapter ends with a summary, review questions, exercises, and lab programming problems.

All programs in the text have been tested using MS-DOS 3.20 and MASM 5.0.

## SUPPLEMENTAL MATERIALS

An Instructor's Manual is available with teaching suggestions and a large bank of test questions. The test questions and answers are also available on disk with software to produce tests to the instructor's specifications. Also available is a program disk giving source statements and executable files of all demonstration programs in the book. Macros and subroutines shown in the text have been grouped into libraries for easier use.

## ACKNOWLEDGMENTS

Many people have contributed to the development and production of this book. Students in my classes of various assembler languages over 28 years have provided a means of testing the approach used here, particularly the use of pseudocode in comments to facilitate structured programming. And my colleagues at Manatee Community College have offered countless examples and suggestions.

Richard J. Bonacci, of Harcourt Brace Jovanovich, oversaw the development of the book from its outset with constant encouragement and careful review. Lynn Edwards provided meticulous editing and guided the transition of manuscript to finished textbook.

The manuscript in its several stages of development was reviewed by Bohdan Stryk, DeVry Institute, Phoenix; Donald Gustafson, Texas Tech University; Jim Leone, Canisius College; Martin Kaliski, California State Polytechnic University, San Luis Obispo; John D. Meinke, Allentown College of St. Francis de Sales; Russell C. Hollingsworth, Tarrant County Community College; Walter Chesbro, Santa Rosa Junior College; Al Clare, Youngstown State, Youngstown, Ohio; Raymond Bell, University of Texas, El Paso; and David Miller, Bemidji State University. I am grateful for the numerous suggestions that came out of their own classroom needs and experiences.

Throughout the entire project, my devoted wife, Joy, has remained a constant source of inspiration and encouragement, and to her I am deeply grateful.

Alton R. Kindred

# CONTENTS

## INTERRUPTS    58

**3**

## PROGRAM LOGIC AND CONTROL    75

**4**

## STRING INSTRUCTIONS    201

**9**

## DISK FILE HANDLING, STRUCTURES, AND RECORDS    216

**10**

## MACRO DEFINITIONS AND CONDITIONAL ASSEMBLY    237

**11**

## ADVANCED ASSEMBLER CONTROL    270

**12**

## LINKING ASSEMBLER LANGUAGE TO OTHER LANGUAGE    310

**13**

## VIDEO MEMORY AND GRAPHICS    340

**14**

## APPENDICES    369

# COMPUTER FUNDAMENTALS

# 1

**OBJECTIVES**

After studying this chapter, you should be able to:

- Name and describe the various parts of a computer system.
- Explain the purpose and functions of the processor.
- Explain segment/offset addressing.
- Describe typical input/output devices.
- Explain the function of the operating system.
- Use ASCII codes to represent character data.
- Convert decimal numbers to or from binary or hexadecimal digits.
- Perform arithmetic on binary and hexadecimal numbers.
- Use DEBUG to enter data into storage, examine storage and registers, and execute instructions.

## THE COMPUTER SYSTEM

People often speak of a computer as a means of processing data. Actually, you should call it a computer system because many different parts and components work together to perform the work you expect to do.

A *system* is defined as a set of interrelated parts or components working together to accomplish some desired function or purpose. A *computer system* has four major groups of components whose purpose is to process basic facts, called *data*, into meaningful information that is useful for record keeping and decision making. This function usually is called *data processing* or *information processing*. Processing includes such activities as recording, classifying, sorting, calculating, summarizing, storing, retrieving, and communicating.

The four major groups of components of the computer system include the following:

1. *Hardware*. Equipment, usually comprised of complex electronic circuits.
2. *Software*. Programs that direct the hardware as to what steps to take.

3. *Personnel.* Includes programmers, systems analysts, operators, and others.
4. *Procedures.* Directions to personnel in handling transactions and papers outside the computer itself.

The text is concerned mainly with the hardware and software of the IBM Personal Computer (PC) and other compatible machines. These machines are small enough to be carried around and are classed as microcomputers. Some reference will be made to personnel and procedures where appropriate.

## HARDWARE

The hardware of the IBM PC and compatible microcomputers is based on the *8088 processor*, which is manufactured by Intel Corporation. The electronic circuits that make up a processor usually are called a *chip*. The 8086 processor is similar to the 8088, except that it moves data between units somewhat faster. The 80286 and 80386 processors are more powerful versions of the 8086/8088 chips. This book will cover the principal hardware features of these processors.

Hardware usually is classified into four groups: (a) memory, (b) processor, (c) secondary storage, and (d) input/output devices. These groups are connected by one or more *buses*, or paths, over which data flows from one group to another. Figure 1-1 shows the relationship between the four hardware components.

### Memory

There are two kinds of memory, RAM and ROM. *RAM* (random access memory) holds programs and data that are being run currently. Data and programs can be moved readily between different locations in RAM or between RAM and input and output devices.

*ROM* (read-only memory) contains data or programs placed there by the manufacturer. You have access to such data or programs, but cannot normally erase them or overwrite them.

**RAM.** RAM, often called *main memory* or *primary storage*, consists of numbered *locations*, also called *addresses*. Each location is called a *byte*, capable of holding a code that represents one letter, digit, or special character of data. The number of bytes is stated in units of *K* (kilobytes), which is actually 1024 bytes. Thus 256K means 256 * 1024, or 262,144 bytes. Memory can contain more than one million bytes.

Each byte holds eight *binary digits*, or *bits*. The binary number system uses only the digits 0 and 1, which can be represented in different mechanical or electronic form.

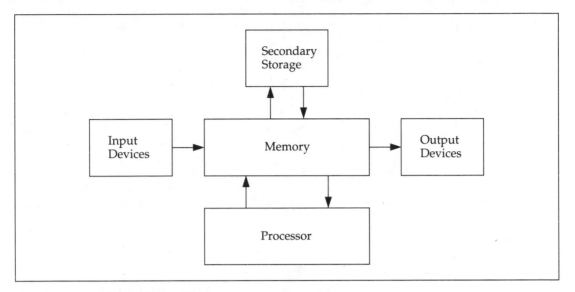

**Figure 1-1    Hardware Components**

In addition to data, computer *instructions* also are represented in the form of bits in special codes called *machine language*. Each instruction occupies from one to six bytes. When programs are to be *run*, or *executed*, their instructions in machine language must be *placed*, or *loaded*, into main storage, usually from a disk. Thus computers are said to have *stored programs*.

Bytes may be grouped together to form binary words. On machines using 8088 chips, groupings of 16 bits are called *words*, those of 32 bits are called *doublewords*, and those of 64 bits are called *quadwords*.

For people, reading and writing long strings of bits are tedious operations, subject to error. Therefore, we usually represent each group of four bits as one *hexadecimal digit*. Four bits can represent 16 different combinations of 0s and 1s. The hexadecimal number system has 16 different digits. The contents of any byte containing eight bits can be shown as two hexadecimal digits. The term *hex* is short for hexadecimal.

Figure 1-2 shows a comparison of decimal, binary, and hex codes for values from 0 through 15. The hexadecimal number system uses the digits A through F as equivalent to the decimal numbers 10 through 15. When there is any question about which number system you are using, you can show binary numbers followed with a b, hex numbers followed with an h, and decimal numbers followed with a d, as in 1101b, or 100d.

***ROM.***    Read-only memory on some machines contains frequently used programs, such as BASIC, or parts of the system software. Such programs may be automatically loaded into RAM when the machine is turned on to make it available for faster use than loading the programs from disk.

| Decimal | Binary | Hex | Decimal | Binary | Hex |
|:-------:|:------:|:---:|:-------:|:------:|:---:|
| 0 | 0000 | 0 | 8 | 1000 | 8 |
| 1 | 0001 | 1 | 9 | 1001 | 9 |
| 2 | 0010 | 2 | 10 | 1010 | A |
| 3 | 0011 | 3 | 11 | 1011 | B |
| 4 | 0100 | 4 | 12 | 1100 | C |
| 5 | 0101 | 5 | 13 | 1101 | D |
| 6 | 0110 | 6 | 14 | 1110 | E |
| 7 | 0111 | 7 | 15 | 1111 | F |

**Figure 1-2    Decimal, Binary, and Hexadecimal Codes**

### The 8086/8088 Processors

The heart of any computer system is the *processor*, or *central processing unit* (CPU). One main duty of the processor is to decode and execute *machine instructions* in main storage. Each instruction consists of one *operation code*, called *op code*, and usually one or more *operands*. The op code corresponds to a verb saying what is to be done. The operands are either actual data to be processed, the addresses of the bytes holding the data, or general registers.

The 8086 and 8088 processors generally are similar except that the 8086 has bus architecture that moves 16 bits at a time, while the 8088 moves only eight bits. The 8088 was used in the IBM PC and XT computers. The 8086 is found in the IBM PS/2 Model 30. These processors will be referred to collectively as the 8088. Appendix A contains a summary of the 8088 instructions.

The 8088 microprocessor contains 14 registers, which are useful in assembler language programming. Each register holds one word of 16 bits. The registers are not a part of main memory. Figure 1-3 shows the registers used on the 8088 processors.

***General Registers.***    The *general registers* may perform binary arithmetic, shift bits to the left or right, and also perform certain logical operations. There are four general registers, designated as AX, BX, CX, and DX. These can be used for performing arithmetic, storing data, and for shifting or rotating bits to the left or right.

Each general register also has some specialized uses. AX is generally used as an accumulator. It holds the results of many arithmetic operations. BX is often used as a base register for addressing data. CX is a counter for certain loops, while DX often holds data during input and output operations.

Each general register also may be used as two separate eight-bit registers. The leftmost eight bits in each register make up the *high byte*, while the

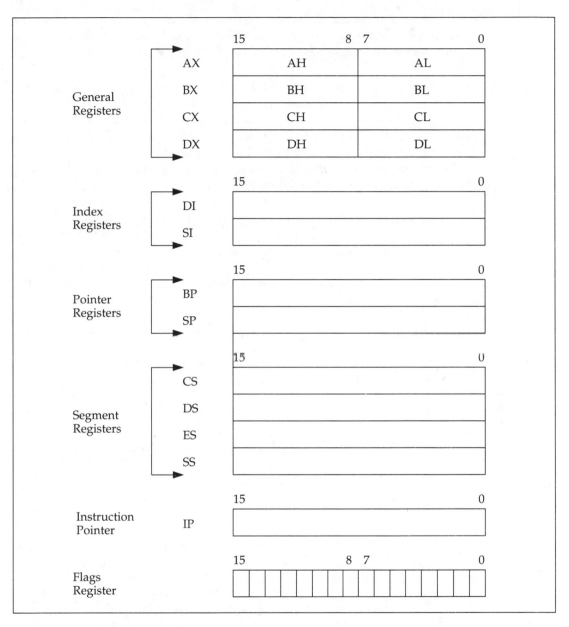

**Figure 1-3    Registers on the 8088 Processor**

rightmost eight bits are the *low byte*. If AX contains 48A6h, then AH contains 48h and AL contains A6h. Similarly, BX can be separated into BH and BL, CX into CH and CL, and DX into DH and DL.

*Index and Pointer Registers.*    Registers SI and DI are index registers, while SP and BP are pointer registers. These are used primarily in addressing data and will be discussed more fully in Chapter 7.

*Segment Registers.*    Programs are divided into as many as four segments. Each segment may be as large as 64K bytes and have a different address. The CS register holds the address of the *code segment*, that is, the part of your program containing the instructions, or code. The DS register holds the address of the *data segment*. ES is an *extra segment* register that may hold the address of other data. SS holds the segment address of the *stack*. Each register will be discussed in Chapter 2.

*Instruction Pointer.*    The IP, or instruction pointer, contains a value that is added to the CS register to form the address of the instruction to be executed next. IP is constantly updated by the 8088 processor as the instructions are executed. IP may be changed through the DEBUG program (discussed later, in this chapter), but is not accessible to the programmer during normal program execution.

*Flag Register.*    The flag (F) register contains 16 bits, of which only nine are used. When a flag bit is 1, the flag is said to be ON, or set. When the bit is 0, that flag is OFF, or reset. The flags are set ON or reset OFF as a result of arithmetic or other operations carried out by the processor. The flags are tested with *conditional jump* instructions so that a jump to some other part of the program may be made when a flag bit is ON and not made if the flag is OFF.

Rather than displaying the flag register in hexadecimal numbers, most system software displays two-letter codes indicating whether each flag is ON or OFF. The flags and their codes are shown in Figure 1-4.

*Segment/Offset Addressing.*    If you could use only one word to address data in storage, you could address only 65536 (64K) bytes (0000h through FFFFh). The 8088 uses a combination of a segment address in CS, DS, ES, or SS, plus an offset of up to 16 bits (FFFFh), to compute the actual, or effective, address. The segment address is multiplied by 10h, or decimal 16, before the addition takes place. In DEBUG, the segment address is listed first, then a colon, and finally the offset. The address 126D:0100 would thus refer to actual address 127D0, computed as follows:

```
Segment address 126Dh * 10h = 126D0h
Plus offset                  +   100h
Actual address                   127D0h
```

This method permits more than one million bytes of main memory to be addressed.

Flags Register

| Bits: | 15 | 14 | 13 | 12 | 11 | 10 | 9 | 8 | 7 | 6 | 5 | 4 | 3 | 2 | 1 | 0 |
|---|---|---|---|---|---|---|---|---|---|---|---|---|---|---|---|---|
| | --- | --- | --- | --- | OF | DF | IF | TF | SF | ZF | -- | AF | -- | PF | -- | CF |

←——— DEBUG CODES ———→

| Bit Number | Flags | ON (1) | OFF (0) |
|---|---|---|---|
| 15 | Unused | | |
| 14 | Unused | | |
| 13 | Unused | | |
| 12 | Unused | | |
| 11 | Overflow flag | OV | NV |
| 10 | Direction flag | DN (Decrement) | UP (Increment) |
| 9 | Interrupt enable flag | EI (Enabled) | DI (Disabled) |
| 8 | Trap flag | * | * |
| 7 | Sign flag | NG (Negative) | PL (Plus) |
| 6 | Zero flag | ZR | NZ |
| 5 | Unused | | |
| 4 | Auxiliary carry flag | AC | NA |
| 3 | Unused | | |
| 2 | Parity flag | PE (Even) | PO (Odd) |
| 1 | Unused | | |
| 0 | Carry flag | CY | NC |

* Trap flag not displayed by DEBUG.

**Figure 1-4    Flags on the 8088 Processor**

Rather than type the actual segment address, you may refer to one of the segment registers followed by a colon and the offset. Any of the following addresses is valid:

```
CS:0 DS:200 SS:FFEE ES:100
```

## The 80286 Processor

The 80286 processor is used in the IBM AT, XT286 and PS/2 Model 50 and 60 and other compatible computers. It has a few more instructions than the 8088 and runs significantly faster. It can be programmed in one of two modes: real address mode or protected virtual address mode. In *real address mode* the 80286 will execute all the instructions found on the 8088 and 8086, and is therefore upwardly compatible with those processors. *Protected virtual address* mode allows use of a larger virtual address space than the actual physical address space. This mode also provides memory protection mechanisms and requires use of special instructions to support operating systems and virtual memory. We will not cover protected virtual address mode in this text.

### The 80386 Processor

The 80386 processor is used in the IBM PS/2 Model 80 computer. It is a major upgrade of the 80286. It can process both 16 bits and 32 bits of data at a time. It can address more memory and has many more features than the 80286 and 8088.

All registers on the 80386, except the segment registers, can be extended to 32 bits. These extended registers are referred to as EAX, EBX, ECX, EDX, EBP, ESI, EDI, ESP, EIP, and Eflags. There are two extra segment registers, FS and GS, in addition to the four found on the 8088. Figure 1-5 shows the registers of the 80386 processor.

The 80386 is designed to support computer systems having multiple input and output stations. It operates in both real address mode and protected virtual address mode. The 80386 can execute more than one program at a time and can even run multiple operating systems at the same time. In this text we will not cover the protected mode and advanced systems programming features of the 80386 processor. Appendix B describes 80186, 80286, and 80386 instructions not found on the 8088 processor.

### Secondary Storage

No matter how much main memory you have, you always need additional *secondary storage*, also called *auxiliary* or *external storage*. Main memory is said to be *volatile* because it does not retain its magnetic properties when power is turned off. It also is relatively expensive. Therefore, some form of magnetic disk storage is needed to hold data files or programs outside of main memory that is readily accessible to the system.

Hardware for secondary storage consists of both devices and media. The *devices* include several types of disk drives that record and sense the magnetic spots that represent data. The media are the disks on which data is recorded. *Flexible (floppy) disks* are 5 1/4 inches in diameter and hold 360K bytes. *Rigid disks* are 3 1/2 inches in diameter and may hold either 720K or 1.44 million bytes. *Hard disks* have capacities of 5 million to 40 million bytes per drive. *Optical disks* and *CD ROMs* (compact disks, read-only memory) can hold hundreds of millions of bytes. *Magnetic tapes* provide high-speed reading and writing that are often used to make copies of disk drives for backup purposes.

### Input/Output Devices

*Input devices* are the machines, such as the keyboards or scanners, that are able to record data in a form that can be converted into binary codes in main memory. The media are the materials, such as visual display screens, that

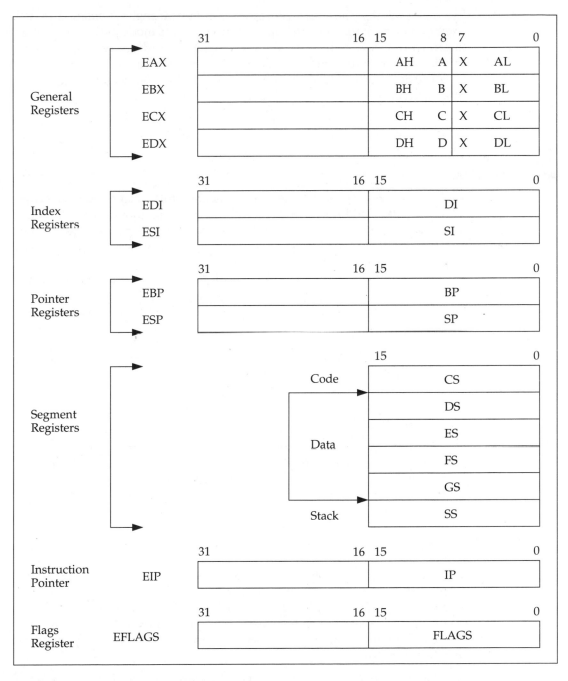

**Figure 1-5    Registers on the 80386 Processor**

actually hold the data. The program reads data from the input device into the main storage of the computer.

After the data has been processed into meaningful information by the program in main memory, the information is sent to an *output device*, such as a printer or visual display terminal. The device records, or writes, the information on a medium, such as paper or the display screen.

The data actually is recorded on the media. The device is the equipment that reads or writes the data on the media.

# SOFTWARE

A *computer program* is a set of instructions to the computer hardware along with the conditions under which they are to be carried out. The entire collection of programs, rules, procedures, and documentation is called *software*. Software is broadly classified as (a) operating systems, or systems software, and (b) applications software.

The *operating system* is concerned with routines that are common to the needs of almost all users, such as loading programs, sorting records, maintaining libraries of files and programs, and carrying out input/output operations.

*Applications software* is designed to perform functions to meet the specific needs of the user, such as billing customers, paying employees, registering students, or making engineering calculations.

## The Operating System

The term *operating system* describes a collection of programs designed to assist in preparing, translating, storing, and executing  programs. Since these programs are normally placed on a disk, the operating system is usually called *DOS*, for *disk operating system*. For computers based on the 8088 chip, the operating system was written by Microsoft and is therefore called *MS-DOS*. IBM provides a version of MS-DOS under the name *PC-DOS*.

A portion of the operating system is copied from disk to main memory when the system is turned on. This operation is called booting up the system. This part of the operating system  remains in main memory during normal operation to carry out commands from the programmer or operator. The symbol A> (or C> for hard-disk users) is displayed on the screen as a prompt to the operator that MS-DOS is ready to receive a command.

Four different programs are used in preparing and executing programs in assembler language:

1.  *DEBUG*. A versatile program that allows you to examine or change the contents of registers and main storage, execute programs one instruction at a time, enter short programs in either assembler or machine language, and perform other useful tasks.

2. *Text editor* or *word processor*. Used to prepare the statements written by the programmer in assembler language. Such statements are called the *source program*. *EDLIN* is a text editor provided with the MS-DOS. Popular word processors that can be available include WordStar, WordPerfect, PFS Write, and others. The source program must be stored on disk as an ASCII file without special codes and symbols often inserted by word processors.

3. *Assembler*. Used to translate the source program into machine language. The translated program is called the *object program*. Several assemblers are available. ASM and MASM are two of them. MASM will be referred to as the general name for an assembler.

4. *Linker*. Called LINK, linker is a program that creates an executable file, called a *load module*, from the object program. LINK may link several object programs together to produce a load module. The load module is in a form that can be loaded into memory and executed immediately. Appendix C lists DOS commands most useful with assembler language.

### Application Programs

The programs that meet the specific information processing needs of the computer user are called application programs. They may be purchased commercially or written by the user. Typical applications include the following: the billing of customers, the registering of students, the reporting of students' grades, the receipt and disbursement of funds, the keeping of accounting records, and the performance of engineering or scientific calculations.

Assembler language can be used to write either systems software or applications software.

## DATA CODES

All computers represent data internally with codes consisting entirely of 0 and 1. Such codes are called *binary codes*, and the digits 0 and 1 are called *bits*, short for binary digits. Letters, decimal digits, and special characters are represented with groups of eight bits, which occupy one *byte* of storage. Binary numbers are represented in the form of *words*, having typical lengths of 16, 32, or 64 bits.

### ASCII Codes

The American Standard Code for Information Interchange (ASCII) codes are used with microcomputers to represent eight-bit characters. Most larger IBM mainframes use the Extended Binary Coded Decimal Interchange Code (EBCDIC). Figure 1-6 depicts the most common characters found on the

| Decimal | Hex | Character | Decimal | Hex | Character |
|---------|-----|-----------|---------|-----|-----------|
| 32 | 20 | Space | 81 | 51 | Q |
| 33 | 21 | ! | 82 | 52 | R |
| 34 | 22 | " | 83 | 53 | S |
| 35 | 23 | # | 84 | 54 | T |
| 36 | 24 | $ | 85 | 55 | U |
| 37 | 25 | % | 86 | 56 | V |
| 38 | 26 | & | 87 | 57 | W |
| 39 | 27 | ' | 88 | 58 | X |
| 40 | 28 | ( | 89 | 59 | Y |
| 41 | 29 | ) | 90 | 5A | Z |
| 42 | 2A | * | 91 | 5B | [ |
| 43 | 2B | + | 92 | 5C | \ |
| 44 | 2C | , | 93 | 5D | ] |
| 45 | 2D | – | 94 | 5E | |
| 46 | 2E | . | 95 | 5F | _ |
| 47 | 2F | / | 96 | 60 | ` |
| 48 | 30 | 0 | 97 | 61 | a |
| 49 | 31 | 1 | 98 | 62 | b |
| 50 | 32 | 2 | 99 | 63 | c |
| 51 | 33 | 3 | 100 | 64 | d |
| 52 | 34 | 4 | 101 | 65 | e |
| 53 | 35 | 5 | 102 | 66 | f |
| 54 | 36 | 6 | 103 | 67 | g |
| 55 | 37 | 7 | 104 | 68 | h |

**Figure 1-6    ASCII Codes for Common Characters**

microcomputer keyboard, along with their binary and hex equivalent ASCII codes. Appendix D presents all of the ASCII codes.

### Binary Numbers

The *value* of a number depends on two things: (a) the value of *each digit* used by the number system, and (b) the place in the number where each digit occurs, called its *place value*. You already are familiar with the place value of decimal numbers. The digit just left of the decimal point has a place value of one. As you move left, the place values become 10, 100, 1000, and so forth. These are the powers of 10, since there are 10 digits in the decimal number system. The number 325 has the value of (3 * 100) + (2 * 10) + (5 * 1) = 325.

Binary numbers use only the digits 0 and 1. Any value larger than 1 requires more than one digit. You need two digits to represent the values 2

| Decimal | Hex | Character | Decimal | Hex | Character |
|---------|-----|-----------|---------|-----|-----------|
| 56 | 38 | 8 | 105 | 69 | i |
| 57 | 39 | 9 | 106 | 6A | j |
| 58 | 3A | : | 107 | 6B | k |
| 59 | 3B | ; | 108 | 6C | l |
| 60 | 3C | < | 109 | 6D | m |
| 61 | 3D | = | 110 | 6E | n |
| 62 | 3E | > | 111 | 6F | o |
| 63 | 3F | ? | 112 | 70 | p |
| 64 | 40 | @ | 113 | 71 | q |
| 65 | 41 | A | 114 | 72 | r |
| 66 | 42 | B | 115 | 73 | s |
| 67 | 43 | C | 116 | 74 | t |
| 68 | 44 | D | 117 | 75 | u |
| 69 | 45 | E | 118 | 76 | v |
| 70 | 46 | F | 119 | 77 | w |
| 71 | 47 | G | 120 | 78 | x |
| 72 | 48 | H | 121 | 79 | y |
| 73 | 49 | I | 122 | 7A | z |
| 74 | 4A | J | 123 | 7B | { |
| 75 | 4B | K | 124 | 7C | | |
| 76 | 4C | L | 125 | 7D | } |
| 77 | 4D | M | 126 | 7E | ~ |
| 78 | 4E | N | 127 | 7F | DEL |
| 79 | 4F | O | | | |
| 80 | 50 | P | | | |

and 3, three digits to represent 4, 5, 6, and 7, and so forth. As you move left, the place value of each digit increases in powers of 2, so that each place value is double that of the preceding place. The relationship between the place value and the powers of 2 is shown below for the rightmost twelve bits of a binary number:

| $2^{11}$ | $2^{10}$ | $2^9$ | $2^8$ | $2^7$ | $2^6$ | $2^5$ | $2^4$ | $2^3$ | $2^2$ | $2^1$ | $2^0$ |
|------|------|-----|-----|-----|-----|-----|-----|-----|-----|-----|-----|
| 2048 | 1024 | 512 | 256 | 128 | 64 | 32 | 16 | 8 | 4 | 2 | 1 |

***Unsigned Binary Numbers.***  A place value table is useful to convert decimal numbers to binary or binary numbers to decimal. For unsigned numbers, you assign a place value to every bit in the number. Unsigned numbers of 4, 8, or 16 bits often are used by the operating system to represent addresses, lengths of operands in the instructions, and lengths of keys or records in files.

To represent the value of the numbers in the following table, add the place value of the positions that contain 1 bits and ignore the 0 bits. The binary numbers at the left are equivalent to the decimal values at the right. For example, in the first number shown, 64 + 8 + 4 + 1 = 77.

### BINARY PLACE VALUES

| 128 | 64 | 32 | 16 | 8 | 4 | 2 | 1 | DECIMAL VALUE |
|-----|----|----|----|---|---|---|---|---------------|
| 0 | 1 | 0 | 0 | 1 | 1 | 0 | 1 | 77 |
| 0 | 0 | 1 | 0 | 1 | 0 | 1 | 1 | 43 |
| 1 | 1 | 0 | 0 | 1 | 0 | 0 | 0 | 200 |
| 0 | 1 | 1 | 1 | 1 | 1 | 1 | 1 | 127 |
| 1 | 1 | 1 | 1 | 1 | 1 | 1 | 1 | 255 |

*Signed Binary Numbers*.    To represent both positive and negative binary numbers, the leftmost bit designates the sign, 0 for positive and 1 for negative. The remaining bits represent the place values. Because fewer bits represent the value of a signed binary number, its magnitude is only about half the size of an unsigned number. A negative number is represented in *twos complement* form. The twos complement is formed in this way:

1.   Write the number in positive form.
2.   Reverse all the 0 bits to 1 and all 1 bits to 0. The result is called the *ones complement*.
3.   Add 1 to the ones complement, forming the twos complement.
    We can form the binary value -77 as shown below:

### BINARY PLACE VALUES

| SIGN | 64 | 32 | 16 | 8 | 4 | 2 | 1 | DECIMAL VALUE | |
|------|----|----|----|---|---|---|---|---------------|--|
| 0 | 1 | 0 | 0 | 1 | 1 | 0 | 1 | 77 | (Positive number) |
| 1 | 0 | 1 | 1 | 0 | 0 | 1 | 0 | | (Ones complement) |
| | | | | | | | +1 | | (Add 1) |
| 1 | 0 | 1 | 1 | 0 | 0 | 1 | 1 | -77 | (Twos complement) |

The same principle applies with larger numbers, such as words of 16 bits or doublewords of 32 bits, or quadwords of 64 bits. The leftmost bit is always the sign. More place values are needed to represent larger numbers. You can expand any number to more bits by *propagating*, or copying, the sign bit into the additional places to the left. For example, the value –77 in eight-bit form is 1011 0011, equivalent to B3h. If you expand it to 16 bits, the binary value is 1111 1111 1011 0011, or FFB3h. Most negative words or doublewords can be recognized as having one or more leading Fh digits.

It is rather tedious to convert decimal numbers to signed binary or vice versa by going through all three steps shown. However, there are two shortcuts that can simplify the process. In the first method, when the sign bit of 1 tells you that the number is negative, add the place value of each 0 rather than the value of each 1. Adding the place value of the 0 bits will give one less than the value you seek. Then add 1 and reverse the sign to get the correct value.

In the example above, the sign bit of 1 indicates the number –77 is negative. Adding the place value of the 0 bits gives 64 + 8 + 4, or 76. Adding 1 gives 77. Reversing the sign gives –77.

As another example, the eight-bit number 1100 1101 has 0 bits in the 32, 16, and 2 place value positions. Adding them together, we get 32 + 16 + 2 = 50. Adding 1 gives 51. Reversing the sign gives –51. The binary number 1100 1101 = –51.

A second shortcut method for recognizing negative numbers is to assign the sign bit a *negative value* equal to the place value it would have if not used as a sign. Then add the value of the 1 bits as with positive numbers. Using this method with 1100 1101, value the sign bit as –128. The values of the other 1 bits are 64, 8, 4, and 1. Adding them together, we get – 128 + 64 + 16 + 4 + 1 = –51.

***Overflow in Binary Arithmetic.***    Binary addition of a pair of bits follows these simple rules:

```
0 + 0 = 0    0 + 1 = 1    1 + 0 = 1    1 + 1 = 10    (Zero
                                                      with a
                                                      carry)
```

Binary subtraction is performed by adding the twos complement of the number to be subtracted. Add the sign bit just like any other bit. Any carry out of the sign bit is discarded.

When a binary number is too large for the number of digits used to represent it, *overflow* occurs. This happens when the sign bit is set opposite to what it should be. Note these examples:

### BINARY PLACE VALUES

|     | SIGN | 64 | 32 | 16 | 8 | 4 | 2 | 1 | DECIMAL EQUIVALENT |
|-----|------|----|----|----|---|---|---|---|---------------------|
| (1) | 0 | 1 | 1 | 0 | 0 | 1 | 0 | 1 | 101 |
|     | 0 | 0 | 0 | 1 | 0 | 1 | 1 | 1 | +  23 |
|     | 0 | 1 | 1 | 1 | 1 | 1 | 0 | 0 | = 124 (Valid; no carry into or out of the sign bit) |
| (2) | 1 | 0 | 1 | 1 | 0 | 1 | 1 | 1 | –73 |
|     | 1 | 1 | 0 | 1 | 0 | 0 | 0 | 0 | +( –48) |
| 1   | 1 | 0 | 0 | 0 | 0 | 1 | 1 | 1 | =(–121) (Valid; carry both into |

```
                                                       and out
                                                       of the
                                                       sign bit)
(3)   0   1   1   0   0   1   0   1           101
      0   1   0   0  ·1   0   0   1          + 73
      1   0   1   0   1   1   1   0          = 174 (Invalid;
                                             carry into
                                             but not
                                             out of
                                             sign bit)
(4)   1   0   0   0   0   1   1   0           -122
      1   0   0   1   1   1   0   1          +(-99)
      1   0   0   1   0   0   0   1   1      =(-221) (Invalid;
                                             no carry
                                             in but
                                             carry out
                                             of sign
                                             bit)
```

In an eight-bit signed number, the maximum values are 127 and -128. Any result exceeding these values causes *overflow*. In the tabulation above, example (1) shows no carry into or out of the sign position, and the result is valid. Example (2) shows a carry into the sign position, but also out of the sign position (dropped), and the result is valid.

In example (3), the carry into the sign position causes what should be a positive number to have a negative sign. If the sign bit had had a place value of 128, the result would have been correct, but since that position is reserved for the sign alone, the result is incorrect, and the overflow flag (OF) is set ON.

Example (4) also shows overflow. The maximum allowable value is -128, but the desired sum is -221. Because there was no carry into the sign position, what should be a negative number appears to have a positive sign and is therefore incorrect. Here again, the overflow flag is set ON.

The rules for determining overflow for addition and subtraction of signed binary numbers of any size are as follows:

1.  All corresponding bits, including sign bits, of both numbers are added together.
2.  Subtraction is performed by adding the twos complement of the number to be subtracted.
3.  A carry out of the sign position is dropped, and the carry flag is set ON.
4.  If there is no carry into the sign position and no carry out of it, the result is valid.
5.  If there is a carry into the sign position and also a carry out of it, the result is valid.
6.  If there is a carry into the sign position but no carry out of it, overflow occurs, and the overflow flag is set ON.
7.  If there is no carry into the sign position but there is a carry out of it, overflow occurs, and the overflow flag is set ON.

## Hexadecimal Numbers

Hexadecimal numbers are used rather than decimal numbers for many purposes on computers because they are easier for human beings to convert to and from binary numbers. As shown in Figure 1-2, each hex digit can be converted directly to four bits.

Two hex digits can represent the contents of any eight-bit byte. Thus they may show machine instructions, constants in assembler programs, addresses, and printouts of main storage.

Hex numbers can be converted to and from decimal numbers, but the process is more complex than conversion too and from binary. The simplest way to convert hex to decimal is to use a place value table. Place values of hex digits are in powers of 16, as contrasted with the place values of decimal digits in powers of 10. The place values of the different hex digits, right to left, are 1, 16, 256, 4096, 65536, and so forth. Each place is 16 times the value of the digit to its right.

As mentioned earlier, to distinguish hex numbers from decimal, follow hex numbers with the letter h, as in 12A7h.

For practice, convert the hex number 947h to decimal, using the place value table in Figure 1-7. This table shows the result in each position when the place value is multiplied by the value of the hexadecimal digit.

| Hex Digit | <--------- Decimal Equivalents --------------------> | | | | | |
|---|---|---|---|---|---|---|
| | X00000 | 0X0000 | 00X000 | 000X00 | 0000X0 | 00000X |
| 0 | 0 | 0 | 0 | 0 | 0 | 0 |
| 1 | 1048576 | 65536 | 4096 | 256 | 16 | 1 |
| 2 | 2097152 | 131072 | 8192 | 512 | 32 | 2 |
| 3 | 3145728 | 196608 | 12288 | 768 | 48 | 3 |
| 4 | 4194304 | 262144 | 16384 | 1024 | 64 | 4 |
| 5 | 5242880 | 327680 | 20480 | 1280 | 80 | 5 |
| 6 | 6291456 | 393216 | 24576 | 1536 | 96 | 6 |
| 7 | 7340032 | 458752 | 28672 | 1792 | 112 | 7 |
| 8 | 8388608 | 524288 | 32768 | 2048 | 128 | 8 |
| 9 | 9437184 | 589824 | 36864 | 2304 | 144 | 9 |
| A | 10485760 | 655360 | 40960 | 2560 | 160 | 10 |
| B | 11543336 | 720896 | 45056 | 2816 | 176 | 11 |
| C | 12582912 | 786432 | 49152 | 3072 | 192 | 12 |
| D | 13631488 | 851968 | 53248 | 3328 | 216 | 13 |
| E | 14680064 | 917504 | 57344 | 3584 | 228 | 14 |
| F | 15728640 | 983040 | 61440 | 3840 | 240 | 15 |

**Figure 1-7   Place Values of Hexadecimal Digits**

The value of the 900h in the third digit from the right is decimal (9 * 256),or 2304. The value of the 40h in the second digit is decimal (4 * 16), or 64. The value of the 7h in the rightmost digit is decimal (7 * 1), or 7. Adding the decimal values of the three digits, we get 2304 + 64 + 7 = 2375.

To get the decimal equivalent of B97Ch:

```
B000h = 11 *  4096 = 45056
0900h =  9 *   256 =  2304
0070h =  7 *    16 =   112
000Ch = 12 *     1 =    12
B97Ch =                47484
```

To convert the decimal value 795 to hex, proceed as follows: find the largest value in the table that does not exceed 795. This is 768 decimal, or 300h. Subtract 768 from 795 leaving 27 still to be converted. The largest number on the table that does not exceed 27 is 16 decimal, or 10h. Subtract 16 from 27 leaving 11 decimal, which is Bh. Add the three hex values 300h+10h+Bh= 31Bh, the hex number that is equivalent to decimal 795.

For another example, convert decimal value 4967 to hex.

```
Original value               4967
Subtract largest value       4096        = Hex value 1000h
Leaving                       871
Subtract largest value        768        = Hex value 0300h
Leaving                       103
Subtract largest value         96        = Hex value 0060h
Leaving                         7         = Hex value 0007h
Add hex values to give hex equivalent = Hex value 1367h
```

All addresses in assembler listings and linker maps are given in hex. You often need to add or subtract hex numbers to determine the number of bytes between addresses. The simplest way to perform hex addition is to convert each digit mentally to decimal, add the two, and reconvert to hex. Instead of carrying when the sum reaches 10, as you do in decimal addition, you carry only when the sum reaches 16 (10h) in hex addition. Note the following example:

```
        DECIMAL    HEX

            09      09h
           +12     +0Ch
            21      15h
```

The sum of the two decimal values is 21, which is 5 more than 16. In the hex number, record the 5h and carry the 16 (10h) to the next position.

Here are some more examples:

```
Carries =>      1         1        111
    456h       72Dh      3ACh      0ABEh
   +789h      +657h     +83Fh     +0FEDh
    BDFh       D84h      BEBh      1AABh
```

## EXPLORING DEBUG

DEBUG is a useful program provided with MS-DOS. It provides many ways to help the assembler programmer. With DEBUG you can examine the contents of memory and internal registers, execute instructions one at a time, save files to disk and load them back into memory, assemble and disassemble instructions, and do other operations. Advanced versions of DEBUG named SYMDEB and CODEVIEW are available with versions 4.0 and 5.0 of the MASM assembler.

From working with high-level languages or software packages, you probably already know how to boot up MS-DOS, that is, to read a part of MS-DOS into main memory where it resides during normal operation. In case you don't, here are the steps for a floppy disk system with two drives:

1.  With power off, place a system disk containing COMMAND.COM into disk drive A and turn power ON.
2.  After a few seconds, when requested, enter current date in form MM/DD/YY (month, day, year) and current time as HH:MM (hours, minutes). Press <ENTER> after each.
3.  When the screen displays A> (the DOS symbol to prompt a response), you may enter any MS-DOS command or load programs from either disk. If a program to be loaded is on drive B, the program name must be preceded with the drive code and a colon, as in A> B:PROG1.

For a hard disk drive (usually drive C), when you turn power on, answer the prompts for date and time by pressing <ENTER>. The DOS prompt for a hard disk system is normally C>. Type in any command or program name. You normally will have standard operating procedures prescribed for any computer installation. Follow them carefully.

Throughout this book, examples will presume you are using a two-drive, floppy disk system. To load DEBUG, place a disk containing DEBUG into drive A. At the A> prompt, type DEBUG. When loaded, DEBUG will display its *prompt*, a hyphen (-). The prompt is an indicator that you may enter a *command*. Each command consists of a single letter, which may be either upper or lower case. The command may be followed by additional operands. Appendix E summarizes the DEBUG commands. Some of the more useful commands are explained in the sections that follow. DEBUG considers all numbers to be hexadecimal. You can leave DEBUG whenever you see the prompt by typing Q (for quit).

### Hexadecimal Addition and Subtractions

The H (hex) command will display the sum and difference of any two hexadecimal numbers between 0000 and FFFF. Numbers are considered to be signed. You need not type leading zeros. Here are some examples:

| COMMAND | RESULT |
|---------|--------|
| -H 5 2 | 0007 0003 |
| -H 94 87 | 011B 000D |
| -H 4 5 | 0009 FFFF |

Confirm these answers by reviewing the preceding section on hexadecimal arithmetic. Note that FFFFh is equivalent to decimal -1. Only four hex digits are retained. Any carries beyond the leftmost digit are dropped. The result will be invalid if the sign in the leftmost bit is incorrectly changed. The result will be displayed even though it may be invalid. Don't always accept computer results without question. Consider these examples of invalid addition:

| COMMAND | RESULT |
|---------|--------|
| -H 7FFF 7FFF | FFFE 0000 |
| -H 8000 8000 | 0000 0000 |

7FFFh is the largest positive number that can be represented in 16 bits (0111 1111 1111 1111, or decimal 32767). When it is added to itself, the sum is 1111 1111 1111 1110, apparently a negative number. When adding the leftmost pair of 1 bits, there was a carry into the sign position, but no carry out of it. Therefore, overflow occurred.

8000h is the largest negative number that can be represented in 16 bits (1000 0000 0000 0000, or decimal -32768). When the leftmost 0 bits are added, there is no carry into the sign position, but adding the two 1-bit signs causes a carry out of the sign position, and overflow occurs.

Try other hex digits to be sure you understand each result. Note that overflow cannot occur when adding one positive and one negative number.

### Examining and Modifying Registers

You may examine the contents of all registers through DEBUG by typing the R (register) command. Here is an example:

```
-R
AX=0000 BX=0000 CX=0000 DX=0000
SP=FFEE BP=0000
SI=0000 DI=0000
DS=126D ES=126D SS=126D CS=126D
IP=0100 NV UP EI PL NZ NA PO NC
126D:0100 0000          ADD     (BX+SI),AL
```

The contents of registers often will vary from those shown in these exercises. They are shown here purely as examples. Flags are shown in two-character codes as presented earlier in Figure 1-4.

The command R followed by the two-letter register name will display the contents of that register and permit you to change those contents. You must change the entire word. You cannot change AH or AL independently in this way. In addition to displaying the registers, DEBUG also displays the word or instruction at the address of CS+IP and attempts to *disassemble*, or to convert machine code to assembler code, that instruction.

To change AX register to FACE and BL to 25 and see the changes, enter:

```
-R AX
AX 0000
:FACE
-R BX
BX 0000
:0025
-R
AX=FACE BX=0025 CX=0000 DX=0000
SP=FFEE BP=0000 SI=0000 DI=0000
DS=126D ES-126D SS=126D CS=126D
IP=0100 NV UP EH PL NZ NA PO NC
```

DEBUG normally clears the general registers, index registers, and the BP pointer register when it is first loaded. In the example above, all of the segment registers contain the same address. This will not necessarily be true when debugging a specific program. MS-DOS assigns these segment addresses according to the type of program you have written. We will discuss this topic in more detail in Chapter 2.

### Memory Dumps

The D (dump) command is used to display the contents of memory. You may follow the command with the segment and offset address at which the dump is to start. Eight lines are displayed, with 16 bytes per line. The address appears to the left of each line, followed by 16 sets of two hex digits each, separated by a space. To the right of the line appear 16 characters. If the byte contains a printable ASCII character, that character is displayed; if the byte is unprintable, a period is shown instead. If you then type another D command, the next 128 bytes will be displayed in eight lines.

Figure 1-8 shows a memory dump of the lowest 256 bytes of main storage. These bytes do not contain text, so that very few characters are printable. They actually are four-byte addresses of DOS and BIOS routines that service interrupts. Interrupts will be discussed in Chapter 3.

## PROGRAM 1: ASSEMBLING AND TRACING A SHORT PROGRAM

You can use DEBUG to enter source statements of short programs in assembler language, translate (assemble) them into machine language, and execute them. You also can use DEBUG to enter instructions and data directly in machine language. Only hex numbers of up to four digits can be used. For

```
B>a:debug
-d 0:0
0000:0000  86 51 BC 02 44 0C 70 00-A5 01 70 00 44 0c 70 00   .Q..D.p...p.D.p.
0000:0010  44 0C 70 00 54 FF 00 50-53 FF 00 F0 53 FF 00 F0   D.p.T..PS...S...
0000:0020  28 02 70 00 A5 02 70 00-24 03 70 00 9E 03 70 00   +.p...p.$.p...p.
0000:0030  18 04 70 00 92 04 70 00-0C 05 70 00 44 0C 70 00   ..p...p...p.D.p.
0000:0040  65 F0 00 F0 71 FE 00 F0-81 FE 00 F0 DF 17 70 00   e...q.........p.
0000:0050  39 E7 00 F0 CD 34 00 F0-2E E8 00 F0 02 01 E5 0B   9...............
0000:0060  6F E4 00 F0 54 1E 70 00-6E FE 00 F0 3E 0C 70 00   o...T.p.n...>.p.
0000:0070  53 FF 00 F0 00 E0 00 F0-22 05 00 00 A8 C0 00 F0   s......."......
0000:0080  6C 13 8C 02 8D 13 8C 02-F5 02 39 0C 2E 03 39 0C   l.........9...9.
0000:0090  BD 02 39 0C 09 15 8C 02-4C 15 8C 02 FE 5D 8C 02   ..9.....L....]..
0000:00A0  72 13 8C 02 7A 01 70 00-72 13 8C 02 72 13 8C 02   r...z.p.r...r...
0000:00B0  72 13 8C 02 72 13 8C 02-57 02 18 0B F2 1D 70 00   r...r...W.....p.
0000:00C0  EA 73 13 8C 02 13 8C 02-72 13 8C 02 72 13 8C 02   .s......r...r...
0000:00D0  72 13 8C 02 72 13 8C 02-72 13 8C 02 72 13 8C 02   r...r...r...r...
0000:00E0  72 13 8C 02 72 13 8C 02-72 13 8C 02 72 13 8C 02   r...r...r...r...
0000:00F0  72 13 8C 02 72 13 8C 02-72 13 8C 02 72 13 8C 02   r...r...r...r...
```

**Figure 1-8    Dump of Lowest 256 Bytes of Main Memory**

longer programs, you may use the MASM or ASM assembler, which accepts statements written with decimal numbers or ASCII characters.

To watch the actual execution of a program, you may create a program to add two hex numbers. The steps are to put 5h into AH, put 2h into AL, add the two together, and return to DOS. You will enter the source statements in assembler language and let DEBUG assemble the statements into machine language. The program begins at an offset of 100h from the address in the code segment for reasons that will be discussed in Chapter 2.

The A (assemble) command followed by the offset address directs DEBUG to assemble the statements as you enter them. (DEBUG automatically supplies the code segment address in CS register). DEBUG responds with the address where the machine language will be placed. As you enter each statement, DEBUG responds with the next available address, and you enter another statement. You need not put the letter h following each hex number, since DEBUG accepts only hex numbers. Stop by pressing <ENTER> alone.

```
-A 100
126D:0100 MOV AH,5
126D:0102 MOV AL,2
126D:0104 ADD AH,AL
126D:0106 INT 20
126D:0108 <ENTER>
```

Next, examine these locations and confirm that your statements were correctly translated by issuing the U (unassemble) command with offset of 100. This command attempts to translate each byte of main storage back into assembler language. Where the byte contains data rather than instructions, the results are meaningless, as at offset 0108 below.

```
-U 100
126D:0100 B405            MOV AH,05
126D:0102 B002            MOV AL,02
126D:0104 00C4            ADD AH,AL
126D:0106 CD20            INT 20
126D:0108 0000            ADD (BX+SI),AL
```

You can see that the program has been translated, and that it occupies the eight bytes from 0100 through 0107 in the code segment that starts at 126D. The object code itself is B405B00200C4CD20. The last statement disassembled at 126D:0108 is the first of a series of bytes containing hex zeros left from the previous program. DEBUG translates these statements as shown.

You now can execute this program one statement at a time with the T (trace) command. First, display the current setting of the registers with the R command. The address of the first instruction to be executed is at CS address 126D and offset 0100. IP contains this offset of 0100. As each instruction is executed, IP will be increased to point to the next instruction.

```
-R
AX=0000  BX=0000  CX=0000  DX=0000
SP=FFEE  BP=0000  SI=0000  DI=0000
DS=126D  ES=126D  SS=126D  CS=126D
IP=0100    NV UP EI PL NZ NA PO NC
126D:0100 B405            MOV    AH,05
-T
AX=0500  BX=0000  CX=0000  DX=0000
SP=FFEE  BP=0000  SI=0000  DI=0000
DS=126D  ES=126D  SS=126D  CS=126D
IP=0102    NV UP EI PL NZ NA PO NC
126D:0102 B002            MOV    AH,02
-T
AX=0502  BX=0000  CX=0000  DX=0000
SP=FFEE  BP=0000  SI=0000  DI=0000
DS=126D  ES=126D  SS=126D  CS=126D
IP=0104    NV UP EI PL NZ NA PO NC
126D:0104 00C4            ADD    AH,AL
-T
AX=0702  BX=0000  CX=0000  DX=0000
SP=FFEE  BP=0000  SI=0000  DI=0000
DS=126D  ES=126D  SS=126D  CS=126D
IP=0106    NV UP EI PL NZ NA PO NC
126D:0106 CD20            INT    20
-T
AX=0702  BX=0000  CX=0000  DX=0000
SP=FFEE  BP=0000  SI=0000  DI=0000
DS=126D  ES=126D  SS=126D  CS=0287
IP=136C    NV UP DI PL NZ NA PO NC
0287:136C B400            MOV    AH,OO
-
```

From the above listings, you can see in AX that the number 05 is moved into AH, then 02 is moved into AL, and finally the sum 07 appears in AH. In the last listing of the registers CS contains 0287 and IP contains 136C. This is the address within DOS to which control is transferred when a program is completed.  Do not attempt to trace through DOS.

### Entering Machine Language Directly

Now that you know that the machine code is for your program is B405B00200C4CD20 you can enter the code directly through DEBUG with the E (enter) command. Let us demonstrate by first changing the eight bytes at 126D:0100 back to zeros.

The command E followed by an address displays the byte at that address followed by a period. To change it, simply type the two hex digits you want in that address. DEBUG then displays the contents of the next byte. If you don't want to change it, press the space bar to display the next byte. Continue to enter new data or leave it unchanged as long as you wish. The E command is terminated by pressing the <ENTER> key. You can go back to the preceding byte at any time by pressing the minus (-) key, and you can go forward by pressing the space bar.

To change bytes 126D:0100 to all zeros, first issue the command E 126D:0100. The screen will look like this:

```
-E 126D:0100 B4.
```

In each position, the number to the left of the period is displayed by DEBUG, and the number to the right is the one we enter. Press the space bar below each pair of zeros, as shown below:

```
-E 126D:0100 B4.00   05.00   B0.00   02.00   00.00   C4.00
CD.00   20.00   00. <ENTER>
```

The D (dump) command will show that you have changed these bytes:

```
-D 126D:0100
126D:0100  00 00 00 00 00 00 00 00 00 00 00 00 00 00 00

00 ...............
```

Now you can enter the machine language codes:

```
-E 126D:0100 00.B4   00.05   00.B0   00.02   00.00   00.C4
00.CD 00.20   00.<ENTER>
```

Next, unassemble these statements and see that you have correctly reentered the program.

```
-U 126D:0100
126D:0100 B405          MOV AH,05
126D:0102 B002          MOV AL,02
```

```
126D:0104 00C4          ADD  AH,AL
126D:0106 CD20          INT  20
126D:0108 0000          ADD  (BX+SI),AL
```

You now can trace through the program once again to watch the registers as each instruction is executed. But beware! Recall that the contents of CS and IR were changed to 0287 and 136C, respectively, when you returned to DOS with the INT 20 instruction earlier. You may need to reset those registers in this way:

```
-R CS
0287
:126D
-R IP
136C
:0100
```

Now you can execute the entire program at once with the G (go) command. This will go to the instruction specified by CS and IP registers and continue until the appropriate return to DOS is reached. A message is displayed if the program executes correctly:

```
-G
Program terminated normally
```

## Saving and Loading Programs

After creating a machine language program through DEBUG, you can save it on disk. We will presume the system disk is in drive A and the data disk in drive B. First you must give the program a name with the N (name) command:

```
-N B:SAMPLE1.COM
```

The extension COM to the filename SAMPLE1 is applied to machine language programs that can be contained fully within one 64K segment. For a COM program, the segment addresses in CS, DS, SS, and ES all will be the same, and the offset address of the first instruction in the program will be 100h. This program meets these requirements.

Before you save the program, you must specify the length of the program in registers BX:CX, where BX holds the high-order digits and CX holds the low-order digits of the length. This program is eight bytes long. BX already contains zeros. You can place the length in CX with:

```
-R CX
0000
:0008
```

The command to write to disk is W (write). When used without another operand, W saves the program named by the N command with the length specified in BX:CX.

```
-W
```

You should see the red light for drive B turn on briefly as the program is written to disk. At this point you could quit DEBUG with the Q command or do any other operations within DEBUG. If you should leave DEBUG, you could display the directory for drive B with:

```
A>DIR B:
```

and confirm that SAMPLE1.COM is recorded with a length of eight bytes.

There are two possible ways to load the SAMPLE1.COM program back into main storage. The first is to load it with DEBUG by giving the file name after DEBUG:

```
A> DEBUG B:SAMPLE1.COM
```

DEBUG will automatically place the same address into all segment registers and 100h into IP. The segment address will not necessarily be the same one used previously. DEBUG seems to choose segment addresses at random.

The second way to load the file is to load DEBUG without another operand:

```
A> DEBUG
```

Then you must specify with the N (name) command the desired file name to be loaded and, finally, load the file with the L (load) command:

```
-N B:SAMPLE1.COM
-L
```

You now can dump storage, trace through your statements, execute the entire program with the G (go) command, add more instructions, save the program under a different name, or do any other operations permitted through DEBUG.

## SUMMARY

The four components of a computer system are hardware, software, personnel, and procedures. The hardware consists of memory, the processor, secondary storage, and input/output devices. Memory is divided into numbered locations called bytes.

Each byte holds a code of eight bits consisting of 0s and 1s only. The 0s and 1s make up the binary number system. The codes represent both program instructions being executed and data to be processed into information. The processor contains the control unit, which decodes and executes instructions; the arithmetic-logic unit, which performs arithmetic operations; and various registers. Secondary storage is primarily in the form of magnetic disk drives. Input/output devices include keyboards, display screens, printers, audio devices, and other units.

Software is classified as systems software that provides programs common to most users, and applications software that meets the specific requirements of different users. The operating system is a collection of systems software programs that perform operations such as loading and storing programs, reading and writing records to files, translating programs into machine language, and sorting records within files. The operating system used with IBM personal computers and compatible machines is called MS-DOS, because it was written by Microsoft, Inc.

The American Standard Code for Information Interchange (ASCII) is used to represent individual letters, digits, or special characters in eight bits each. Binary numbers may be represented in 16, 32, or 64 bits called words, doublewords, or quadwords. Binary numbers may be signed or unsigned. Signed binary numbers are positive if the leftmost bit is a 0 and negative if it is a 1. Negative numbers are represented in twos complement form.

In the addition of both positive and negative numbers, all bits are added, including the sign. Carries out of the sign bit are dropped. Overflow occurs if the carry out of the sign bit is different from the carry into it. Overflow means that the correct result was too large to be contained in the number of bits provided.

Hexadecimal (hex) numbers have 16 different digits. Each digit represents the value contained in four bits. Hex digits are used as a short form to represent long strings of bits.

DEBUG is an MS-DOS program that allows examination of main storage and the 14 registers contained in the 8088 chip. Commands consist of a single letter. The H command gives the sum of the difference between two hex numbers. The R command displays the contents of the 14 registers, and also permits the contents of any specific register to be changed. Four of the registers hold the addresses of the code, data, extra, and stack segments. This address reflects the start of the segment. An offset is added to the segment address to refer to any location within the segment. The D command displays the contents of 128 bytes of main storage in both hex and character form, with 16 bytes per line.

The A (assemble) command converts statements written in assembler language into machine language, while the U (unassemble) command does the reverse. The T (trace) command allows only one instruction of a program at a time to be executed and displays the 14 registers after each instruction. The G (go) command runs the entire program. The E command permits hex digits to be entered directly into main storage.

The N command allows a name to be given to a program. The W command writes a program to disk, and the L command loads it from disk into main storage.

## QUESTIONS

1. What is the main function of a computer system?
2. Name the four major groups of components of a computer system.
3. Describe the organization of main storage.
4. Name the parts of the central processing unit and describe their functions.
5. Name some of the principal input/output devices.
6. What is the difference between systems software and applications software?
7. What four programs of MS-DOS are of special interest to the assembler language programmer?
8. What is the relationship between binary and hexadecimal number systems?
9. How are negative numbers represented in binary?
10. What is meant by overflow in binary addition, and how do we determine that it has occurred?
11. Describe the steps in booting up MS-DOS.
12. Name the four general registers and explain how each is normally used. Into what eight registers may they be divided?
13. What is meant by segment/offset addressing? What four registers may contain segment addresses?
14. What is meant by assembling and unassembling instructions?
15. In what form does DEBUG display a dump of main memory?
16. Describe what happens in tracing a program.
17. What two steps must you take before you can write a program to disk using DEBUG?

## EXERCISES*

1. Using a place value table for an eight-bit unsigned binary number, convert the following decimal numbers to binary:

   31    57    84    106    127    155    189    240

2. Using a place value table for an eight-bit signed binary number, convert the following decimal numbers to binary:

   48    96    125    -1    -19    -64    -100    -128

3. Write the decimal value for each of these signed binary numbers:

   01010101    10101010    00010011    11110000    10000001

4. Add the following binary numbers. Check the results in decimal.

   ```
    00001111     00001010     00110011     11110000     11001100
   +00001100    +00101010    +11001101    +00111100    +11101011
   ```

5. Add the following binary numbers. Mark any answers in which overflow occurred:

   ```
    00101010     01100110     01111111     01111111     10010101
   +01000100    +01000000    +11111100    +01010101    +10111111
   ```

6.  Using a hex place value table, convert the following unsigned decimal numbers to hex:

    33   59   86   108   255   512   4095   5000

7.  Convert the following unsigned hex numbers to decimal:

    40   87   100   125   207   4AB   CAD   BEEF

8.  Add the following hex unsigned hex numbers:

    ```
     1234    5793    47AD    9999    FF29    BEAD
    +1345   +4321   +9904   +0BAD   +FFED   +DEAF
    ```

9.  Referring to the ASCII character table in this chapter (see Figure 1-6), show the two-digit hex code for each letter of the following:

    Your name   MS-DOS   $1,234.56   IBM-PC   DEBUG

10. Using DEBUG, place the following hex values into the registers shown:

    AX=4328   CX-0005   ES-4800   SI-0060   DX-FFFF

11. Using DEBUG, unassemble the instructions at the address 7600:0100.

12. Using DEBUG, enter in hex the ASCII values for your name at address 7600:0100. Then dump memory starting at that location.

---

*NOTE: Answers to exercises appear in Appendix F.

# LAB PROBLEMS

1.  Load DEBUG and, at the address provided by MS-DOS in CS and IP, assemble the following statements:

    ```
    MOV AX,0078
    MOV BX,1234
    ADD AX,BX
    INT 20
    ```

    Then unassemble these statements to see that they were correctly translated. Trace through the instructions, stopping when the address in CS changes to one supplied by MS-DOS following the INT 20 instruction. Reset the values in CS and IP to those at which you started the program. Give the program the name B:PROG1.COM. Put the program length in CX and zero in BX. Write the program to disk. Quit DEBUG and display the directory to drive B to ensure that the program was saved.

2.  At the MS-DOS A>, type DEBUG B:PROG1.COM. When DEBUG is loaded, unassemble statements at the address specified by CS and IP. Confirm that they are the program you entered in Lab 1. Reassemble the program, changing the third statement to SUB AX,BX. Trace through the instructions, noting that the sum in AX is negative (EE44). Save this program under the name B:PROG1A.COM.

# GETTING STARTED IN ASSEMBLER LANGUAGE

# 2

## OBJECTIVES
After studying this chapter, you should be able to:

- Describe the steps in the overall assembly process.
- Name and describe the types of statements used in assembler language.
- Identify the segments of a program.
- Define the beginning and end of programs, segments, and procedures.
- Explain the difference between data constants and storage definitions.
- Explain differences between COM and EXE programs.
- Name and describe the inputs and outputs of the assembler.
- Explain the function of the linker and its inputs and outputs.
- Use DEBUG to examine and trace COM and EXE programs.

## OVERVIEW OF THE ASSEMBLY PROCESS

Several steps are necessary to produce an assembler language program and get it ready for execution. These steps require use of at least three and sometimes four different programs.

First, you must write the source program in assembler language. You may use EDLIN, a utility program provided by DOS, or a word processor to write this program and save it as a disk file. You should assign a file name with an extension of .ASM to the source program.

Next, load the assembler (MASM or ASM) and submit your source program to it for translation. The assembler produces an object program and saves it with a file name with extension of .OBJ. It also may produce two optional files, one with an extension of .LST for listing on the printer and another with .CRF for showing a cross-reference of names used in the program.

The third step is to submit the object program to LINK, a DOS program that produces a load module which is given a file name with extension of

.EXE.LINK also may combine our object module with other object modules previously assembled. LINK may produce an optional map (with filename and extension .MAP) naming the various object modules that have been combined.

A load module with .EXE extension is now ready to be loaded and executed. However, depending upon how you have written your source program, you may wish to convert the EXE program to an executable load module with an extension of .COM in the file name. Another DOS utility named EXE2BIN performs this conversion. Later in this chapter we shall discuss differences between EXE and COM programs.

Once the load module is in the desired EXE or COM form, you may load it into memory and execute it merely by typing its name when DOS displays the A> prompt. It is not necessary to type the EXE or COM extension. Example:

```
A> B:PROGRAM1
```

Figure 2-1 shows the steps in creating an assembler language program.

## TYPES OF STATEMENTS

Statements that you write in assembler language are called *source statements*. Each statement may have up to four optional fields and is limited to a single line (brackets enclose optional items). The statement syntax is:

[name] [operation] [operands] [;comments]

where *name* identifies the statement so that it can be referred to elsewhere in the program, *operation* defines what the statement is to do, *operands* describe the registers or data to be operated on by the statement, and *comments* supply additional information not processed by the assembler.

Each field, except comments, must be separated from other fields by a space or tab character. Uppercase or lowercase letters may be used. Statements generally may be written in free form, but it is common practice to start fields in specific columns to make programs more readable. In this book, the name field is started in column 1, the operation field in column 11, the operands field after the operation, and comments in column 36. Comments must be preceded by a semicolon (;).

The name of a variable or instruction is also called a *symbol*. A symbol naming an instruction is called a *label* and must be followed by a colon (:). The symbol may be of any length, but only the first 31 characters are recognized by the assembler. It may contain letters, digits, question marks, at (@) signs, underscores, dollar signs, and periods. However, the first character of the symbol may not be a digit, and a period when used must be the first character. The assembler will recognize either uppercase or lowercase letters. *Reserved names* are words having special meaning to the assembler. Reserved names may not be used as names of instructions or data.

| Inputs | Program | Outputs |
|---|---|---|
| Programmer's logical plan | EDLIN or word processor | Source program [Macros] [Subroutines] |
| Source program [INCLUDE modules] [Macro libraries] | MASM or other assembler | Object module [Listing module] [Cross-reference] |
| Object modules [Object libraries] | LINK | EXE load module [Map] |
| [EXE load module | EXE2BIN | COM load module] |
| Input data | COM or EXE load module | Output data |

*Note:* [ ] denote optional items or steps.

**Figure 2-1    Creating an Assembler Language Program**

There are four general types into which source statements may be divided: (a) instructions, (b) directives, (c) macros, and (d) comments. A discussion of these source statements follows.

## Instructions

*Instructions* indicate what actions the computer should take. They are translated by the assembler directly into machine language object code. One instruction in assembler language produces one machine language instruction.

Operation fields usually are called *op codes* in assembler language. They are short words of two to six letters corresponding to verbs that describe an operation or action to be taken. Only those words defined within assembler language may be used as op codes. The words are *abbreviations* or *mnemonics*, terms that are an aid to memory. MOV (move), CMP (compare), and ADD are three of the mnemonics widely used in assembler language.

*Operands* refer to data to be processed by the op codes. Operands may be the names of registers, names of data fields, character strings enclosed in quotation marks, or numbers. Operands usually are separated by a comma.

Decimal, binary, or hexadecimal numbers may be operands. Decimal numbers require no special identification, but may end with the letter D (upper- or lowercase) for clarity if desired. The number 256 may be written as

256, 0256, or 256d. Binary numbers must end with the letter B (upper- or lowercase). Hex numbers must end with the letter H (upper- or lowercase) and may not begin with the digits A through F. A leading zero must precede any hex number starting with A through F to keep the number from being confused with a word. Examples: 0FEEDh, 0A4h, 0Bh.

### Directives

*Directives*, also called *pseudo-operations (pseudo-ops)*, are statements that instruct the assembler to do something when the program is being assembled rather than when the program is being executed. Except for definitions of data constants, directives are not converted into machine language. A complete list of directives appears in Appendix G.

### Macros

*Macros* are single statements used in the operation field that may have operands that cause one or more source statements to be placed into the program by the assembler. Macros are a type of shorthand that allow us to write only one statement instead of all the statements the macro produces.

Before any macro can be used, it must first be defined to show the statements that are to be inserted, or generated, in the source program. Macros will be discussed in detail in Chapter 11.

### Comments

A well-documented program contains *comments* which identify the program, describe its functions, and explain individual instructions. Comments are valuable to describe special uses of registers or the conditions under which certain actions are taken.

In this text we shall use comments to reflect program logic through pseudocode. These comments parallel the machine instructions to provide structured programming. Chapter 4 will emphasize comments in this context.

*Full-line comments* may be written by placing a semicolon (;) in the first column of the line. *Partial-line comments* may be written after the operands of instructions, pseudo-ops, or macros if preceded by a semicolon.

## DEFINING SEGMENTS

Programs are typically divided into three or more *segments*. A segment is a collection of instructions or data whose addresses are relative to the same segment register. The segments we may use are:

| Name | Register | Contents |
|------|----------|----------|
| Code segment | CS | Instructions |
| Data segment | DS | Data constants and variable fields |
| Extra segment | ES | Additional data |
| Stack segment | SS | Area for saving words from registers and memory |
| Extra segment | FS | Additional data (80386 only) |
| Extra segment | GS | Additional data (80386 only) |

Each segment is normally limited to 64K, but under some conditions may be larger. Exceptions will be discussed in Chapter 12.

Versions 1.0 through 4.0 of the MASM assembler required full segment definitions. Starting with MASM 5.0 a simplified system of segment directives was implemented. We will use full definitions in our sample programs, but will explain the simplified form in Chapter 12.

## The Code Segment

The code segment contains machine instructions and (later) macros that specify the actions to be taken to process data. The code segment is divided into one or more *procedures*, classified as NEAR or FAR. *Near procedures* must all be contained in the same segment, while *far procedures* may be in different segments. We will explain these details later in the text. For now, let's see how the code segment is defined.

The directives

```
CODE       SEGMENT
           ASSUME CS:CODE
PROGNAME   PROC NEAR

PROGNAME   ENDP
CODE       ENDS
```

designate the start and end of the code segment named CODE which encloses a near procedure named PROGNAME. The name of each segment must appear in the SEGMENT statement at the beginning and the ENDS statement at the end of each segment. The name of each procedure must appear in the PROC statement at the beginning and the ENDP statement at the end of each procedure. Each procedure must be completely *nested*, or enclosed, within the code segment.

The directive

```
ASSUME CS:CODE
```

tells the assembler that it should calculate all offsets from the location of CODE in main memory. This address of CODE is placed in the CS register by DOS when the program is loaded into memory.

## The Data Segment

The data segment contains definitions of constants and storage space for variable data used by the program. It may be defined with the statements

```
DATA        SEGMENT
            . .
DATA        ENDS
```

Between the SEGMENT statement and the ENDS statement are the data definitions.

An ASSUME statement is required to specify the address of the data segment that will be in the DS register. The same ASSUME statement used in the code segment also can designate the address to be in the DS register. The statement

```
        ASSUME CS:CODE, DS:DATA
```

would typically be used. The programmer is responsible for actually placing the correct address in the DS register. This will be discussed in the sample programs later in this chapter.

***Defining Constants.***    The DB (define byte) directive allows you to define one or more bytes and assign values to the bytes. You also may give a name to the byte and assign values to the bytes. You also may give a name to the byte, or the first byte of the string, if more than one byte is defined. You may put one or more ASCII characters between single or double quotation marks, or you may specify any value from 0 to 255 as an unsigned decimal, hex, or binary number or values from -128 to 127 as a signed number. You also may use commas to separate several values in a single DB statement.

You may define more than one occurrence of a byte by writing the number of occurrences followed by the word DUP and the value to be repeated enclosed in parentheses.

Here are some examples, showing the hex codes to the left of the DB statements:

| Object Code | Instruction |
|---|---|
| 01 02 03 | DB 1,2,3 |
| 31 32 33 | DB '1','2', '3' |
| 41 42 43 44 | DB 'ABCD' |
| 30 30 30 30 30 | DB 5 DUP ('0') |
| FF FF FF | DB 3 DUP (0FFh) |
| 48 45 4C 4C 4F 0D 0A 24 | DB 'HELLO',13,10,'$' |

In the last example, the value 13 is the code for a *cursor return*, 10 is a *line feed*, and the $ indicates the end of a string to be printed or displayed by DOS. A line feed moves the cursor to the next line on the screen or printer, while a cursor return moves the cursor to the leftmost position on a line.

The DW (define word) directive creates a two-byte constant having unsigned values from 0 to 65535 or signed values from -32768 to 32767:

| Object Code | Instruction |
|---|---|
| 12 00 34 00 | `DW 12h, 34h` |
| FF FF | `DW 65535` |
| 08 00 08 00 | `DW 2 DUP (1000b)` |
| FF FF | `DW -1` |

Note that words are stored with the *least significant byte* (LSB) to the left of the *most significant byte* (MSB), as in the first and third examples above. The actual values are 0012 and 0034, respectively, in the first example and 0008 and 0008 in the third. Some versions of MASM show words in their normal order on program listings, but always store them in main memory with the LSB to the left of the MSB.

The DD, DF, and DQ directives create four-byte, six-byte, and eight-byte integers respectively. Words of this size cannot be processed through 16-bit registers and are used primarily with 8087 or 80386 processors. The DT (define tenword) directive will be discussed in Chapter 8.

*Defining Storage.*    The DB and DW directives also are used to define areas of storage where data will be put later. In these cases, no values are specified. You may reserve a single byte, a single word, or any specified number of each. A question mark (?) indicates that no value is placed in the area reserved. A number followed by the word DUP can specify the number of bytes or words to be reserved. The question mark following DUP is placed in parentheses.

The following examples reserve one byte, one word, eight bytes, and 10 words, respectively:

Instruction

```
DB ?
DW ?
DB 8 DUP (?)
DW 10 DUP (?)
```

The DD, DF, DQ, and DT directives also can be used to reserve space for larger numbers.

## The Stack Segment

The *stack* is an area of storage where the contents of various 16-bit registers may be saved as desired. It may be any size desired up to 64k. For most of the programs in this book, we will use a stack of 256 bytes, defined as follows:

```
STACK     SEGMENT STACK
          DB 32 DUP ('STACK  ')
STACK     ENDS
```

These statements create an area holding the word STACK followed by three spaces repeated 32 times in the 256-byte area. Such a stack is easy to recognize when you examine your object program in memory through DEBUG.

The address where the stack begins is placed by DOS in the SS (stack segment) register. The SP (stack pointer) register is initially set by DOS to the highest word in the stack. SP is adjusted everytime a word is added to or removed form the stack to specify the offset from SS to the address where the next word is to be placed. This location is called the *top of the stack*.

The same ASSUME statement that give the addresses in CS and DS also may tell MASM the address of the stack, as in

```
ASSUME CS:CODE, DS:DATA, SS:STACK
```

The stack will be discussed briefly later in this chapter and more fully in Chapter 6.

## COM VERSUS EXE PROGRAMS

DOS recognizes two kinds of executable load modules—those with an extension of .COM and those with .EXE. The program created in Chapter 1 using DEBUG was a COM program. All programs processed through LINK are EXE programs. There are a number of important differences between these two types of programs.

We shall explain the differences in purpose and format between COM and EXE programs and give an overview of the steps in creating, assembling, linking, and executing each type of program.

### COM Programs

The COM extension designates a program that can be completely contained within one 64k segment. COM programs usually are short and not capable of being combined with programs written in other languages. DOS creates a 256-byte (100h) *program segment prefix* (PSP) in front of the program when it is loaded form disk into main storage for execution. The PSP and program are loaded just above the resident portion of DOS. The *resident portion* of DOS is that part of the operating system placed in memory when the system is booted up and remains there throughout normal operation of the system.

The address of the PSP for a COM program is placed by DOS into all four segment registers when the program is loaded. Recall from Figure 1-3 that the segment registers are code (CS), data (DS), stack (SS), and extra (ES). The first instruction in the code segment must be at an offset of 100h. This is why we placed the offset of 100h in the instruction pointer (IP) register when we wrote our program in Chapter 1 with DEBUG.

Figure 2-2 shows the relationship between the segment registers, the PSP, and the rest of the program. COM load modules are efficient for short programs because they require less space on disk and less time to load.

The code segment for a COM program should start this way:

```
CODE        SEGMENT
            ORG 100H
            ASSUME CS:CODE,DS:CODE, ES:CODE, SS:CODE
PROCNAME    PROC NEAR
```

These statements give the name CODE to the address where the PSP is loaded, tell the assembler that all four segment registers will contain that address, and indicate the first statement in a procedure named PROCNAME will originate (ORG) at an offset of 100h.

The code segment should return to DOS with either an INT 20h or these statements, which place 4Ch into AH and 00 into AL at the same time:

```
            MOV AX, 4C00h
            INT 21h
PROCNAME    ENDP
```

No separate data segment is defined in a COM program. Data and the stack are in the same segment with the program code. (You may define any

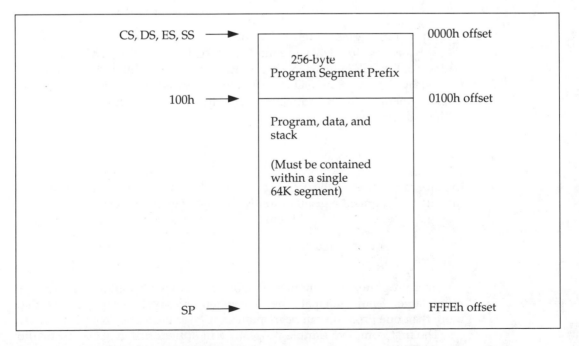

**Figure 2-2    Arrangement of a COM Program**

data constants or storage locations between the ENDP statement for the last procedure and the ENDS statement for the code segment.)

No separate stack segment is defined in a COM program. The stack pointer (SP) is set by MS-DOS initially at FFFEh so that words are placed on the stack at even numbered addresses at the high end of the segment containing the code.

The precise DOS commands to assemble the COM program, link the object module, and convert the resulting EXE form to COM form will be shown later in the chapter.

## EXE Programs

Programs assembled by MASM are normally written as EXE programs and processed by LINK into load modules with the EXE extension. Such files have a block of header information giving control information useful to DOS. The header is stored on disk ahead of the object code. Figure 2-3 shows the arrangement of an EXE program when loaded into memory for execution. Note its characteristics.

Separate code, data, and stack segments must be defined. Each can have a maximum size of 64K.

The ASSUME statement usually appears just after the CODE SEGMENT statement and reads:

```
ASSUME   CS:CODE,DS:DATA,SS:STACK,ES:DATA
```

A program segment prefix (PSP) of 256 bytes is placed by DOS in front of the EXE load module when the module is loaded from disk. DOS places the address of the PSP in registers DS and ES because sometimes data in the PSP is used by the program. DOS places the correct addresses of the code and stack segments into CS and SS, respectively. The first executable statements in the code segment are usually:

```
MOV AX,DATA
MOV DS,AX
```

to place the address of the data segment into DS. Addresses cannot be moved directly to a segment register but only through a general register.

The code segment should return to DOS with:

```
MOV AX, 4C00h
INT 21h
```

EXE programs are far more flexible than COM programs and can be much larger. They anticipate the time when DOS will be expanded so that more than one program can be in main storage at the same time.

The first complete sample program will appear first in COM form and then in EXE form.

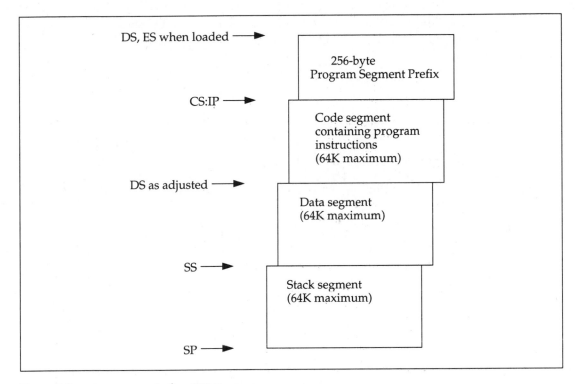

**Figure 2-3    Arrangement of an EXE Program**

## PROGRAM 2A: COM PROGRAM TO PRINT FOUR-LINE NAME AND ADDRESS

For our first complete demonstration program, we will define and print out a four-line name and address. Here we introduce all the required parts of a program and provide an outline form, called a *template* or *skeleton*, into which later programs can be fitted. Figure 2-4 shows a listing of the complete COM program. We will discuss each part in detail.

### Program Description and Comments

The first statement

```
PAGE 50,132
```

is not a comment but a directive telling the assembler to arrange the listing file to print 50 lines per page (leaving margins of eight lines at top and bottom of 11-inch paper) and make each line 132 characters long. At time of printing you can compress the print on most printers and show each source statement, with the translated object code, on a single printed line. The PAGE directive is optional in the source program.

```
          PAGE 50,132
;------------------------------------------------------------------------
; Program name:  PROG2A.ASM
;
; Author:        Alton R. Kindred
;
; This COM program displays name, company, address, and city, state,
; and zip code on four lines.
;------------------------------------------------------------------------
CODE     SEGMENT
         ORG 100h
         ASSUME CS:CODE,DS:CODE,SS:CODE,ES:CODE
PROG2A   PROC NEAR
         MOV DX,OFFSET MYNAME      ;display name
         MOV AH,9
         INT 21h
         MOV DX,OFFSET COMPANY     ;display company name
         MOV AH,9
         INT 21h
         MOV DX,OFFSET ADDRESS     ;display address
         MOV AH,9
         INT 21h
         MOV DX,OFFSET CITYSTZIP   ;display city, state, and zip
         MOV AH,9
         INT 21h
         INT 20h                   ;return to DOS
PROG2A   ENDP
;------------------------------------------------------------------------
;                    Data Definitions
;
MYNAME    DB 'Alton R. Kindred',13,10,'$'
COMPANY   DB 'Manatee Community College',13,10,'$'
ADDRESS   DB '5840 26th Street West',13,10,'$'
CITYSTZIP DB 'Bradenton, FL 34207',13,10,'$'
;------------------------------------------------------------------------
CODE     ENDS
         END PROG2A
```

**Figure 2-4    COM Source Program to Print a Four-Line Name and Address**

Comments must begin with a semicolon (;). To improve the appearance of our source program, we use a frame with hyphens at the top and bottom and semicolons down the left margin to enclose our program description and comments. We also use comments with only a hyphen on the line to separate different parts of the program.

Program names follow the rules for file names under DOS. The first character must be a letter, and there must be no more than eight letters or digits in the name. Following the period is the file extension (.ASM) indicating that this is an assembler source program. Another comment identifies the author. The program description may be as short or long as necessary to describe the purpose of the program.

## The Segment

A COM program must be contained within a single segment. The following statements define a segment named CODE:

```
CODE        SEGMENT
            ORG 100h
            ASSUME CS:CODE, DS:CODE, SS:CODE
            ..
CODE        ENDS
            END PROG2A
```

The SEGMENT and ENDS directives designate the beginning and end of the segment. The directive

```
    ORG 100h
```

tells the assembler to start (originate) the machine code at an offset of 100h from the start of the code segment. When the program is loaded into memory for execution, the instruction pointer (IP) will contain the offset of 100h.

The ASSUME statement indicates that all four segment registers will contain the address of CODE. This address will be placed by DOS into these registers when the program is loaded into memory. ES will not actually be used in this program.

The last statement

```
    END PROG2A
```

identifies for the assembler the last statement to be assembled and gives the address (PROG2A) of the first instruction to be executed.

In COM programs no stack segment is defined. The stack occupies the same segment as the instructions, and the SS register will contain the address of CODE. The stack pointer (SP) is normally set by DOS to FFFEh so that words are placed on the stack near the high end of the code segment. The stack will be discussed more fully in Chapter 6.

The segment is divided into two parts, (a) a procedure named PROG2A that contains the instructions and (b) data definitions.

*Instructions.*    The instructions are contained in a procedure defined with these statements:

```
PROG2A      PROC NEAR
            ..
PROG2A      ENDP
```

in which *near procedures* all must be contained within the same segment, while *far procedures* may be in different segments. We will explain these details regarding near and far procedures in Chapter 6.

The instructions display on the screen the four lines of name and address defined in the data definitions. The interrupt (INT 21h) is a DOS utility that permits input and output in a number of different forms. The value in the AH register at the time the interrupt is executed determines what operation takes place. The code 9 in AH causes a string of characters to be displayed on the screen. The address of the line to be displayed must be in the DX register before the interrupt is executed.

The MOV (move) instruction is one of the most widely used machine instructions to move data or address from one location or register to another. It has the general form.

```
MOV destination, source
```

where *destination* may be a register or a memory location and *source* may be a register, memory location, or an immediate value (an actual number). The instructions

```
MOV DX,OFFSET MYNAME
MOV AH,9
INT 21h
```

get ready to print the MYNAME field described later in the program. The OFFSET operator specifies that the *address* of MYNAME rather than the *word* at MYNAME should be moved to the DX register. The data contained in the MYNAME field must be a string of characters ending with a dollar sign required by INT 21h.

We use these three instructions to place the offset address of COMPANY, ADDRESS, and CITYSTZIP into DX and display each of the other three lines.

The final instruction INT 20h causes the COM program to return to DOS when it is completed.

***Data Definitions.***    The data in a COM program occupies the same segment as the instructions. However, to separate it logically from the instructions we place it after the procedure containing the instructions but before the end of the segment.

The following constants define the name, company, address, and city, state, and zip:

```
MYNAME     DB 'Alton R. Kindred',13,10,'$'
COMPANY    DB 'Manatee Community College',13,10,'$'
ADDRESS    DB '5840 26th Street West', 13,10,'$'
CITYSTZIP  DB 'Bradenton, FL 34207',13,10,'$'
```

Each line is followed by a cursor return (code 13), line feed (code 10), and dollar sign ($). The cursor return moves the cursor to the left of the screen, and the line feed moves it to the next line. The dollar sign is required by DOS to indicate the end of the string of characters to be processed by INT 21h.

The symbol MYNAME rather than NAME identifies the first line because of the fact that NAME is a reserved name to the assembler and cannot be used as the name of a string.

## WRITING THE SOURCE PROGRAM

Now that you have seen the form of an assembler language COM source program, you need to prepare it for input to the assembler in the form of text using ASCII characters. You may use EDLIN, a line editor provided with DOS, or any more suitable word processing program that produces an ASCII file.

With EDLIN or a word processor you can create new files of source statements and save them on disk. You can update existing files by deleting, editing, inserting, and displaying lines in the files. You also can search for, delete, or replace text within one or more lines in a file. Appendix H shows how to use EDLIN and gives a complete list of the EDLIN commands.

The advantage of a word processor over EDLIN is that you may use its full-screen editing ability to edit any statement in the program merely by moving the cursor around rather than by having to type and edit each line separately.

Use of special control codes, such as underlining, should be avoided. The assembler is not able to recognize special codes used by some of the word processors. It is the usual practice to save the source statements in ASCII format, which strips away any special codes in the text, and to use an extension of .ASM with the file name.

## ASSEMBLING THE PROGRAM

Once the source program is written and saved on disk, you are ready to submit it to the assembler (MASM or ASM) for translation. From this point on, we will refer to the assembler as MASM. Our programs will be assembled on version 5.0. Versions later than 5.0 should assemble programs written for earlier versions.

Put the system disk containing the MASM into drive A and your data disk holding the source program into drive B. At the A> prompt, type

```
A> MASM
```

DOS loads MASM and displays copyright and version information. MASM asks for the names of various files. Generally, MASM gives each file a specific extension by default. The extension .ASM indicates a source file, .OBJ the object file (the primary output), .LST an optional source listing file, and .CRF an optional cross-reference file. The default for .LST and .CRF is a null file (no file). You should request each file but the cross-reference (which gives an alphabetical list of all names used in the program) The cross-reference listing is unnecessary with the short programs we will use and takes up valuable disk space.

After you respond to various prompts, pressing <ENTER> after each, your screen should look like this:

```
Source filename [.ASM]: B:PROG2A
Object filename [B:PROG2A.OBJ]:
Source listing  [NUL.LST]: B:PROG2A
Cross-reference [NUL.CRF]:
```

The word NUL as the file name for the listing and cross-reference files indicates that no file will be created unless you give a specific name for the file.

After you answer the last prompt, MASM translates your source code into object code in two passes. During the first pass it sets a location counter and determines the offset of every label and instruction from the start of the respective segment. The second pass creates the actual object file and places it on disk.

If you prefer, you can tell the assembler what files you wish in a command line in the following format:

```
A>MASM sourcefile[,objectfile][,[listingfile][,
      [crossreferencefile]]]][;]
```

where the file names give the same information you supplied through the MASM prompts. You may supply your own file names or accept the default choices from MASM for any except the source file by typing only a comma for that file. A semicolon terminates the line and prevents the creation of any following files.

The statement

```
A>MASM B:PROG2A,B:PROG2A,B:PROG2A;
```

indicates you wish to assemble a source file named PROG2A.ASM on drive B and create object file B:PROG2A.OBJ and listing file B:PROG2A.LST. The semicolon prevents creation of a cross-reference file. The assembler will attach the standard extension to the filename unless you give a different extension in the command line.

An even shorter command line can be written if you tell DOS to assign your default disk drive to drive B as follows:

```
A> B:
B> A:MASM PROG2A,,;
```

The assembler will look for PROG2A.ASM on drive B; assign names of PROG2A.ASM, PROG2A.OBJ, and PROG2A.LST, respectively; and place the output files on drive B.

## LOCATING AND REMOVING ERRORS

There are two major types of programming errors. *Errors in syntax* violate some rule of assembler language, such as using an invalid mnemonic or failing to use an ENDS directive paired with a SEGMENT directive. Errors in syntax can be detected by the assembler and are shown on the assembler listing file.

*Errors in logic* occur when you write instructions in the correct form but use them to do the wrong thing or the right thing in the wrong sequence. Logical errors are not detected by the assembler, but can be found only by running the program after it has been linked and seeing if it produces the expected results.

Some common syntax errors include the following:

1. Failure to show segment names on both SEGMENT and ENDS directives.
2. Failure to show procedure name on both PROC and ENDP directives.
3. Failure to include the final END directive and to show as an operand the name of the first instruction to be executed.
4. Misspelling reserved names.
5. Using reserved names for symbols or labels.
6. Failure to use a colon following the label of an instruction.
7. Improper nesting of procedures within the code segment.
8. Omitting the semicolon preceding comments.

Some common logical errors include the following:

1. Failure to end a string of characters with a dollar sign.
2. Failure to use the operator OFFSET when moving an address to a register.
3. Reversing the first and second operands in instructions.

We will discuss detection and correction of errors as we cover additional features throughout the text.

If the assembler finds no errors in your source program, after a few moments it will display:

```
Warning  Severe
Errors   Errors
0        0
```

and return to the DOS A> prompt.

If there are errors, you must remove them and reassemble the program. The LST file can be a great help in locating errors. The assembler will indicate each error and give the probable reason for it. You can examine the listing on the screen by entering the DOS command:

```
A> TYPE B:PROG2A.LST or B> TYPE PROG2A.LST
```

The listing should look like Figure 2-5. On the screen, each line extending beyond 80 characters will wrap around to the next line.

At the left of each line is shown the offset in hex of each statement and label from the start of the current segment. To the right of the offset is the object code for the machine instructions or the ASCII code for each constant we have defined, both in hex. Still further to the right is each source statement just as it was presented to the assembler.

The last page of the listing is the symbol table. It gives information about each segment and the offset and type of each symbol or label.

You can divert the listing to the printer and display 132 characters per line in compressed format by entering at the A> prompt:

```
A> MODE LPT1:132,6
A> TYPE B:PROG2A.LST > PRN
```

The DOS utility program MODE must be on the system disk on drive A. Some printers have external buttons that can be pressed to produce compressed print without the DOS MODE utility.

Finding errors is easier on a hard copy (printed) listing. It provides a permanent record of both the source and object program for future reference.

## LINKING THE PROGRAM

LINK is a DOS utility program that converts one or more object files into an EXE executable load module and stores it on disk. You load LINK at the DOS A> prompt by typing:

```
A> LINK
```

LINK responds with copyright information and then asks for the name of the object module (or modules). You enter B:PROG2A. LINK responds with the name of the EXE file and asks if you wish to produce a list file that gives a map of segment addresses. Specify B:PROG2A as the name for the map listing. LINK asks if any libraries of procedures are to be searched. You have no library at this time and merely press <ENTER> The screen will look like this following your conversation with LINK:

```
Object Modules [.OBJ]: B:PROG2A
Run File [B:PROG2A.EXE]:
List File [NUL.MAP]: B:PROG2A
Libraries [.LIB]:
```

LINK will produce the message

```
Warning: No stack segment
```

Microsoft (R) Macro Assembler Version 5.00          9/19/89 15:04:27
                                                      Page      1-1


PAGE 50,132
    ; ------------------------------------------------------------------
    ; Program name:  PROG2A.ASM
    ;
    ; Author:        Alton R. Kindred
    ;
    ; This COM program displays name, company, address, and city, state,
    ; and zip code on four lines.
    ;------------------------------------------------------------------
0000CODE         SEGMENT
0100             ORG 100h
          ASSUME CS:CODE,DS:CODE,SS:CODE,ES:CODE
0100PROG2A      PROC NEAR
0100  BA 011E R      MOV DX,OFFSET MYNAME    ;display name
0103  B4 09          MOV AH,9
0105  CD 21          INT 21h
0107  BA 0131 R      MOV DX,OFFSET COMPANY   ;display company name
010A  B4 09          MOV AH,9
010C  CD 21          INT 21h
010E  BA 014D R      MOV DX,OFFSET ADDRESS   ;display address
0111  B4 09          MOV AH,9
0113  CD 21          INT 21h
0115  BA 0165 R      MOV DX,OFFSET CITYSTZIP;display city, state, and zip code
0118  B4 09          MOV AH,9
011A  CD 21          INT 21h
011C  CD 20          INT 20h                 ;return to DOS
011EPROG2A      ENDP
    ;------------------------------------------------------------------
    ;                     Data Definitions
    ;
011E  41 6C 74 6F 6E 20 52      MYNAME    DB 'Alton R. Kindred',13,10,'$'
      2E 20 4B 69 6E 64 72
      65 64 0D 0A 24
0131  4D 61 6E 61 74 65 65      COMPANY   DB 'Manatee Community College',13,10,'$'
      20 43 6F 6D 6D 75 6E
      69 74 79 20 43 6F 6C
      6C 65 67 65 0D 0A 24
014D  35 38 34 30 20 32 36      ADDRESS   DB '5840 26th Street West',13,10,'$'
      74 68 20 53 74 72 65
      65 74 20 57 65 73 74
      0D 0A 24
0165  42 72 61 64 65 6E 74      CITYSTZIP DB 'Bradenton, FL 34207',13,10,'$'
      6F 6E 2C 20 46 4C 20
      33 34 32 30 37 0D 0A
      24
;------------------------------------------------------------------
Microsoft (R) Macro Assembler Version 5.00          9/19/89 15:04:27
                                                      Page      1-2


**Figure 2-5    Assembler Output Listing of PROG2A**

```
017BCODE        ENDS
          END PROG2A
Microsoft (R) Macro Assembler Version 5.00              9/19/89 15:04:27
                                                            Symbols-1


Segments and Groups:

                N a m e              Length AlignCombine Class

CODE . . . . . . . . . . . . . .     017BPARANONE

Symbols:

                N a m e              Type Value Attr

ADDRESS . . . . . . . . . . .        L BYTE014DCODE


CITYSTZIP . . . . . . . . . .        L BYTE0165CODE
COMPANY . . . . . . . . . . .        L BYTE0131CODE


MYNAME . . . . . . . . . . . .       L BYTE011ECODE


PROG2A . . . . . . . . . . . .       N PROC0100CODELength = 001E


. . . . . . . . . .      TEXT   prog2a



    37 Source  Lines
    37 Total   Lines
     8 Symbols

  51176 + 405528 Bytes symbol space free

      0 Warning Errors
      0 Severe  Errors
```

**Figure 2-5**    *continued*

which can be ignored with a COM program. If LINK detects any other error, it is most likely that you have incorrectly spelled the name of a file in a prompt or command line. Correct the name and run LINK again.

As with MASM, instead of responding to the  prompts you may give LINK a command line to designate the desired files. The format is:

```
A> LINK objectfiles[,[executablefile][,[mapfile]
   [,[libraryfiles]]]][;]
```

where *objectfiles* and *libraryfiles* are input and *executablefile* and *mapfile* are output. The following command line would expect B:PROG2A.OBJ as the input file, give the name B:PROG2A to the EXE file and the MAP file, and tell LINK that there is no LIB file to be searched:

```
A> LINK B:PROG2A,B:PROG2A,B:PROG2A;
```

or, if you have assigned drive B as the default drive:

```
B> A:LINK PROG2A,,;
```

would produce the same result more easily.

You may ask DOS to display the LINK map file by typing:

```
A> TYPE B:PROG2A.MAP
```

and the map appears as follows:

```
LINK: warning L4021: no stack segment
Start    Stop    Length  Name         Class
00000H  0017AH  0017BH  CODE
Program entry point at 0000:0100
```

The map shows the starting point of the program within the code segment and specifies the length of the segment.

At this point you could request a directory of your data disk:

```
A> DIR B:
```

and find that you have five or six versions of PROG2A. They have extensions of ASM, BAK (if you used EDLIN or certain word processors), OBJ, LST, MAP, and EXE. The files for ASM and LST are much longer than the others. This is due to the number of comments and labels used in the source code. Object code contains no comments and labels. A BAK file is produced each time you update a source file with EDLIN or some word processors. The previous version of the file is given the extension BAK, while the new version is named with extension ASM. Eventually, you may wish to erase all of these files except ASM and EXE to save disk space.

## EXECUTING EXE2BIN

If you had written an EXE program, you could now execute it by typing

```
A> B:PROG2A
```

However, you wrote this program to be run as a COM program. So you must now submit the EXE version produced by LINK to EXE2BIN to convert it to COM. EXE2BIN does not provide any prompts, so you must specify the name of the EXE and COM files as a command line when you load EXE2BIN for execution:

```
A> EXE2BIN B:PROG2A.EXE B:PROG2A.COM
```

If you have correctly spelled both file names and EXE2BIN runs successfully, you can then take two steps to confirm that both the COM and EXE files are on your data disk and then erase the EXE version:

```
A> DIR B:
A> ERASE B:PROG2A.EXE
```

You can print or display ASM, LST, or MAP files since they are created using ASCII characters, but you cannot print or display OBJ, COM, or EXE files since they are in machine code.

## EXECUTING THE PROGRAM

You now can run the COM load module by typing:

```
A> B:PROG2A or A> B:PROG2A.COM
```

You should see the program output on the screen as the four lines you defined as constants, followed by the A prompt upon return to DOS:

```
Alton R. Kindred
Manatee Community College
5840 26th Street West
Bradenton, FL 34207
A>
```

If you do not get these results, you must determine the cause of the logic error. First, carefully examine the source statements and mentally step through the program. If this does not give a clue as to the error, load the program with DEBUG and trace through the program, examining the registers and lines of output if any. In a short program such as PROG2A you should find any error fairly easily.

When the error is found, reload EDLIN or other word processor, make the corrections, and repeat the process of assembly, linking, and execution.

## PROGRAM 2B: EXE PROGRAM TO PRINT 4-LINE NAME AND ADDRESS

Figure 2-6 presents an EXE version of the same program. We have changed the program name to B:PROG2B.ASM to keep it separate from B:PROG2A.ASM. For an EXE program, you must define separate segments for code, data, and stack. It is common practice to define the data segment first so that the assembler can calculate the offsets of data elements before they are referred to in the code segment:

```
DATA       SEGMENT
           (DB or DW statements here)
```

```
          PAGE 50,132
;-------------------------------------------------------------------------------
; Program name:  PROG2B.ASM
;
; Author:        Alton R. Kindred
;
; This EXE program displays name, company, address, and city, state,
; and zip code on four lines.
;-------------------------------------------------------------------------------
DATA        SEGMENT
MYNAME      DB 'Alton R. Kindred',13,10,'$'
COMPANY     DB 'Manatee Community College',13,10,'$'
ADDRESS     DB '5840 26th Street West',13,10,'$'
CITYSTZIP   DB 'Bradenton, FL 34207',13,10,'$'
DATA        ENDS
;-------------------------------------------------------------------------------
STACK       SEGMENT STACK
            DB 32 DUP ('STACK   ')
STACK       ENDS
;-------------------------------------------------------------------------------
CODE        SEGMENT
            ASSUME CS:CODE,DS:DATA,SS:STACK
PROG2B      PROC FAR
            MOV AX,DATA             ;load DS with data segment address
            MOV DS,AX
            MOV DX,OFFSET MYNAME    ;display name
            MOV AH,9
            INT 21h
            MOV DX,OFFSET COMPANY   ;display company
            MOV AH,9
            INT 21h
            MOV DX,OFFSET ADDRESS   ;display address
            MOV AH,9
            INT 21h
            MOV DX,OFFSET CITYSTZIP ;display city, state, and zip
            MOV AH,9
            INT 21h
            MOV AX,4C00h            ;return to DOS
            INT 21h
PROG2B      ENDP
CODE        ENDS
            END PROG2B
```

**Figure 2-6    EXE Version of Program to Print a Four-Line Name and Address**

```
     DATA        ENDS
```

Next, define the stack segment. The maximum size can be 64K bytes, but you rarely need more than a few hundred. Reserve 256 bytes as a standard size for the stack, and fill them with 32 repetitions of the word 'STACK' followed by three spaces so that the stack can readily be seen if you display memory while using DEBUG.

```
     STACK       SEGMENT STACK
```

```
            DB 32 DUP ('STACK ')
STACK       ENDS
```

Note that the word STACK must appear as an operand as well as the name in the SEGMENT directive.

In the code segment, change the ASSUME statement to show that different addresses will be in the segment registers. Omit ES, since you do not use it in your program, and since the programmer must put the desired address in ES in an EXE program.

```
ASSUME CS:CODE,DS:DATA,SS:STACK
```

DOS places the correct addresses in CS and SS when the program is loaded for execution, but DS and ES contain the address of the program segment prefix (PSP). The ASSUME statements tell the assembler what address should be in the segment registers when the program is run. But the programmer is responsible for placing the correct address in DS (and ES if used). You cannot place a memory address directly into a segment register, so first place the address of DATA into AX and then transfer it to DS:

```
MOV AX,DATA
MOV DS,AX
```

Also change the PROG2B procedure from near to far. A near procedure can be called only from within the segment in which it appears. A far procedure can be called from another segment.

Another difference between EXE programs and COM programs is the way of returning to DOS when the program is finished. In EXE programs the preferred method for MASM versions 4.0 and 5.0 is to use the INT 21h with 4Ch in AH and 00h in AL. Do this by:

```
MOV AX,4C00h
INT 21h
```

To prepare this program for execution, follow all the steps described previously for the COM program, except you need not use EXE2BIN. After executing LINK, you can run the EXE load module by typing:

```
A> B:PROG2B or A> B:PROG2B.EXE
```

You should get exactly the same output as you did from the COM program.

The map produced by LINK for an EXE program will differ from one for a COM program, since there are three separate segments instead of only one. By typing

```
A> TYPE B:PROG2B.MAP
```
you will see the listing of this map as follows:

```
    Start Stop Length Name                 Class
00000H 0005CH 0005DH DATA
00060H 0015FH 00100H STACK
00160H 00185H 00026H CODE
Program entry point at 0016:0000
```

# SUMMARY

A program written in assembler language is the source program. The assembler translates it into an object program in machine language. Then the linker converts the object program into a load module, suitable for execution. More than one object program may be combined into a single load module.

Source program statements are instructions, directives, macros, or comments. Statements have four optional fields: name or symbol, operation, operand, and comment.

Programs are divided into segments, each of which can be as large as 64K. The code segment contains instructions, the data segment contains constants and storage areas to be used by the program, and the stack contains an area in which to save and retrieve the contents of registers and memory locations.

A COM program must be contained within a single segment. All segment registers contain the same address. The first executable instruction begins at an offset of 100h. An EXE program requires separate addresses for each segment. Each load module produced by the linker bears the extension .EXE. EXE programs intended to be run as COM programs must be converted by the DOS utility EXE2BIN.

Each program should begin with comments that give the name of the program, author, data, purpose of the program, and other pertinent details.

Source statements may be written using EDLIN or a word processing program. EDLIN is a line editor that permits lines to be inserted, deleted, modified, listed, copied, or moved. Source statements may be saved on disk and loaded into main storage for further processing. Source programs created by word processors must be saved in ASCII format.

The assembler reads in the source program and creates an object file and, optionally, a list file and cross-reference file. The list file shows an object code to the left of each source statement with statements identifying any errors detected.

The linker produces an EXE load module and an optional map giving the location of object modules linked together. The linker can search a library file for object modules to be linked together automatically.

If the program was written as a COM program, the EXE load module must be converted to a COM load module by using the DOS utility EXE2BIN. Then the EXE load module is deleted from the program disk.

# QUESTIONS

1. What four programs are required to produce a COM program and make it ready for execution?
2. Describe the major differences between a COM program and an EXE program.
3. What is the program segment prefix? What is its size? Who or what creates it?

4. Where must the first executable statement be in a COM program?

5. In EXE programs, what segment registers are loaded correctly by DOS? What registers must be loaded by the program?

6. Name and describe the four fields that may appear in statements.

7. What is meant by a program template or skeleton?

8. What directive is used to tell the assembler what addresses will be in the segment registers?

9. In the MOV statement, which operand is the source and which is the destination?

10. What is the last statement in the source program? What does its operand normally refer to?

11. What code appears at the end of a character string to be displayed by the DOS INT 21h instruction?

12. What is the maximum decimal value that can be assigned to a constant defined by the DB directive? The maximum value for a DW constant?

13. What is the name of the DOS utility programs that can produce source programs? How else may source programs be written?

14. What is the required output of the assembler? What optional output may be requested?

15. What are two ways that we can give LINK the names of the object modules to be linked into a load module?

16. What is the purpose of EXE2BIN?

## EXERCISES

1. Draw three columns down a sheet of paper. In the left column, write the name of a program use to create, assemble, link, or convert an assembler language program. In the middle column give the extension for the file name (if any) used as input to the program. In the right column, give the extension for each file that may be produced as output by the program.

2. Write statements to define the code segment, a procedure named PROGA, the origin, and the ASSUME statement for a COM program. Show statements indicating the end of the procedure, the segment, and the program.

3. Write statements to define a stack segment of 128 bytes, filling it with the correct number of constants consisting of the word 'STACK' followed by three blanks.

4. Write statements to define a data segment for an EXE program. Define in it constants showing your name, address, and city, state, and zip. Include a line feed, cursor return, and dollar sign in each constant.

5. Using EDLIN or your preferred word processor, insert five lines of your choice. Then insert two new lines at the original line three. List your text if necessary to see the renumbering.

6. Using text created in exercise 5, copy the first two lines and place them at the end of your text. Then delete the first two lines. List entire text to see the results.

7. Create a source program named EX7 in COM format containing these machine instructions:

```
MOV AX,5
MOV BL,300
INT 20h
```

Assemble the program and create a LST file. Display the LST file on your screen by typing at the A> prompt:

```
A> TYPE EX7.LST
```

Note the error diagnostic. See if you can correct it.

## LAB PROBLEMS

1. Write an EXE program to display your name and address on three lines using only one INT 21h statement with function code 9 in AH. (Hint: Put a dollar sign only at the end of the last line of the name and address constants.) Assemble the program, correct any errors, link it, and run it. Copy the screen output to the printer by pressing <SHIFT> and <PRT-SCR> at the same time.

2. Write a COM program to display a line showing 'MAIN HEADING', then a blank line, then three columns headed 'COLUMN 1', 'COLUMN 2', AND 'COLUMN 3', with three spaces between column headings. Assemble, link, use EXE2BIN, and run the program. Copy screen output to the printer.

# INTERRUPTS

# 3

**Objectives**

After studying this chapter, you should be able to:

* Define interrupts.
* Describe how interrupt numbers refer to the position of the interrupts in main storage.
* Explain the difference between DOS interrupts and BIOS interrupts.
* Describe requirements for the most common keyboard input functions.
* Set up data in the proper form for screen output functions.
* Explain differences between output to the screen and to the printer.
* Manipulate the cursor through use of BIOS interrupts.

## OVERVIEW OF INTERRUPTS

The INT (interrupt) instruction provides a way to utilize routines provided through DOS and BIOS (basic input/output system). These routines provide some of the most useful input and output services needed by the programmer. No useful program can be written without the input and output of data. Therefore, the means of getting data into the computer from the keyboard and displaying the results of the program on the screen are introduced early in the text.

Most computers can execute only one instruction at a time. Once a program starts running, it will monopolize the computer unless there is some way to interrupt its operation in some way. The computer operator may wish to interrupt a program in order to run a more urgent one. A terminal operator may wish to interrupt a network system to notify it that a message is ready for transmission. The machine itself may interrupt execution of a program because of invalid data or instructions.

Thus, there may be both *hardware* and *software interrupts*. We are most concerned with the software interrupts.

On the 8088 computers, there are 256 possible interrupt numbers, specified as INT 00h through INT 0FFh. The first 1024 bytes of main memory

(00000h to 003FFh) are reserved for the 256 addresses of the interrupt-handling routines. Each address consists of two words, or four bytes. These addresses are stored in segment-offset form, where the offset is the first word and the segment address is the second word. We might call each of these addresses a *pointer* to the routine that will do the work we want done.

To execute an INT instruction, the processor multiplies the interrupt number by four to calculate the offset in low memory where the pointer to the interrupt-handling routine is stored. For example, INT 00h refers to the two words at 0000:0000 (00h * 04h = 0000h). INT 20h refers to two words at 0000:0080 (20h * 04h = 0080h).

Here is how the INT 21h instruction is executed. First, the processor pushes three registers on to the stack: the flags register, the current code segment (CS), and the current instruction pointer (IP). Recall that CS:IP contain the address of the instruction following INT 21h as the interrupt begins execution. Thus, the return address when the interrupt is completed has been saved on the stack.

Next, the processor calculates the address of the interrupt pointer (21h * 04h = 0084h). It then places the word at 0000:0084 into IP and the next word at 0000:0086 into CS. CS:IP now contain the start address of the interrupt-handling routine, and that routine begins to execute.

The interrupt routine usually ends with an IRET (interrupt return) instruction, which pops the saved register contents off the stack in reverse order, first IP, then CS, and last the flags. CS:IP again point back to the instruction following INT 21h, and the program continues.

The interrupt routines normally save the contents of all registers that they use except for those that hold addresses of data to be sent between our program and the interrupt routines.

We will discuss the stack and the PUSH and POP operations more fully in Chapter 6.

In general, INT 00h through INT 1Fh are reserved for hardware interrupts; however, INT 10h through 1Fh are presently used by DOS to refer to routines provided by the basic input/output system (BIOS), which are in read-only memory (ROM) in certain machines and are therefore called *hardware dependent*. INT 20h through 0FFh are available to DOS as software interrupts. Interrupt routines are changed from time to time as new versions of DOS appear, and some former interrupt numbers have been superseded by newer numbers.

## HARDWARE INTERRUPTS

The first five interrupts are used by all 8088 systems, regardless of the operating system or application. They are seldom used by the beginning programmer, but will be summarized here as general information.

INT 0 (*divide overflow*) is caused whenever the result of division is too large to fit into the quotient register. An attempt to divide by zero will also cause this interrupt.

INT 1 (*single step*) is used only by DEBUG in trace instructions. It is effective only if the trap flag is set.

INT 2 (*non-maskable interrupt*) is used by the IBM PC to handle keyboard input.

INT 3 (*breakpoint*), like INT 1, is used by DEBUG to permit an interruption at a specific point when running a program.

INT 4 (*overflow*) will execute if INTO is specified and the overflow flag is set. The instruction INTO (interruption on overflow) may be placed in a program after a signed arithmetic operation to test if overflow occurred.

INT 5 *through INT 0Dh* are hardware interrupts used by the 80286 processor.

## DOS FUNCTION INTERRUPTS

DOS interrupts 20h through FFh are usually called *high-level interrupts* because they are controlled by DOS. They generally carry out input/output operations to the keyboard, screen, printer, and disk files. Some of their functions are somewhat less efficient than BIOS interrupts, but they are less likely to be affected by hardware changes because the operating system is intended for use among different types of hardware. In general, DOS interrupts should be used instead of BIOS interrupts wherever programs are intended to be used with many types of hardware.

DOS uses eight interrupts, INT 20h through INT 27h, and has INT 28h through INT 3Fh reserved, but INT 21h is by far the most common and useful. As information, the eight are:

1. *INT 20h terminate program* (COM program only).
2. *INT 21h DOS function call.*
3. *INT 22h address for program termination.*
4. *INT 23h ctrl-break exit address.*
5. *INT 24h critical error handler.*
6. *INT 25h absolute disk read.*
7. *INT 26h absolute disk write.*
8. *INT 27h terminate but stay resident.*

Information about interrupts other than INT 21h is contained in the *DOS Technical Reference Manual*, available when you purchase DOS software. Use of INT 21h in connection with disk files will be covered in Chapter 10.

## Keyboard Input Functions

INT 21h handles several DOS routines for getting data from the keyboard into memory. Before the interrupt is executed, a number called a *function code* must be placed in AH to specify exactly what operation is to be performed. For some keyboard input functions, AL receives a byte representing the key that was pressed. For other, AL receives a status code indicating the result of the interrupt. We will discuss some of the most useful functions and give examples of how they can be used in programs.

*Function 1, Character Input with Echo*.    When AH = 1, INT 21h waits for a key to be pressed and then places its ASCII value in AL. This function also displays the key on the screen at the current cursor location. This function will recognize the <CTRL-BREAK> and <CTRL-PRTSCR> combinations. <CTRL-BREAK> terminates your program and returns to DOS <CTRL-PRTSCR> turns the screen print feature on or off.

Certain function keys or keys pressed in combination with the <CTRL>, <ALT>, or <SHIFT> keys return two-byte *extended codes*, of which the first byte is always 00h and the second is the function code. These codes, in addition to requiring special programming, print meaningless data on the screen. Typing extended codes should be avoided when AH = 1.

To get the letter A into AL and also echo it on the screen, use:

```
MOV AH,1
INT 21h
```

When these instructions are executed, the program pauses until you press some key. If you press A, the code for A (decimal 65 or 41h) will be placed in AL.

*Function 8, Character Input without Echo*.    When AH = 8, the key that is pressed is placed into AL, but is not echoed to the screen. Function 8 works just like Function 1 without the echo. It is the preferred way to analyze the keys that return the two-byte extended codes, since nothing displays on the screen. It can be useful for entering passwords or for answering messages that say, "Press any key to continue."

*Function 7, Unfiltered Character Input without Echo*.    When AH = 7, the function is similar to Function 8, but the<CTRL-BREAK> and <CTRL-PRTSCR> combinations are not recognized. There is no echo on the screen.

*Function 6, Direct Console I/O*.    Function 6 can be used for either keyboard input or screen output. When AH = 6, the input function works like Function 7, except that DL must contain 0FFh (255 decimal) when INT 21h is executed. Unlike Functions 1, 8, and 7, Function 6 does not wait for a key to be pressed, but returns immediately to the program that issues it. If a key has been pressed, AL holds the ASCII code, and the zero flag will be 0, indicating rather oddly "not zero." If no key has been pressed, the zero flag will be set to 1, indicating "result zero."

If DL holds any value other that 0FFh when INT 21h is executed with AH = 6, this function outputs the byte in DL to the screen.

To input a byte from the keyboard without echo, use:

```
MOV AH,6                    ;set function code
MOV DL,0FFh                 ;specify input
INT 21H
```

Upon return, if the zero flag is not set, the byte entered at the keyboard will be in AL. If the zero flag is set, no key was pressed. We shall see how to test flags and take conditional actions in Chapter 4.

**Function 10, Buffered Input.**    This highly useful function is like BASIC's INPUT statement. When AH = 10 (0Ah), it accepts a string of characters from the keyboard and places them into a buffer in main memory. The <ENTER> key (ASCII code 0Dh, or 13 decimal) is the last byte placed in the buffer and terminates the string. The address of the input buffer must be placed into DS:DX before the interrupt is called.

The buffer must be set up a certain way:

> *Byte 0.* The first byte of the buffer must contain a number indicating the maximum number of characters the buffer can hold, including the final <ENTER>.
>
> *Byte 1.* On return from the INT 21h, DOS will indicate the actual numbers of bytes entered, *excluding* the final <ENTER>.
>
> *Byte 2.* This is the first byte of the actual data whose maximum length was specified in Byte 0.

If the next-to-last byte in the buffer is filled, the keyboard will not accept any more data, and DOS sounds the bell if any key other than  <ENTER> is struck.

These statements define a buffer area to hold an input string of no more than 20 bytes, plus <ENTER>, get the string, and place the first byte of the string into AL:

```
BUFFER      DB 21,?,21 DUP(?)        ; in the data segment
            ...
            MOV DX,OFFSET BUFFER     ; in the code segment
            MOV AH,0Ah
            INT 21h
            MOV AL,BUFFER+2
```

If you had entered the message 'HELLO' <ENTER> at the keyboard, the byte at BUFFER+1 would contain 05h indicating the five bytes but not the <ENTER> code.

***Function 11, Get Input Status.*** Most keyboards have a hardware buffer that holds characters typed but not yet sent to memory. This feature is called a *type-ahead buffer,* so that characters will not be lost in case of brief delays, such as the cursor return or movement of a word to the next line if it will not fit on the current line.

When AH = 0Bh, INT 21h checks to see if a character is available from the keyboard buffer. If so, AL will hold 0FFh on return; if not, AL will hold 00h. The actual byte is not placed in AL. If a character is available from the buffer, Functions 1 or 8 can be used to get the character into AL. Like Functions 1 and 8, this function checks for <CTRL-BREAK> and <CTRL-PRTSCR>.

***Function 12, Reset Input Buffer and then Input.*** When AH = 0Ch, this routine first clears the keyboard buffer and then calls one of the other keyboard input routines designated in AL. AL may contain only 1, 6, 7, 8, or 0Ah. Upon return, AL contains the ASCII character code for the key that was struck. Clearing the buffer assures that no key that was struck previously will be placed in AL. This function is usually used along with some prompt to be displayed and answered to be sure that some key previously struck is not interpreted as the response to this prompt.

## Screen Output Functions

Three DOS interrupt functions are commonly used for screen output: two to display a single byte and the other to show a string of bytes on the screen.

***Function 2, Character Output.*** When AH = 02h, the character in DL is displayed on the screen at the current cursor location. Note that, whereas in input functions AL receives the character from the keyboard, in output functions DL holds the character to be displayed. Function 2 will handle control characters, including the tab character, ASCII 9, which advances the cursor to the next preset tab position. Tabs are usually preset by DOS eight characters apart.

The following routine moves the cursor to the next tab position and prints the character 'X':

```
MOV AH,02h              ;tab
MOV DL,09h
INT 21h
MOV AH,02h              ;display an X
MOV DL,'X'
INT 21h
```

Note in the next-to-last statement that we may specify the immediate value for a byte by placing the character between single quotation marks (apostrophe). We also could give the decimal or hex value of the ASCII character. Any of these three statements would move the character X to DL:

```
MOV DL,'X'
MOV DL,88
MOV DL,58h
```

***Function 6, Direct Console I/O.***   This function, mentioned previously under keyboard input functions, will display any character on the screen except 255 (0FFh) that has been placed in DL. As usual, AH must contain the function code 06h. Function 6 does not provide the usual action for the <CTRL-BREAK>, <CTRL-PRTSCR>, or <TAB> keys. If DL contains 0FFh, this function becomes keyboard input and tests whether a key was struck as described under Function 6 in the keyboard input section above.

***Function 9, Output Character String.***   You saw this function in Chapter 2 to print the name and address lines in the sample programs. It prints an entire string, including control codes such as cursor return and linefeed. The string must be ended with a dollar sign ($). AH must contain 9. DS:DX must contain the address of the string to be displayed. Any codes in the string that are not control codes and do not form printable characters are displayed as blank spaces.

The following routine displays a message to press any key, clears the input buffer, receives a response without displaying the key, and displays another prompt:

```
PRESSKEY    DB 'Press any key to continue',13,10,'$'
NEXTMSG     DB 'Insert data disk in drive B',13,10,'$'
            .
            MOV DX,OFFSET PRESSKEY   ;display prompt
            MOV AH,09h
            INT 21H
            MOV AH,0Ch               ;clear input buffer and
            MOV AL,8                  ;get response without echo
            INT 21h
            MOV DX,OFFSET NEXTMSG     ;display next prompt
            MOV AH,9
            INT 21h
```

## The Printer Function

When AH = 5 with INT 21h, the character in DL is sent to the standard printer device (printer number 0). This function prints only one byte. To print a string, you must use a loop that puts the first byte into DL for printing, then modifies the offset to the next byte of the string, moves it to DL, and continues until the entire string has been printed. We will discuss loops and address modification in Chapters 5 and 6.

## Other Functions

Other INT 21h routines perform such operations as program termination, character input and output to ports, disk control, file operations, record operations, directory operations, and miscellaneous system functions. Those related to disk files will be discussed further in Chapter 10. Full details about all DOS interrupts is contained in the appropriate technical reference manuals.

## BIOS FUNCTION INTERRUPTS

The basic input/output system (BIOS) provides a number of routines placed in ROM (read-only memory). They usually are written by a software company other than Microsoft and are specific to the machine that contains the ROM. These BIOS routines may provide for keyboard input, screen output, and other screen-handling routines. As with DOS interrupts, you must place a function code in AH and other values in different registers according to the nature of the function.

Because BIOS routines are placed in read-only memory (ROM), they are called *low-level interrupts*. They are hardware dependent, and may or may not be available on all 8088-based processors. Commercial software programmers might prefer to avoid use of ROM interrupts on software intended for distribution to a wide variety of machines to permit compatibility with future versions of DOS and portability among IBM PC-compatible machines.

INT 10h through INT 1Fh are available to BIOS, although not all are used currently. INT 10h is the most common interrupt.

We will explore a few of the BIOS interrupts that are useful in positioning the cursor and clearing and scrolling the screen. A more detailed analysis of BIOS interrupts will be made in Chapter 14.

### Cursor and Display Handling Functions

Along with the function code placed in AH, most BIOS interrupts require values, or *parameters*, in certain other registers. The parameters are codes that describe attributes or other characteristics of the data to be displayed.

*Function 0, Set Video Mode.*    When AH = 00h, AL may contain any one of many different codes to determine screen size, graphic density, or number of colors. Certain codes pertain only to special machines or monitors. Acceptable values for AL are:

*Text Modes*
```
00h 40 x 25 black-and-white text, color adapter
01h 40 x 25 color text
02h 80 x 25 black-and-white text
03h 80 x 25 color text
```
*Graphics Modes*
```
04h 320 x 200 4-color graphics
05h 320 x 200 4-color graphics (color burst off)
06h 640 x 200 2-color graphics
07h monochrome adapter text display
```

*Extended Graphics Modes*

```
08h 160 x 200 16-color graphics
09h 320 x 200 16-color graphics
0Ah 640 x 200 4-color graphics
0Dh 320 x 200 16-color graphics
0Eh 640 x 200 16-color graphics
0Fh 640 x 350 monochrome graphics
10h 640 x 350 4-color or 16-color graphics (depending on RAM
        available)
```

The following sequence sets the display mode for 80 x 25 black-and-white text:

```
MOV AH,00h                  ;function code to set mode
MOV AL,02h                  ;mode for 80 x 25
                            ;black-and-white
INT 10h
```

**NOTE:**    This function also clears the screen and resets the cursor at the upper left corner of the screen.

*Function 2, Set Cursor Position.*    A *monochrome* (single color) screen has only one page, while a *color/graphics* screen may have four. The page for a monochrome screen is always 0, while pages for a color/graphics screen are 0, 1, 2, and 3. When AH = 02h, the cursor is positioned according to page number, row, and column. Before the interrupt is executed, BH must contain the page number, DH the row ($y$ coordinate), and DL the column ($x$ coordinate). Coordinates are usually expressed as $(x,y)$. (0,0) indicates the leftmost position of the top line on the screen. (79,24) indicates the last position of the bottom line.

The following routine places the cursor on page 0 at the leftmost position of line 10 on page 0.

```
MOV AH,02h
MOV BH,00h
MOV DL,00h
MOV DH,0Ah
INT 10h
```

*Function 3, Read Cursor Position.*    When AH = 03h and BH = page number, INT 10h obtains the current position of the cursor in $x$ and $y$ coordinates. This function returns in CH the starting line for the cursor, in CL the ending line for the cursor (refer to Function 1 in Chapter 14), in DH the $y$ row coordinate, and in DL the $x$ column coordinate. Function 3 is often used to see where the cursor is so that Function 2 can be used to reposition it on the same or a nearby line.

*Function 6, 7, Scroll Page Up or Down.*    Placing 06h in AH allows any part of the current active page to be scrolled up; 07h in AH allows scrolling down. A portion of the page is called a *window*. On input, CH,CL must contain the row and column of the upper left corner of the window, while DH,DL contains the row and column of the lower right corner. AL must specify the number of lines to scroll up or down, and BH the attribute to be used on blank lines. If AL = 0, the entire window is blanked out and set to the attribute in BH.

A common use of this function is to blank the entire screen, using these instructions:

```
MOV CX,0            ;CL and CH = 0 for upper
                    ;left of screen
MOV DL,79           ;for 80 columns; use 39 for
                    ;40 columns
MOV DH,24           ;bottom line
MOV AL,0            ;option to clear entire
                    ;screen
MOV BH,7            ;standard black-on-white
                    ;attribute
MOV AH,6            ;scroll up
INT 10h
```

## Other BIOS Functions

BIOS also has a large number of other functions supporting screen operations with colors, disk operations, reading from and writing to I/O devices, handling the system timer, and other hardware control functions. Some of these will be treated in Chapter 14. Some are similar to DOS interrupt functions covered in Chapter 10, while others are beyond the scope of this book.

## PROGRAM 3: DOS AND BIOS INTERRUPTS

For our next demonstration program, we shall clear the screen, print a message centered on line 10 and another centered on line 15, and display a prompt on the bottom line telling the operator to press any key to continue. Whenever displaying a message, it is common to allow the operator to determine how long a time to allow to read the message. If no pause is allowed, the screen will flash only for an instant before the next screen appears. After the key is pressed, the screen is cleared again, and the program returns to DOS.

We should point out that many of these DOS and BIOS interrupts require use of loops, comparison, and address modification. We will therefore return to them in later chapters after we have studied other programming techniques to permit us to use them effectively.

First, let us consider possible ways to clear the screen. One way would be to print 24 blank lines, which will ultimately scroll everything off the screen. This is a relatively slow technique and certainly not very elegant. Another possibility is to print a string consisting of 24 line feeds and one cursor return followed by a dollar sign:

```
LF24        DB 24 DUP (10),13,'$'
            .
            MOV AH,09h
            MOV DX,OFFSET LF24
            INT 21h
```

This method is still slow and not the best available. We will use BIOS INT 10h, Function 6, to scroll the entire screen up. Figure 3-1 shows the entire program, and the comments identify the statements that clear the screen.

Next we use BIOS INT 10h, Function 2, to set the cursor to line 10, column 24, so that the title will be properly centered. The first title is 32 bytes long. Since there are 80 bytes on the screen, 80 - 32 = 48 spaces are left. We divide this available space by two and center the title 24 spaces from the left margin. We then use DOS INT 21h, Function 9, to output the title.

Then we reset the cursor to line 15, column 32, and display our second title line. Finally we reset the cursor to line 24, column 27, to center the prompt asking to press any key to continue.

INT 21H, Function 8, receives any key pressed without displaying it on the screen. As soon as any key is pressed, the screen is again cleared and the program proceeds to the INT 21h, Function 4C00h, to terminate the program and return to DOS. This program is written as an EXE program. After assembling and linking it, we can execute it without using EXE2BIN, by merely typing

```
A>B:PROG3
```

Figure 3-2 shows the assembler output listing of PROG3.LST, and Figure 3-3 shows the output from the program.

## SUMMARY

Interrupts are software routines provided by DOS and BIOS to handle operations such as setting the cursor, clearing the screen, and performing input/output operations. There are 256 possible interrupts, whose addresses are contained in the first 1024 bytes of main memory. Each address is four bytes long.

DOS interrupts are provided by DOS software. BIOS interrupts usually are provided by the hardware manufacturer and tend to be more hardware dependent, varying from one machine to another.

Interrupts INT 0 through INT 4 are hardware interrupts common to all 8088 processors. Interrupts INT 5 through INT 13 (0Dh) are used by the 80286 processor.

INT 21h is the most widely used DOS interrupt. It serves many different functions, which are specified by the code placed in AH register. Some interrupts require additional information in other registers. The principal functions of INT 21h are to input one character or a string from the keyboard,

```
        PAGE 50,132
;------------------------------------------------------------------------
; Program name:  B:PROG3.ASM
;
; Author:        Alton R. Kindred
;
; This EXE program clears the screen, displays a title centered on line
; 10 and another centered on line 15, and issues a prompt on line 24 to
; press any key to continue.  When any key is pressed, the screen is cleared
; again, and the program returns to DOS.
;------------------------------------------------------------------------
DATA        SEGMENT
TITLE1      DB 'SOFTWARE DEVELOPMENT ENTERPRISES$'
TITLE2      DB 'GENERIC ROUTINE$'
PROMPT      DB 'Press any key to continue. $'
DATA        ENDS
;------------------------------------------------------------------------
STACK       SEGMENT STACK
            DB 32 DUP ('STACK   ')
STACK       ENDS
;------------------------------------------------------------------------
CODE        SEGMENT
            ASSUME CS:CODE,DS:DATA,SS:STACK
PROG3       PROC FAR
            MOV AX,DATA              ;load DS with data segment address
            MOV DS,AX
            MOV AH,6                 ;clear screen
            MOV AL,0
            MOV CX,0                 ;  CH = line 0; CL = column 0
            MOV DH,24                ;  DH = line 24
            MOV DL,79                ;  DL = column 79
            MOV BH,7                 ;  BH = black on white attribute
            INT 10h
            MOV AH,2                 ;set cursor for first title
            MOV BH,0
            MOV DH,10                ;  DH = row 10
            MOV DL,24                ;  DL = column 24
            INT 10h
            MOV AH,9                 ;print first title
            MOV DX,OFFSET TITLE1
            INT 21h
            MOV AH,2                 ;set cursor for second title
            MOV BH,0
            MOV DH,15                ;  DH = row 15
            MOV DL,32                ;  DL = column 32
            INT 10h
            MOV AH,9                 ;print second title
            MOV DX,OFFSET TITLE2
            INT 21h
            MOV AH,2                 ;set cursor for prompt
            MOV BH,0
            MOV DH,24                ;  DH = row 24
            MOV DL,27                ;  DL = column 27
```

**Figure 3-1    Source Program Listing of PROG3**

```
            INT 10h
            MOV AH,9                    ;print prompt
            MOV DX,OFFSET PROMPT
            INT 21h
            MOV AH,8                    ;get response without echo
            INT 21h
            MOV AH,6                    ;clear screen
            MOV AL,0
            MOV CX,0                    ;  CH = line 0; CL = column 0
            MOV DH,24                   ;  DH = line 24
            MOV DL,79                   ;  DL = column 79
            MOV BH,7                    ;  BH = black on white attribute
            INT 10h
            MOV AX,4C00h                ;return to DOS
            INT 21h
PROG3       ENDP
CODE        ENDS
            END PROG3
```

```
Microsoft (R) Macro Assembler Version 5.00              9/19/89 15:04:53
                                                        Page   1-1

            PAGE 50,132
    ;----------------------------------------------------------------------
    ; Program name:   B:PROG3.ASM
    ;
    ; Author:         Alton R. Kindred
    ;
    ; This EXE program clears the screen, displays a title centered on line
    ; 10 and another centered on line 15, and issues a prompt on line 24 to
    ; press any key to continue.  When any key is pressed, the screen is cleared
    ; again, and the program returns to DOS.
    ;----------------------------------------------------------------------
0000    DATA        SEGMENT
0000    53 4F 46 54 57 41 52  TITLE1     DB 'SOFTWARE DEVELOPMENT ENTERPRISES$'
        45 20 44 45 56 45 4C
        4F 50 4D 45 4E 54 20
        45 4E 54 45 52 50 52
        49 53 45 53 24
0021    47 45 4E 45 52 49 43  TITLE2     DB 'GENERIC ROUTINE$'
        20 52 4F 55 54 49 4E
        45 24
0031    50 72 65 73 73 20 61  PROMPT     DB 'Press any key to continue. $'
        6E 79 20 6B 65 79 20
        74 6F 20 63 6F 6E 74
        69 6E 75 65 2E 20 24
004D    DATA        ENDS
    ;----------------------------------------------------------------------
0000    STACK       SEGMENT STACK
```

**Figure 3-2   Assembler Listing of Program 3**

```
0000   0020[       DB 32 DUP ('STACK    ')
  53 54 41 43 4B
  20 20 20
  ]

0100   STACK      ENDS
  ;-------------------------------------------------------------------------
0000   CODE       SEGMENT
                  ASSUME CS:CODE,DS:DATA,SS:STACK
0000   PROG3      PROC FAR
0000   B8 ---- R  MOV AX,DATA             ;load DS with data segment address
0003   8E D8      MOV DS,AX
0005   B4 06      MOV AH,6                ;clear screen
0007   B0 00      MOV AL,0
0009   B9 0000    MOV CX,0                ;  CH = line 0; CL = column 0
000C   B6 18      MOV DH,24               ;  DH = line 24
000E   B2 4F      MOV DL,79               ;  DL = column 79
0010   B7 07      MOV BH,7                ;  BH = black on white attribute
0012   CD 10      INT 10h
```

Microsoft (R) Macro Assembler Version 5.00                9/19/89 15:04:53
                                                          Page    1-2

```
0014   B4 02      MOV AH,2                ;set cursor for first title
0016   B7 00      MOV BH,0
0018   B6 0A      MOV DH,10               ;  DH = row 10
001A   B2 18      MOV DL,24               ;  DL = column 24
001C   CD 10      INT 10h
001E   B4 09      MOV AH,9                ;print first title
0020   BA 0000 R  MOV DX,OFFSET TITLE1
0023   CD 21      INT 21h
0025   B4 02      MOV AH,2                ;set cursor for second title
0027   B7 00      MOV BH,0
0029   B6 0F      MOV DH,15               ;  DH = row 15
002B   B2 20      MOV DL,32               ;  DL = column 32
002D   CD 10      NT 10h
002F   B4 09      MOV AH,9                ;print second title
0031   BA 0021 R  MOV DX,OFFSET TITLE2
0034   CD 21      INT 21h
0036   B4 02      MOV AH,2                ;set cursor for prompt
0038   B7 00      MOV BH,0
003A   B6 18      MOV DH,24               ;  DH = row 24
003C   B2 1B      MOV DL,27               ;  DL = column 27
003E   CD 10      INT 10h
0040   B4 09      MOV AH,9                ;print prompt
0042   BA 0031 R  MOV DX,OFFSET PROMPT
0045   CD 21      INT 21h
0047   B4 08      MOV AH,8                ;get response without echo
0049   CD 21      INT 21h
004B   B4 06      MOV AH,6                ;clear screen
004D   B0 00      MOV AL,0
004F   B9 0000    MOV CX,0                ;  CH = line 0; CL = column 0
0052   B6 18      MOV DH,24               ;  DH = line 24
0054   B2 4F      MOV DL,79               ;  DL = column 79
0056   B7 07      MOV BH,7                ;  BH = black on white attribute
0058   CD 10      INT 10h
```

**Figure 3-2**    *continued*

```
005A  B8 4C00      MOV AX,4C00h              ;return to DOS
005D  CD 21        INT 21h
005F    PROG3      ENDP
005F    CODE       ENDS
                   END PROG3
```
Microsoft (R) Macro Assembler Version 5.00              9/19/89 15:04:53
                                                            Symbols-1


Segments and Groups:

                    N a m e          Length  Align Combine Class

CODE . . . . . . . . . . . . . .     005F PARA NONE
DATA . . . . . . . . . . . . .       004D PARA NONE
STACK  . . . . . . . . . . . . .     0100 PARA STACK

Symbols:

                    N a m e          Type  Value  Attr

PROG3 . . . . . . . . . . . . .      F PROC 0000 CODE Length = 005F
PROMPT  . . . . . . . . . . . . .    L BYTE 0031 DATA

TITLE1 . . . . . . . . . . . .       L BYTE 0000 DATA
TITLE2 . . . . . . . . . . . .       L BYTE 0021 DATA

. . . . . . . . . .     TEXT  prog3

    71 Source  Lines
    71 Total   Lines
     9 Symbols

  51190 + 405514 Bytes symbol space free

     0 Warning Errors
     0 Severe  Errors


**Figure 3-2**   *concluded*




              SOFTWARE DEVELOPMENT ENTERPRISES

                    GENERIC ROUTINE

               Press any key to continue.


**Figure 3-3**   **Output from PROG3**

output a character or a string to the screen, or output a character to the printer.

BIOS INT 10h is used for many functions related to the cursor and the screen. Among these are to set the cursor position, set the video mode (attributes for color, text, or graphics), scroll all or part of the screen up or down, or read or write the attribute and character at the cursor.

## QUESTIONS

1. Explain the relationship between the number of an interrupt and the location in memory of the routine used by that interrupt.
2. In what form are the addresses of the interrupts stored?
3. What is placed on the stack when the INT instruction is executed? What instruction ends each interrupt to return to your program?
4. What interrupt numbers are used by all 8088 systems for hardware interrupts?
5. What determines what function is to take place when INT 21h is used in your program?
6. What is meant by the term "echo" with regard to input from the keyboard?
7. Where does INT 21h place a character received from the keyboard?
8. What is meant by "extended codes" in keyboard input?
9. Describe what is necessary to input a string of characters from the keyboard using Function 10 with INT 21h. Where is the string placed?
10. Where is a single byte placed to be displayed on the screen using Function 2 of INT 21h?
11. Describe Function 9 of INT 21h to output a character string to the screen.
12. What registers are used to refer to the line and column number of the cursor for Functions 2 and 3 with INT 10h?
13. What page numbers may be specified with the standard color/graphics adapter for 40-column displays? For 80-column displays? What page number must be used for graphics mode?
14. What is meant by a "window?" What functions are used to scroll a window up or down?
15. What is a possible reason to limit use of BIOS interrupts in your programs?

## EXERCISES

1. Write a routine that (a) gets a character from the keyboard and displays it on the screen and (b) gets a second character but does not display it.
2. Write a routine to accept a string of up to 20 characters from the keyboard. Show both data definitions and code.
3. Write a routine to display the character A at the current cursor location.
4. Write a routine to move the cursor down by three lines and then return it to the start of the line by writing a single string.

5. Write a routine to issue the prompt "What is your name?" and receive a response of no more than 15 characters.
6. Write a routine to place the cursor at the center of the fourth line.
7. Write a routine to scroll the lower half of the screen down three lines.
8. Write a routine to display five hyphens at the current cursor location.

## LAB PROBLEMS

1. Write a COM program to clear only the lower half of the screen, display a prompt centered on line 15 to enter the operator's name, and move the cursor to the first column of line 18 to show the name typed by the operator.
2. Write an EXE program to clear the screen, set the screen for 40 x 25 black-and-white text, and display your name centered on line 12. Prompt the operator to press any key when ready to end the program.
3. Write an EXE program to clear the screen by using INT 10h Function 6. Note how long this takes. Prompt the operator to press any key to continue. When a key is struck, clear the screen by printing 24 line feeds as a string. Note how long this takes. Again prompt the operator to press any key when ready to end the program.

# PROGRAM LOGIC AND CONTROL

# 4

**OBJECTIVES**

After studying this chapter, you should be able to:
- Name and describe the three basic logical structures.
- Write pseudocode and flowchart symbols to represent the three basic logical structures.
- Describe various forms of comparison.
- Explain how flags are set by comparison and certain other instructions.
- Differentiate between conditional and unconditional jumps.
- Name and use special instructions for control loops.

Up to this point in the text each program has been merely a sequence of instructions from start to finish with no deviation. However, the logic of realistic programs requires that you be able to repeat certain groups of operations or to select one path or another depending upon conditions you encounter. In this chapter you will see the importance of comparison and the setting of the flag register to give your programs flexibility and power to make decisions.

## PROGRAM STRUCTURES

Program logic involves those steps necessary to transform input data into output information. The logic may be expressed in pseudocode, program flowchart, or both.

*Pseudocode* consists of a few capitalized keywords followed by ordinary English terms, indented to show the relationships of the statements. A *program flowchart* uses lines, arrows, and symbols to show the flow of the program logic. Figure 4-1 shows program flowcharting symbols and conventions.

Years of experience have shown that all program logic can be classified under one of three categories:

1. · *Sequence structure.* A series of instructions executed in the order they appear.

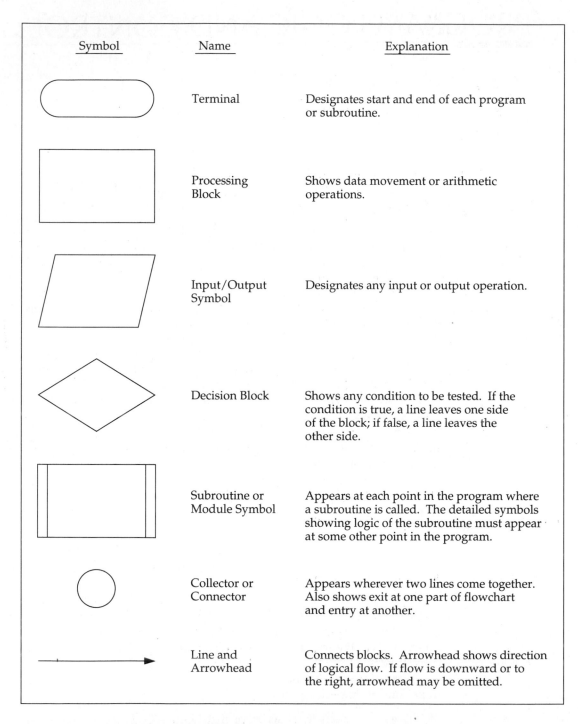

| Symbol | Name | Explanation |
|---|---|---|
| | Terminal | Designates start and end of each program or subroutine. |
| | Processing Block | Shows data movement or arithmetic operations. |
| | Input/Output Symbol | Designates any input or output operation. |
| | Decision Block | Shows any condition to be tested. If the condition is true, a line leaves one side of the block; if false, a line leaves the other side. |
| | Subroutine or Module Symbol | Appears at each point in the program where a subroutine is called. The detailed symbols showing logic of the subroutine must appear at some other point in the program. |
| | Collector or Connector | Appears wherever two lines come together. Also shows exit at one part of flowchart and entry at another. |
| | Line and Arrowhead | Connects blocks. Arrowhead shows direction of logical flow. If flow is downward or to the right, arrowhead may be omitted. |

**Figure 4-1    Program Flowcharting Symbols and Conventions**

2. *Repetition structure.* Usually called a *loop*, repetition structure is a group of instructions that are repeated until some condition occurs that terminates the loop.
3. *Selection structure.* A choice of one logical path if a condition is true and a different path if the condition is false.

Every structure should have a single entry point and a single exit. In other words, you should never jump into or out of the middle of a structure.

## Sequence Structure

The *sequence structure* in programming is simply to execute instructions one after another in the exact order they are written. So far all programs in this text have been sequence structures.

Only the most elementary program can be written using only the sequence structure. Here is pseudocode for the first program in Chapter 1:

```
START
Move first number to AX
Move second number to BX
Add BX to AX
Return to DOS
END
```

Pseudocode for a program or procedure begins with the keyword START. END is usually the last word in a program, and RETURN is the last word in a procedure used as a subroutine.

A program flowchart with the same logic is shown in Figure 4-2.

## Repetition Structures

*Repetition structures*, commonly called *loops*, involve repeating a series of instructions until some condition is encountered that causes the loop to be terminated. Each loop consists of four steps, which need not always be in the same sequence:

1. *Initialize.* This step takes place before the loop actually begins. It sets one or more values to be used the first time the loop is executed. Examples include setting counters, flags, or addresses.
2. *Test.* This step determines whether the loop is to be performed, or repeated. If the test is made at the beginning of the loop, we call it a *pretest loop.* If the test appears at the end of the loop, we call it a *posttest loop.* You will find that a pretest loop might not be executed at all, while a posttest loop always will be executed at least once.
3. *Execute.* This step of the loop carries out the specific processing that you expect to repeat more than once. This might involve doing calculations, displaying results, or reading in more data.

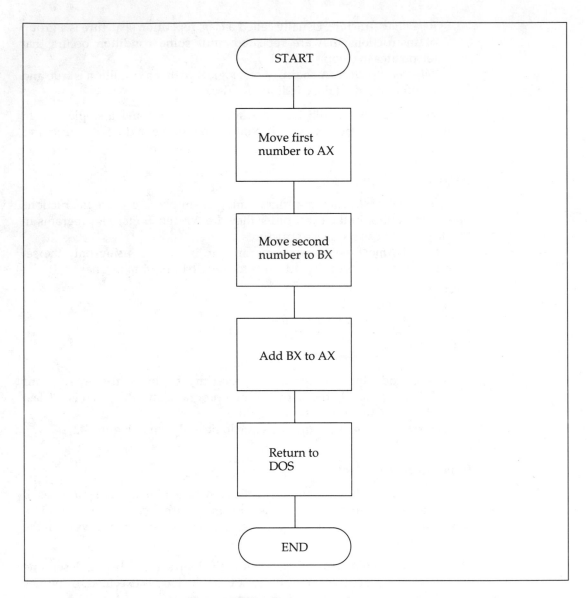

**Figure 4-2**    **Program Flowchart to Add Two Numbers**

4.   *Modify*. this step involves changing one or more initialized values before they are tested again. Examples might include adding to or subtracting from a counter, setting a flag, or changing an address of data. If you fail to modify some value that is tested, you can have an *endless loop*, also called an *infinite*, *uncontrolled*, or *runaway loop*.

**Pretest Loops.**   A *pretest loop* is one in which the test is made at the beginning of the loop, that is, before the execute and modify steps are performed. If the tested condition is true, the loop is performed. If it is false, the loop is terminated. Note that, if the condition is false the first time the condition is tested, the loop will not be executed at all.

Pseudocode throughout this text uses the keywords WHILE and WEND to mark the start and end of pretest loops. Indent the execute and modify steps to show that they are contained within the body of the loop. For example, to print the numbers from 1 to 10, use pseudocode and indicate the parts of the loop as follows:

```
Set number to 1               Initialize
WHILE number <=10             Test
    Print number              Execute
    Add 1 to number           Modify
WEND
```

The phrasing of the condition is important. The loop is executed only so long at the number is less than or equal to 10. If you had initially typed set number to 12, the loop would not be executed at all. Figure 4-3 shows a program flowchart for this pretest loop.

*Posttest Loops.*    The pseudocode for *posttest loops* uses the keywords REPEAT and UNTIL to mark the start and end of the loop. Statements between REPEAT and UNTIL are indented. To print the numbers from 1 to 10 with the test at the end of the loop, the pseudocode is:

```
Set number to 1               Initialize
REPEAT
    Print number              Execute
    Add 1 to number           Modify
UNTIL number > 10             Test
```

Note that the loop does not stop until the number is greater than 10. When it becomes 10, you must still loop back to print the final number. Note also that, even if you set the initial value greater than 10, the loop would still be executed once because the test is not made until the end of the loop.

Figure 4-4 shows the program flowchart for this posttest loop.

## Selection Structures

*Selection structures* often are called *IF-THEN* or *IF-THEN-ELSE* structures after the names used to implement them in a number of high-level programming languages such as COBOL, BASIC, and Pascal. You may use one-way selection or two-way selection.

*One-way Selection.*    In *one-way selection* you take some action if the condition is true and omit that action if the condition is false. In pseudocode, the keywords are IF, THEN, and ENDIF. All statements between IF and ENDIF are indented. Pseudocode for one-way selection looks like this:

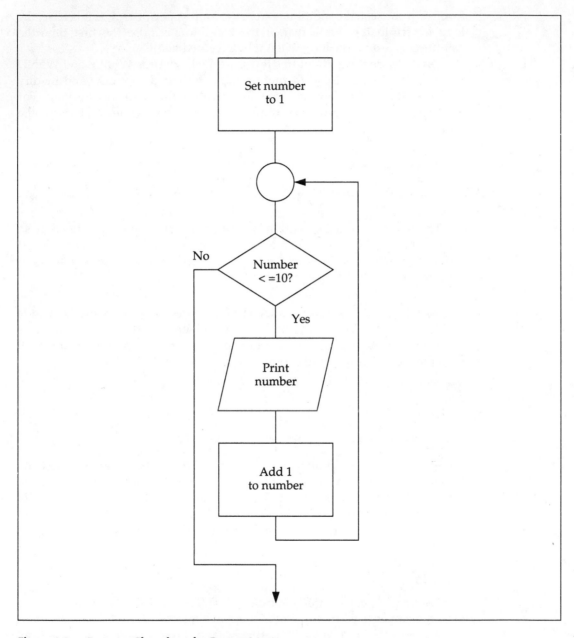

**Figure 4-3     Program Flowchart for Pretest Loop**

```
IF a condition is true
    THEN do something
ENDIF
```

If the condition is true, the THEN part of the structure is carried out. Any number of statements can be included under THEN. If the condition tested is

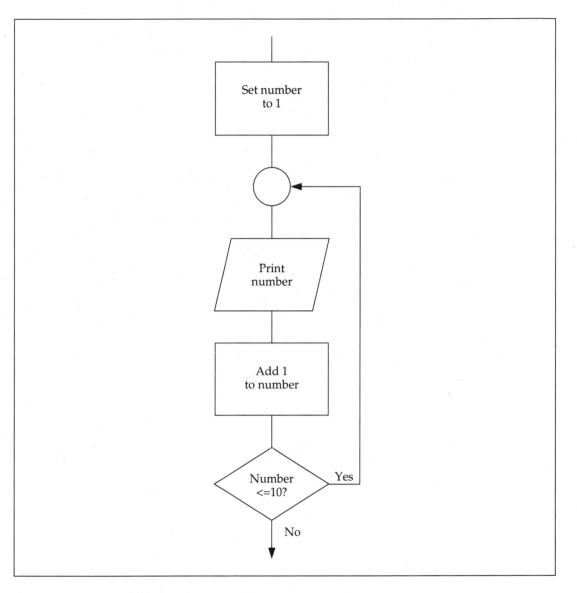

**Figure 4-4    Program Flowchart for Posttest Loop**

false, the THEN part of the structure is skipped, and the statements following ENDIF are executed.

Figure 4-5 shows a program flowchart for one-way selection.

***Two-way Selection.***    With *two-way selection* you have two choices, a THEN part and an ELSE part. You must be careful that only one of these two parts is executed for any one condition. A generalized form of pseudocode for two-way selection is:

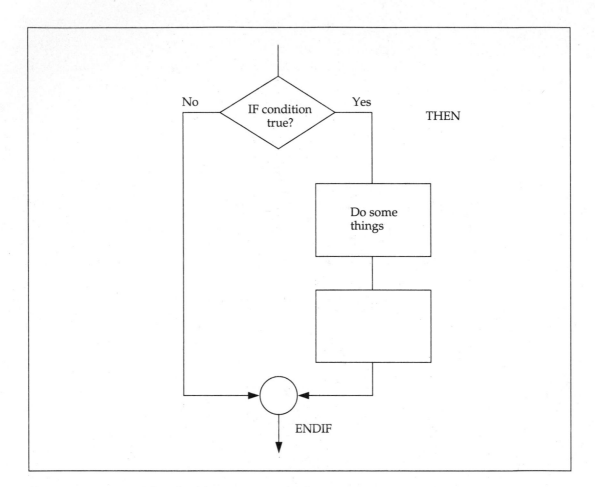

**Figure 4-5    Program Flowchart for One-Way Selection**

```
IF a condition is true
    THEN do something
ELSE
    Do something else
ENDIF
```

Figure 4-6 shows a flowchart example of two-way selection.

## COMPARISON

In assembler language you test conditions for both repetition and selection structures by comparing certain values and then jumping to some other instruction according to the setting of certain flags. Some arithmetic operations set the flags so that the compare instruction is not required, and a few

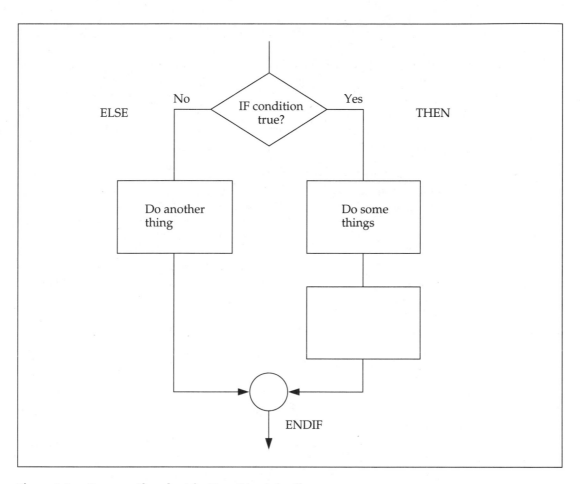

**Figure 4-6    Program Flowchart for Two-Way Selection**

instructions contain both the comparison and the test as a part of the instructions themselves.

The CMP (compare) instruction compares two hex numbers. Both numbers must be of the same length, either bytes or words, except that an eight-bit immediate value may be compared with a word register. The numbers may represent either pure binary or ASCII codes. The general form of the CMP instruction is: CMP first, second where *first* may represent registers or data in memory and *second* may represent registers, data in memory, or immediate values. However, both operands may not be memory locations.

FORMAT                          EXAMPLE

```
CMP accumulator,data       CMP AX,05h
CMP register,data          CMP BX,0FFFFh
CMP register,register      CMP AL,BL
CMP register,memory        CMP CX,WORD
```

```
CMP memory,data          CMP BYTE,'A'
CMP memory,register      CMP WORD,CX
```

In effect, CMP subtracts the second operand from the first and sets one or more of the flags accordingly. A 1 bit (TRUE) sets a flag ON, while a 0 bit (FALSE) sets it OFF. Neither operand is actually changed. CMP operates the same regardless of the type of data being compared. The flags may be interpreted differently depending upon the type of data being compared.

The arithmetic flags are designated as follows:

AF = auxiliary carry flag  CF = carry flag
OF = overflow flag         PF = parity flag
SF = sign flag             ZF = zero flag

AF (auxiliary carry flag) will be discussed in Chapter 8.

CF (carry flag) is set to 1 if the result of an arithmetic operation on unsigned numbers becomes less than 0 or exceeds 255 (0FFh) for byte instructions or 65535 (0FFFFh) for word instructions. It also is set by certain shift instructions.

OF (overflow flag) is set whenever the result of signed numbers exceeds the allowable range. This range is -128 to 127 for bytes and - 32768 to 32767 for words.

PF (parity flag) is used primarily with communications software. It is set if the result of an operation has an even number of 1 bits in the lower byte.

SF (sign flag) is 1 if the result of an operation is negative and 0 if it is positive. This is a copy of the leftmost bit of the result, which indicates the sign in signed binary numbers.

ZF (zero flag) is 1 if the result of an operation is zero and 0 if the result is not zero. (Caution: This can be very confusing.)

The remaining three flags, DF (direction flag), IF (interrupt enable flag), and TF (trap flag), are not set by comparison or arithmetic operations. Instructions that set these and other flags are presented in Appendix I.

## CONDITIONAL JUMPS

A *conditional jump* is an instruction that tests one or more flags that may be set by a comparison, some arithmetic instructions, or some interrupts. The instruction may test if a flag *is* or *is not* set to 1. If the condition being tested is true, then a jump, or transfer of control, is made to the label named as the operand. If the condition is not true, the next instruction in sequence is executed.

All conditional jumps are *short jumps*, which are limited to 127 bytes forward or 128 backward. You will see later how to overcome this limitation if you have to jump a longer distance within your program.

## Conditional Jumps after Comparison

A conditional jump may follow a comparison of either signed or unsigned data. Instructions used for signed comparisons are different from those used for unsigned comparisons. Those with abbreviations for below or above are used for *unsigned comparison*, while those with greater or less are used for *signed comparisons*.

In Table 4-1, all of the conditional jumps are listed and the flags that are tested are shown. In every instance following a comparison, the first operand is being compared with the second. For example, JA means to jump if first is above the second. Note that some of the instructions are equivalent. For example, jump if greater (JG) is equivalent to jump if not less than or equal (JNLE).

## Conditional Jumps after Other Instructions

Any of the six arithmetic flags may be set by certain, but not all, arithmetic instructions. ADC (add carry), ADD, NEG (negate), SBB (subtract borrow), SCAS (scan string), and SUB (subtract) can set any of the six arithmetic flags. DEC (decrement) and INC (increment) can set any except CF (carry flag). The logical instructions AND, OR, XOR (exclusive OR), and TEST can set all but AF (auxiliary carry flag), and will always set CF and OF to 0. The shift instructions SHR (shift right), SHL (shift left), SAL (shift arithmetic left), and SAR (shift arithmetic right), can set all but AF. Rotate instructions ROL (rotate left), ROR (rotate right), RCL (rotate through carry left), and RCR (rotate through carry right) can set CF and OF only, as can the multiply instructions MUL (multiply) and IMUL (signed multiply). The instruction summary in Appendix I shows all possible flag settings by instructions.

In general, move instructions and jump instructions do not set any of the flags. There are a few other instructions that have no effect on flags.

# UNCONDITIONAL JUMPS

The JMP (jump) instruction transfers control to some other point in the program without regard to any flag settings. It is like the GOTO statement in other programming languages.

There are five possible kinds of unconditional jumps, depending upon the label of the target instruction to which the jump is made. The assembler will choose the correct kind of jump according to the definition of the target label. A *near jump*, or *intra segment direct jump*, can jump up to 32767 bytes forward or -32768 bytes backward within the code segment. The op code of the machine instruction requires one byte, and the target address for the jump requires two bytes. Instead of the actual offset of the target address, the distance between the instruction *following JMP* and location of the target label

Table 4-1
Conditional-Jump Instructions

| | | | | |
|---|---|---|---|---|
| | | **Instructions after Comparing First Operand with Second** | | |
| Result of Compare | **Signed Operands** Instruction | Jump If | **Unsigned Operands** Instruction | Jump If |
| = | JE | ZF=1 | JE | ZF=1 |
| <> | JNE | ZF=0 | JNE | ZF=0 |
| > | JG/JNLE | ZF=0 And SF=0F | JA/JNBE | CF=0 AND ZF=0 |
| >= | JGE/JNL | SF=0F | JAE/JNB | CF=0 |
| < | JL/JNGE | SF<>0F | JB/JNAE | CF=1 |
| <= | JLE/JNG | ZF=1 And SF<>0F | JBE/JNA | CF=0 |

Meaning of Letters

J = Jump
A = Above (unsigned comparisons
B = Below (unsigned comparisons
E = Equal

G = Greater than (signed comparisons)
L = Less than (signed comparisons)
N = Not

---

**Instructions Based on Single Flag Setting**

| Instruction | Meaning | Jump If |
|---|---|---|
| JC | Jump if carry | CF=1 |
| JNC | Jump if no carry | CF=0 |
| JO | Jump if overflow | OF=1 |
| JNO | Jump if no overflow | OF=0 |
| JP | Jump if parity | PF=1 |
| JNP | Jump if no parity | PF=0 |
| JPE | Jump if parity even | PF=1 |
| JPO | Jump if parity odd | PF=0 |
| JS | Jump if sign flag set | SF=1 |
| JNS | Jump if sign flag clear | SF=0 |
| JZ | Jump if zero | ZF=1 |
| JNZ | Jump if not zero | ZF=0 |

---

**Instruction Based on Single Register Setting**

| Instruction | Meaning | Jump If |
|---|---|---|
| JCXZ | Jump if CX is zero | CX=0 |

is used. The first byte is the least significant byte (LSB) and the second is the most significant byte (MSB). This distance is added to IP to compute the target address when the JMP is executed. Examples:

| OBJECT CODE | INSTRUCTION | EXPLANATION |
|---|---|---|
| E9 08 01 | JMP WEND01 | ;WEND01 is 264 (0108h) ;bytes forward |
| E9 F8 FE | JMP WHILE01 | ;WHILE01 is -264 (FEF8) ;bytes backward |

A *short jump* is identical to a near jump except that only one byte in the JMP instruction contains the distance, which cannot exceed 127 (7Fh) bytes forward and -128 (80h) bytes backwards. The assembler will automatically use short jumps wherever possible. On a *forward jump*, that is, where the target address is ahead of the JMP instruction, the assembler assumes that a near jump will be required and provides two bytes for the target address. Then if the target is fewer than 127 bytes ahead, it creates a short jump and turns the second byte into a NOP (no-op) instruction. You can tell the assembler to use a short jump by using the SHORT operator preceding the target address. Examples:

| OBJECT CODE | INSTRUCTION | EXPLANATION |
|---|---|---|
| EB 6E 90 | JMP WEND02 | ;WEND02 is 110 (6Eh) ;bytes ahead ;90h is NOP to fill ;extra byte |
| EB 6E | JMP SHORT WEND02 | ;WEND02 is 110 (6Eh) ;bytes ahead |
| EB F9 | JMP WHILE02 | ;WHILE02 is -7 (F9h) ;bytes back |

As noted earlier, all conditional jumps and all LOOP instructions are short jumps.

A *far jump*, or *inter segment jump*, transfers control to another segment or to a label that is the name of a far procedure. It requires four bytes in the JMP instruction for the target address, two for the segment address and two for the offset. Both addresses are set to 0000 by the assembler and filled in by LINK. The assembler listing usually shows the segment address as ----. Both addresses have the LSB preceding the MSB. Normally we use a far jump only for programs with more than one code segment. Example:

| OBJECT CODE | INSTRUCTION | EXPLANATION |
|---|---|---|
| EA 0000 --- | JMP FARPROC | ;address of FARPROC ;must be supplied ;by LINK |

There are two kinds of *indirect jumps*: intra segment jumps within the same segment and inter segment jumps between different segments. Indirect jumps are those in which the address of the next instruction is held in a data table or in a general register instead of being a part of the JMP instruction itself. One byte is required for the op code and one byte for a code representing the form of indirect address. If the indirect address includes a constant, then the constant is the third and possibly the fourth byte of the instruction. Examples:

| OBJECT CODE | INSTRUCTION | EXPLANATION |
|---|---|---|
| FF 24 | JMP [SI] | ;24h is code for SI<br>;register |
| FF 21 | JMP [BX][DI] | ;21h is code for BX<br>;and DI registers |
| FF 60 02 | JMP [BX+SI]+2 | ;60h is code for BX<br>;and SI plus<br>;constant ;02h is<br>;the constant |

## WRITING STRUCTURES IN ASSEMBLER LANGUAGE

An effective way to provide structured programming in assembler language is to use pseudocode as comments along with source statements in the code segment. You then can use the keywords WHILE, WEND, REPEAT, UNTIL, IF, THEN, ELSE, and ENDIF as labels to control the statements to which you jump. Jumps, both conditional and unconditional, make the program flow agree with the pseudocode. A few examples will illustrate this approach.

### Simple Structures

WHILE and WEND are the keywords used as labels to identity a pretest loop in your source code. To avoid the possibility of using the same label twice, or of using an assembler language reserved word, we will attach a two-digit number following the keyword. The general format follows:

```
WHILEnn:   The statements at WHILEnn test if the loop
           should be performed. If not, jump to WENDnn.
           Following WHILEnn are the statements executed
           by the loop. At least one of these statements
           must change some value that is tested to see if
           the loop is to be continued. The loop must end
           with a jump to WHILEnn.
           JMP WHILEnn
WENDnn:
```

Example: Here is a pretest loop to input a character from the keyboard, display it upon the screen, and continue until <ENTER> is pressed:

```
                MOV AH,1                      ;Get a character and display
                                              ;it
                INT 21h
WHILE01:        CMP AL,13                     ;WHILE character is not
                                              ;<ENTER> (13)
                JE WEND01
                MOVE AH,1                     ; Get another character and
                                              ; display it
                INT 21h
                JMP WHILE01
WEND01:                                       ;WEND
```

Note how indentation is used in the comments to show the start and end of each structure at the same column, while statements included within the structure are indented to the right. However, do not indent the labels of the statements themselves, since a label begins in column 1 of the source statement. Also note that MASM allows a label such as WEND01 on a line without an instruction. This feature allows you to match the labels and the pseudocode closely.

REPEAT and UNTIL are the labels that identify a posttest loop. They too are followed by a two-digit number to be consistent with other labels.

```
REPEATnn:
                These are statements to be executed by the
                loop. One or more statements must modify the
                condition tested to see if the loop is to
                continue. The last statements in the loop
                provide a test of the condition and conditional
                jump to REPEATnn if the condition is met. If
                the condition is not met, the program falls
                through to the UNTILnn.
UNTILnn:
```

Example: Here is a posttest loop to input a character from the keyboard without echo on the screen until the character 'Y' is pressed, and then display the Y.

```
REPEAT01:                                     ;REPEAT
                MOV AH,8                      ; Input a character without
                                              ; echo
                INT 21h
                CMP AL,'Y'
                JNE REPEAT01
UNTIL 01:                                     ;UNTIL character = 'Y'
                MOV DL,AL                     ;Move character to DL
                MOV AH,2                      ;Display the character
                INT 21h
```

IF, THEN, and ENDIF are labels that identify one-way selection. However, since several of these are reserved words in assembler language, you must append a two-digit number to make each label unique.

```
IFnn:           Here the condition is tested. If not true, jump
                to ANDIFnn.
```

```
THENnn:     Here the statements are to be executed if the
            condition is true.
ENDIFnn:
```

Example: this routine inputs a character without echo and displays it if it is a 'Y':

```
            MOV AH,8                ;Input a character
                                    ;without echo
            INT 21h
IF01:       CMP AL,'Y'              ;IF character = 'Y'
            JNE ENDIF01
THEN01:     MOV DL,AL               ; THEN move character
                                    ; to DL
            MOV AH,2                ; Display it
            INT 21h
ENDIF01:                           ;ENDIF
```

IF, THEN, ELSE, and ENDIF are labels that specify two-way selection.

```
IFnn:       Here the condition is tested. If not true, jump
            to ELSEnn.
THENnn:     Here the statements are to be executed if the
            condition is true.
            They terminate with an unconditional jump to
            ENDIFnn.
            JMP ENDIFnn
ELSEnn:
            Here the statements are to be executed if the
            condition is false.
            When they are finished, program logic falls
            through to ENDIFnn.
ENDIFnn:
```

Example: This routine accepts a character from the keyboard without echo. If a flag contains the character 'P', the character is output to the printer; otherwise, it is displayed on the screen.

```
            MOV AH,8                ;Input character without echo
            INT 21h
            MOV DL,AL               ;Move character to DL for
                                    ;output
IF02:       CMP FLAG,'P'            ;IF flag = 'P'
            JNE ELSE02
THEN02:     MOV AH,5                ; THEN print character
            INT 21h
            JMP ENDIF02
ELSE02:     MOV AH,2                ;ELSE display character
            INT 21h
ENDIF02:                           ;ENDIF
```

## Nested Structures

Any structure may be nested within any other structure. For example, a loop may be contained within the THEN or the ELSE part of a selection structure, or within another loop. Use indentation to clarify the nesting. Each structure contained within another is indented further. Statements between IF and ELSE are indented, as are those between ELSE and ENDIF. Statements between WHILE and WEND are indented, and also those between REPEAT and UNTIL. The example below shows an IF-THEN structure nested in a WHILE-WEND loop.

Example: Most of the special control codes such as line feeds, carriage returns, tabs, and backspaces are lower than 32 decimal, or 20h. To input characters until <ENTER> is pressed, but display only codes of 20h or higher, you might write:

```
            MOV AH,8             ;Get character without echo
            INT 21h
WHILE02:    CMP AL,13            ;WHILE character is not
                                 ;<ENTER> (13)

            JE WEND02
IF03:       CMP AL,32            ; IF character = 32 (blank)
            JB ENDIF03
THEN03:     MOV DL,AL            ;   THEN display character
            MOV AH,2
            INT 21h
ENDIF03:                         ; ENDIF
            MOV AH,8             ; Get another character
                                 ; without echo

            INT 21h
            JMP WHILE02
WEND02:                          ;WEND
```

## Compound Conditions

Compound conditions are two or more simple conditions connected with AND or OR. With AND both or all of the simple conditions must be true for the compound condition to be true. For example, both conditions must be true for eligibility if you say "IF a person is over 62 years old AND that person has 10 quarters of social security coverage, THEN that person is eligible for retirement benefits."

With OR, if either or any of the simple conditions is true, the result is true. For example, "IF you have a car OR I have a car, THEN we can take a ride." Only one simple condition must be true to execute the THEN action.

Example: This routine shows a pretest loop with a nested compound IF structure. It will input characters until <ENTER> is pressed, but will display only the decimal digits 0 through 9. All other characters will be ignored (except the <ENTER>).

```
            MOV AH,8             ;Get character without echo
            INT 21h
WHILE03:    CMP AL,13            ;WHILE character is not <ENTER>
                                 ;(13)

            JE WEND03
IF04:       CMP AL,'0'           ; IF character NOT < '0'
```

```
                    JB ENDIF04
AND04:              CMP AL,'9'                 ; AND character NOT > 9'
                    JA ENDIF04
THEN04:             MOV DL,AL                  ;  THEN display character (0-9)
                    MOV AH,2
                    INT 21h
ENDIF04:                                       ; ENDIF
                    MOV AH,8                    ; Get another character without
                                               ; echo
                    INT 21h
                    JMP WHILE03
WEND03:                                         ;WEND
```

Note that the conditional jumps at IF04 and AND04 are exactly opposite from the pseudocode. This is because you must ignore any character less than 0 and greater than 9. Thus you jump to ENDIF04 if either condition is true. That leaves you at THEN04 if the character is NOT less than 0 and NOT greater than 9.

## Special Looping Instructions

In controlling loops up to now, the examples have used separate instructions to modify the variable or counter used in the condition, to make a comparison to test the condition, and to decide which conditional jump to use. The 8088 machine language has several special instructions that combine these three steps.

The LOOP instruction uses the CX register as a counter. When LOOP is executed, the instruction subtracts one from CX and jumps to the specified label if CX is not zero. CX must be properly initialized. The example below shows a loop to print 10 hyphens on a line:

```
                    MOV CX,10               ;Set counter to 10
                    MOV DL,'-'              ;Display a hyphen
REPEAT02:                                   ;REPEAT
                    MOV AH,2
                    INT 21h
                    LOOP REPEAT02           ; Subtract 1 from counter
UNTIL02:                                     ;UNTIL counter = 0
```

We can move the hyphen to DL in the initialization section of the loop because it does not change during execution of the loop.

For additional versatility, several variations of the LOOP instruction are available. LOOPE (loop if equal) and LOOPZ (loop if zero) operate alike. They subtract 1 from CX and loop back if CX is not zero and the zero flag is *set*. The zero flag is not affected by the LOOP instruction itself, but is set if the result of a previous comparison or arithmetic instruction was zero. LOOPNE (loop if not equal) and LOOPNZ (loop if not zero) also are alike. They subtract 1 from CX and loop back if CX is not zero and the zero flag is *not set*. This means the result of some previous operation did not set this flag.

Failure to initialize CX can cause problems with the LOOP instruction. CX is decremented before it is checked for zero. If CX contains zero when the LOOP instruction is executed, the result will be -1 (0FFFFh), identical to 65535. Thus, the loop will be executed 65535 more times before CX again becomes zero.

The JCXZ can detect this condition and prevent the loop from being executed if CX initially contains zero. This example shows how:

```
IF05:          JCXZ ENDIF05           ;IF CX is < > 0
THEN05:                               ;   THEN
REPEAT03:                             ;   REPEAT
          (statements within loop)    ;      statements within loop
          LOOP REPEAT03               ;      Subtract 1 from CX
UNTIL03:                              ;   UNTIL CX = 0
ENDIF05:                              ;ENDIF
```

## PROGRAM 4: DEMONSTRATION OF STRUCTURES

Program 4 (Figure 4-7) combines typical sequence, repetition, and selection structures. This program does the following operations:

1.  Clears the screen.
2.  Spaces down five lines.
3.  Inputs characters from the keyboard, printing only 0 through 9 until <ENTER> is pressed.
4.  Inputs a line from the keyboard, displays a message, and prints the line 10 times.
5.  Asks the operator if he or she wishes to continue and repeats until 'N' or 'n' is entered.

This program has one major REPEAT01-UNTIL01 loop that continues until the operator enters a negative response of 'N' or 'n' to the prompt. Nested within this loop are three other loops. the first loop (REPEAT02-UNTIL02) displays a line feed five times. The next loop (WHILE01-WEND01) contains a nested compound IF01-THEN01 structure to test whether the keyed character is between 0 and 9 so that it will be printed. If the keyed character is below 0, a jump is made to ENDIF01. Then if the keyed character is above 9, a jump is made to ENDIF01. Only if the character is equal to or greater than 0 AND less than or equal to 9 can the THEN01 part of the structure be executed.

The third loop (REPEAT03-UNTIL03) repeats 10 times, displaying the contents of a buffer containing a string entered by the operator. Note that the byte at BUFFER+1 contains the length of the string. This byte is placed into CL as required by function 40h of INT 21h to print a string that need not be ended with a dollar sign.

```
            PAGE 50,132
;-------------------------------------------------------------------
; Program name:    B:PROG4.ASM
                ;
; Author:   Alton R. Kindred
;
; This program demonstrates sequence, repetition, and selection structures.
; It clears the screen, spaces down five lines, prompts the operator to enter
; any number of decimal digits, prints only digits between 0 and 9 until
; <ENTER> is pressed, asks the operator to input a line from the keyboard,
; prints the line 10 times, and asks the operator if he/she wishes to continue.
; Program continues until operator types 'N' or 'n'.
;-------------------------------------------------------------------
DATA        SEGMENT                    ;segment for data
MSG1        DB 'Press any keys ending with <ENTER>.',13,10
            DB 'Only decimal digits will print: $'
MSG2        DB 'Type a line ended with <ENTER>'
CRLF        DB 13,10,'$'
MSG3        DB 10,10,'Here is the line you typed: $'
MSG4        DB 'Do you wish to continue? (Y/N) $'
BUFFER      DB 80,?, 80 dup (?)
DATA        ENDS
;-------------------------------------------------------------------
STACK       SEGMENT STACK              ;stack segment
            DB 32 DUP ('STACK   ')
STACK       ENDS
;-------------------------------------------------------------------
CODE        SEGMENT                    ;segment for code
            ASSUME CS:CODE,DS:DATA,SS:STACK
PROG4       PROC FAR                   ;for proper return to DOS
            MOV AX,DATA                ;set up data segment in DS
            MOV DS,AX
REPEAT01:                              ;REPEAT
            MOV AX,0002h               ;  set mode and clear screen
            INT 10h
            MOV CX,5                   ;  set line counter to 5
REPEAT02:                              ;  REPEAT
            MOV DL,10                  ;    feed a line
            MOV AH,2
            INT 21h
            LOOP REPEAT02              ;    subtract 1 from line counter
UNTIL02:                              ;  UNTIL line counter = 0
            MOV DX,OFFSET MSG1         ;  display prompt for digits
            MOV AH,9
            INT 21h
            MOV AH,8                   ;  get character without echo
            INT 21h
WHILE01:    CMP AL,13                  ;  WHILE character  ENTER
            JE WEND01
IF01:       CMP AL,'0'                 ;    IF character = '0'
            JB ENDIF01
AND01:      CMP AL,'9'                 ;    AND character < '9'
            JA ENDIF01
THEN01:     MOV DL,AL                  ;      THEN display character
```

**Figure 4-7    Source Listing of Program 4**

```
              MOV  AH,2
              INT  21h
ENDIF01:                              ;     ENDIF
              MOV  AH,8               ;     get another character
              INT  21h
              JMP  WHILE01
WEND01:                               ; WEND
              MOV  DX,OFFSET CRLF     ; return cursor
              MOV  AH,9
              INT  21h
              MOV  DX,OFFSET MSG2     ; display prompt
              MOV  AH,9
              INT  21h
              MOV  DX,OFFSET BUFFER   ; get a string
              MOV  AH,10
              INT  21h
              MOV  DX,OFFSET MSG3     ; display message after 2 line feeds
              MOV  AH,9
              INT  21h
              MOV  DX,OFFSET CRLF     ; return cursor
              MOV  AH,9
              INT  21h
              MOV  CX,10              ; set line counter to 10
REPEAT03:                             ;   REPEAT
              PUSH CX                 ;     save line number
              MOV  BX,1               ;     get file handle to screen
              MOV  DX,OFFSET BUFFER+2 ;     print the string
              MOV  CL,BUFFER+1
              MOV  AH,40h
              INT  21h
              MOV  DL,10              ;     return cursor
              MOV  AH,2
              INT  21h
              MOV  DL,13
              MOV  AH,2
              INT  21h
              POP  CX                 ;     restore line counter
              LOOP REPEAT03           ;     subtract 1 from line counter
UNTIL03:                              ;   UNTIL line counter = 0
              MOV  DX,OFFSET MSG4     ; ask if to continue
              MOV  AH,9
              INT  21h
              MOV  AH,1               ; get response
              INT  21h
              CMP  AL,'N'
              JE   UNTIL01
              CMP  AL,'n'
              JE   UNTIL01
              JMP  REPEAT01
UNTIL01:                              ;UNTIL response = 'N' or 'n'
              MOV  AX,4C00h           ;return to DOS
              INT  21h
PROG4         ENDP                    ;end of procedure declaration
;--------------------------------------------------------------------------
CODE          ENDS                    ;end of segment code declaration
              END  PROG4              ;end of program
```

**Figure 4-7**    *concluded*

The test of the operator's response to the question 'Do you wish to continue? (Y/N)' actually tests only the negative response. Any other character typed would cause the outer loop to be repeated. It is not possible to use the statement JNE REPEAT01 following CMP AL, 'N' and CMP AL, 'n' because the conditional jump is more than 127 bytes. To overcome this problem we use the conditional jump JE UNTIL01 and follow it with an unconditional jump to REPEAT01 if the character was not an 'N' or 'n'. Unconditional jumps can be of any length.

Figure 4-8 shows sample output from program 4.

## SUMMARY

Program structures include the sequence structure, repetition structure or loop, and selection structure. Program logic for each structure may be expressed in pseudocode or as a program flowchart.

The sequence structure is merely one instruction after another with no variation.

Repetition structure contains four steps, which are not always executed in the same order: initialize, test, execute, and modify. A pretest loop makes the test before doing the execute and modify steps; a posttest loop tests after executing and modifying.

Selection structure may involve one-way or two-way selection. One-way selection, or IF-THEN structure, does an action if a condition is true and omits it if the condition is false. Two-way selection, or IF-THEN-ELSE structure, does the actions specified by THEN if the condition is true and those designated by ELSE if the condition is false.

Pseudocode uses the keywords WHILE and WEND to designate a pretest loop and REPEAT and UNTIL to designate a posttest loop. IF, THEN, and ENDIF are used to specify one-way selection, and IF, THEN, ELSE, and ENDIF are used to specify two-way selection. Statements between these keywords are indented to help to emphasize statements dependent upon the conditions.

Most conditions depend upon the comparison between two values. Certain flags in the flag register are set depending upon the results of the comparison. Certain arithmetic operations also set flags, but not all do.

Conditional jumps transfer control to other locations if the flags are set to indicate that the tested condition is true. Unconditional jumps transfer control without regard to the setting of the flags. Unconditional jumps are of five possible kinds, depending upon the label of the instruction to which the jump is made: near, short, far, indirect near, and indirect far.

Program logic in assembler may be made clear by using pseudocode as comments throughout the source code, and by identifying the corresponding statements with labels WHILE, WEND, REPEAT, UNTIL, IF, THEN, ELSE,

```
Press any keys ending with <ENTER>.
Only decimal digits will print:   035827
Type a line ended with <ENTER>:
OK, here is a line.

Here is the line you typed:
OK, here is a line.
OK, here is a line.
OK, here is a line.
OK, here is a line.
OK, here is a line.
OK, here is a line.
OK, here is a line.
OK, here is a line.
OK, here is a line.
OK, here is a line.
Do you wish to continue? (Y/N) n
B>
```

**Figure 4-8    Output from Program 4**

and ENDIF. To avoid duplication of labels a two-digit suffix may be attached to the keyword used as a label, as in IF01 or WHILE20.

Structures may be nested within other structures. An IF-THEN-ELSE structure may be contained between a WHILE and its corresponding WEND or between a REPEAT-UNTIL pair. Or any structure may be contained entirely within the THEN or the ELSE portion of an IF structure. The beginning or ending part of any nested structure may not overlap into another structure.

Compound conditions consist of two or more simple conditions. Where the simple conditions are connected by AND, all conditions must be true for the action to be taken. Where they are connected by OR, the action is taken if at least one of the simple conditions is true.

## QUESTIONS

1. Define pseudocode. What are its advantages over program flowcharting?
2. Describe program flowcharting symbols used for each of the following: terminal, processing, input/output, decision, subroutine, connector.
3. Give an example of the sequence structure.
4. What is the difference between a pretest loop and posttest loop? What pseudocode keywords are used to designate each? Which type of loop will always be executed at least once?
5. Name the four parts of a loop, and describe the purpose of each.
6. What keywords are used in pseudocode to indicate one-way selection? Two-way selection?

7. How many different types of operands may be used in compare (CMP) instructions? What type may not be used for both operands?
8. Name the six arithmetic flags. What other flags are there?
9. What are short jumps? What is their limit?
10. Name the principal kinds of instructions that do not set flags.
11. Explain the difference between intra segment and inter segment jumps.
12. What is meant by nested structures? Give an example of incorrect nesting.
13. Explain the difference between compound conditions with AND and those with OR.
14. Name several instructions used in looping that combine several operations into one. What register is used with these instructions?

## EXERCISES

1. Write pseudocode for a routine to count to 100 by fives. Use a pretest loop.
2. Draw a program flowchart to count to 50 by twos. Use a posttest loop.
3. Write a segment of a program flowchart to perform a heading subroutine if a line counter is equal to or greater than 50. Whether or not the heading is printed, print a detail line and add 1 to the line counter. Use the subroutine symbol for the heading routine.
4. Write pseudocode for the following program segment: Read in employee name, hours worked, and hourly rate of pay. If hours worked are greater than 40, regular pay is hours * rate, and overtime pay is zero. If hours are less than or equal to 40, regular pay is 40 * rate and overtime pay is (hours - 40) * rate * 1.5. Regardless of hours worked, gross pay is regular pay + overtime pay.
5. Write an assembler routine to display your name five times on the screen. Use AX as a counter for a pretest loop. Use naming conventions described in the chapter and pseudocode as comments.
6. Write an assembler routine to display a line of 80 hyphens across the screen. Use CX as the counter and the LOOP instruction for a posttest loop. Set the cursor at the start of the line before entering the loop.
7. Write an assembler routine that issues a prompt to the keyboard operator to set the CAPS LOCK ON, then press any keys, and press <ENTER> to stop. Input the key without echo. Display each letter of the alphabet on the screen but ignore any other keys that are pressed. Stop when <ENTER> is pressed.

## LAB PROBLEMS

1. Write a program that uses a posttest loop to display the 26 letters of the alphabet. Start with MOV DL, 'A'. Use CX as the counter and the LOOP instruction. In the loop, add 1 to DL and space once between letters. Then space down five lines and use the same technique to display the decimal digits 0 through 9.
2. Write an assembler program to issue a prompt to the operator to enter any line of data. Display the line five times on the screen. Ask if the operator wishes to continue. Repeat until the operator answers 'N' or 'n'.

# ARITHMETIC OPERATIONS

# 5

**OBJECTIVES**

After studying this chapter, you should be able to:

- Explain how negative numbers are formed and processed.
- Perform addition and subtraction on eight-bit and 16-bit numbers.
- Increment and decrement registers and values in main storage.
- Perform multiplication and division on eight-bit and 16-bit numbers.
- Explain logical operations on binary numbers and describe how they are used in programming.
- Describe the various shifting and rotating operations.
- Input characters and convert them to numeric form.
- Convert numbers in main storage into printable form.

## NEGATIVE NUMBERS

In Chapter 1 we saw that binary numbers could be expressed as unsigned or signed values. You will recall that the leftmost bit of a byte or word represents the sign of the number, with 0 indicating positive and 1 indicating negative. Whether the number is signed or unsigned depends entirely upon the way you treat it. For example, the binary number 10000000 (80h) is 128 decimal if you regard it as unsigned and -128 if you think of it as signed. Similarly, 11111111 (FFh) can represent 255 decimal if unsigned or -1 if signed.

The arithmetic-logic unit operates on signed and unsigned values in exactly the same fashion. For example, FFh added to 01h (255 + 1 decimal) in an eight-bit register produces a result of 00 and sets the carry flag. This indicates overflow of an unsigned value, since the correct sum of 100h (256 decimal) is too large to be represented in eight bits.

For the same values, if you consider FFh to be -1 decimal and 01h to be +1 decimal, then the result of 00 is correct. In this instance, you would test the overflow flag rather than the carry flag to see if overflow occurred. The overflow flag is set to zero, since the signed result is valid.

Conversely, the sum of 7Fh and 7Fh gives a sum of FEh (127 + 127 = 254). Since there is no carry, this is a valid unsigned sum, but an incorrect signed sum, and the overflow flag would be set. In summary, test the carry flag to see if overflow occurred on unsigned numbers, and test the overflow flag for signed numbers.

## THE ADD, SUBTRACT, AND NEGATE INSTRUCTIONS

The ADD instruction allows you to add to registers or memory addresses. Its format is:

```
ADD destination,source
```

The value at *source* is added to *destination* and the sum appears at destination. As with the MOV instruction, *source* can be an immediate value, a general register, or a memory location. A general register is any register except the segment registers, flag register, or IP. *Destination* can be a general register or memory location. However, both operands cannot be memory locations.

ADD can be used with either bytes or words, but the operands cannot be mixed. Immediate values are made to be either one or two bytes according to the type of register or the storage definition (DB or DW) to which it is to be added. Here are some valid examples:

```
ADD AL,BL            ;byte addition between
                     ;registers
ADD AX,DX            ;word addition between
                     ;registers
ADD AL,250           ;add immediate to byte
                     ;register
ADD AX,5000          ;add immediate to word
                     ;register
ADD WORD,DX          ;add word register to storage
ADD BYTE,CL          ;add byte register to storage
ADD BH,BYTE          ;add storage to byte register
ADD CX,WORD          ;add storage to word register
```

Here are some invalid examples of ADD:

```
ADD CX,BH            ;wrong size registers
ADD WORD1,WORD2      ;both operands in storage
ADD AL,500           ;immediate value too large
```

The SUB (subtract) instruction has the format:

```
SUB destination,source
```

SUB works just like ADD, except that source is subtracted from destination. Actually, source is converted to its 2s complement (negative form) and added to destination. The difference is stored at destination. Source may be a general register, a storage location, or an immediate value. Destination may be a general register or a storage location. Both operands may not be storage locations. Examples are identical to those given for ADD above, with the op code of SUB instead.

The NEG (negate) instruction changes the sign of a number. A positive number becomes negative, and a negative number becomes positive. The format of NEG is:

```
NEG operand
```

where *operand* can be any general byte or word register or a storage location. You can use NEG when some value needs to be subtracted from an immediate value, such as 50. You cannot subtract from an immediate value. But if the value you want subtracted is in AL, you can write:

```
NEG AL
ADD AL,50
```

AL will then contain 50 plus the negative of the original value in AL, that is AL = 50 - AL.

Three flags help you to interpret the results of addition and subtraction. The sign flag is a copy of the leftmost bit in the result, 0 if positive and 1 if negative. The carry flag is set to 1 when a carry results from adding the leftmost bits of the two operands. The overflow flag is set whenever the addition or subtraction exceeds the range for signed numbers. The allowable range is 127 to 128 for bytes and 32767 to -32768 for words.

ADD, SUB, and NEG all set these three flags, but certain other arithmetic instructions do not. When in doubt, check Appendix I.

## INCREMENTING AND DECREMENTING

The INC (increment) and DEC (decrement) instructions change the content of a register or storage location by 1. INC adds 1 and DEC subtracts 1. The format of both instructions is:

```
INC operand
DEC operand
```

where *operand* can be a byte or a word. INC and DEC both set the sign and overflow flags, but not the carry flag.

INC and DEC are useful for counting or for modifying addresses in the index or base registers. We will cover addressing techniques in Chapter 7.

The following example processes a loop 256 times:

```
          MOV AL,0
REPEAT01:
          (Statements executed in the loop)
          INC AL (or DEC AL)
          JNZ REPEAT01
UNTIL01:
```

It is strange to note that you get exactly the same result whether you increment or decrement AL. If you increment AL, it is not zero from 01h through FFh. When you increment AL the 256th time, the FFh becomes 00h, and the zero flag is set to 1 but not the carry flag. If you decrement AL, the 00h becomes FFh (-1) after the first DEC is executed, and then you decrement 255 more times before AL becomes 00h.

## MULTIPLICATION

Many processors prior to the 8088 did not have hardware multiply and divide instructions. These operations had to be done by subroutines. Even now, multiplication and division are somewhat more restricted than addition and subtraction.

The MUL (multiply) instruction produces the product of two numbers, which can be either two bytes or two words. Its format is:

```
MUL source
```

where *source* can be a byte or a word in a general register or storage location, but not an immediate value. If source is a byte, the contents of source are multiplied by the value in AL, and the product appears in all of AX. If source is a word, the contents of source are multiplied by the value in AX, and the product appears in DX and AX. DX contains the high-order (leftmost) word of the product.

The general rule for multiplication is that the length of the product is equal to the sum of the lengths of the two numbers being multiplied. Thus, two bytes multiplied produce a two-byte product, and two words produce a two-word product.

Here are some examples of byte multiplication:

CONTENTS BEFORE MULTIPLYING

| INSTRUCTION | AL | SOURCE | RESULT IN AX |
|---|---|---|---|
| MUL BL | 10h | 02h | 0020h |
| MUL AL | FFh | FFh | FE01h |
| MUL BYTE | 40h | 82h | 2080h |

Here are some examples of word multiplication:

CONTENTS BEFORE MULTIPLYING

| INSTRUCTION | AX | SOURCE | RESULT IN DX-AX |
|---|---|---|---|
| MUL BX | 0100h | 0100h | 00010000h |
| MUL AX | 0400h | 0400h | 00100000h |
| MUL WORD | 6430h | 0210h | 00CEA300h |

**NOTE:**    MUL AL or MUL AX squares the value in AL or AX.

MUL works properly only with unsigned numbers. The IMUL instruction works exactly like MUL, but takes the sign into account on signed numbers. MUL with signed numbers, or IMUL with unsigned numbers, produces meaningless results. When both numbers being multiplied have the same sign, the product is positive; when the signs differ, the product is negative.

MUL and IMUL do not set any flags except CF and OF. Both of these flags are set if the product for byte multiplication exceeds eight bits or the product of word multiplication exceeds 16 bits.

## DIVISION

The DIV (divide) instruction likewise can work with bytes or words. The format for DIV is:

```
DIV source
```

where *source* can be any general byte register or a memory location. Source cannot be an immediate value.

With byte division, the number to be divided (dividend) is stored in AX. After being divided by the source byte, AL holds the quotient and AH holds the remainder. Here are a few examples of byte division:

### CONTENTS BEFORE DIVIDING

| INSTRUCTION | AX | SOURCE | REMAINDER IN AH | QUOTIENT IN AL |
|---|---|---|---|---|
| DIV BL | 0042h | 10h | 02h | 04h |
| DIV BYTE | 0100h | 19h | 06h | 0Ah |
| DIV DH | 0FFFh | FFh | 0Fh | 10h |

To divide a single byte in AL by another byte at source, it is necessary to set AH to 0. For example, to divide decimal 144 by decimal 20, you might write:

```
MOV AL,144
MOV AH,0
MOV BL,20
DIV BL
```

After division, AH will contain the remainder of 4 and AL will hold the quotient of 7. Without the instruction MOV AH,0, the dividend would be considered to include whatever the previous contents of AH might have been.

With word division, the dividend is stored in DX and AX, with the most significant word in DX and the least significant in AX. After division, DX holds the remainder and AX the quotient. Here are some examples, using decimal values for easier verification:

CONTENTS BEFORE DIVIDING

| INSTRUCTION | DX-AX | SOURCE | REMAINDER IN DX | QUOTIENT IN AX |
|---|---|---|---|---|
| DIV DX | 65535 | 655 | 35 | 100 |
| DIV WORD | 25217 | 25 | 17 | 1008 |

There are two possible error conditions in division. First, division by zero is always impossible. You will recall that INT 00h is invoked by the hardware whenever this condition occurs. Second, if a very large number is divided by a very small one, the quotient may be too large to fit into its designated register. Consider the following example, using decimal numbers:

```
MOV AX,60000
MOV BL,10
DIV BL
```

Clearly, the quotient in this example should be 6000, far too large to fit into the single byte register AL. This condition also produces an interrupt because of divide overflow, and the program will be terminated.

You can recognize a divide overflow condition by examining the contents of the registers in hex before division takes place. If that portion of the quotient in the high order register (AH for byte division or DX for word division) is equal to or larger than the divisor (source), then divide overflow is bound to occur. Note this example:

```
MOV AX,100h         ; AH = 01h, AL = 00h
MOV BL,01h          ; BL = 01h
DIV BL              ; AH = 00h, AL should hold
                    ; 100h
```

Clearly, AL cannot hold the quotient of 100h, since FFh is the largest number that can be contained in any single byte. Similarly, if the part of the dividend in DX with byte division is greater than the divisor, the quotient will be too large to be contained in AX, and divide overflow will occur.

DIV works correctly only with unsigned numbers. For signed numbers, use IDIV. This instruction takes the sign bits of both operands into account. If both signs are alike, the quotient is positive; if signs are different, the quotient is negative. The remainder always has the sign of the dividend.

## LOGICAL OPERATIONS

There is a group of instructions closely related to the arithmetic operations that usually are classified as logical operations. These operations are based on a form of logic developed by an Englishman, George Boole, in the 19th century. They are often called *Boolean algebra* or *Boolean logic*. They involve operations between corresponding bits in a pair of bytes or words.

The bits in one number of the pair may be changed by certain rules. There is never a carry or a borrow with logical operations.

All logical operators have the same format:

OPERATOR destination,source

where *destination* and *source* may be the same combinations used with ADD and SUB. Destination is modified according to the function specified in OPERATOR. The functions are AND, OR, XOR, and NOT. TEST is a related instruction that does not change the contents of destination, but senses whether specified bits are 1 or 0.

These five instructions all clear the carry and overflow flags to 0 and set the zero, sign, and parity flags to either 0 or 1 as appropriate.

We use these terms in ordinary English, and we have introduced them in Chapter 4 in connection with compound conditions.

## AND

The term AND used in a compound condition implies that the entire condition is true only if both, or all, of the simple conditions are true. In logical operations, a 1 bit designates true and a 0 bit means false. The AND instruction causes the bit in any position in destination to be set to 1 only if it was already 1 and the corresponding bit in source is also 1. In every other case, that bit is set to zero.

Logical operations often are represented as truth tables. The table for AND is:

```
1 AND 1 = 1
1 AND 0 = 0
0 AND 1 = 0
0 AND 0 = 0
```

Here are some examples of AND using bytes:

| Destination before AND | 00110011 | 01010101 | 00010001 | 11111111 |
|---|---|---|---|---|
| Source before AND | 10101010 | 00001111 | 11001100 | 10000001 |
| Destination after AND | 00100010 | 00000101 | 00000000 | 10000001 |

The most common use of AND is to set a specified bit to zero. Whether any given bit in destination is 0 or 1, you can make it a 0 by placing a 0 in the corresponding position in source. This is like setting a bit switch OFF. You should place a 1 in each bit position that you do not wish to change. If you AND any byte or word against a source containing all 0s, then all bits in destination also become 0s.

You may prefer to use binary numbers rather than decimal or hex when working with logical operations. For example, the decimal number 128, the hex number 80h, and the binary number 10000000b all are exactly the same value. However, the last form is much clearer to indicate exactly which bit is a 0 and which is a 1. This is especially true where the second operand (source) in a logical operation is an immediate value. We will show further examples throughout this chapter.

## OR

OR instructions follow this table:

```
1 OR 1 = 1
1 OR 0 = 1
0 OR 1 = 1
0 OR 0 = 0
```

You can see that the result is 1 if either or both of the corresponding bits is 1. That is like saying that a compound condition is true if any of the simple conditions is true. Here are some examples with bytes:

| | | | | |
|---|---|---|---|---|
| Destination before OR | 01010101 | 11110000 | 11001100 | 10000001 |
| Source before OR | 11101110 | 00001100 | 10101010 | 00001000 |
| Destination after OR | 11111111 | 11111100 | 11101110 | 10001001 |

**NOTE:**    From these examples, wherever you put a 1 in source, the corresponding bit in destination becomes a 1. Wherever you put a 0 in source, the corresponding bit in destination remains unchanged.

OR is often used to set any desired bit in destination to 1, like setting a switch ON.

## XOR

XOR (exclusive OR) sets a bit in destination to 1 if its corresponding bit in source is different and to 0 if the bit in source is the same. Here is the truth table:

```
1 XOR 1 = 0
1 XOR 0 = 1
0 XOR 1 = 1
0 XOR 0 = 0
```

Here are some examples of the XOR instruction using bytes:

| | | | | |
|---|---|---|---|---|
| Destination before XOR | 10101010 | 11110000 | 11101110 | 10000001 |
| Source before XOR | 11101110 | 10101010 | 11101110 | 11111111 |
| Destination after XOR | 01000100 | 01011010 | 00000000 | 01111110 |

The third column above illustrates a common use of XOR, that is, to set a register, byte, or word to zero by operating on itself. Since all bits in both operands are identical, all bits are set to 0. The fourth column above illustrates another use of XOR, to reverse the bits in a field. Any position containing a 1 in source reverses the setting of the corresponding bit in destination.

A third use of XOR is unusual. The contents of any two bytes or words can be swapped, or interchanged, by executing XOR three successive times.

Note the following example. Assume that AL contains 00001111 and BL contains 10101010:

|  | CONTENTS OF AL | CONTENTS OF BL |
|---|---|---|
| At start | 00001111 | 10101010 |
| XOR AL,BL | 10100101 | 10101010 |
| XOR BL,AL | 10100101 | 00001111 |
| XOR AL,BL | 10101010 | 00001111 |

This last technique can be used to advantage in sorting operations. No other register or storage area need be used to hold one operand temporarily as the items are being interchanged.

## NOT

NOT reverses all of the bits in the operand specified. It has the format:

```
NOT source
```

Thus, it forms the 1s complement of *source*. Its truth table is:

```
NOT 0 = 1
NOT 1 = 0
```

It is different from NEG (negate), which forms the 2s complement of a byte or word.

## TEST

TEST provides a way of testing the bits in a general register or byte or word in main storage. It has the format:

```
TEST destination,source
```

It is identical to AND except that the result of the operation is not stored, that is, *destination* is not changed when operated on by the bits of *source*.

TEST sets the zero, sign, and parity flags so that a conditional jump may be made based on the value of the register or storage location tested.

Examples:

```
(1)        TEST AH,80h            ;test sign bit in AH
           JS ELSE01              ;jump if sign = 1 (negative)
(2)        TEST AL,01100001b      ;test bits 6, 5, and 1
           JZ ENDIF02             ;jump if all are 0
```

## SHIFTING AND ROTATING

Most computers provide the ability to move the bits in a general register or addressed memory location to the left or right. Shifting the contents of a register to the left one bit multiplies the value of the number in that register by 2. Shifting to the right divides the number by 2 (unrounded). Thus, shifting performs a fast way of multiplying or dividing by powers of 2. The number of bit positions shifted designates the power of 2 by which the value is multiplied or divided.

## Shifting

There are four *shift operations*: SHL (shift left), SHR (shift right), SAL (shift arithmetic left), and SAR (shift arithmetic right). All have this format:

```
OPERATION source,count
```

where *source* can be any general register or word location. *Count* can be either the number 1 or CL register, where CL contains the number of positions to be shifted. All of the shift instructions set the overflow, sign, zero, and parity flags according to the result produced.

**SHL and SAL.**    SHL and SAL are identical. Recall that the bits are numbered in descending order from left to right. In bytes, bits are numbered from 7, the leftmost being the most significant bit, to 0, the rightmost being the least significant bit. In words, they are numbered from 15 on the left to 0 on the right.

On a left shift of one bit, bit 7 is moved to the carry flag, all other bits are shifted left one position, and a 0 fills in bit 0. This has the effect of multiplying the value by 2. If the sign is changed, the overflow flag is set to 1. Consider this example:

```
MOV AL,00110011b          ; value 51 decimal
SHL AL,1
```

After this operation is completed, AL contains 01100110b, or 102 decimal. Another execution of SHL AL,1 would produce 11001100b, or 204 decimal.

**SHR.**    This form of the shift right instruction should be used with unsigned numbers. When SHR is executed, the least significant bit, bit 0, is moved into the carry flag, all other bits are shifted one position to the right, and bit 7 is filled with a 0. The effect of SHR is to divide an unsigned number by 2. For example:

```
MOV AL,00110011b          ;value 51
SHR AL,1
```

When SHR has been executed, AL contains 00011001b, or 25 decimal. This is half of the original value of 51, unrounded. Whenever bit 0 contains a 1 before the shift, we know the original number is odd; the shifted result cannot contain a fraction, so the result will always be an unrounded integer.

**SAR.**    SAR is used to shift signed numbers to the right. Like SHR, SAR shifts bit 0 to the carry flag and shifts all other bits to the right one position.

However, bit 7, the sign bit, in addition to being shifted to bit 6, also is shifted back into bit 7. This is called *sign propagation* and has the effect of preserving the same sign the number originally had. Here is an example:

```
MOV AL,11111000B          ;value -8
SAR AL,1
```

The result in AL is 11111100b, or -4 decimal. An SHR shift would have produced 01111100b, changing the result to positive, and giving a completely different value to the number after shifting.

Figure 5-1 shows the effect of each of the shift instructions.

## Rotating

There are four *rotate instructions*: ROL (rotate left), ROR (rotate right), RCL (rotate through carry left), and RCR (rotate through carry right). The format of each of these instructions is similar to the shift instructions:

```
OPERATION source,count
```

where *source* can be a byte or word in a general register or memory location, and *count* is 1 or CL. CL must contain the number of bits to be rotated if more than 1.

Rotate instructions set only the carry and overflow flags. Other arithmetic flags are not affected. The rotate instructions differ from shifts mainly in that bits shifted out one end of the register, byte, or word are shifted back in the other end.

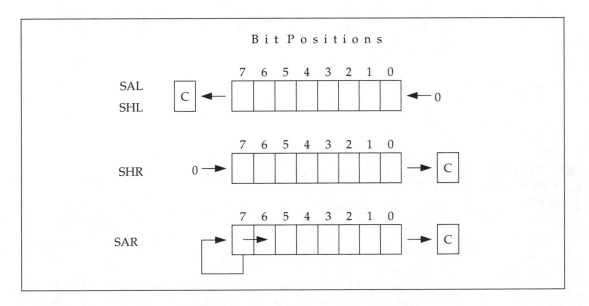

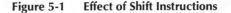

**Figure 5-1    Effect of Shift Instructions**

*ROL*.    ROL rotates the number to the left. Bit 7 is moved into the carry flag, but also into bit 0. All other bits are moved one position to the left. For example:

```
MOV AL,11100010b
ROL AL,1
```

would leave 11000101b in AL and set the carry flag.

*ROR.*    ROR works like ROL but in the opposite direction. ROR moves bit 0 into the carry flag and also to bit 7, and moves all other bits one position to the right. In this example:

```
MOV AL,00001111b
ROR AL,1
```

AL contains 10000111b, and the carry flag is set.

*RCL.*    RCL moves all bits to the left one position. Bit 7 moves to the carry flag, but the previous contents of the carry flag are moved to bit 0. In effect, the carry flag serves as an additional bit in the rotate. In this example, assume the carry flag was previously a 1:

```
MOV AL,01010101b
RCL AL,1
```

AL now contains 10101011b, and the carry flag contains 0.

*RCR.*    RCR moves all bits to the right one position. Bit 0 moves to the carry flag, and the previous contents of the carry flag are moved to bit 7. RCR is just like RCL but in the opposite direction. In this example, again assume that the carry flag is set to 1:

```
MOV AL,01010101b
RCR AL,1
```

AL now contains 10101010b, and the carry flag contains 1.

Figure 5-2 shows the movement of the bits in the rotate instructions.

## CONVERTING NUMBERS TO PRINTABLE CHARACTERS.

One problem common to all microcomputers is the fact that binary numbers cannot be printed in their numeric form. You must design routines to convert numbers to strings of ASCII characters having the correct code for printing. These routines make use of the arithmetic, logical, and shifting operations just discussed.

We will present two useful routines, one to convert either a byte or a word to two or four hexadecimal digits and the other to convert a word to five decimal digits for printing or display upon the screen.

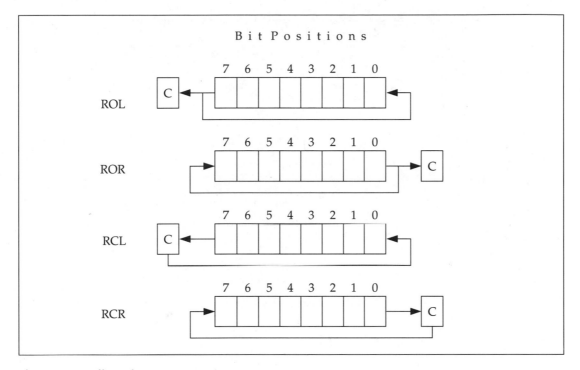

**Figure 5-2    Effect of Rotate Instructions**

### Displaying Hex Digits

As you know, a hex digit occupies four bits and can have values from 0h through Fh. The hex digits 0 through 9 must be converted to the ASCII characters 30h through 39h to print correctly. Somehow, we must get each hex digit into the right half of a byte and add 30h to print these values. However, 3Ah is not the ASCII code for the character A; it is 41h. Therefore, to print correctly the hex digits A through F, we must add the 30h and then add 7h.

We can write one routine that will convert one byte to two hex digits or one word to four hex digits. To be consistent with some of the interrupts discussed in Chapter 3, we will place the byte to be displayed in DH and the word in DX. We also will need to put a 2 in CX as a counter to display two hex digits or 4 in CX to display four digits. We will call the routine DSPHEX and later write it as a subroutine that can be called whenever we wish to use it.

We also will have to use the stack, which we will discuss more fully in Chapter 6. For now, let us merely explain that a PUSH operation places a word on the stack and a POP retrieves a word from the stack. The last word placed on the stack is the first word retrieved.

Figure 5-3 shows the DSPHEX routine. Let us explain each instruction. Assume the byte in DH contains C4h, DL contains 00h (DX = C400h), and CX

```
;-------------------------------------------------------------------------------
;                               DSPHEX Routine
;-------------------------------------------------------------------------------
; Displays two or four hex digits representing one byte or one word.
; At entry:  For byte, DH contains byte; CX contains 2.
;            For word, DX contains word; CX contains 4.
;
REPEAT01:                               ;REPEAT
            PUSH CX                     ;   save counter
            MOV CL, 4                   ;   rotate digit to right 4 bits
            ROL DX,CL
            POP CX                      ;   restore counter
            PUSH DX                     ;   save hex data
            AND DL,00001111b            ;   set zone bits to 0
            ADD DL,30h                  ;   make 0-9 printable
IF01:       CMP DL,39h                  ;   IF digit 9
            JBE ENDIF01
THEN01:     ADD DL,7                    ;     THEN make A-F printable
ENDIF01:                                ;   ENDIF
            MOV AH,2                     ;   display the character
            POP DX                      ;   retrieve hex data
            LOOP REPEAT01               ;   subtract 1 from CX
UNTIL01:                                ;UNTIL CX = 0
```

**Figure 5-3    Routine to Display Byte or Word in Hex**

contains 2. The instruction PUSH CX saves the number of digits to be displayed and allows us to use CL. MOV CL,4 sets the count for the ROL instruction. After ROL DX,CL is executed to rotate DX four bits to the left, DX contains 400Ch. POP CX retrieves the count of 2 from the stack, and PUSH DX places the value 400Ch on the stack.

AND DL,0Fh sets the leftmost four bits of DL to 0 and leaves the rightmost four bits as they were. DL now contains 0Ch. The leftmost four bits in a byte often are called the *zone bits* and the rightmost the *numeric bits*. We shall refer to them with these terms.

After ADD DL,30h is executed, DL contains 3Ch. The CMP DL,39h tests whether the ASCII character in DL is greater than the character '9'. Since 3Ch is greater than 39h, we execute the ADD DL,7 instruction. DL now contains 43h, the ASCII code for the character 'C', the first hex digit to be printed.

INT 21h will display on the screen any character in DL if AL contains 2. We already have the correct character in DL, so we execute MOV AL,2 and then INT 21h to display the character 'C'.

Next we POP the rotated number back into DX. DX now contains 400Ch that was saved. The LOOP instruction subtracts 1 from CX and loops back to repeat the process for the second digit (4).

This time ROL DX,CL leaves 00C4h in DX. The AND DL,0Fh leaves 04h in DL. The ADD DL,30h gives 34h in DL. This is the correct code for the character '4', and also less than 39h, so 7 is not added, and the character '4' is printed. When the LOOP instruction is executed CX becomes 0, and the routine is ended.

To display four hex digits of a word in DX, CX must contain the count of 4, and the routine passes through the loop four times. The ROL instruction takes the leftmost hex digit (4 bits) of DX and places it in the rightmost four bits of DL so that the AND and ADD operations will correctly prepare that digit for display in ASCII code.

## Displaying Decimal Digits

A second useful routine is to take a word containing four hex digits and display it as a five-digit decimal number. For this routine, we use successive division by 10, so that the remainder will always be between 0 and 9. Then we make this remainder printable by adding 30h. One complication is the fact that the first remainder we get from dividing is the last digit to be printed. We get around this problem by placing each digit on the stack as we get it in printable form, and then retrieve the digits from the stack in reverse order to display them.

We shall call this routine DSPDEC and later make it into a subroutine for general use. Figure 5-4 shows the DSPDEC routine.

This routine expects that the word to be displayed is in DX. The instruction MOV CX,5 sets up a loop so that we can create five printable decimal digits. MOV AX,DX moves the word to be displayed into position for dividing, and XOR DX,DX sets the high order register of the dividend to 0. We then move decimal number 10 into BX and divide BX into the number.

```
;----------------------------------------------------------------------
                          DSPDEC Routine
;----------------------------------------------------------------------
; Displays a word from DX upon screen as decimal number of five digits.
; At entry:  DX contains word.

          MOV CX,5                  ;set counter for 5 digits
          MOV AX,DX                 ;put dividend in AX
REPEAT01:                           ;REPEAT
          XOR DX,DX                 ;   clear remainder
          MOV BX,0010               ;   divide DX-AX by 10
          DIV BX
          ADD DL,30h                ;   make remainder printable
          PUSH DX                   ;   push digit on stack
          LOOP REPEAT01             ;   subtract 1 from counter
UNTIL01:                            ;UNTIL counter = 0
          MOV CX,5                  ;set counter for 5 digits
REPEAT02:                           ;REPEAT
          POP DX                    ;   retrieve digit from stack
          MOV AH,2                  ;   display the digit
          INT 21h
          LOOP REPEAT02             ;   subtract 1 from counter
UNTIL02:                            ;UNTIL counter = 0
```

**Figure 5-4    Routine to Display Word in Decimal**

Following division, the remainder, which must be between 0 and 9, is in DX, and the quotient is in AX. We add 30h to DL making the remainder printable with ASCII code from 30h through 39h, and push DX on the stack for later use. The next time through the loop, the previous quotient is in AX, and the XOR instruction clears the remainder from DX. When we divide again, the new remainder is in DX and the new quotient is in AX. We repeat this process five times to produce the five digits.

The loop at REPEAT01 through UNTIL01 creates the five printable digits and PUSHes them on the stack. The loop at REPEAT02 through UNTIL02 POPs the digits off the stack in reverse order in DL, puts the proper code 2 into AH, and calls INT 21h to display each digit.

Since the largest value that can be in a word is FFFFh, the largest decimal value we can print is 65535. If the number is shorter, there will be leading zeros printed.

## CONVERTING CHARACTER DIGITS TO NUMBERS

Digits entered at the keyboard are in ASCII code and not in pure binary numeric form. We must, therefore, use a routine to convert hex digits entered at the keyboard into hex numbers. A separate routine is needed to convert decimal digits into hex numbers for internal processing.

### Converting Hex Characters to Numbers

If we key in the hex digits 1234h at the keyboard, they are entered as the ASCII codes 31 32 33 34h (spaces between bytes to be more readable). The hex digits ABCD are represented by ASCII codes 41 42 43 44h. To key in four hex digits and store their numeric value in a word, we must adjust the rightmost four bits of the byte to the correct hex value, strip off the leftmost four bits of each word, add the hex digits to a word, and then shift the digit four bits to the left. Repeating this process four times will produce the correct number.

We shall call this routine INPHEX. Figure 5-5 shows the complete routine. This routine will accept any number of hex digits until the <ENTER> key is pressed. However, only the last four digits entered are retained in the word. The result is accumulated in DX and appears there when finished.

The XOR DX,DX instruction sets DX to 0. The next three instructions get whatever key is pressed on the keyboard and put it in AL. CMP AL,13 tests to see if the <ENTER> key was pressed. If so, JE WEND01 jumps to the end of the routine.

Only the digits 0-9, A-F, and a-f can be valid hex digits. First we compare AL with '0' and then with '9'. If the key pressed is between '0' and '9', we jump to THEN01. If it is not between '0' and '9', the OR AL, 20h instruction sets bit 5 to a 1. The digits 'A' through 'F' have ASCII codes of 41h through

```
;--------------------------------------------------------------------------
;                              INPHEX Routine
;--------------------------------------------------------------------------
; This routine receives any number of hex digits from keyboard and converts
; them to a word in DX.  Invalid characters are ignored. Input is terminated
; by <ENTER>. Only the last four hex digits are retained.
; At entry:      No parameters.
; At exit:       DX contains word.
;
                XOR DX,DX                   ;set DX to zero
                MOV AH,1                    ;get digit in AL
                INT 21h
WHILE01:        CMP AL,13                   ;WHILE digit <> <ENTER>
                JE WEND01
IF01:           CMP AL,'0'                  ;  IF digit => '0'
                JBENDIF01
AND01:          CMP AL,'9'                  ;  AND digit <='9'
                JNA THEN01
OR01:           OR AL,00100000b            ;  OR digit => 'a'
                CMP AL,'a'
                JB ENDIF01
AND01A:         CMP AL,'f'                 ;  AND digit <= 'f'
                JA ENDIF01
THEN01:                                    ;    THEN
IF02:           CMP AL,'9'                 ;    IF digit > '9'
                JNA ENDIF02
THEN02:         SUB AL,7                   ;      THEN subtract 7
ENDIF02:                                   ;      ENDIF
                AND AL,00001111b           ;      set zone bits to 0
                MOV CL,4                   ;      shift DX left 4 bits
                SHL DX,CL
                ADD DL,AL                  ;      add digit to DL
ENDIF01:                                   ;    ENDIF
                MOV AH,1                   ;    get another digit
                INT 21h
                JMP WHILE01
WEND01:                                    ;WEND
```

**Figure 5-5    Routine to Convert Input Hex Digits to a Word**

46h. Lowercase digits 'a' through 'f' are represented by 61h through 66h.
Rather than test whether these digits are upper- or lowercase, we will use the
instruction OR AL,00100000h to convert the leftmost four bits from 4h to 6h.
Then we need only to test whether the characters are not lower than 'a' and
not greater than 'f' to arrive at THEN01.

We can be at THEN01 only if the character entered is between '0' and '9'
or between 'a' and 'f'. If the character is greater than '9', we must subtract 07h
to convert the rightmost four bits to their correct hex value. In other words, if
the character were 'a' (61h), by subtracting 07h we make it 5Ah. The
rightmost four bits are the correct hex value.

The instruction AND AL,0Fh changes the leftmost four bits to 0s and
guarantees that the hex value in AL must be between 00h and 0Fh. We used

SHL DX,CL to shift DX four bits to the left and then add AL to DL. The hex value of the first digit we typed is now in the leftmost four bits of DL.

We then get another digit into AL and return to see if <ENTER> is pressed. This process continues to convert each hex character to a hex digit, shift the previous contents of DX left four bits, and add in the new hex value. If we enter more than four digits, the earlier digits are shifted left out of DX, and only the last four digits are retained.

## Converting Decimal Characters to Numbers

The next routine developed is to accept decimal characters from the keyboard and convert them to four hex digits stored in DX. The process is stopped by entering <ENTER>. If we enter a decimal number larger than 65535, the result will be the difference between the number and 65535. This is called *modulus 65535*.

The process first is to set DX-AX to zeros to be used for multiplication. Then we input a character, be sure it is between '0' and '9', strip off the leftmost four bits, multiply DX-AX by 10 decimal, and add the number to AX. Figure 5-6 shows the routine, called INPDEC.

The two XOR instructions set AX and DX to zeros. We push AX on the stack, since we need AH for the command for the INT 21h to input a digit and AL to receive the digit keyed in by the operator. MOV BL,AL transfers the digit to BL for additional processing, and POP AX restores AX to the zeros placed there by our first instruction.

CMP BL,13 tests if the <ENTER> key was pressed. If so, we jump to WEND01 to end the routine. If not, we test if the digit is between '0' and '9'. If not, we jump to ENDIF01 and get another digit. If between '0' and '9', we set the zone bits to zero, making BL a hex value from 00h through 09h. XOR BH,BH sets BH to zero, so that the entire register BX has a value from 0000h through 0009h. We then multiply DX-AX by 10 decimal and add BX to AX. Then we input another digit and repeat the process. The final result in AX is transferred to DX before leaving the routine.

If we enter in succession the four digits 2345, the routine proceeds as follows:

| DIGIT | DX-AX AFTER MULTIPLYING BY 10 | AX AFTER ADDING DIGIT IN HEX | IN DECIMAL |
|---|---|---|---|
| 2 | 0000 0000 | 0002 | 0002 |
| 3 | 0000 0014 | 0017 | 0023 |
| 4 | 0000 00E6 | 00EA | 0234 |
| 5 | 0000 0924 | 0929 | 2345 |

We can see that if we enter digits that exceed 65535, part of the product will be in DX each time we multiply by 10. Only the part in AX (0FFFFh or less) is retained.

```
;---------------------------------------------------------------------
;                          INPDEC Subroutine
;---------------------------------------------------------------------
; This routine inputs up to five decimal digits and converts them to a 16-bit
; word.  Entry is terminated when <ENTER> is pressed. Only digits 0-9 are
; accepted.  Values greater than 65535 are reduced modulus 65535.
; At entry:       No parameters
; At exit:        DX contains word.
;
            XOR AX,AX                   ;clear AX and DX
            XOR DX,DX
            PUSH AX
            MOV AH,1                     ;get digit in AL
            INT 21h
            MOV BL,AL                    ;move it to BL
            POP AX
WHILE01:    CMP BL,13                    ;WHILE digit <> <ENTER>
            JE WEND01
IF01:       CMP BL,'0'                   ;  IF digit => 0
            JL ENDIF01
AND01:      CMP BL,'9'                   ;  AND digit <= 9
            JA ENDIF01
THEN01:     AND BL,00001111b             ;    THEN set zone bits to 0
            XOR BH,BH                    ;    make digit a word
            MOV CX,10                    ;    multiply AX by 10
            MUL CX
            ADD AX,BX                    ;    add digit to AX
ENDIF01:                                 ;  ENDIF
            PUSH AX                      ;  get another digit into AL
            MOV AH,1
            INT 21h
            MOV BL,AL                    ;  move it to BL
            POP AX
            JMP WHILE01
WEND01:                                  ;WEND
            MOV DX,AX                    ;move AX to DX
```

**Figure 5-6    Routine to Convert Input Decimal Digits to a Word**

## PROGRAM 5: NUMERIC CONVERSION

Program 5, shown in Figure 5-7, combines several of the routines described in this chapter. First, we issue a prompt requesting the operator to enter four digits, which are stored as a word and displayed in decimal form. Then we ask for five decimal digits with value not greater than 65535, which also are stored as a word and displayed in hex form. We then ask if the operator wishes to continue. We repeat this procedure until the operator responds 'N' or 'n'.

We have placed a cursor return (13) and line feed (10) in front of each prompt. This guarantees that each prompt will start on a new line. We do not

```
          PAGE 50,132
;-------------------------------------------------------------------------
; Program name:  PROG5.ASM
;
; Author:   Alton R. Kindred
;
; This program issues a prompt requesting the operator to enter up to four hex
; digits which are stored as a word and displayed in decimal form.  Then it
; asks for up to five decimal digits with value not greater than 65535, which
; are also stored as a word and displayed in hex form.  It then asks if the
; operator wishes to continue.  It repeats this procedure until the operator
; responds 'N' or 'n'.
;-------------------------------------------------------------------------
DATA       SEGMENT                        ;segment for data
PROMPT1    DB 13,10,'Enter up to four hex digits: $'
PROMPT2    DB 13,10,'Enter up to five decimal digits (0-65535): $'
PROMPT3    DB 13,10,'Continue (Y/N)? $'
WORD1      DW ?
WORD2      DW ?
DECVAL     DB 13,10,'Decimal value = $'
HEXVAL     DB 13,10,'Hex value    = $'
DATA       ENDS
;-------------------------------------------------------------------------
STACK      SEGMENT STACK                  ;stack segment
           DB 32 DUP ('STACK   ')
STACK      ENDS
;-------------------------------------------------------------------------
CODE       SEGMENT                        ;segment for code
PROG5      PROC FAR                       ;for proper return to DOS
           ASSUME CS:CODE,DS:DATA,SS:STACK
           MOV AX,DATA                    ;set up data segment in DS
           MOV DS,AX
REPEAT01:                                 ;REPEAT
           MOV DX,OFFSET PROMPT1          ;  prompt for hex digits
           MOV AH,9
           INT 21h
           XOR DX,DX                      ;  set DX to zero
           MOV AH,1                       ;  get digit in AL
           INT 21h
WHILE01:   CMP AL,13                      ;  WHILE digit <> <ENTER>
           JE WEND01
IF01:      CMP AL,'0'                     ;    IF digit <> '0'
           JB ENDIF01
AND01:     CMP AL,'9'                     ;    AND digit <= '9'
           JNA THEN01
OR01:      OR AL,20h                      ;    OR digit => 'a'
           CMP AL,'a'
           JB ENDIF01
AND01A:    CMP AL,'f'                     ;    AND digit <= 'f'
           JA ENDIF01
THEN01:                                   ;      THEN
IF02:      CMP AL,'9'                     ;      IF digit  > '9'
```

**Figure 5-7    Program 5: Numeric Conversions**

```
            JNA ENDIF02
THEN02:     SUB AL,7                    ;           THEN subtract 7
ENDIF02:                                ;           ENDIF
            AND AL,00001111b            ;        set zone bits to 0
            MOV CL,4                    ;        shift DX left 4 bits
            SHL DX,CL
            ADD DL,AL                   ;        add digit to DL
ENDIF01:                                ;      ENDIF
            MOV AH,1                    ;      get another digit
            INT 21h
            JMP WHILE01
WEND01:                                 ;   WEND
            MOV WORD1,DX                ;   save first word
            MOV DX,OFFSET DECVAL        ;   identify decimal value
            MOV AH,9
            INT 21h
            MOV CX,5                    ;   set counter for 5 digits
            MOV AX,WORD1                ;   put dividend in AX
REPEAT02:                               ;   REPEAT
            XOR DX,DX                   ;      clear remainder
            MOV BX,0010                 ;      divide by 10
            DIV BX
            ADD DL,30h                  ;      make remainder printable
            PUSH DX                     ;      push digit on stack
            LOOP REPEAT02               ;      subtract 1 from counter
UNTIL02:                                ;   UNTIL counter = 0
            MOV CX,5                    ;   set counter for 5 digits
REPEAT03:                               ;   REPEAT
            POP DX                      ;      retrieve digit from stack
            MOV AH,2                    ;      display digit
            INT 21h
            LOOP REPEAT03               ;      subtract 1 from counter
UNTIL03:                                ;   UNTIL counter = 0
            MOV DX,OFFSET PROMPT2       ;   issue prompt for decimal number
            MOV AH,9
            INT 21h
            XOR AX,AX                   ;   clear AX and DX
            XOR DX,DX
            PUSH AX                     ;   save AX
            MOV AH,1                    ;   get digit in AL
            INT 21h
            MOV BL,AL                   ;   move digit to BL
            POP AX                      ;   restore AX
WHILE02:    CMP BL,13                   ;   WHILE digit <> <ENTER>
            JE WEND02
IF03:       CMP BL,'0'                  ;      IF digit => '0'
            JL ENDIF03
AND03:      CMP BL,'9'                  ;      AND digit <= '9'
            JA ENDIF03
THEN03:     AND BL,0fh                  ;         THEN set zone bits to 0
            XOR BH,BH                   ;         make digit a word
            MOV CX,0010                 ;         multiply AX by 10
            MUL CX
            ADD AX,BX                   ;         add digit to AX
ENDIF03:                                ;      ENDIF
```

**Figure 5-7**    *continued*

```
              PUSH AX                  ;      get another digit
              MOV AH,1
              INT 21h
              MOV BL,AL                ;      put digit in BL
              POP AX
              JMP WHILE02
WEND02:                                ;   WEND
              MOV WORD2,AX             ;   save second number
              MOV DX,OFFSET HEXVAL     ;   identify hex value
              MOV AH,9
              INT 21h
              MOV DX,WORD2             ;   move number to DX
              MOV CX,4                 ;   set counter for four digits
REPEAT04:                             ;   REPEAT
              PUSH CX                  ;      save counter
              MOV CL,4                 ;      rotate digit to right 4 bits
              ROL DX,CL
              POP CX                   ;      restore counter
              PUSH DX                  ;      save hex data
              AND DL,00001111b         ;      set zone bits to 0
              ADD DL,30h               ;      make 0-9 printable
IF04:         CMP DL,39h               ;      IF digit  9
              JBE ENDIF04
THEN04:       ADD DL,7                 ;         THEN make A-F printable
ENDIF04:                               ;      ENDIF
              MOV AH,2                 ;      print the digit
              INT 21h
              POP DX                   ;      retrieve hex data
              LOOP REPEAT04            ;      subtract 1 from counter
UNTIL04:                               ;   UNTIL counter = 0
              MOV DX,OFFSET PROMPT3    ;   ask whether to continue
              MOV AH,9
              INT 21h
              MOV AH,1                 ;   get response
              INT 21h
              OR AL,00100000b          ;   make response lowercase
              CMP AL,'n'               ;
              JE UNTIL01
              JMP REPEAT01
UNTIL01:                               ;UNTIL response = 'n'
              MOV AX,4C00h             ;return to DOS
              INT 21h
PROG5         ENDP                     ;end of procedure declaration
;-----------------------------------------------------------------------
CODE          ENDS                     ;end of segment code declaration
              END PROG5                ;end of program
```

**Figure 5-7**    *concluded*

put a cursor return and line feed at the end of the prompt so that the cursor will remain on the same line to receive the response from the keyboard.

We have used the OR instruction to change any uppercase letter typed in response to the prompt 'Continue? (Y/N)' into a lower case letter. Thus we have to test only for an 'n' to determine when to stop the program. Because every conditional jump is limited to 127 bytes, we make a short jump to UNTIL01 if the response to the last prompt is 'n' and follow it with an unconditional jump to REPEAT01 for any other response. An unconditional jump, as discussed in Chapter 4, can be of any length.

Figure 5-8 shows the output from Program 5.

## SUMMARY

Negative numbers are represented in 2s complement form. To form the negative of any number, first change all 1 bits in the number to 0 and all 0 bits to 1. This is the 1s complement. Add 1 to the result, giving the 2s complement. The leftmost bit of the signed number represents the sign, 0 if positive and 1 if negative.

Overflow occurs whenever the result of an arithmetic operation produces a result too large for the space it is to occupy. When two unsigned numbers are added, the carry flag indicates overflow has occurred. When two signed numbers are added, the overflow flag indicates overflow. The same flags indicate overflow in subtraction.

In addition and subtraction (ADD and SUB) the first operand is considered the destination and the second operand is considered the source. The source and destination are added or subtracted, and the result replaces the original value in destination. Destination may be a general register or a storage location. Source may be a general register, a storage location, or an immediate value.

The negate (NEG) instruction only has one operand, called the source. This instruction forms the 2s complement, or negative, of the source and places it back into the same location. Addition, subtraction, and negation can all be done on eight- or 16-bit numbers.

```
B>prog5

Enter up to four hex digits:   4F50
Decimal value = 20304
Enter up to five decimal digits (0-65535):   32567
Hex value        = 7F37
Continue (Y/N)? y
Enter up to four hex digits:   FFFF
Decimal value = 65535
Enter up to five decimal digits (0-65535): 10000
Hex value        = 2710
Continue (Y/N)? n
B>
```

**Figure 5-8    Output from Program 5**

Increment (INC) and decrement (DEC) instructions change the value in the destination field by 1. These instructions set any of the arithmetic flags except the carry flag.

Multiplication of eight-bit numbers requires the multiplicand to be in AL and the multiplier in another byte register or a byte in storage. The product occupies AX. Sixteen-bit multiplication requires the multiplicand to be in AX and the multiplier in another word register or a word in storage. The product occupies DX for the leftmost 16 bits of the product and AX for the rightmost 16 bits.

Division can be done with bytes or words. Byte division requires the dividend to be in AX, with the divisor in a byte register or byte in storage. The quotient will be in AL and the remainder in AH. For word division, the dividend occupies DX and AX and the divisor is in another word register or word in storage. The quotient will be in AX and the remainder in DX. Divide overflow occurs when an attempt is made to divide by zero or when the quotient is too large to be contained in the specified register.

Logical operations modify a bit in a byte or word on the basis of the corresponding bit in another byte or word. AND operations set a bit in destination to 1 only if it and its corresponding bit in source are both 1s. OR sets a bit in destination to 1 if either or both corresponding bits in source and destination are 1s. XOR sets the bit in destination to 1 if the corresponding bits in destination and source are different. NOT reverses the bits in the operand destination, forming the 1s complement. TEST works like AND and sets flags without actually changing the bits in destination. Each of these logical operations will set the carry and overflow flags to 0 and the zero, sign, and parity flags according to the result of the operation.

Shifting operations to the left move the leftmost bit in a register or location in storage to the carry flag, shift other bits one position to the left, and fill in the rightmost bit with 0. Two right shifts work differently. Both move the rightmost bit to the carry flag and shift the other bits right one position. But SHR fills the leftmost bit with 0, while SAR moves the leftmost (sign) bit both to bit 6 and also back to itself.

Rotate instructions move the bits to the left or right, but also wrap the bits moved out of one end of the register or storage location back into the opposite end.

Arithmetic, logical, and shift or rotate instructions may be combined to convert character data from the keyboard into numeric data to be stored in memory, or may convert numeric data into decimal or hexadecimal characters to be displayed on the screen or printed as output.

# QUESTIONS

1. How are negative numbers represented?

2. What types of data can be the destination operand in addition or subtraction? What can be the source operand?

3. What is meant by the negate instruction? What kind of data can be negated?

4. In what ways do INC and DEC instructions differ from ADD and SUB instructions? How do they affect the flags?

5. What registers are used in byte multiplication? Where does the product appear? What registers are used in word multiplication, and where is the product?

6. Explain byte and word division and the location of the result after each.

7. Explain the effect of each of the following logical instructions: AND, OR, XOR, NOT.

8. What is the purpose of the TEST instruction? To which of the other logical operations is it most similar?

9. Describe what happens on a shift instruction. What two instructions are identical?

10. Explain the difference between the SHR and the SAR instructions.

11. What is the major difference between the shift instructions and the rotate instructions?

12. Explain the difference between the ROL and the RCL instructions; between the ROR and RCR instructions.

## EXERCISES

1. Write instructions to add unsigned numbers in AX and BX and jump to ELSE01 if the result is overflow.

2. Write instructions to add signed numbers in AL and BYTE1 and jump to ELSE01 if overflow occurs.

3. Write a SUB instruction to subtract 3 from BX.

4. Write one or more DEC instructions to subtract 3 from BX.

5. Write instructions to multiply 55 by 17 using byte multiplication, then using word multiplication.

6. Write instructions to divide 65000 by 3. Would this produce divide overflow?

7. Write instructions to divide 65000h by 3h. Would this produce divide overflow?

8. Write a logical operation to set bit 4 of AL to 0 without changing any of the other bits in AL.

9. Write a logical operation to set bit 3 of AH to 1 without changing any of the other bits in AH.

10. Write instructions that will jump to ENDIF if bit 5 of BH is set to 1?

11. Write an XOR instruction that will reverse the setting of all bits in DX. What other logical instruction could do the same thing?

12. Write rotate and other necessary instructions to swap the contents of AH and AL.

13. Write a shift instruction that will move the contents of DH into DL and set DH to zeros.

14. Write necessary instructions to take the hex value C (12 decimal) in AX and cause it to display on the screen as the character C.

## LAB PROBLEMS

1.  Write an assembler program that will display a prompt to enter a line of key-strokes ended with <ENTER>. As each key is pressed, display the character on the screen, space once, and display it as two hex digits. Issue another prompt to see if the operator wished to continue. Continue until the operator enters 'N' or 'n' to the second prompt.

2.  Write a routine to key in two decimal numbers between 0 and 65535. Convert each number to a word in storage. Display each number in hex. Then multiply the two numbers together and display the product in hex. Your output should be similar to that below:

```
Enter number between 0 and 65535: 240
Enter number between 0 and 65535: 48
00F0 * 30 = 00002D00
Do you wish to continue (Y/N)?
```

Continue until operator responds 'N' or 'n'.

# SUBROUTINES AND THE STACK

# 6

**OBJECTIVES**

After studying this chapter, you should be able to:

- Describe the operation of the stack and its purpose.
- Distinguish between near and far subroutines.
- Explain the difference between internal and external subroutines and the relationship between EXTRN and PUBLIC statements.
- Explain the use of registers, flags, memory locations, and the stack for passing parameters to and from subroutines.
- Describe techniques for removing parameters from the stack upon return from a subroutine.

## STACK OPERATIONS

The *stack* is one of the segments typically found in a program. It is used to save the contents of registers and, occasionally, storage locations so that they can be used for other purposes. Only words can be placed on the stack. The operation of placing a word on the stack is called a *PUSH*, while removing a word from the stack is called a *POP*.

Words are placed on the stack from top down, that is, from the highest-numbered location in storage to the lowest-numbered locations. The address of the stack is placed by DOS in the SS register when the program is loaded. The SP (stack pointer) is initialized to point to the top of the stack.

In COM programs the SS (stack segment) register contains the same address as the code and data segments. The SP (stack pointer) is initialized to FFFEh when a COM program is loaded.

In EXE programs SS has a separate address from that of the other segments, and SP contains the length of the stack. For example, in programs with a stack of 256 bytes (100h), SP is initialized to 100h. You must ensure that that stack is large enough to hold all the words you expect to PUSH on it. For all programs in this text, a stack of 256 bytes is adequate.

The PUSH operation first subtracts 2 from SP and then places the specified word on the stack at the address specified by SS:SP. That address is called the *top of the stack*. Thus, for an EXE program SP is reduced to FEh for the first PUSH, and the first word is at SS:FEh, which becomes the new top of the stack.

A POP operation moves the word at the top of the stack into the specified register or storage location and then adds 2 to SP. Thus, the stack operates on a last in, first out basis. You must normally POP words off the stack in the reverse order they were PUSHed on the stack.

If you wish to save the contents of AX, BX, and CX so that they can be used for a different purpose, you would write:

```
PUSH AX
PUSH BX
PUSH CX
```

After you have finished using these registers, you could restore their original contents by writing:

```
POP CX
POP BX
POP AX
```

You can use the stack to exchange the contents of AX and BX in this way:

```
PUSH AX
PUSH BX
POP AX
POP BX
```

To define the stack segment, you normally use:

```
STACK       SEGMENT STACK
            DB 32 DUP ('STACK    ')
STACK       ENDS
```

This definition shows the string STACK followed by three spaces repeated 32 times to occupy 256 bytes. This makes the stack easy to find in any display of storage through DEBUG. Naturally anything PUSHed on the stack will replace the strings at the top of the stack and work downward in memory.

You can define the stack using any number of bytes or words. For example,

```
DW 128 DUP (?)
```

also defines a stack of 256 bytes with no specified contents, and

```
DW 128 DUP (0)
```

defines a stack of 256 zeros.

# SUBROUTINES

A *subroutine* is a short program that does one specific task. In a sense, DOS considers each program to be a subroutine from which you return at the end to DOS. You can write a subroutine one time in a program and use it many times from different points in the program. You may even assemble one or more subroutines separately from your program and have LINK combine the object code of the subroutine with the object code of your program.

Each subroutine should begin with comments that clearly identify the name of the subroutine and what it does. The comments also should tell what data will be in certain registers when the subroutine is entered and when the subroutine returns to the calling program. The subroutine should PUSH on the stack any registers it will use and POP them off before returning to the calling program.

The CALL statement is used to leave the main program and execute a subroutine, and the RETURN statement is used in the subroutine to return to the main program. The CALL statement contains the name of the subroutine to be executed. A subroutine in turn may CALL another subroutine, which RETURNs to the first subroutine. This nesting of subroutines can give great flexibility to programming.

The CALL statement PUSHes the address of the following instruction on the stack and then jumps to the subroutine that is named. The RETURN statement POPs the address to return to the instruction following the CALL.

## Near Subroutines

*Near subroutines* must be in the same code segment as the program which calls them. They often are called *intra segment direct calls*. With near subroutines, only the contents of the IP (instruction pointer) are pushed on the stack, since the main program and the subroutine will use the same address in CS. The CALL statement then places the offset address of the subroutine in IP so that it will be the next instruction executed.

The intra segment direct call is much like a JMP instruction except that it saves the address in IP on the stack, whereas JMP does not.

The RETURN statement at the end of the subroutine POPs the return address from the stack and places it in IP so that the next instruction executed will be the one following the CALL. The assembler generates a near RETURN, called an *intra segment return*, for a near subroutine.

A near subroutine is identified in the PROC statement naming the subroutine with the attribute NEAR:

```
SUB1      PROC NEAR
          (Code statements for the subroutine are here.)
SUB1      ENDP
```

### Far Subroutines

*Far subroutines* may be in different segments from the program that calls them. They are called *inter segment direct calls*. A CALL to a far subroutine pushes both CS and IP on the stack. Then the CALL places the address of the subroutine in both CS and IP and the program jumps to the subroutine.

Upon completion of the subroutine, the RETURN from a far subroutine POPS the return address from the stack into both CS and IP and the program returns to the statement following the CALL. The assembler assures that a far RETURN will be generated for a far subroutine. This is called an *inter segment return*.

A far procedure is defined in this way:

```
SUB2      PROC FAR
          (All code statements for the subroutine are here.)
SUB2      ENDP
```

### The PUBLIC Statement

If a subroutine is to be used by many programs, such as one to convert a word to four hex digits as described in Chapter 5, you may wish to assemble it separately. The PUBLIC directive identifies one or more subroutines that may be called by a different program from the one in which they were assembled. You may combine several subroutines into a single assembly or assemble each subroutine separately.

The PUBLIC directive normally appears after the ASSUME statement at the start of the code segment, although it can be anywhere in the source file. To assemble SUB1 and SUB2 together, you might write:

```
CODE      SEGMENT
          ASSUME CS:CODE
          PUBLIC SUB1, SUB2
SUB1      PROC NEAR
          (Statements in SUB1 ending with RETURN)
SUB1      ENDP
SUB2      PROC FAR
          (Statements in SUB2 ending with RETURN)
SUB2      ENDP
CODE      ENDS
          END
```

You normally use no operand with the final END statement when you assemble subroutines. The assembler determines the address of the first instruction executed from the END statement in the main program. Each subroutine returns to the program that called it, so that the subroutine never is executed independently.

### The EXTRN Statement

If subroutines are assembled separately from the main program, you must use the EXTRN (external) directive in the main program that calls them to identify those subroutines to the assembler. Otherwise, the assembler will indicate the name of each subroutine to be undefined. Of course, each subroutine must be named in a PUBLIC directive in the separate assembly. The assembler makes note of these names and leaves their addresses blank, and the linker supplies the necessary addresses in the CALL instructions.

Both near and far subroutines may be named in the same EXTRN statement. Any EXTRN directives should appear in the code segment containing the CALL statement, usually just after the ASSUME statement. Here is an example:

```
EXTRN SUB1:NEAR,SUB2:FAR
```

## Placing Subroutines

There are four ways you can place a subroutine for use with your main program: (a) write it as a procedure in the same code segment as your main program; (b) write it as a separate ASM program and use the INCLUDE statement to bring into your main program before assembly; (c) assemble it separately and tell LINK to attach it to your object code after you assemble your main program; or (d) assemble it separately, put it into a library, and have LINK search the library for it.

The first two methods have the advantage of showing your subroutines with the main program listing, but they do require that you assemble the same subroutine each time it is used in a program. They increase the length of the ASM, OBJ, and LST versions of your program. The second two methods reduce assembly time and disk volume, but require that you keep good documentation to know what subroutines are in your libraries and how to use them.

Let us illustrate each of these techniques with a short subroutine we will call DSPLINE called by a main program called TESTSUB.

*Writing Subroutine with Main Program.* Here the main program TESTSUB1 defines four lines containing a name and address. It supplies the offset of each line in DX and then calls the internal subroutine DSPLINE to display the line of the screen. Figure 6-1 shows the program.

*Using INCLUDE Statement.* Here the subroutine was stored as a separate source program under the name DSPLINE.SUB. The INCLUDE directive in the main program TESTSUB2 after the main procedure and before the end of the code segment tells the assembler to copy the subroutine at that place. Since it is assembled with the main program, EXTRN and PUBLIC statements are not needed. Figure 6-2 shows the main program and Figure 6-3 the subroutine.

*Assembling and Linking Subroutine Separately.* Here the subroutine was written separately as in the preceding section, but was assembled

```
          PAGE 50,132
;---------------------------------------------------------------------
; Program name:  TESTSUB1.ASM
;
; Author:   Alton R. Kindred
;
; This program defines a four-line name and address.  It puts the address of
; each line into DX and calls a subroutine to display it on the screen.  The
; subroutine is written and assembled with the main program.
;---------------------------------------------------------------------
DATA      SEGMENT                       ;segment for data
NAMEX     DB 13,10,'Honorable Samuel B. Preston$'
TITLEX    DB 13,10,'Circuit Judge, Fourth Circuit$'
ADDRESS   DB 13,10,'Manatee County Courthouse$'
CITY      DB 13,10,'Bradenton, FL 34205$'
DATA      ENDS
;---------------------------------------------------------------------
STACK     SEGMENT STACK                 ;stack segment
          DB 32 DUP ('STACK   ')
STACK     ENDS
;---------------------------------------------------------------------
CODE      SEGMENT                       ;segment for code
          ASSUME CS:CODE,DS:DATA,SS:STACK
TESTSUB1  PROC FAR                      ;for proper return to DOS
          MOV AX,DATA                   ;set up data segment in DS
          MOV DS,AX
          MOV DX,OFFSET NAMEX           ;display name
          CALL DSPLINE
          MOV DX,OFFSET TITLEX          ;display title
          CALL DSPLINE
          MOV DX,OFFSET ADDRESS         ;display address
          CALL DSPLINE
          MOV DX,OFFSET CITY            ;display city, state, and zip
          CALL DSPLINE
          MOV AX,4C00h                  ;return to DOS
          INT 21h
TESTSUB1  ENDP                          ;end of procedure declaration
;---------------------------------------------------------------------
;                             DSPLINE Subroutine
;---------------------------------------------------------------------
; This subroutine displays a string upon the screen.  The string must end with
; a dollar sign ($).
; At entry:  DS:DX points to first byte of string.
;
DSPLINE   PROC NEAR
          PUSH AX
          MOV AH,9
          INT 21h
          POP AX
          RET
DSPLINE   ENDP
CODE      ENDS                          ;end of segment code declaration
          END TESTSUB1                  ;end of program
```

**Figure 6-1    Subroutine Assembled with Main Program**

```
           PAGE 50,132
;-------------------------------------------------------------------------------
; Program name:  TESTSUB2.ASM
;
; Author:    Alton R. Kindred
;
; This program defines a four-line name and address.  It puts the address of
; each line into DX and calls a subroutine to display it on the screen.  The
; separate ASM subroutine is included and assembled with the main program.
;-------------------------------------------------------------------------------
DATA       SEGMENT                    ;segment for data
NAMEX      DB 13,10,'Honorable Samuel B. Preston$'
TITLEX     DB 13,10,'Circuit Judge, Fourth Circuit$'
ADDRESS    DB 13,10,'Manatee County Courthouse$'
CITY       DB 13,10,'Bradenton, FL 34205$'
DATA       ENDS
;-------------------------------------------------------------------------------
STACK      SEGMENT STACK              ;stack segment
           DB 32 DUP ('STACK    ')
STACK      ENDS
;-------------------------------------------------------------------------------
CODE       SEGMENT                    ;segment for code
TESTSUB2   PROC FAR                   ;for proper return to DOS
           ASSUME CS:CODE,DS:DATA,SS:STACK
           MOV AX,DATA                ;set up data segment in DS
           MOV DS,AX
           MOV DX,OFFSET NAMEX        ;display name
           CALL DSPLINE
           MOV DX,OFFSET TITLEX       ;display title
           CALL DSPLINE
           MOV DX,OFFSET ADDRESS      ;display address
           CALL DSPLINE
           MOV DX,OFFSET CITY         ;display city, state, and zip
           CALL DSPLINE
           MOV AX,4C00h               ;return to DOS
           INT 21h
TESTSUB2   ENDP                       ;end of procedure declaration
;-------------------------------------------------------------------------------
           INCLUDE DSPLINE.SUB        ;include subroutine
CODE       ENDS                       ;end of code segment
           END TESTSUB2               ;end of program
```

**Figure 6-2    Main Program with INCLUDE Statement**

separately and stored on disk as DSPLINE.OBJ. Note that in this case DSPL-INE must be identified as PUBLIC. Figure 6-4 shows the separately assembled subroutine.

The main program TESTSUB3 must identify DSPLINE as EXTRN and NEAR, since DSPLINE was given the NEAR attribute in the subroutine. Figure 6-5 shows the main program that calls the external subroutine.

After assembling TESTSUB3, you must direct LINK to combine the two object modules. This command line could be used:

```
;--------------------------------------------------------------------------
;                     DSPLINE.SUB Subroutine
;--------------------------------------------------------------------------
; This subroutine displays a string upon the screen.  The string must end with
; a dollar sign ($).  This subroutine is to be INCLUDEd in the source program.
; It should be saved under the name DSPLINE.SUB.
; At entry:  DS:DX points to first byte of string.
;
DSPLINE    PROC NEAR
           PUSH AX
           MOV AH,9
           INT 21h
           POP AX
           RET
DSPLINE    ENDP
```

**Figure 6-3    Separate Subroutine to be Included and Assembled**

```
;--------------------------------------------------------------------------
;                     DSPLINE Subroutine
;--------------------------------------------------------------------------
; This subroutine displays a string upon screen.  The string must end with
; a dollar sign ($). The subroutine is to be assembled separately and the OBJ
; file will be linked to the main program.
; At entry:  DS:DX points to first byte of string.
;
CODE       SEGMENT
           ASSUME CS:CODE
           PUBLIC DSPLINE
DSPLINE    PROC NEAR
           PUSH AX
           MOV AH,9
           INT 21h
           POP AX
           RET
DSPLINE    ENDP
CODE       ENDS
           END
```

**Figure 6-4    Subroutine Assembled Separately**

```
A>LINK B:TESTSUB3 + B:DSPLINE,B:TESTSUB3,B:TESTSUB3;
```

This line tells link to combine TESTSUB and DSPLINE, both on drive B, and produce an EXE module and a MAP file, both named TESTSUB3, also on drive B. Unless the drive and full filename appear, LINK will look on drive A for the object files and put the EXE file on drive A.

The MAP file for TESTSUB3 looks like this:

```
          PAGE 50,132
;------------------------------------------------------------------------
; Program name:  TESTSUB3.ASM
;
; Author:   Alton R. Kindred
;
; This program defines a four-line name and address.  It puts the address of
; each line into DX and calls the DSPLINE subroutine to display it on the
; screen.  The subroutine has been assembled separately and must be linked
; to the main program.
;------------------------------------------------------------------------
DATA        SEGMENT                    ;segment for data
NAMEX       DB 13,10,'Honorable Samuel B. Preston$'
TITLEX      DB 13,10,'Circuit Judge, Fourth Circuit$'
ADDRESS     DB 13,10,'Manatee County Courthouse$'
CITY        DB 13,10,'Bradenton, FL 34205$'
DATA        ENDS
;------------------------------------------------------------------------
STACK       SEGMENT STACK              ;stack segment
            DB 32 DUP ('STACK   ')
STACK       ENDS
;------------------------------------------------------------------------
CODE        SEGMENT                    ;segment for code
            ASSUME CS:CODE,DS:DATA,SS:STACK
TESTSUB3    PROC FAR                   ;for proper return to DOS
            EXTRN DSPLINE:NEAR
            MOV AX,DATA                ;set up data segment in DS
            MOV DS,AX
            MOV DX,OFFSET NAMEX        ;display name
            CALL DSPLINE
            MOV DX,OFFSET TITLEX       ;display title
            CALL DSPLINE
            MOV DX,OFFSET ADDRESS      ;display address
            CALL DSPLINE
            MOV DX,OFFSET CITY         ;display city, state, and zip
            CALL DSPLINE
            MOV AX,4C00h               ;return to DOS
            INT 21h
TESTSUB3    ENDP                       ;end of procedure declaration
CODE        ENDS                       ;end of code segment
            END TESTSUB3               ;end of program
```

**Figure 6-5    Main Program to Call External Subroutines**

| START | STOP | LENGTH | NAME | CLASS |
|-------|------|--------|------|-------|
| 00000H | 00070H | 00071H | DATA | |
| 00080H | 0017FH | 00100H | STACK | |
| 00180H | 001A1H | 00022H | CODE | |
| 001B0H | 001B6H | 00007H | CODE | |
| Program entry point at 0018:0000 | | | | |

     Note that two procedures are shown in the code segment. The main
program starts at 0018:0000 (absolute address 00180h) with a length of 22h

(34 decimal) bytes. The subroutine DSPLINE occupies seven bytes starting at 001B:0000, which is the same as 0018:0030.

The command line may be shortened as follows:

```
A>B:
B>A:LINK TESTSUB3 + DSPLINE,,TESTSUB3;
```

In this case, all files (except LINK) are assumed to be on drive B, the default drive. The EXE file is given the name of the first object file specified (TESTSUB3) by default, since we do not give any other name as the second operand in the LINK command line. We must give the name to be assigned to the MAP file as the third operand. Either a plus sign or space can separate the names of all object files to be linked together. The first file named is assumed to be the main program. The name of each object module to be combined must appear on the command line. If there are more object files to be combined than will appear on one line, make the last character on the command line a plus sign. LINK will then issue a prompt to ask for the names of the remaining object files.

A group of subroutines may be combined into a single code segment and assembled as one unit named, say, SUBS.ASM. The object file, SUBS.OBJ, could then be linked to a main program SAMPLE with this command line:

```
B>A:LINK SAMPLE + SUBS,;
```

All of the subroutines contained in SUBS are available to the calling program. The only objection to this procedure is that all of the subroutines in SUBS are linked to SAMPLE, whether or not they actually are used. It usually is better to find a way to link only those subroutines actually called by the main program.

***Creating an Object File Library.***    Figure 6-6 shows a group of useful subroutines that are required for most of the programs appearing in the rest of this book. Each subroutine is written so that it can be assembled separately. By using EDLIN or a word processor, you can separate these subroutines and store on your program disk as CLRSCN.ASM, DSPCHR.ASM, and so forth.

Each subroutine is named in a separate procedure and given the PUBLIC attribute so that it can be assembled separately and used by any program that designates it as EXTRN.

These subroutines fall into two categories. CLRSCN, DSPCHR, DSPLINE, DSPLNCNT, INPCHR, INPLINE, and PRTCHR are adapted from BIOS and DOS interrupts discussed in Chapter 3. DSPHEX, DSPDEC, INPDEC, and INPHEX are routines shown in Chapter 5 and made into external subroutines. These four subroutines call one or more of the interrupt subroutines.

DSPBIN, not previously mentioned, displays the contents of a byte as eight bits. It uses the technique of isolating each bit by rotating it from DL to DH, making it into a printable character, and displaying it on the screen using DSPCHR subroutine.

```
          PAGE 50,132
;----------------------------------------------------------------------------
; PROGRAM NAME:    SUBS.ASM
;
; AUTHOR:  Alton R. Kindred
;
; These are subroutines to be assembled separately and linked to any object
; modules of programs that call them.
;----------------------------------------------------------------------------
;                              CLRSCN Subroutine
;----------------------------------------------------------------------------
; Clears screen and positions cursor at top left.
; No parameters required.
;
CODE      SEGMENT
          ASSUME CS:CODE
          PUBLIC CLRSCN
CLRSCN    PROC NEAR
          PUSH AX
          PUSH BX
          PUSH CX
          PUSH DX
          MOV CX,0                    ;upper left (col 0, row 0)
          MOV DL,79                   ;lower right (col 79)
          MOV DH,24                   ;    "    "   (row 24)
          MOV AL,0                    ;clear all screen option
          MOV BH,7                    ;white on black
          MOV AH,7                    ;scroll down
          INT 10h
          MOV BH,0                    ;set current page
          MOV DX,0                    ;set cursor at upper left
          MOV AH,2
          INT 10h
          POP DX
          POP CX
          POP BX
          POP AX
          RET
CLRSCN    ENDP
CODE      ENDS
          END
;----------------------------------------------------------------------------
;                              DSPCHR Subroutine
;----------------------------------------------------------------------------
; Displays a character from DL upon screen.
; At entry:  DL contains character to be displayed.
;
CODE      SEGMENT
          ASSUME CS:CODE
          PUBLIC DSPCHR
DSPCHR    PROC NEAR
          PUSH AX
          MOV AH,2
          INT 21h
```

**Figure 6-6    Useful External Subroutines to be Assembled Separately**

```
                POP AX
                RET
DSPCHR          ENDP
CODE            ENDS
                END
;-------------------------------------------------------------------------
;                               DSPLINE Subroutine
;-------------------------------------------------------------------------
; Displays a string upon screen.  String must end with dollar sign ($).
; At entry:  DS:DX points to first byte of string.
;
CODE            SEGMENT
                ASSUME CS:CODE
                PUBLIC DSPLINE
DSPLINE         PROC NEAR
                PUSH AX
                MOV AH,9
                INT 21h
                POP AX
                RET
DSPLINE         ENDP
CODE            ENDS
                END
;-------------------------------------------------------------------------
;                               DSPLNCNT Subroutine
;-------------------------------------------------------------------------
; Displays a string upon screen.  Need not end with dollar sign ($), but CX
; must contain number of characters in string.
; At entry:  CX contains numbers of characters in string.
;            DS:DX points to first byte of string.
;
CODE            SEGMENT
                ASSUME CS:CODE
                PUBLIC DSPLNCNT
DSPLNCNT        PROC NEAR
                PUSH AX
                PUSH BX
                MOV AH,40h              ;print string function
                MOV BX,1               ;set handle for screen
                INT 21h
                POP BX
                POP AX
                RET
DSPLNCNT        ENDP
CODE            ENDS
                END
;-------------------------------------------------------------------------
;                               INPCHR Subroutine
;-------------------------------------------------------------------------
; Gets a character when keyboard is pressed, displays it on the screen,
; and returns it in AL.
; At entry:  No parameters.
; At exit:   AL contains character keyed.
CODE            SEGMENT
                ASSUME CS:CODE
                PUBLIC INPCHR
INPCHR          PROC NEAR
```

**Figure 6-6**   *continued*

```
                 MOV    AH,1
                 INT    21h
                 RET
INPCHR           ENDP
CODE             ENDS
                 END
;------------------------------------------------------------------------------
;                            INPLINE Subroutine
;------------------------------------------------------------------------------
; Clears keyboard buffer, gets input from keyboard, displays it on the screen,
; and stores it in an internal buffer.
; At entry:   DS:DX points to first byte of buffer.
;             Byte 1 of buffer contains number of characters to be entered.
; At exit:    Byte 2 of buffer contains number of characters entered,
;             excluding <ENTER>.
;             Bytes 3-n of buffer contain string entered.
;
CODE             SEGMENT
                 ASSUME CS:CODE
                 PUBLIC INPLINE
INPLINE          PROC NEAR
                 PUSH   AX
                 MOV    AH,0Ah
                 INT    21h
                 POP    AX
                 RET
INPLINE          ENDP
CODE             ENDS
                 END
;------------------------------------------------------------------------------
;                            PRTCHR Subroutine
;------------------------------------------------------------------------------
; Prints a byte from DL on line printer.
; At entry:   DL contains byte for printer.
;
CODE             SEGMENT
                 ASSUME CS:CODE
                 PUBLIC PRTCHR
PRTCHR           PROC NEAR
                 PUSH   AX
                 MOV    AH,5
                 INT    21h
                 POP    AX
                 RET
PRTCHR           ENDP
CODE             ENDS
                 END
;------------------------------------------------------------------------------
;                            DSPHEX Subroutine
;------------------------------------------------------------------------------
; Displays two or four hex digits representing one byte or one word.
; At entry:   For byte, DH contains byte; CX contains 2.
;             For word, DX contains word; CX contains 4
;
CODE             SEGMENT
                 ASSUME CS:CODE
                 PUBLIC DSPHEX
```

**Figure 6-6**    *continued*

```
DSPHEX      PROC NEAR
REPEAT01:                               ;REPEAT
            PUSH CX                     ;   save counter
            MOV CL,4                    ;   rotate digit to right 4 bits
            ROL DX,CL
            POP CX                      ;   restore counter
            PUSH DX                     ;   save hex data
            AND DL,0Fh                  ;   set zone bits to 0
            ADD DL,30h                  ;   make 0-9 printable
IF01:       CMP DL,39h                  ;   IF digit  9
            JBE ENDIF01
THEN01:     ADD DL,7                    ;      THEN make A-F printable
ENDIF01:                                ;   ENDIF
            MOV AH,2                    ;   display the digit
            INT 21h
            POP DX                      ;   retrieve hex data
            LOOP REPEAT01               ;   subtract 1 from CX
UNTIL01:                                ;UNTIL CX = 0
            RET
DSPHEX      ENDP
CODE        ENDS
            END
;-------------------------------------------------------------------------------
;                               DSPDEC Subroutine
;-------------------------------------------------------------------------------
; Displays a word from DX upon screen as decimal number of five digits.
; At entry:  DX contains word.
;
CODE        SEGMENT
            ASSUME CS:CODE
            PUBLIC DSPDEC
DSPDEC      PROC NEAR
            PUSH DX                     ;save registers
            PUSH CX
            PUSH BX
            PUSH AX
            MOV CX,5                    ;set counter for 5 digits
            MOV AX,DX                   ;put dividend in ax
REPEAT02:                               ;REPEAT
            XOR DX,DX                   ;   clear remainder
            MOV BX,0010                 ;   divide by 10
            DIV BX
            ADD DL,30h                  ;   make remainder printable
            PUSH DX                     ;   push digit on stack
            LOOP REPEAT02               ;   subtract 1 from counter
UNTIL02:                                ;UNTIL counter = 0
            MOV CX,5                    ;set counter for 5 digits
REPEAT03:                               ;REPEAT
            POP DX                      ;   retrieve digit from stack
            MOV AH,2                    ;   display the digit
            INT 21h
            LOOP REPEAT03               ;   subtract 1 from counter
UNTIL03:                                ;UNTIL counter = 0
            POP AX                      ;restore registers
            POP BX
            POP CX
            POP DX
```

**Figure 6-6**    *continued*

```
                RET
DSPDEC          ENDP
CODE            ENDS
                END
;-------------------------------------------------------------------------------
;                           DSPBIN Subroutine
;-------------------------------------------------------------------------------
; Displays DL as eight-bit binary number.
; At entry:  DL contains byte.
;
CODE            SEGMENT
                ASSUME CS:CODE
                PUBLIC DSPBIN
DSPBIN          PROC NEAR
                PUSH DX             ;save registers
                PUSH CX
                MOV CX,8            ;set counter for 8 bits
REPEAT04:                           ;REPEAT
                ROL DX,1            ;  move bit to DH
                AND DH,01h          ;  erase other bits in DH
                ADD DH,30h          ;  make bit printable
                PUSH DX
                MOV DL,DH           ;  print the bit
                MOV AH,2
                INT 21h
                POP DX
                LOOP REPEAT04       ;  subtract 1 from counter
UNTIL04:                            ;UNTIL counter = 0
                POP CX              ;restore registers
                POP DX
                RET
DSPBIN          ENDP
CODE            ENDS
                END
;-------------------------------------------------------------------------------
;                           INPDEC Subroutine
;-------------------------------------------------------------------------------
; This routine inputs up to five decimal digits and converts them to a 16-bit
; word.  Entry is terminated when <ENTER> is pressed.  Only digits 0-9 are
; accepted.  Values greater than 65535 are reduced modulus 65535.
; At entry:      No parameters
; At exit:       DX contains word.
;
CODE            SEGMENT
                ASSUME CS:CODE
                PUBLIC INPDEC
INPDEC          PROC NEAR
                PUSH AX             ;save registers
                PUSH BX
                PUSH CX
                XOR AX,AX           ;clear AX and DX
                XOR DX,DX
                PUSH AX
                MOV AH,1            ;get digit in AL
                INT 21h
                MOV BL,AL           ;move it to BL
                POP AX
```

**Figure 6-6**     *continued*

```
WHILE01:  CMP BL,0Dh                ;WHILE digit <> <ENTER>
          JE WEND01
IF02:     CMP BL,'0'                ;  IF digit => 0
          JL ENDIF02
AND02:    CMP BL,'9'                ;  AND digit <= 9
          JA ENDIF02
THEN02:   AND BL,0Fh                ;     THEN make zone bits 0
          XOR BH,BH                 ;     make digit a word
          MOV CX,10                 ;     multiply AX by 10
          MUL CX
          ADD AX,BX                 ;     add digit to AX
ENDIF02:                            ;  ENDIF
          PUSH AX
          MOV AH,1                  ;  get another digit
          INT 21h
          MOV BL,AL
          POP AX
          JMP WHILE01
WEND01:                             ;WEND
          MOV DX,AX                 ;move AX to DX
          POP CX                    ;restore registers
          POP BX
          POP AX
          RET
INPDEC    ENDP
CODE      ENDS
          END
;-------------------------------------------------------------------------
;                         INPHEX Subroutine
;-------------------------------------------------------------------------
; This routine receives any number of hex digits from keyboard and converts
; them to a word in DX.  Invalid characters are ignored.  Input is terminated
; by <ENTER>.  Only the last four digits are retained.
; At entry:      No parameters.
; At exit:       DX contains word.
;
CODE      SEGMENT
          ASSUME CS:CODE
          PUBLIC INPHEX
INPHEX    PROC FAR
          PUSH AX                   ;save registers
          PUSH CX
          XOR DX,DX                 ;set DX to zero
          MOV AH,1                  ;get digit in AL
          INT 21h
WHILE02:  CMP AL,13                 ;WHILE digit <> <ENTER>
          JE WEND02
IF05:     CMP AL,'0'                ;  IF digit => '0'
          JB ENDIF05
AND05:    CMP AL,'9'                ;  AND digit <= '9'
          JNA THEN05
OR05:     OR AL,20h                 ;  OR digit => 'a'
          CMP AL,'a'
          JB ENDIF05
```

**Figure 6-6** *continued*

```
AND05a:     CMP AL,'f'               ;   AND digit <= 'f'
            JA ENDIF05
THEN05:                              ;     THEN
IF06:       CMP AL,'9'               ;     IF digit > '9'
            JNA ENDIF06
THEN06:     SUB AL,7                 ;       THEN subtract 7
ENDIF06:                             ;     ENDIF
            AND AL,0Fh               ;     zap left nibble
            MOV CL,4                 ;     shift DX left 4 bits
            SHL DX,CL
            ADD DL,AL                ;     add digit to DL
ENDIF05:                            ;   ENDIF
            MOV AH,1                 ;   get another digit
            INT 21h
            JMP WHILE02
WEND02:                              ;WEND
            POP CX                   ;restore registers
            POP AX
            RET
INPHEX      ENDP                     ;end of procedure
CODE        ENDS                     ;end of code segment
            END                      ;end of assembly
```

**Figure 6-6**  *concluded*

As you assemble each subroutine, save the object file on drive B. To create a library of object modules, use a command line in this format:

```
LIB oldlibrary [/PAGESIZE:number][commands][,
[listfile][,[newlibrary]]][;]
```

LIB is the name of a DOS utility that creates and maintains the library. *Oldlibrary* is the name of the library, which DOS gives the extension of LIB. If the named *oldlibrary* does not exist, DOS creates a new one. The *commands* name the object modules to be added to or deleted from the library. *Listfile* gives the name of an optional file that shows the modules contained in the library. *Newlibrary* is an optional name for the revised library. If *newlibrary* is omitted, the new library receives the name of *oldlibrary* with an extension of LIB, and *oldlibrary* retains its old name with an extension of BAK.

To create a library and put into it all the object modules created from Figure 6-6, write these command lines:

```
B>A:LIB ASSEM + CLRSCN + DSPCHR + DSPLINE +
DSPLCNT + INPCHR + INPLINE;
B>A:LIB ASSEM + PRTCHR + DSPHEX + DSPDEC +
INPDEC + INPHEX;
B>A:LIB ASSEM + DSPBIN, ASSEM.LST;
```

These lines create a library file named ASSEM.LIB on drive B and put into it each object module, all on drive B. The semicolon terminates each command. The listfile ASSEM.LST is created only by the third command, after all modules have been put into the library. There also will be an oldlibrary file called ASSEM.BAK on drive B.

```
CLRSCN............clrscn          DSPBIN............dspbin
DSPCHR............dspchr          DSPDEC............dspdec
DSPHEX............dsphex          DSPLINE...........dspline
DSPLNCNT..........dsplncnt        INPCHR............inpchr
INPDEC............inpdec          INPHEX............inphex
INPLINE...........inpline         PRTCHR............prtchr


clrscn              Offset: 00000010H  Code and data size:  21H
  CLRSCN


dspchr              Offset: 00000090H  Code and data size:  7H
  DSPCHR


dspline             Offset: 000000f0H  Code and data size:  7H
  DSPLINE


dsplncnt            Offset: 00000150H  Code and data size:  cH
  DSPLNCNT


inpchr              Offset: 000001c0H  Code and data size:  5H
  INPCHR


inpline             Offset: 00000220H  Code and data size:  7H
  INPLINE


prtchr              Offset: 00000280H  Code and data size:  7H
  PRTCHR


dsphex              Offset: 000002e0H  Code and data size:  1fH
  DSPHEX


dspdec              Offset: 00000360H  Code and data size:  27H
  DSPDEC


inpdec              Offset: 000003e0H  Code and data size:  3aH
  INPDEC


dspbin              Offset: 00000470H  Code and data size:  1cH
  DSPBIN


inphex              Offset: 000004e0H  Code and data size:  35H
  INPHEX
```

**Figure 6-7    Library Listing File ASSEM.LIB**

Figure 6-7 shows the listing file ASSEM.LST for the library ASSEM.LIB at this point. At the start of the listing, modules are listed in alphabetic order. Then the modules appear in the order in which they were placed, showing the number of bytes each module requires. New modules are added to the end of the library.

Library files also can be used with prompts and response files. See the Microsoft Macro Assembler 5.0 manual for additional details.

Other commands useful with LIB are:

+ Add a named module to the library; also combine two libraries.

- Delete the named module from the library.

-+Delete the named module from the library, then add the module with the same name. Modules always are added at the end of the library.

* Copy the named module from the library into an object file with the same name.

-* Copy the named module from the library into an object file with the same name, then delete it from the library.

Now that a library file is present, you can use this command line:

```
B>A:LINK TESTSUB3,TESTSUB4,TESTSUB4,ASSEM
```

This line loads LINK from drive A. TESTSUB3 may be used again as our main program, but we change the name of the EXE and MAP files to TES-TSUB4 to distinguish them from the files created in the section, Assembling and Linking Subroutines Separately. This command line tells LINK to link TESTSUB3.OBJ with object modules named as EXTRN in TESTSUB3.OBJ that appear in ASSEM.LIB, and create a load file named TESTSUB4.EXE and a map named TESTSUB4.MAP. This is the first time we have used the fourth operand in the LINK command line to specify the library to be searched. We must name the MAP file as the third operand, because the default name of this file is NUL.MAP, meaning that no map is created unless a name is given.

## PASSING PARAMETERS

Subroutines normally need to receive data or the addresses of data from the main program in order to work on the values and to return results. These values or addresses are called *parameters*. The four chief ways of passing parameters to subroutines or back to main programs are through a register, a memory location, a flag, or the stack.

### Using Registers

Passing parameters through registers is the simplest of the four approaches named. Many of the routines shown in Chapter 5 can be made easily into subroutines using this approach.

You might write a subroutine called DSPCHR (display character) that would display any character in DL upon the screen. The main program would show:

```
                    MOV DL, 'X'
                    CALL DSPCHR
```

to display the character 'X'.

The subroutine, based on INT 21h, which also requires the character displayed to be in DL, is written:

```
DSPCHR      PROC NEAR
            PUSH AX
            MOV AH,2
            INT 21h
            POP AX
            RET
DSPCHR      ENDP
```

Passing parameters in registers is appropriate for numeric calculations such as functions. The value is sent to the subroutine in one register, such as AX, and the function is returned in the same or a different register.


### Using Flags

Many DOS interrupts, especially those for disk operations, set flags to indicate error conditions. If one of the last instructions in the subroutine sets the desired flag, the flag register will be unchanged by later instructions such as POP, MOV, or RET.

There are three instructions that set the carry flag as a signal to the main program of something that happened in the subroutine. CLC (clear carry) sets the carry flag to 0. STC (set carry) makes the carry flag a 1. CMC (complement carry) reverses the setting of the flag. If the setting was 0, it becomes 1; if 1, it becomes 0.

Upon return from the subroutine, the main program can execute a JC (jump on carry) or JNC (jump if no carry) to test the condition that was set.


### Using Memory Locations

Where data is in a memory location, you can refer to that location by name if the subroutine was included in the same assembly as the calling program. But you cannot use that name if the subroutine is assembled separately, since the code segment of the object module contains only numbers and addresses. Hence, you put the *address* of the data into a register.

We already have used this technique when we put the address of a string to be displayed by DSPLINE into DX. We also could put the address of a string of numbers, or the address of an array of words or bytes into registers. For example, a subroutine to sort an array of 100 words needs only the address of the first word in the array to be able to do the sorting. Base register BX, or index registers SI and DI, which can be used for indirect addressing as discussed in Chapter 7, often are used for this purpose.

### Using the Stack

You may push values or address on the stack before issuing the CALL statement. High-level languages, such as FORTRAN, COBOL, Pascal, and BASIC, often use this technique. We will explore use of subroutines with high-level languages in Chapter 13.

One problem with using the stack for parameters is that, while you can push as many values as you wish on the stack before calling the subroutine, you cannot simply pop them off in reverse order, because the return address is now also on the stack when you reach the subroutine. Get around this problem by using BP to address various locations within the stack. BP and SP are the only registers that can refer to stack offsets.

As an example of passing parameters via the stack, assume that SUB1 is a near procedure that requires two parameters, called N1 and N2, and that it is to return the result to the calling program in AX. A possible solution might be:

```
MAINPROG    PUSH N1
            PUSH N2
            CALL SUB1
            MOV ANSWER,AX
            (More program statements)
            .
SUB1        PUSH BP                    ;save BP
            MOV BP,SP                  ;get stack pointer address
                                       ;into BP
            MOV AX,[BP+6]              ;get first parameter into AX
            MOV BX,[BP+4]              ;get second parameter into BX
            (Do other processing)      ;use the parameters
            MOV AX,RESULT              ;put result into AX
            POP BP                     ;restore BP
            RET 4                      ;remove parameters from stack
```

Figure 6-8 shows the position of the parameters and the return address on the stack and the position to which BP points. The lowest address of the stack is at the top of the figure, and the highest address is at the bottom. The highest addresses on the stack represent anything previously pushed on the stack that has not been popped off. Then you see the parameter N1, followed by the parameter N2, then the return address (offset only for a near procedure), then the contents of BP. The stack pointer SP points to the contents of BP, and we put this address into BP. Then you can see that the return address is at BP+2, the address of N2 at BP+4, and the address of N1 at BP+6.

In the subroutine, you refer to BP+6 to move N1 into AX and BP+4 to move N2 into BX. At the end of the subroutine, you POP BP, adding 2 to SP. If you executed a normal return (RET), you would POP the return address and add 2 to SP. Upon return to the main program, SP would be 4 less than it should be because of the two parameters that were pushed on to the stack but never popped off. The RET 4 instruction not only pops the return address from the stack, but also adds 4 to SP to set it to its correct value.

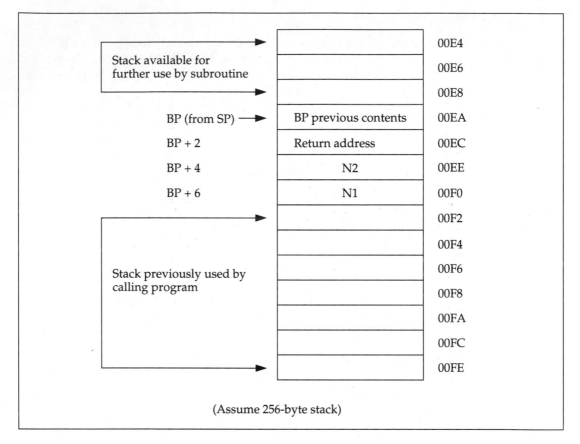

Figure 6-8    **Passing Parameters Via the Stack**

The RET instruction may be used in the format

```
RET n
```

where *n* indicates the number of extra bytes to be added to SP when the return address is popped from the stack.

Remember also that if a far subroutine is called, both CS and IP are placed on the stack, and the return address occupies four bytes instead of two. Thus, if SUB1 were a far procedure, the address of N1 would be in BP+8 and that of N2 would be in BP+6. You still would end with RET 4 because the two extra parameters would still occupy four bytes as they did before.

## PROGRAM 6: USING EXTERNAL SUBROUTINES

Figure 6-9 shows the source listing of program 6, which makes extensive use of the subroutines placed in ASSEM.LIB in this chapter. It displays a

```
          PAGE 50,132
;-----------------------------------------------------------------------------
; Program name:  PROG6.ASM
;
; Author:   Alton R. Kindred
                   ;
; This program displays a prompt asking for a decimal number between 0 and
; 65535.  It converts the number to a binary word and stores it.  Then it asks
; for and receives another similar number and stores it.  Next, it adds the
; numbers together.  Then it prints out the two numbers and their sum in both
; hex and decimal numbers.  It continues until the response 'N' or 'n' is
; received to a prompt asking if the operator wishes to continue.
;-----------------------------------------------------------------------------
DATA       SEGMENT                      ;segment for data
NUMBER1    DW ?
NUMBER2    DW ?
SUM        DW ?
PROMPT1    DB 13,10,'Enter a number between 0 and 65535: $'
PROMPT2    DB 13,10,'Do you wish to continue (Y/N)?  $'
HEADING    DB 13,10,'  Results in hex           Results in decimal',10,13,'$'
PLUS       DB ' + $'
EQUAL      DB ' = $'
SPACE5     DB '     $'
DATA       ENDS
;-----------------------------------------------------------------------------
STACK      SEGMENT STACK                ;stack segment
           DB 32 DUP ('STACK    ')
STACK      ENDS
;-----------------------------------------------------------------------------
CODE       SEGMENT                      ;segment for code
           ASSUME CS:CODE,DS:DATA,SS:STACK
PROG6      PROC FAR                     ;for proper return to DOS
           EXTRN DSPLINE:NEAR,INPDEC:NEAR,DSPCHR:NEAR,DSPDEC:NEAR
           EXTRN DSPHEX:NEAR,INPCHR:NEAR
           MOV AX,DATA                  ;set up data segment in DS
           MOV DS,AX
REPEAT01:                              ;REPEAT
           MOV DX,OFFSET PROMPT1    ;   issue prompt for number
           CALL DSPLINE
           CALL INPDEC              ;   get first number
           MOV NUMBER1,DX           ;   save first number
           MOV DX,OFFSET PROMPT1    ;   issue another prompt
           CALL DSPLINE
           CALL INPDEC              ;   get another number
           MOV NUMBER2,DX           ;   save it
           MOV AX,NUMBER1           ;   add the two numbers
           ADD AX,NUMBER2
           MOV SUM,AX               ;   save the sum
           MOV DX,OFFSET HEADING    ;   display heading
           CALL DSPLINE
           MOV DX,NUMBER1           ;   display first number in decimal
           CALL DSPDEC
           MOV DX,OFFSET PLUS       ;   display plus sign
```

**Figure 6-9    Source Listing of Program 6**

```
           CALL DSPLINE
           MOV DX,NUMBER2              ; display second number in decimal
           CALL DSPDEC
           MOV DX,OFFSET EQUAL        ; display equal sign
           CALL DSPLINE
           MOV DX,SUM                 ; display sum in decimal
           CALL DSPDEC
           MOV DX,OFFSET SPACE5       ; display 5 spaces
           CALL DSPLINE
           MOV DX,NUMBER1             ; display first number in hex
           MOV CX,4
           CALL DSPHEX
           MOV DX,OFFSET PLUS         ; display plus sign
           CALL DSPLINE
           MOV DX,NUMBER2             ; display second number in hex
           MOV CX,4
           CALL DSPHEX
           MOV DX,OFFSET EQUAL        ; display equal sign
           CALL DSPLINE
           MOV DX,SUM                 ; display sum in hex
           MOV CX,4
           CALL DSPHEX
           MOV DX,OFFSET PROMPT2      ; ask to continue (Y/N)
           CALL DSPLINE
           CALL INPCHR                ; get response
           OR AL,20h                  ; make response lowercase
           CMP AL,'n'
           JE UNTIL01
           JMP REPEAT01
UNTIL01:                             ;UNTIL response = 'n'
           MOV AX,4C00h               ;return to DOS
           INT 21h
PROG6      ENDP                       ;end of procedure declaration
CODE       ENDS                       ;end of segment code declaration
           END PROG6                  ;end of program
```

**Figure 6-9    concluded**

prompt asking that a number be entered in decimal. The number is converted to a binary word and stored. Then a second number is requested and stored. Then the two numbers are added together. The original numbers and their sum are then displayed as both hex and decimal characters. It should be noted that, if the number entered is greater than 65535 or if the sum exceeds 65535, the result will be 65535 less than it should be, since the largest number that can be contained in a 16-bit register is 65535.

The procedure is repeated until the operand responds 'N' or 'n' to a prompt.

After this source program is assembled, it may be linked to the subroutines as follows:

```
B> A:LINK PROG6,,PROG6,ASSEM
```

This command line links main program PROG6.OBJ to subroutines stored in ASSEM.LIB and creates a load file named PROG6.EXE and a link map named PROG6.MAP. Only the subroutines actually called by PROG6 will be linked to the EXE module. Figure 6-10 shows a listing of PROG6.MAP. Each entry after the first in the CODE segment is one of the subroutines from ASSEM.LIB listed as an EXTRN in PROG6.

Figure 6-11 shows some sample output from the program.

```
Start  Stop   Length Name              Class
00000H 0008EH 0008FH DATA
00090H 0018FH 00100H STACK
00190H 00226H 00097H CODE
00230H 00236H 00007H CODE
00240H 00244H 00005H CODE
00250H 0026EH 0001FH CODE
00270H 00296H 00027H CODE
002A0H 002D9H 0003AH CODE
002E0H 002E6H 00007H CODE


Program entry point at 0019:0000
```

**Figure 6-10    Listing of PROG6.MAP**

```
B>prog6

Enter a number between 0 and 65535: 15439
Enter a number between 0 and 65535: 2048
  Results in decimal      Results in hex
15439 + 02048 = 17487      3C4F + 0800 = 444F
Do you wish to continue (Y/N)?  y
Enter a number between 0 and 65535:  55000
Enter a number between 0 and 65535:  25000
  Results in decimal      Results in hex
55000 + 25000 = 14464      D6D8 + 61A8 = 3880
Do you wish to continue (Y/N)? n
B>
```

**Figure 6-11    Output from Program 6**

## SUMMARY

The stack is one of the segments found in a program. It provides up to 64K bytes for temporary storage of words by the program. Words are PUSHed on to the stack and POPped off.

The address of the stack is placed in the SS register by DOS when the program is loaded into storage. IP points to the top of the stack where the most recent word was PUSHed. Words are placed on the stack from the top down and removed in reverse order.

A subroutine is a short program that does one specific task. It usually is placed at one place in the program, but called from various points as needed. The CALL statement is used to save the return address on the stack and then to go to the subroutine. The RETURN statement retrieves the return address from the stack and returns to the main programs.

A near subroutine pushes only the IP register on the stack, since it is in the same segment as the calling program. A far subroutine pushes both the CS and IP registers on the stack, since it may be in a different code segment from the calling program. Subroutines are identified as near or far in the PROC statement giving the name of the subroutine. The RETURN statement pops one word from the stack for a near subroutine and two words for a far subroutine.

Subroutines may be made available to calling programs in any of four ways: (a) assembled with them as part of the source code; (b) saved on disk as separate source modules and named in an INCLUDE statement in the source module; (c) assembled separately with the object module saved on disk and named on a LINK command line to be attached to the object module of the calling program; or (d) assembled separately with the object module placed in a library to be attached by LINK when the library is named in the command line.

Subroutines assembled separately must designate each procedure as PUBLIC, and the calling program must identify each subroutine as EXTRN.

Parameters are values or addresses needed by the subroutine. They may be passed to the subroutine by the calling program through registers, by setting flags, by giving the address of memory locations, or by pushing data on the stack. The BP register may be used as an offset to SS to refer to data placed on the stack.

## QUESTIONS

1. Define the stack and name several of its uses.
2. What is meant by the top of the stack? What registers are used to point to it?
3. Explain what happens on a PUSH operation; a POP operation.
4. What addresses are placed in SS and SP when a COM program is loaded? An EXE program?
5. Explain how the stack can be used to exchange the contents of two registers.
6. What is a subroutine, and why is it used?
7. Explain the difference between CALL and JMP instructions as they affect the registers and the stack.
8. What is meant by the nesting of subroutines?
9. What are the differences between near and far subroutines?
10. Where is the PUBLIC statement placed, and what is its purpose?
11. Where is the EXTRN statement placed, and what is its purpose?

12. Explain four different ways of relating a subroutine to its calling program.
13. Explain how to create a subroutine library. How is the library name made known to LINK?
14. What are parameters? Why are they important to subroutines?
15. How are memory locations used as parameters to external subroutines?
16. What base register normally is used to refer to addresses within the stack instead of in the data segment? Can it be used with DS and ES?
17. Why is the RET *n* (where *n* is an integer) sometimes needed to return from a subroutine? What determines the value of *n*?

# EXERCISES

1. Write statements to define a stack segment of 128 bytes containing binary zeros.
2. For the stack defined in exercise 1, show the value in SP when the program is first loaded, after the first PUSH, and after the second PUSH if no POP is issued.
3. Write PROC and ENDP statements to define a near subroutine name SUB1.
4. Write statements to PUSH registers AX, CX, and DX upon entering SUB1 and POP them back into the correct registers before returning to the calling program.
5. Write statements to identify SUB2 as a far subroutine to be assembled separately.
6. Write statements in a calling program to designate SUBA and SUBB as external subroutines.
7. Write an external near subroutine named SPACE5 that returns the cursor and spaces down five lines. Then write the necessary DOS statements to assemble it separately and link to a program called MAINPROG. Assume all data is on drive B.
8. Write DOS statements to create a library of subroutines named SUB.LIB and place into it the SPACE5 subroutine from exercise 7. Then link the library to a program named MAINPROG.
9. Write a near subroutine named MULTX that multiplies one word in BX and another in CX together so that the product is in DX-AX. Return to the calling program.
10. Write a program that pushes on the stack two words to be multiplied together and then calls a subroutine named DIFFSTK that subtracts the second word from the first and returns the difference in AX. Then write the DIFFSTK subroutine, saving and restoring any work registers that you use.

# LAB PROBLEMS

1. Modify the SUBS.ASM source file shown in this chapter so that each subroutine is a separate source module. Assemble each procedure separately and save the object file on disk. You will be able to link these subroutines to many of your later programs.
2. Write a program that calls whatever external subroutines you need from lab problem 1. The program should display a prompt asking you to enter two

numbers in decimal between the range from 0 through 65535. Input the numbers, convert them to hex words, and store them. Then multiply the two words together. Display the two numbers and the product in hex. Repeat until you respond 'N' or 'n' to a question whether you wish to continue. Hint: Use DSPHEX subroutine twice to display the two-word product, first with the high-order word and then with the low- order word.

# ADDRESSING MODES

# 7

## OBJECTIVES

After studying this chapter, you should be able to:

- Explain the difference between constant and variable operands.
- Describe six different addressing modes and give examples of each.
- Explain use of the PTR instruction to eliminate ambiguity.
- Describe and give examples of segment overrides.
- Explain three instructions for specialized addressing.
- Use address modification to process strings and arrays of bytes or words.

## CONSTANT AND VARIABLE OPERANDS

Most computer instructions consist of one operation (op) code and two operands. The first operand is usually designated destination and the second source. When symbols are used as operands, their offsets are place in the instruction as constants.

Operands we have used so far—general registers, offsets of symbols, and immediate data—all are constants. Any reference to AX is always to AX, although the contents of AX can change. A storage location named PROMPT always is the same offset throughout the program. The immediate value 50 always is 50.

Four registers—SI, DI, BX, and BP—can hold an offset that can be varied to point to different locations as the program progresses. This ability is called *indirect addressing*.

## DIRECT MODE ADDRESSING

As we have seen, addresses are made up of two parts, the segment address and the offset. The *segment address* is a base point, usually that of the start of the data segment in the DS register, while the *offset* is the number of bytes between the address in DS and the location of some symbol. The segment address and offset added together give the *actual*, or *effective, address*.

*Direct mode addressing* names a symbol as one of the operands. The assembler substitutes for that symbol the offset of its location from the start of the data segment. The data at that location is used in the instruction. The name of the symbol refers directly to the data stored at its location.

The symbol always is at a constant location. However, you can use a *displacement*, an additional constant preceded with a plus or minus sign, to refer to another constant location. This form usually is called a *relative address*, since it is related to the address of the named symbol.

You might define a data segment as follows:

| OFFSET | NAME | INSTRUCTION | REMARKS |
|--------|------|-------------|---------|
| 0000 | DATA | SEGMENT | |
| 0000 | WORDS | DW 15,300 | ;2 words occupy 4 bytes |
| 0004 | SAVE | DW ? | ;2 more bytes here |
| 0006 | BYTES | DB 225,'A',0 | ;3 bytes here |
| 0009 | DATA | ENDS | |

In the code segment we can use direct mode addressing as in the following instructions:

| INSTRUCTION | OFFSET OF DATA | VALUE OF DATA |
|-------------|----------------|---------------|
| MOV AX,WORDS | 0000 | 15 |
| CMP AX,WORDS+2 | 0002 | 300 |
| MOV DL,BYTES | 0006 | 255 |
| MOV SAVE,BX | 0004 | Whatever was in BX |
| CMP BYTES+1,DL | 0007 | 'A' or 41h |
| MOV BYTES-2,BX | 0004 | Whatever was in BX |

Note that the word named SAVE at offset 0004 also can be addressed as WORDS+4 or BYTES-2 or any other name with a displacement that produces an offset of 0004. We also may put the displacement in brackets. BYTES[2] is the same address as BYTES+2.

## REGISTER INDIRECT MODE ADDRESSING

Only in direct mode is the address made up entirely of constants. All other addressing modes refer to one or more base or index registers. The contents of these registers can vary, and the address is said to be *variable*. This usually is called *indirect addressing*, because the register contains the address of the data rather than the data itself. Indirect addressing is widely used to process tables of words or individual bytes within strings.

Only SI, DI, BX, and BP registers can be used in *register indirect mode addressing*. The desired offset is placed into one of these registers, and the register is enclosed in brackets. The contents of that register can be modified with each execution of a loop to point to data at another offset. Indirect mode can be used with either the source or destination operand, but not with both. Note these examples:

```
MOV  AX,[SI]
ADD  [DI],BL
CMP  AH,[BX]
MOV  [BP],DX
```

Remember that both operands cannot refer to memory locations. The following instructions are invalid:

```
MOV  [DI],[SI]
ADD  SUM,[BX]
```

In register indirect mode addressing, either a base register or an index register may be used, but only one register may be used with only one operand. The offset in the indirect register is added to the segment address to form the effective address of the data to be processed.

## BASED MODE ADDRESSING

*Based mode addressing* uses one of the base registers, BX or BP, together with a constant. The sum of the contents of the base register plus the constant is the offset portion for the effective address. The constant may be the name of a memory location or a displacement. Here are some examples:

```
MOV AX,WORD[BX]
ADD AX,[BX+2]
SUB AX,[BX]+4
MOV [BP],AX
CMP [BP-1],DL
```

Note that the displacement may be placed either inside the brackets with the base register or outside them. Either the destination or source operands, but not both, may be based.

## INDEXED MODE ADDRESSING

*Indexed mode addressing* is identical to based mode except that one of the index registers, SI or DI, is used. The desired value previously must have been placed in SI or DI. Here are some examples:

```
MOV TABLE[DI],'A'
ADD AX,[SI]-2
CMP DX,[SI+4]
```

## BASED INDEXED MODE ADDRESSING

*Based indexed mode addressing* uses one base register and one index register to form the effective address of one operand. The only possible combinations are BP + SI, BP + DI, BX + SI, and BX + DI. The contents of the two registers are added together, and their sum is the address of the data. Note these examples:

```
MOV AX,[BP][SI]
MOV DX,[BX+DI]
MOV [SI+BP],CX
```

Either the base or the index register may be named first. Both must be in brackets, but there may be either one or two sets of brackets.

## BASED INDEXED MODE WITH DISPLACEMENT ADDRESSING

This last addressing mode is the most complex of all. It is a combination of based indexed mode addressing with a constant. The constant may be in two parts. Part of the constant may be the name of a memory location. The constant may be inside or outside of the brackets. Here are some examples:

```
MOV AX,[BP+SI+2]
ADD AX,4+[BP+SI]
MOV [BX][DI]+6,AX
CMP DX,WORD[BP][SI]+2
```

## THE PTR OPERATOR

Any of the addressing modes can refer to either the source or destination operand, but not to both in the same instruction. Where one of the operands is a general register, the assembler can tell whether the effective address is that of a word or a byte:

```
MOV AX,[BX+2]          ;source is a word to match AX
ADD AL,[BX+4]          ;source is a byte to match AL
```

However, if the destination operand is indirect and the source data is immediate, the assembler cannot tell whether the source is a byte or a word. For example,

```
CMP [DI],25h
```

is ambiguous. The assembler has no way of knowing whether to create the immediate value 25h if DI points to a byte or 0025h if DI points to a word. In such a case, you may use the PTR operator to specify the size, as in these examples:

```
CMP BYTE PTR [DI],25h    ;DI points to a byte
CMP WORD PTR [BP+DI],1234h ;BP+DI points to a word
```

If the name of a memory location is part of the effective address, the length may not be ambiguous. If you define WORDS in the data segment as:

```
WORDS      DW 12345,5000,2500,1250
```

then the instruction

```
CMP WORDS[BP+2],5000
```

clearly refers to a word and not a byte.

## SEGMENT OVERRIDES

All addresses in memory consist of a segment address plus an offset. The segment address may be in CS with the offset normally in IP for instructions, the stack address in SS uses the offset in SP, and for most data the assembler assumes that DS will contain the segment address.

Sometimes we wish to override these automatic segment usages. BP normally is assumed to refer to addresses within the stack segment. If we wish BP to refer to locations within the data segment, we use the segment override:

```
MOV AX,DS:[BP]
```

to associate BP with DS. ES often is used in segment overrides in referring to data, as in:

```
MOV AX,ES:WORD+2
```

Of course, ES must contain the proper segment address designated in an ASSUME statement.

If it is necessary to use the PTR operand, it should precede the segment override. Sometimes in subroutines you may use CS to refer to data placed after the RET statement.

```
CODE       SEGMENT
SUBPROG    PROC NEAR
           (Other subroutine code)
           MOV BYTE PTR CS:TABLE[DI],5 ;moves byte with value of
                                       ;5
           (Other subroutine code)
           MOV WORD PTR CS:TABLE[DI],5 ;moves word with value of
                                       ;5
           RET
TABLE      DB DUP 10 (?)
SUBPROG    ENDP
CODE       ENDS
           END
```

Sometimes you might have two data segments, one based on DS and one on ES. Indirect addressing is normally used with DS. To use BP or SI with ES, you could write a segment override to refer to a byte as follows:

```
CMP BYTE PTR ES:[BP+SI],'Y'
```

## SPECIALIZED ADDRESSING

There are several specialized instructions useful with memory addressing. They include LDS (load data segment), LES (load extra segment), LEA (load effective address), XCHG (exchange), and XLAT (translate).

### LDS and LES

These two instructions are used to load the DS or ES register with a value at an addressed memory location. The format of these two instructions is the same:

```
LDS destination,source
LES destination,source
```

where *destination* is any general register and *source* is an addressed memory location that should contain two adjacent words. The first word goes into the destination register, and the second word into DS if LDS is used or ES if LES is used.

The PTR instruction with the operand DWORD is used with LES or LDS to ensure that a doubleword of four bytes is intended as the memory location. In the data segment, a pseudo-op DD (define doubleword) may be used to define the four-byte areas. If you use this definition:

```
DBLWORD    DD FAR_ADDR1,FAR_ADDR2,FAR_ADDR3
```

then the instruction

```
LDS SI,DBLWORD[BP]+4
```

would put the first word of the addressed doubleword into SI and the second word into DS. Since DBLWORD is defined as DD (four bytes), no PTR instruction is necessary. But if you do not use the name, you must tell the assembler the correct length with a PTR instruction:

```
LES DI,DWORD PTR [BX][SI]
```

or some other addressing mode.

### LEA

The LEA (load effective address) instruction has this format:

```
LEA destination,source
```

where *destination* can be any general word-sized register and *source* is any addressed memory location. In this case, the address and not the contents of the memory location is placed in the register.

When used without a base or index register:

```
LEA SI,PROMPT
```

is equivalent to

```
MOV SI,OFFSET PROMPT
```

However, any use of standard MOV instruction with OFFSET is invalid with indirect addressing. Instead, you must use something like

```
LEA SI,TABLE[SI][BX]+2
```

to compute an effective address involving base or index registers.

## XCHG

The XCHG (exchange) instruction has the format

```
XCHG destination,source
```

and exchanges, or swaps, the contents of the *source* and *destination*. Destination and source may be general byte or word registers or addressed memory locations, but both operands cannot be in memory. No flags are set by XCHG. Unlike MOV, which copies source into destination, XCHG changes the contents of both operands. Here is an example:

```
XCHG AX,TABLE[SI]+2
```

This instruction is especially useful in sorting routines, where values must be exchanged to place them into the desired sequence.

## XLAT

The XLAT (translate) instruction has this form:

```
XLAT source-table
```

XLAT allows any byte in AL to be translated to any other desired byte according to the construction of *source-table*. BX must hold the address of source-table. The byte in AL is considered an offset into the table, and the byte at the addressed location in the table is moved into AL, replacing the original value there.

For example, if AL holds 04h and source-table contains '01234567890', then AL is replaced by '4' or 34h, the value at source-table+4. The table must be defined as bytes, and may contain as many as 256 bytes. If your table is shorter than 256 bytes, then values such as FFh will be translated incorrectly.

XLAT can be used in routines such as DSPDEC and DSPHEX to translate any decimal or hex value into printable form. It also can convert ASCII code into other codes such as EBCDIC (Extended binary coded decimal interchange code), used on many IBM mainframes.

## EXAMPLES OF ADDRESS MODIFICATION

Nearly the remainder of this text will be devoted to use of addressing modes to work through strings of bytes or arrays of words. Here we will show a few of the more common applications.

### Displaying a String

Instead of displaying a line of characters using DSPLINE or DSPLNCNT subroutines, you may wish to display one byte at a time, so that you can stop when you encounter a cursor return (13) or any other special character. Assume you have just used INPLINE and have a string starting at BUFFER+2. You can display the string in this fashion:

```
          LEA SI,BUFFER+2          ;set address of string
REPEAT01:                          ;REPEAT
          MOV DL,[SI]              ; move byte to DL
          CALL DSPCHR              ; display the byte
          INC SI                   ; set address to next byte
          CMP DL,13                ; test for cursor return
          JNE REPEAT01
UNTIL01:                           ;UNTIL byte is cursor return
```

If you do not wish to display the cursor return, you can write a pretest loop to terminate the loop when the character 13 (0Dh) is in DL:

```
          LEA [SI],BUFFER+2        ;set address of string
          MOV DL,[SI]             ;move byte to DL
WHILE01:  CMP DL,13               ;WHILE byte <> cursor return
                                  ; (13)
          JE WEND01
          CALL DSPCHR             ; display the byte
          INC SI                  ; increment byte address
          MOV DL,[SI]             ; move next byte to DL
          JMP WHILE01
WEND01:                           ;WEND
```

### Blanking Out an Area

You may wish to clear a 20-byte field called NAMEX to spaces before moving some data into it. This routine does the job:

```
          LEA SI,NAMEX            ;set address of field
          MOV CX,20              ;set counter to 20
REPEAT02:                         ;REPEAT
```

```
            MOV [SI],' '            ; move space to byte
            INC SI                  ; set address to next byte
            LOOP REPEAT02           ; subtract 1 from counter
UNTIL02:                            ;UNTIL counter = 0
```

## Building an Array of Integers

You can use INPDEC or INPHEX to create a word in DX and then store that word in an array. You can repeat this process for 5, 10, or 100 times to build an array of word integers. Let's make an array of 10 integers. We will omit prompts to keep the example short. The array in the data segment is defined thus:

```
ARRAY       DB 10 DUP (?)
```

Our routine works this way:

```
            LEA DI,ARRAY            ;set address of first word
                                    ;in array
            MOV CX,10               ;set counter to 10
REPEAT03:                           ;REPEAT
            CALL INPHEX             ; get a word in DX
            MOV [DI],DX             ; move word to array address
            ADD DI,2               ; set address to next word
            LOOP REPEAT03           ;subtract 1 from counter
UNTIL03:                            ;UNTIL counter = 0
```

We might use two INC DI statements in place of ADD DI,2. They would require less space and probably execute as fast.

## Averaging an Array of Integers

To get the average of the array you have just created, use this routine. This short example ignores the possibility that adding the 10 numbers might possibly produce overflow.

```
            LEA SI,ARRAY           ;set address of first word
            MOV CX,10              ;set counter to 10
            XOR AX,AX             ;clear sum
REPEAT 04:                         ;REPEAT
            ADD AX,[SI]            ; add word to sum
            INC SI                 ; increment word address by 2
            INC SI
            LOOP REPEAT04          ; subtract 1 from counter
UNTIL04:                           ;UNTIL counter = 0
            XOR DX,DX             ;clear high order dividend
            MOV BX,10              ;set divisor to 10
            DIV BX                ;divide sum by 10
            MOV AVERAGE,AX         ;save average
            MOV DX,AX             ;display average in decimal
            CALL DSPDEC
```

## Averaging Each Row of a Two-Dimensional Array

This next example is somewhat more complex. We define an array having five rows, each with 10 words. We define a separate array called AVERAGES, with space for five values, one for each row.

We use SI to point to each word in the row, BX to point to each row, and DI to point to the word in AVERAGES. We use nested loops. The outer loop modifies BX and DI, while the inner loop modifies SI. The offsets for the five rows, relative to array, are 0, 20, 40, 60, and 80, respectively. The offsets for the words within the rows or for the words within the AVERAGES array are 0, 2, 4, and so forth. We show the data segment entries.

```
ARRAY       DW 10 DUP (?)
            DW 10 DUP (?)
            DW 10 DUP (?)
            DW 10 DUP (?)
            DW 10 DUP (?)
AVERAGES    DW 5 DUP (0)
```

We assume that ARRAY already has been loaded with appropriate values. The code segment routine is as follows:

```
            XOR BX,BX               ;set row offset to 0
            XOR DI,DI               ;set AVERAGES offset to 0
            MOV CX,5                ;set row counter to 5
REPEAT05:                           ;REPEAT
            XOR AX,AX               ;  set row total to 0
            PUSH CX                 ;  save row counter
            MOV CX,10               ;  set column counter to 10
            XOR SI,SI               ;  set column offset to 0
REPEAT06:                           ;  REPEAT
            ADD AX,ARRAY[BX][SI]    ;    add word in column to row
                                    ;    total
            INC SI                  ;    add 2 to column offset
            INC SI
            LOOP REPEAT06           ;  subtract 1 from column
                                    ;  counter
UNTIL06:                            ;  UNTIL column counter = 0
            MOV CX,10               ;  set divisor to 10
            XOR DX,DX               ;  clear high word of dividend
            DIV CX                  ;  divide row total by 10
            MOV AVERAGE[DI],AX      ;  move row average to array
            ADD BX,20               ;  set row offset to next row
            ADD DI,2                ;  set AVERAGES address to
                                    ;  next word
            POP CX                  ;  restore row counter
            LOOP REPEAT05           ;  subtract 1 from row counter
UNTIL05:                            ;UNTIL row counter = 0
```

By wise use of the stack, we can use CX as both the row counter and the column counter. We also can use it to hold the divisor for computing the row average. Note that the ADD instruction in the REPEAT06 loop uses based indexed mode with displacement addressing, where ARRAY is the constant, BX the base register holding offset for the row, and SI the index register holding offset for the column within the row.

## PROGRAM 7: ADDRESS MODIFICATION

Program 7 (Figure 7-1) changes the DSPDEC subroutine to use the XLAT and XCHG instructions and assembles the subroutine with the main procedure. The program directs the keyboard operator to enter up to 20 decimal numbers (0–65535) which are placed in an array of words. DI is used as a pointer to the position in the array where the word is to be stored, and DI is incremented by 2 for each new word. Input is terminated when the operator presses <ENTER> without entering a number, that is, the value of the word entered is 0.

The number of words entered is counted in CX and used as the basis for computing the location of the last word stored. The formula for calculating the position of any item in an array or table is $(N-1)*L$, where N is the number of the item within the array and L is the length of each item in the array. For example, the fifth word in array has a displacement of 8 from the start of the array, since $(5-1)*2 = 8$.

The words are retrieved from the array in reverse order, displayed in decimal, and then the number of words and the largest word entered are displayed in decimal. The largest word is found by placing a 0 in a word named LARGE, comparing each word with LARGE as it is retrieved, and replacing LARGE with any larger word from the array. The process is repeated until the operator answers 'N' or 'n' to a prompt.

External subroutines are linked to program 7 from ASSEM.LIB and EXE and MAP files are created with this command line:

```
B> A:LINK PROG7,,PROG7,ASSEM;
```

Figure 7-2 shows output from program 7.

## SUMMARY

Operands in machine instructions may be constant or variable. Registers, immediate values, and names of memory locations are constant. Base and index registers are variable, since their contents may be changed each time the instruction is repeated that contains them.

Base and index registers, when enclosed in brackets, contain indirect addresses, that is, the address of the data to be operated on instead of the data itself.

Six addressing modes are discussed.

```
            PAGE 50,132
;-------------------------------------------------------------------------------
; Program name:  PROG7.ASM
;
; Author:   Alton R. Kindred
;
; This program prompts the operator to enter decimal numbers between 0 and
; 65535.  The numbers are converted to binary words and placed in an array.
; Entry of numbers is terminated by pressing <ENTER> alone.  The program counts
; the number of words entered, finds the largest number, and displays the
; numbers from the array in reverse order, the count, and the largest number, in
; decimal.  The program continues until the operator response 'N' or 'n'
; to a prompt.
;-------------------------------------------------------------------------------
DATA        SEGMENT                     ;segment for data
PROMPT1     DB 13,10,'Enter up to 20 numbers between 0 and 65535'
            DB 13,10,'Press <ENTER> alone to stop.',13,10,'$'
PROMPT2     DB 13,10,'Continue? (Y/N) $'
CRLF        DB 13,10,'$'
ARRAY       DW 20 dup (?)
COUNT       DW ?
LARGE       DW ?
OUTMSG      DB 13,10,'Numbers in reverse order of entry',13,10,'$'
COUNTMSG    DB 13,10,'Numbers entered: $'
LARGEMSG    DB '   Largest number: $'
DATA        ENDS
;-------------------------------------------------------------------------------
STACK       SEGMENT STACK               ;stack segment
            DB 32 DUP ('STACK   ')
STACK       ENDS
;-------------------------------------------------------------------------------
CODE        SEGMENT                     ;segment for code
            ASSUME CS:CODE,DS:DATA,SS:STACK
PROG7       PROC FAR                    ;for proper return to DOS
            EXTRN DSPLINE:NEAR,INPCHR:NEAR,DSPCHR:NEAR,INPDEC:NEAR
            MOV AX,DATA                 ;set up data segment in DS
            MOV DS,AX
REPEAT01:                               ;REPEAT
            LEA DX,PROMPT1              ;  display prompt for numbers
            CALL DSPLINE
            XOR CX,CX                   ;  set word counter to 0
            XOR DI,DI                   ;  set array offset to 0
            XOR AX,AX                   ;  set array total to 0
            CALL INPDEC                 ;  get a number
            PUSH DX                     ;  save number
            LEA DX,CRLF                 ;  return cursor
            CALL DSPLINE
            POP DX                      ;  restore number
WHILE01:    CMP DX,0                    ;  WHILE number <> 0
            JE WEND01
            ADD AX,DX                   ;    add number to array total
            MOV ARRAY[DI],DX            ;    move number to array
            INC CX                      ;    add 1 to word counter
            ADD DI,2                    ;    set array offset to next word
```

**Figure 7-1     Source Listing of Program 7**

```
              CALL INPDEC           ;     get another number
              PUSH DX               ;     save number
              LEA DX,CRLF           ;     return cursor
              CALL DSPLINE
              POP DX                ;     restore number
              JMP WHILE01
WEND01:                             ;   WEND
              MOV COUNT,CX          ;   save count
              MOV LARGE,0           ;   set largest number to 0
              LEA DX,OUTMSG         ;   describe numbers in reverse order
              CALL DSPLINE
              MOV SI,CX             ;   move word counter to index
              DEC SI                ;   subtract 1 from index
              SHL SI,1              ;   double index to point to last word
REPEAT02:                           ;   REPEAT
              LEA DX,CRLF           ;     return cursor
              CALL DSPLINE
              MOV DX,ARRAY[SI]      ;     move word to DX
IF01:         CMP DX,LARGE          ;     IF number > largest
              JNA ENDIF01
THEN01:       MOV LARGE,DX          ;       THEN make number largest
ENDIF01:                            ;     ENDIF
              CALL DSPDEC           ;     display word in decimal
              DEC SI                ;     subtract 2 from index
              DEC SI
              LOOP REPEAT02         ;     subtract 1 from word counter
UNTIL02:                            ;   UNTIL word counter = 0
              LEA DX,COUNTMSG       ;   identify count
              CALL DSPLINE
              MOV DX,COUNT          ;   display count
              CALL DSPDEC
              LEA DX,LARGEMSG       ;   identify largest number
              CALL DSPLINE
              MOV DX,LARGE          ;   display largest number
              CALL DSPDEC
              LEA DX,PROMPT2        ;   prompt whether to continue
              CALL DSPLINE
              CALL INPCHR           ;   get response
              OR AL,00100000b       ;   make response lowercase
              CMP AL,'n'
              JE UNTIL01
              JMP REPEAT01
UNTIL01:                            ;UNTIL response is 'N' or 'n'
              MOV AX,4C00h          ;return to DOS
              INT 21h
;
PROG7     ENDP                      ;end of procedure declaration
;----------------------------------------------------------------------------
;                          DSPDEC Subroutine
;
; This subroutine converts a 16-bit binary word into a string of five decimal
; digits and prints them out.  It makes use of the XLAT instruction to
; convert each decimal digit into a printable character.  It in turn calls the
; external subroutine DSPCHR to display the decimal character.
; Upon entry:  Word must be in DX.
; Upon exit:   All registers restored.
```

**Figure 7-1** *continued*

```
;---------------------------------------------------------------------
DSPDEC      PROC NEAR
            PUSH DX                     ;save registers
            PUSH CX
            PUSH BX
            PUSH AX
            MOV CX,5                    ;set counter for 5 digits
            MOV AX,DX                   ;put word in AX as dividend
REPEAT03:                              ;REPEAT
            XOR DX,DX                   ;   clear remainder
            MOV BX,0010                 ;   divide by 10
            DIV BX
            XCHG AX,DX                  ;   swap quotient and remainder
            LEA BX,CS:TABLE             ;   convert remainder to printable digit
            XLAT CS:TABLE
            PUSH AX                     ;   save digit on stack
            XCHG AX,DX                  ;   swap quotient and remainder
            LOOP REPEAT03               ;   subtract 1 from counter
UNTIL03:                               ;UNTIL counter = 0
            MOV CX,5                    ;reset counter to 5
REPEAT04:                              ;REPEAT
            POP DX                      ;   retrieve digit from stack into DX
            CALL DSPCHR                 ;   print it
            LOOP REPEAT04               ;   subtract 1 from counter
UNTIL04:                               ;UNTIL counter = 0
            POP AX                      ;restore registers
            POP BX
            POP CX
            POP DX
            RET
TABLE       DB '0123456789'
DSPDEC      ENDP
CODE        ENDS                        ;end of segment code declaration
            END PROG7                   ;end of program
```

**Figure 7-1** *concluded*

1. Direct mode addressing refers to the name of a memory location as a constant.
2. Register indirect mode addressing uses either one base register or one index register to contain the address of either the source or destination operand, but not both.
3. Based mode addressing uses either BX or BP with an optional constant to refer to one operand.
4. Indexed mode uses either SI or DI with an optional constant to refer to one operand.
5. Based indexed mode combines one base register and one index register to form the address of one operand.
6. Based indexed mode with displacement addressing combines based indexed mode with a constant displacement in the form of the name of a memory location or number of bytes.

```
B> prog7

Enter up to 20 numbers between 0 and 65535
Press <ENTER> alone to stop.
4825
39946
127
9087
14


Numbers in reverse order of entry

00014
09087
00127
39946
04825
Numbers entered: 00005    Largest number: 39946
Continue? (Y/N) n
B>
```

**Figure 7-2    Output from Program 7**

Where there is any doubt of the length of an operand referred to indirectly, the PTR instruction with WORD or BYTE preceding the indirect register tells the assembler the correct length.

Normally, data offsets are combined with the DS segment register, while code offsets for instructions are combined with the CS register. A segment override permits other registers to be used with offsets. As an example, CS:DATAITEM might be used in a subroutine to refer to a piece of data in the code segment where no data segment is declared.

Several instructions are used for specializing addressing. LDS and LES permit a word from the source operand in memory to be placed in the register named as destination and the following word to be placed in DS (for LDS) or ES (for LES). LEA permits indirect addresses to be computed as effective addresses and then loaded into the destination register. XCHG exchanges the contents of source and destination. XLAT translates a byte in AL according to the data in a table in the position indexed by the byte in AL.

Indirect addressing is widely used for processing individual bytes in strings of characters or processing words in arrays. The value in the indirect register must be incremented or decremented by one or two each time a loop is repeated to process that next byte or word.

## QUESTIONS

1.   What is meant by a constant operand? A variable operand?

2. Is use of immediate data considered direct mode addressing? Why or why not?

3. What registers may be used in register indirect mode addressing? May they be used for both operands in an instruction? Why or why not?

4. What registers are used in based mode addressing? Give two examples.

5. What base register normally requires a segment override for use with the data segment? Why?

6. What registers are used in indexed mode addressing? Give two examples.

7. What registers may be combined in based indexed mode addressing? What registers may not be combined? Give two examples.

8. What are the possible combinations in based indexed mode addressing? Give three examples showing different uses of brackets.

9. What is the purpose of the PTR instruction? Give examples of its use with bytes and with words.

10. What is meant by segment override? When is it necessary? Give two examples.

11. Describe the operation of the LDS and LES instructions.

12. Explain the difference between the MOV and the LEA instructions in computing offset addresses.

13. Explain the function of the XCHG instruction.

14. Explain the function of the XLAT instruction. How does it relate to indirect addressing?

## EXERCISES

1. Write direct mode addressing instructions to swap the contents of WORD1 and WORD2 in memory.

2. Use register indirect mode addressing in a loop to copy the first five words from ARRAY1 into ARRAY2. Remember that both operands in an instruction may not refer to memory locations.

3. Write a loop to place the even numbers from 2 through 20 into ARRAY1 and the function $N*2-1$ for values of $N$ from 2 through 20 into ARRAY2. Use based mode addressing for ARRAY1 and indexed mode addressing for ARRAY2.

4. You have a two-dimensional array with five rows and five columns. Use BX to refer to the rows and DI to refer to the columns. Write nested loops to put the values 11, 12, 13, 14, 15 into row 1; 21, 22, 23, 24, 25 into row 2; and so forth.

5. Use based indexed mode with displacement addressing to compare adjacent items in an array of 20 words; that is, the first item with the second, the second with the third, and so forth. Whenever the lower item of the pair has a value larger than the higher item of the pair, exchange them.

6. Write a routine to count and get the average of all nonzero bytes in a byte array named BYTARRAY with 100 elements. Store the count in a byte named COUNT and the average in a word named AVERAGE.

7. Write a routine to find the largest and the smallest value in an array of words named ARRAY. Place the largest value in LARGE and the smallest in SMALL.

## LAB PROBLEMS

1. Write a program to key in 10 hex numbers and place them in ARRAY. Then display the numbers in two columns, with the hex value in the lefthand column and the decimal value in the righthand column. Display headings over each column. Repeat until the operator responds 'N' or 'n' to a prompt asking whether to continue. Use subroutines in SUBS.

2. Define a 26-byte table consisting of the letters of the alphabet. Prompt the keyboard operator to enter a word terminated with <ENTER>. In three columns, each with headings, display each letter of the word, the hex value of the letter, and the offset in decimal of that letter from the start of the table. Repeat as long as the operator wishes to continue.

# ADVANCED ARITHMETIC

# 8

## OBJECTIVES

After studying this chapter, you should be able to:

* Describe how to perform arithmetic operations on numbers longer than one word.
* Describe how to compare long strings of bytes or words.
* Display long hexadecimal numbers in decimal or hex form.
* Explain subroutines that permit keyboard entry of decimal numbers of up to 25 digits and hex numbers of up to 20 digits.
* Define unpacked and packed binary-coded decimal numbers.
* Perform arithmetic and adjustment on unpacked and packed BCD numbers.
* Create libraries of external subroutines.

## MULTIWORD ADDITION

In any type of addition in any number base, a *carry* occurs when the sum of two digits is greater than the largest digit in that number base. These examples of decimal and hex addition demonstrate what should be familiar to most of us:

|                | DECIMAL ADDITION | HEX ADDITION |
|----------------|:----------------:|:------------:|
| Carries        | 11               | 1 1          |
| First Number   | 42783            | 5A491        |
| Second Number  | 36454            | 299B6        |
| Sum            | 79237            | 83E47        |

In decimal addition, the carry results when the sum of two digits exceeds nine, the largest decimal digit. In hex addition, the carry occurs when the sum exceeds Fh (decimal 15), the largest hex digit.

Whenever two words are added in a computer, any carry generated within the word is automatically added to the sum of the next digits to the left. This is automatically done by the hardware of the computer, so that you are barely aware of the fact that a carry has taken place.

But if the carry is produced when adding the leftmost digits of a pair of words, there is no room within the register or word in memory to store the carry, and *overflow* occurs. You then need more digits to represent the correct value of the sum. You can represent longer numbers by using more than one word.

Whenever overflow occurs, the carry flag is set. The ADC (add carry) instruction works just like ADD, except that it also adds 1 to the sum if the carry flag was previously set.

Assume you have one 32-bit number in AX and BX, with the leftmost bits in AX, and another in CX and DX, with the leftmost bits in CX. You can add them together with these instructions:

```
        ADD BX,DX                 ;if sum > 16 bits, carry
                                  ;flag = 1
        ADC AX,CX                 ;carry, if any, is included
                                  ;in sum
```

You can use a loop to add numbers of almost any length. Figure 8-1 shows the generalized MULTIADD subroutine to add two numbers that can contain any reasonable number of words. Both numbers must be of the same length and arranged with the least significant word to the left and the most significant word to the right. The sum is placed in a separate location.

The MULTIADD subroutine expects SI to contain the address of the first number, DI the address of the second number, and BX the address of the sum. CX specifies the number of words to be added. Along with DI, SI, CX, and BX, we save AX, since it is used as the accumulator for addition. To ensure that there is no carry added into the first pair of numbers, the CLC (clear carry flag) instruction is used before entering the REPEAT-UNTIL loop.

In addition to the ADC instruction, the two ADD instructions that adjust addresses also might produce a carry that sets the carry flag. PUSHF places the flag register on the stack to save the flag set by the ADC, and POPF restores it after the two ADD instructions.

The MULTIADD subroutine can be modified to perform addition on multiple bytes instead of multiple words by changing AX to AL in each reference and adding 1 instead of 2 to DI, SI, and BX.

## MULTIWORD SUBTRACTION

A *borrow* occurs in subtraction whenever you subtract a digit from a smaller digit. The next most significant digit is reduced by 1. Borrows within a word are handled automatically by the hardware, but if the leftmost digit subtracted results in a borrow, the carry flag is set. The SBB (subtract with borrow) instruction subtracts a 1 from the result if the carry flag was set previously.

You can use the MULTIADD subroutine to perform multiword subtraction by merely changing the ADC instruction to SBB. Another useful subrou-

```
;-----------------------------------------------------------------------
; Program name:  MULTIADD.ASM
;
; Author:  Alton R. Kindred
;
; This routine adds two numbers each containing any desired number of words
; and stores the sum in a separate location.  Both numbers must contain the
; least significant byte at the left and the most significant byte at the
; right.
; At entry:  SI points to leftmost byte of first number
;            DI points to leftmost byte of second number
;            BX points to leftmost byte of sum
;            CX contains count of words in each number
; At exit:   BX points to leftmost byte of sum
;            AX used but saved.
;-----------------------------------------------------------------------
CODE      SEGMENT
          ASSUME CS:CODE
          PUBLIC MULTIADD
MULTIADD  PROC NEAR
          PUSH DI               ;save registers
          PUSH SI
          PUSH CX
          PUSH BX
          PUSH AX
          CLC                   ;clear carry flag
REPEAT:                         ;REPEAT
          MOV AX,[SI]           ;  move word of N1 to AX
          ADC AX,[DI]           ;  add word of N2 to AX
          MOV [BX],AX           ;  store sum
          PUSHF                 ;  save carry flag
          ADD SI,2              ;  increment N1 pointer
          ADD DI,2              ;  increment N2 pointer
          ADD BX,2              ;  increment sum pointer
          POPF                  ;  restore carry flag
          LOOP REPEAT           ;  subtract 1 from word counter
UNTIL:                          ;UNTIL word counter = 0
          POP AX                ;restore registers
          POP BX
          POP CX
          POP SI
          POP DI
          RET                   ;return
MULTIADD  ENDP
CODE      ENDS
          END
```

**Figure 8-1    MULTIADD Subroutine**

tine can be put in your collection by writing MULTISUB with only the ADC instruction changed to SBB and with appropriate changes to comments. There is no practical limit to the length of the numbers that can be subtracted. The same technique can be used when the number consists of multiple bytes.

## MULTIWORD COMPARISON

You can compare numbers consisting of more than one word. Start with the most significant words of the two numbers. If they are equal, you compare the next most significant. If at any point the words are different, there is no need to compare the rest of the words.

You need some way to tell when all words have been compared to know if the numbers are equal. CX is normally used as a counter to control the number of words compared. CX becomes zero only when you have compared all the words in the number without finding any that are different. If any word is not equal to its corresponding word in the other number, the JNE (jump if not equal) instruction terminates the loop.

The MULTICMP subroutine in Figure 8-2 compares any number of words using the technique just described. When you enter the subroutine, SI must point to the last word (most significant word) of the first number and DI to the last word (MSW) of the second number. Both numbers should be arranged with the least significant word to the left (lowest-numbered address) and the most significant word to the right (highest-numbered address). CX must contain the number of words to be compared. Upon return from subroutine, the flags will be set just as they would after a single word comparison. You may write a conditional jump instruction immediately after the CALL MULTICMP instruction in the calling program.

## MULTIWORD MULTIPLICATION

You also can multiply numbers having more than one word each. The procedure is more complex than that of multiword addition, subtraction, or comparison. The numbers to be multiplied must contain the same number of words, with the least significant word to the left and the most significant word to the right. The product will have twice the number of words that either number has.

We will demonstrate a subroutine that will multiply two five-word numbers together to produce a 10-word product.

The algorithm is this:

1. Set all words of the product to zeros.
2. Multiply the first word of the first number by the first word of the second number.
3. Add the product to the first two words of the product area.
4. Modify addresses to the next word of the first number and the next word of the product area.
5. Repeat steps 2, 3, and 4 for each word in the first number.
6. Modify address to the second word of the second number.

```
;-----------------------------------------------------------------------
; Program name:  MULTICMP.ASM
;
; Author:  Alton R. Kindred
;
; This routine compares two numbers that may contain any number of words.  Each
; number must have the least significant byte to the left and the most
; significant byte to the right.
; At entry:  SI contains address of rightmost word of N1
;            DI contains address of rightmost word of N2
;            CX contains number of words in number
; At exit:   Flags are set as with single word compare
;            All registers preserved
;-----------------------------------------------------------------------
CODE       SEGMENT
           ASSUME CS:CODE
           PUBLIC MULTICMP
MULTICMP   PROC NEAR
           PUSH DI                  ;save registers
           PUSH SI
           PUSH CX
           PUSH AX
REPEAT:                            ;REPEAT
           MOV AX,[SI]             ;   move word of N1 to AX
           CMP AX,[DI]             ;   compare with word in N2
           PUSHF                   ;   save flags
           SUB SI,2                ;   set N1 address to next word
           SUB DI,2                ;   set N2 address to next word
           POPF                    ;   restore flags
           JNE UNTIL
           LOOP REPEAT             ;   subtract 1 from word counter
UNTIL:                            ;UNTIL last word compared or words <>
           POP AX                  ;restore registers
           POP CX
           POP SI
           POP DI
           RET                     ;return
MULTICMP   ENDP
CODE       ENDS
           END
```

**Figure 8-2 • MULTICMP Subroutine**

7. Repeat steps 2 through 6 until every word in the first number has been multiplied by each word of the second number and the resulting products added to the product area.

Figure 8-3 shows the MULTIMUL subroutine that performs this procedure. To call the subroutine, put the address of the first number in SI, the address of the second number in DI, and the address of the product area in BX.

```
;------------------------------------------------------------------------------
; Program name:  B:MULTIMUL.ASM
;
; Author:    Alton R. Kindred
;
; This routine multiplies two five-word hex numbers together and produces a
; 10-word product.  All numbers are arranged with least significant word to the
; left of the number.
; At entry:  SI contains address of first number.
;            DI contains address of second number.
;            BX contains address of product.
; At exit:   BX points to leftmost word of product.
;            All registers saved.
;------------------------------------------------------------------------------
CODE        SEGMENT                     ;segment for code
            PUBLIC MULTIMUL
            ASSUME CS:CODE
MULTIMUL    PROC NEAR                   ;for proper return to DOS
            PUSH AX                     ;save registers
            PUSH CX
            PUSH DX
            PUSH SI
            PUSH DI
            PUSH BX                     ;save product address
            MOV CX,10                   ;set word counter to 10
            XOR AX,AX                   ;set AX to zeros
REPEAT01:                               ;REPEAT
            MOV [BX],AX                 ;   move zeros to word in product
            ADD BX,2                    ;   increment product address
            LOOP REPEAT01               ;   subtract 1 from word counter
UNTIL01:                                ;UNTIL word counter = 0
            MOV CX,5                    ;set N2 counter to 5
            POP BX                      ;restore product address
REPEAT02:                               ;REPEAT
            PUSH CX                     ;   save registers
            PUSH DI
            PUSH BX
            MOV CX,5                    ;   set N1 counter to 5
            PUSH SI                     ;   save N1 address
            CLC                         ;   clear carry flag
            PUSHF                       ;   save carry flag
REPEAT03:                               ;   REPEAT
            MOV AX,[SI]                 ;      multiply word of N1 by word of N2
            MOV DX,[DI]
            MUL DX
            POPF                        ;      restore carry flag
            ADC [BX],AX                 ;      add part product to product
            ADC [BX+2],DX
            PUSHF                       ;      save carry
            ADD SI,2                    ;      increment N1 address
            ADD BX,2                    ;      increment product address
            LOOP REPEAT03               ;      subtract 1 from N1 counter
UNTIL03:                                ;   UNTIL N1 counter = 0
```

**Figure 8-3    MULTIMUL Subroutine**

```
              POPF                    ;  restore carry
              POP SI                  ;  restore registers
              POP BX
              POP DI
              POP CX
              ADD DI,2                ;  set N2 address to next word
              ADD BX,2                ;  set product address to next word
              LOOP REPEAT02           ;  subtract 1 from N2 counter
UNTIL02:                              ;UNTIL N2 counter = 0
              POP DI                  ;restore registers
              POP SI
              POP DX
              POP CX
              POP AX
              RET                     ;return
MULTIMUL      ENDP                    ;end of procedure declaration
CODE          ENDS                    ;end of segment code declaration
```

**Figure 8-3**    *concluded*

The loop REPEATO1-UNTILO1 sets the product area to zeros. The loop REPEATO2-UNTILO2 successively moves from one word to the next in the second number and in the product area. The nested loop REPEATO3-UNTILO3 multiplies each of the five words in the first number by one word of the second number and adds the partial products into the final product area.

The process is just what you do in ordinary multiplication. Assume that one decimal digit in the following example corresponds to one word in the MULTIMUL subroutine. You wish to multiply the number 98765 by 12345. The operation proceeds like this:

|  | PARTIAL PRODUCTS | FINAL PRODUCT |
|---|---|---|
| Set product to zeros | 0000000000 | 0000000000 |
| Multiply 98765 by 5 | 493825 | 493825 |
| Multiply 98765 by 4 | 395060 | 4444425 |
| Multiply 98765 by 3 | 296295 | 34073925 |
| Multiply 98765 by 2 | 197530 | 231603925 |
| Multiply 98765 by 1 | 098765 | 1219253925 |

## MULTIWORD NUMBER CONVERSION

In Chapter 5, we described the DSPDEC and DSPHEX routines that convert hex data in main storage into decimal or hex characters for display on the screen. We also described the INPDEC and INPHEX routines to convert decimal or hex characters from the keyboard to a hex word in main storage.

## Displaying Large Numbers in Decimal

Advanced techniques are necessary to convert numbers longer than one word for input or output. Assume that you have an 80-bit binary number (10 bytes or five words long) that you wish to print as a decimal string. Follow the same principle used in DSPDEC, whereby you repeatedly divide the number by 10 and use the remainder to form the decimal digit to be displayed. The remainder from the first division is the rightmost digit of the string to be printed. The remainder of each successive division becomes the next digit to the left until the quotient becomes zero.

The problem with numbers longer than a word is that there are no hardware instructions to divide the entire number at once. You only can divide two words by one word and create a one-word quotient and one-word remainder. You must be able to repeat this process on different parts of the number until the entire number has been divided by 10.

Just as with long division, first divide the high-order section of the dividend by the divisor, record the quotient so far, and bring down the remainder. Next to the remainder, bring down the next part of the dividend, divide again, record the quotient so far, and bring down the next remainder. Continue this process until the quotient is zero. The final remainder is the remainder of the entire divide operation. Figure 8-4 shows the HEX5DEC subroutine to convert a five-word hex number into a 25-byte decimal string.

At entry, this subroutine requires SI to point to the most significant word of a five-word hex number and DI to point to the leftmost byte (lowest-numbered address) of the decimal string area.

It begins by saving registers used. The first loop, REPEAT01, sets the string area to spaces (' ' or 20h).

The next loop, REPEAT02, saves the source pointer, clears the quotient flag and the remainder in DX to zeros, sets a counter for five words to be divided, and sets the source pointer to the rightmost (high-order) word.

The inner loop, REPEAT03, saves the word counter, gets the first word, divides it by 10, moves the quotient back to the original word, ORs the quotient against the quotient flag, and sets the pointer to the next word. This procedure continues until all five words have been divided.

Instructions between UNTIL3 and UNTIL2 handle the results of the first full division and set up for the second division. The final remainder in DL from the first division must be between 0 and 9, since 10 was the divisor. The remainder is made printable by ORing with 30h and is stored in the last byte of the string. Then the remainder is returned to its numeric form in DL with an AND instruction, the string pointer is decremented, and a test is made of the quotient flag. If the flag is not zero, the REPEAT2 loop is repeated until the final quotient of the five-word division is zero.

To print the full 25-byte decimal number after leaving the subroutine, set a pointer such as SI to the leftmost byte of the string area, display the character, and increment and display 24 more times. Any bytes not required

```
;-------------------------------------------------------------------------
; Program name:  HEX5DEC.ASM
;
; Author:  Alton R. Kindred
;
; This routine converts an 80-bit binary integer into a 25-byte decimal
; string.
; At entry:  SI points to leftmost word of 80-bit binary integer
;            DI points to leftmost byte of 25-byte area for decimal string
; At exit:   DI points to 25-digit decimal string
;            AX, BX, CX, DX are used but preserved
;-------------------------------------------------------------------------
CODE        SEGMENT
            PUBLIC HEX5DEC
            ASSUME CS:CODE
HEX5DEC     PROC NEAR
            PUSH AX                    ;save registers
            PUSH BX
            PUSH CX
            PUSH DX
            MOV AL,' '                 ;move space to AL
            MOV CX,25                  ;set byte count to 25
REPEAT1:                               ;REPEAT
            MOV [DI],AL                ;  move space to byte
            INC DI                     ;  increment byte address
            LOOP REPEAT1               ;  subtract 1 from count
UNTIL1:                                ;UNTIL count = 0
REPEAT2:                               ;REPEAT
            PUSH SI                    ;  save source pointer
            MOV BX,0                   ;  clear quotient flag
            MOV CX,5                   ;  set word counter to 5
            MOV DX,0                   ;  clear remainder
            ADD SI,8                   ;  point to high order word
REPEAT3:                               ;  REPEAT
            PUSH CX                    ;    save word counter
            MOV AX,[SI]                ;    get 16-bit word
            MOV CX,10                  ;    set divisor to 10
            DIV CX                     ;    divide word by 10
            MOV [SI],AX                ;    save quotient
            OR BX,AX                   ;    OR quotient against quotient flag
            SUB SI,2                   ;    point to next 16-bit word
            POP CX                     ;    restore count
            LOOP REPEAT3               ;    subtract 1 from word counter
UNTIL3:                                ;  UNTIL counter = 0
            OR DL,30h                  ;  make remainder printable digit
            DEC DI                     ;  adjust string pointer
            MOV [DI],DL                ;  move digit to string area
            AND DL,0CFh                ;  restore remainder to numeric
            POP SI                     ;  restore source pointer
            CMP BX,0                   ;  test quotient flag
            JNZ REPEAT2
UNTIL2:                                ;UNTIL quotient flag = 0
            POP DX                     ;restore registers
            POP CX
```

**Figure 8-4    HEX5 DEC Subroutine**

```
              POP  BX
              POP  AX
              RET                       ;return
HEX5DEC       ENDP
CODE          ENDS                      ;end of segment code declaration
              END                       ;end of program
```

**Figure 8-4**    *concluded*

to display the decimal value will contain spaces, so that the 25-byte decimal number will be displayed right-justified.

If you know that the number to be displayed is actually no larger than, say, 10 decimal digits, you might set the pointer to STRING+15 and repeat the loop to display only the 10 bytes.

## Displaying Large Hex Numbers

Large numbers may be displayed in hex by using the DSPHEX subroutine in a loop. No other conversion techniques are necessary, since you can make a hex digit display as a hex character. The following routine will display a five-word number as 20 hex digits. We presume the most significant word is stored at the left.

```
              LEA  SI,WORD+8            ;set address to most
                                       ;significant word
              MOV  CX,5                 ;set word counter to 5
REPEAT01:                              ;REPEAT
              MOV  DX, [SI]             ; move word to DX
              PUSH CX                   ; save word counter
              MOV  CX,4                 ; set counter for 4 digits
              CALL DSPHEX               ; display word in hex
              POP  CX                   ; restore word counter
              SUB  SI,2                 ; set address to next word
              LOOP REPEAT01             ; subtract 1 from word
                                       ; counter
UNTIL01:                               ;UNTIL word counter = 0
```

## Entering Large Numbers in Hex

Entering large numbers poses one special problem: the numbers are entered from left to right, but they should be stored in words right justified. The INPHEX subroutine, described in Chapter 5, handles only one to four digits. We need a special routine to enter more than four digits.

Our algorithm is this:

1.   Enter a character and verify that it is a valid hex digit.
2.   If so, continue; if not, get another.
3.   Convert the hex character to a one-word hex value and push it on the stack.
4.   Count the number of hex characters entered.
5.   Continue until <ENTER> is pressed.

6.   If any hex characters were entered, retrieve the words from the stack and store the digits in the string area from the last byte down to the first.

7.   Pad the rest of the 20-byte string area with zeros. This has the effect of right justifying the digits in the number.

8.   Set AX to zero to form hex words.

9.   Shift AX left four bits and add in the digits, from the most significant (leftmost) digit.

10.  After each four digits have been added to AX, store the resulting word.

11.  Continue until all 20 digits have been formed into five words.

The MULTINHX subroutine, shown in Figure 8-5, performs this operation. Upon entry, SI must contain the address of the least significant word of the five-word area, and DI must point to the 20-byte string area.

The routine between IF01 and ENDIF01 is similar to that used in the INPHEX routine. It tests that the character entered is between '0' and '9' or between 'a' and 'f'. Uppercase characters 'A' through 'F' are converted to lowercase with the instruction OR AL,20h. The instruction SUB AL,7 at THEN02 followed by AND AX,000Fh converts the characters 'a' through 'f' to the hex values A through F.

Any hex digits entered are pushed on the stack so that they can be retrieved in reverse order. If any hex digits were entered, the routine at REPEAT01-UNTIL01 retrieves the last digit entered, stores it as the least significant byte in the string area, and continues until all digits entered have been retrieved from the stack. The loop at WHILE01-WEND01 pads the leading bytes of the string area with zeros. If no hex digits were entered, the string area is padded with 20 zeros.

The REPEAT03-UNTIL03 loop retrieves the 20 digits from the string area, places them in words in groups of four, and stores the words in the area pointed to by SI. The words are stored with the most significant word to the right.

### Entering Large Numbers in Decimal

To enter large numbers as decimal digits, start in much the same way as you do with hex digits. Enter the digit, verify that it is between '0' and '9', convert it to a numeric value between 0 and 9, and push it on the stack. Continue this process until <ENTER> is pressed, counting the number of digits entered. Since one word will hold values up to 65535 decimal, you provide for 25 digits to be held in the five words.

If any digits were entered, retrieve the digits from the stack and place them on the string of bytes, working from the last byte downward. Next, fill in any unused bytes with leading zeros. If no digits were entered, 25 bytes of zeros are placed in the string area.

Figure 8-6 shows the MULTINDC subroutine. At REPEAT02, set the five words to zeros. The two nested loops REPEAT03-UNTIL03 and REPEAT04-UNTIL04 complete the process of converting the decimal digits into hex

```
;----------------------------------------------------------------------------
; Program name: B:MULTINHX.ASM
;
; Author:   Alton R. Kindred
;
; This routine accepts a string of up to 20 characters from the keyboard, tests
; that they are valid hex digits, and converts them to a five-word hex number.
; At entry:  SI points to leftmost word of the five-word area
;            DI points to leftmost byte of 25-byte string area
; At exit:   Number is in five-word area, least significant word first
;----------------------------------------------------------------------------
CODE        SEGMENT                         ;segment for code
            PUBLIC MULTINHX
            ASSUME CS:CODE
MULTINHX    PROC NEAR
            PUSH AX                          ;save registers
            PUSH BX
            PUSH CX
            PUSH DX
            PUSH ES
            PUSH SI
            PUSH DI
            PUSH BP
            MOV BX,DI           ;set string address
            MOV BP,SI           ;set word address
            XOR CX,CX           ;clear byte counter
            MOV AH,1            ;get a byte
            INT 21h
WHILE:      CMP AL,13           ;WHILE byte <> ENTER
            JE WEND
IF01:       CMP AL,'0'          ;   IF byte => '0'
            JB ENDIF01
AND01:      CMP AL,'9'          ;   AND byte <= '9'
            JNA THEN01
            OR AL,20h
OR01:       CMP AL,'a'          ;   OR byte => 'a'
            JB ENDIF01
AND01a:     CMP AL,'f'          ;   AND byte <= 'f'
            JA ENDIF01
THEN01:                         ;      THEN
IF02:       CMP AL,'9'          ;      IF byte > '9'
            JNA ENDIF02
THEN02:     SUB AL,7            ;        THEN convert 'a'-'f' to A-F
ENDIF02:                        ;      ENDIF
            AND AX,000Fh        ;      zap zone bits
            PUSH AX             ;      save byte on stack
            INC CX              ;      add 1 to byte counter
ENDIF01:                        ;   ENDIF
            MOV AH,1            ;   get another byte
            INT 21h
            JMP WHILE
WEND:                           ;WEND
            MOV DI,19           ;set string address to last byte
IF04:       JCXZ ENDIF04        ;IF CX <> 0
```

**Figure 8-5     MULTINHX Subroutine**

```
THEN04:                               ;    THEN
REPEAT01:                             ;    REPEAT
          POP AX                      ;       restore byte
          MOV [BX][DI],AL             ;       move byte to string address
          DEC DI                      ;       subtract 1 from string address
          LOOP REPEAT01               ;       subtract 1 from byte counter
UNTIL01:                              ;    UNTIL byte counter = 0
ENDIF04:                              ;ENDIF
WHILE01:  CMP DI,0                    ;WHILE string address => 0
          JNGE WEND01
          MOV BYTE PTR [BX][DI],0     ;    move 0 to string address
          DEC DI                      ;    subtract 1 from string address
          JMP WHILE01
WEND01:                               ;WEND
          MOV DI,0                    ;set string offset to 0
          MOV SI,8                    ;set address of most significant word
          XOR AX,AX                   ;clear AX
          MOV CX,4                    ;set digit counter to 4
REPEAT03:                             ;REPEAT
          PUSH CX                     ;    save digit counter
          MOV CX,4                    ;    shift left 4 bits
          SHL AX,CL
          ADD AL,[BX][DI]             ;    add digit
          INC DI                      ;    add 1 to string address
          POP CX                      ;    restore digit counter
          DEC CX                      ;    subtract 1 from digit counter
IF03:     CMP CX,0                    ;    IF digit counter = 0
          JNE ENDIF03
THEN03:   MOV DS:[BP][SI],AX          ;       THEN store word
          MOV CX,4                    ;       reset digit counter to 4
          SUB SI,2                    ;       subtract 2 from word address
ENDIF03:                              ;    ENDIF
          CMP DI,20
          JB REPEAT03
UNTIL03:                              ;UNTIL string offset => 20
          POP BP                      ;restore registers
          POP DI
          POP SI
          POP ES
          POP DX
          POP CX
          POP BX
          POP AX
          RET
MULTINHX  ENDP                        ;end of procedure declaration
;
CODE      ENDS                        ;end of segment code declaration
          END                         ;end of program
```

**Figure 8-5**    *concluded*

```
;------------------------------------------------------------------------------
; Program name: B:MULTINDC.ASM
;
; Author:   Alton R. Kindred
;
; This routine accepts a string of up to 25 characters from the keyboard, tests
; that they are valid decimal digits, and converts them to a five-word hex
; number.
; At entry:  SI points to leftmost word of the five-word area
;            DI points to leftmost byte of 25-byte string area
; At exit:   Number is in five-word area, least significant word first
;------------------------------------------------------------------------------
CODE        SEGMENT                     ;segment for code
            PUBLIC MULTINDC
            ASSUME CS:CODE
MULTINDC    PROC NEAR
            PUSH AX                     ;save registers
            PUSH BX
            PUSH CX
            PUSH DX
            PUSH SI
            PUSH DI
            PUSH BP
            MOV BX,DI                   ;set string address
            MOV BP,SI                   ;set word address
            XOR CX,CX                   ;clear byte counter
            MOV AH,1                    ;get a byte
            INT 21h
WHILE:      CMP AL,13                   ;WHILE byte <> ENTER
            JE WEND
IF01:       CMP AL,'0'                  ;  IF byte => '0'
            JB ENDIF01
AND01:      CMP AL,'9'                  ;  AND byte <= '9'
            JA ENDIF01
THEN01:     AND AX,000Fh                ;    THEN zap zone bits
            PUSH AX                     ;    save byte on stack
            INC CX                      ;    add 1 to byte counter
ENDIF01:                                ;  ENDIF
            MOV AH,1                    ;  get another byte
            INT 21h
            JMP WHILE
WEND:                                   ;WEND
            MOV DI,24                   ;set string address to last byte
IF02:       JCXZ ENDIF02                ;IF CX <> 0
THEN02:                                 ;  THEN
REPEAT01:                               ;  REPEAT
            POP AX                      ;    restore byte
            MOV [BX][DI],AL             ;    move byte to string address
            DEC DI                      ;    subtract 1 from string address
            LOOP REPEAT01               ;    subtract 1 from byte counter
UNTIL01:                                ;  UNTIL byte counter = 0
ENDIF02:                                ;ENDIF
WHILE01:    CMP DI,0                    ;WHILE string address => 0
            JNGE WEND01
```

**Figure 8-6    MULTINDC Subroutine**

```
                    MOV BYTE PTR [BX][DI],0    ;   move 0 to string address
                    DEC DI                     ;   subtract 1 from string address
                    JMP WHILE01
WEND01:                                        ;WEND
                    XOR SI,SI                  ;set word offset to 0
                    MOV CX,5                   ;set word counter to 5
                    XOR AX,AX                  ;set AX to 0
REPEAT02:                                      ;REPEAT
                    MOV DS:[BP][SI],AX         ;   move zeros to word
                    ADD SI,2                   ;   add 2 to word address
                    LOOP REPEAT02              ;   subtract 1 from word counter
UNTIL02:                                       ;UNTIL word counter = 0
                    MOV DI,0                   ;set string offset to 0
REPEAT03:                                      ;REPEAT
                    MOV SI,8                   ;   set address of most significant word
                    MOV AX,DS:[BP][SI]         ;   get word
                    MOV DX,10                  ;   multiply by 10
                    MUL DX
                    MOV DS:[BP][SI],AX         ;   store word back
                    MOV CX,4
REPEAT04:                                      ;   REPEAT
                    MOV AX,DS:[BP][SI-2]       ;      get adjacent word
                    MOV DX,10                  ;      multiply by 10
                    MUL DX
                    MOV DS:[BP][SI-2],AX       ;      restore word
                    ADD DS:[BP][SI],DX         ;      add carry from multiply
                    SUB SI,2                   ;      set address to next word
                    LOOP REPEAT04              ;      subtract 1 from word counter
UNTIL04:                                       ;   UNTIL word counter = 0
                    ADD AL,[BX][DI]            ;   add byte to number
                    ADC AH,0                   ;   add carry if any
                    ADC WORD PTR DS:[BP][SI+2],0  ; add carry if any to next word
                    MOV DS:[BP][SI],AX         ;   store word
                    INC DI                     ;   increment byte address
                    CMP DI,25
                    JB REPEAT03
UNTIL03:                                       ;UNTIL byte address > 24
                    POP BP                     ;restore registers
                    POP DI
                    POP SI
                    POP DX
                    POP CX
                    POP BX
                    POP AX
                    RET
MULTINDC            ENDP                       ;end of procedure declaration
CODE                ENDS                       ;end of segment code declaration
                    END                        ;end of program
```

**Figure 8-6**   *concluded*

words. The idea is to multiply all five words by 10 and then add the most significant digit to the least significant position in the least significant word. This process is repeated 25 times, moving from the most significant digit to the least significant. As each word is multiplied by 10 in AX and DX, the AX portion of the product is replaced in its original word, and the DX portion is added to the next higher significant word. Since you are multiplying AX by 10, the portion of the product in DX can never exceed 9.

This routine will work correctly for any decimal number up to 24 digits and for any 25-digit number not greater than 1,208,925,819,614,629,174, 706,175 (FFFF FFFF FFFF FFFF FFFFh).

## EXTENDING BYTES AND WORDS

There are times when you wish to extend a byte into a word or a word into a doubleword before doing calculations. The 8088 family of processors provides two useful instructions for this purpose.

The CBW (convert byte to word) instruction converts a byte in AL into a word in AX by extending the sign (leftmost bit) of AL into AH. This preserves the sign of the number for later calculations. The previous value in AH is destroyed. For example:

```
Value in AX:      ?? 3C     ?? FF     ?? 80
AX after CBW:     00 3C     FF FF     FF 80
```

For unsigned or positive numbers, you can extend a byte to a word by putting the byte in AL and moving 0 to AH, but this technique gives incorrect values for negative numbers. In the second column above, FFh as a signed number in AL is -1 decimal. If we move 00 to AH, the value in AX becomes 00FFh, or 255 decimal. Extending the sign preserves the same value no matter how long the extended number may be.

The CWD (convert word to doubleword) instruction converts a word in AX into a doubleword with the sign bits extended throughout DX. The high-order bits of the doubleword are in DX and the low-order bits in AX, just as the result of binary multiplication appears.

A common use of CBW and CWD is to extend a signed number before dividing. The IDIV instruction rather than DIV must be used when dividing signed numbers.

## BCD (BINARY-CODED DECIMAL) DATA

In addition to pure binary numbers, you may express numbers in BCD (binary-coded decimal) form. Any value between 0 and 9 may be expressed in four bits. You may put either one or two decimal digits per byte.

*Unpacked BCD data* has one decimal digit per byte, in the rightmost four bits. The leftmost four bits are always zeros. *Packed BCD data* contains two four-bit decimal digits per byte. The two forms of BCD data are compared with pure binary numbers expressed as hex digits in the examples below. Spaces are left between bytes for clarity.

| DECIMAL VALUE | HEX FORM | UNPACKED BCD | PACKED BCD |
|---|---|---|---|
| 3 | 03 | 03 | 03 |
| 13 | 0D | 01 03 | 13 |
| 35 | 23 | 03 05 | 35 |
| 128 | 80 | 01 02 08 | 01 28 |
| 511 | 01 FF | 05 01 01 | 05 11 |

## Data Definitions

Unpacked numbers are sometimes called *ASCII numbers*, because they can readily be printed or displayed by adding 30h to each byte. For example, the ASCII number 05h with 30h added gives 35h, which prints as the character 5. To define constant unpacked BCD data, you use DB (define byte) or DW (define word) directives followed by the decimal digits making up the value. For DB directives, digits must be separated by commas. When using DW directives, remember that words are actually placed in storage with the least significant byte first. Although you can arrange the digits with the least significant digit on the left as you do with binary numbers, it is common with BCD numbers to arrange the most significant digit on the left. Then, when you view storage through DEBUG you see the decimal digits in their customary sequence. Note the following examples:

```
UNPK511   DB 5,1,1      ; value 511 form 05 01
                        ; 01
UNPK5000  DB 5,0,0,0    ; value 5000 form 05 00
                        ; 00 00
UNPK51    DW 0105h      ; value 51 form 05 01
```

Packed BCD numbers usually are called *decimal numbers* to distinguish them from ASCII numbers. Later sections will emphasize the distinctions. To define packed BCD data, you may define two hex digits per byte, so long as you do not exceed the decimal value nine in either four-bit value:

```
PK511   DB 05h,11h      ; value 0511 form 05 11
PK5000  DB 50h,00h,     ; value 5000 form 50 00
PK1024  DW 2410h        ; value 1024 form 10 24
PK5678  DW 7856h        ; value 5678 form 56 78
```

The assembler provides DT the (define tenword) directive to define packed BCD numbers. The 10-byte numbers provide for a maximum of 18 digits in the rightmost nine bytes. The leftmost byte is reserved for the sign, 00h indicating positive and 80h indicating negative. Negative numbers appear in their normal notation, not as complements. The most significant digit is to the left. Here are some examples:

```
TW1 DT 9876543          ; form 00 00 00 00 00 00 09
                        ; 87 65 43
```

```
TW2 DT 123456789123456789  ; form 00 12 34 56 78 91 23
                           ; 45 67 89
    TW3 DT -5566778899      ; form 80 00 00 00 00 55 66
                           ; 77 88 99
```

In working with tenwords, the programmer is responsible for testing the signs of the numbers and selecting the correct operations accordingly.

## ASCII Adjustments

The 8088 family of processors does not have specific arithmetic instructions to process BCD data. Instead, the regular binary arithmetic instructions are used. Six special instructions are provided to adjust the results into correct form, four for unpacked (ASCII) data, and two for packed (decimal) data. The programmer is responsible for making these adjustments. The adjustment usually follows immediately after the arithmetic instruction on the BCD numbers.

*AAA (ASCII Adjust for Addition).* The *AAA instruction* requires no operand. It uses AL and AH registers to adjust the result of binary addition. AAA works on the byte in AL. If that byte contains a value between 00 and 09, and the CF (carry flag) and AF (auxiliary carry flag) are set to zero, no change is made in AL, and the flags remain at zero. When an adjustment is made, 6 is added to AL, the left half of AL is cleared, AH is incremented by 1, indicating a carry, and the CF and AF carry flags are set to 1. The adjustment is made under two conditions: (a) if the value in AL is between 0Ah and 0Fh, and (b) if the value in AL is greater than 10h and the AF flag is set to 1. The AF (auxiliary carry flag) is set to 1 any time there is a carry from bit 3 to bit 4, indicating a carry out of a four-bit number.

Let us look at some examples of adjustment after ASCII addition:

| FIRST BYTE | SECOND BYTE | SUM | FLAGS SET | ADJUSTMENT MADE | AX INCREMENTED |
|---|---|---|---|---|---|
| 03 | 04 | 07 | None | None | No |
| 07 | 05 | 0C | None | 02 | Yes |
| 09 | 09 | 12 | AF | 08 | Yes |
| 01 | 09 | 0A | None | 00 | Yes |

Figure 8-7 shows the ADDASC subroutine, which will add and adjust ASCII numbers of any specified length. Upon entry, SI must point to the LSB of the first number, DI to the second number, BX to the area for the sum, and CX must contain the number of bytes to be added.

AH is not used in this subroutine. Whenever a carry results in adjusting the sum, the CF flag is set, and the carry is added to the next most significant byte the next time through the loop. INC (increment) instructions do not affect the carry flag, so that the carry produced by the adjustment is added by the ADC instruction to the next byte the next time through the loop.

```
;-----------------------------------------------------------------------
; Program name:  B:ADDASC.ASM
;
; Author:  Alton R. Kindred
;
; This routine adds and adjusts two unpacked (ASCII) BCD numbers and stores
; the sum in a separate location.  Both numbers and the sum must have the least
; significant byte to the right.
; Upon entry:  SI points to the LSB of the first number
;              DI points to the LSB of the second number
;              BX points to the LSB of the sum area
;              CX contains the number of bytes
; Upon exit:   All registers preserved
;-----------------------------------------------------------------------
CODE      SEGMENT
          PUBLIC ADDASC
          ASSUME CS:CODE
ADDASC    PROC NEAR
          PUSH AX                    ;save registers
          PUSH BX
          PUSH SI
          PUSH DI
          CLC                        ;clear carry flag
REPEAT:                              ;REPEAT
          MOV AL,[SI]                ;  get byte of first number
          ADC AL,[DI]                ;  add byte with carry if any
          AAA                        ;  adjust sum to ASCII
          MOV [BX],AL                ;  store byte in sum
          DEC SI                     ;  decrement addresses
          DEC DI
          DEC BX
          LOOP REPEAT                ;  subtract 1 from byte counter
UNTIL:                              ;UNTIL byte counter = 0
          POP DI                     ;restore registers
          POP SI
          POP BX
          POP AX
          RET                        ;return
ADDASC    ENDP
CODE      ENDS
          END
```

**Figure 8-7    ADDASC Subroutine**

In ASCII addition, the programmer is responsible for ensuring that valid ASCII digits are used. The AAA instruction makes no tests for valid data, and gives no special indication if final results are not valid ASCII digits. If a carry results from adjusting the leftmost digit of the sum, the last carry is lost, and the sum will be truncated.

**AAS (ASCII Adjust for Subtraction).**    The *AAS instruction* is used with no operand to adjust the result of subtraction on ASCII numbers. It makes use of the AL and AH registers to adjust the result of the borrow (carry).

AAS works like AAA, except that the adjustment is made by subtracting 6 from the value in AL. Digits are tested and flags are set as they are in AAA. AH is decremented when an adjustment is made, to reflect the borrow from the next most significant digit. Whenever we subtract a larger ASCII byte from a smaller one, the result is negative, and the leftmost four bits of the difference will be 1111b, or Fh. The AAS instruction properly adjusts for this difference. Here are some examples:

| FIRST DIGIT | SECOND DIGIT | DIFFERENCE | FLAGS SET | ADJUSTMENT MADE | BORROW FROM AH? |
|---|---|---|---|---|---|
| 09 | 07 | 02 | None | No | No |
| 04 | 06 | FE | Both | 08 | Yes |
| 07 | 02 | 05 | None | No | No |
| 01 | 08 | F9 | Both | 03 | Yes |

The ADDASC subroutine can be converted to SUBASC subroutine by making only two changes: (a) change the ADC (add carry) instruction to SBB (subtract with borrow), and (b) change the AAA instruction to AAS.

If the entire second number is larger than the first number, the difference after adjustment will appear in 10s complement form. This means that we have borrowed as far as possible, but one additional borrow would be necessary for the correct difference. We usually can recognize 10s complement numbers as having several leading nines. Note these examples:

| | | |
|---|---|---|
| First number: | 01 02 03 04 05 | 00 00 07 08 09 |
| Second number | 00 06 05 04 03 | 00 00 09 01 03 |
| Difference (adjusted): | 00 05 08 00 02 | 09 09 08 07 06 |
| Result | Valid | Invalid; 10s complement |

***AAM (ASCII Adjust for Multiplication).*** AAM converts the result of one-byte multiplication of ASCII digits into two ASCII digits. It uses only AL and AH. The result of the multiplication in AL must be between 00h and 99h. When AAM is executed, the product is adjusted to BCD digits, the leftmost four bits in AL are transferred to AH, and the leftmost four bits in AL are set to zeros. Thus, AH contains the leftmost digit of the product in ASCII numeric form, and AL contains the rightmost digit. The previous contents of AH are destroyed.

AAM makes no checks for the validity of the data in AX. If the number is invalid, AAM returns invalid digits; no flags are set.

Suppose you have multiplied 9 by 3 and have the product (001Bh or 27 decimal) in AX. AAM adjusts the product to show 0207h in AX. AAM also can be used to convert any value in AL between 00h and 99h into two BCD unpacked digits.

Here is an example of possible use of AAM to print the product of ASCII multiplication:

CONTENTS OF AX

```
MOV AL,09        ;put multiplicand in AL        ?? 09
MOV BL,03        ;put multiplier in BL          -?? 09
MUL BL           ;multiply                      00 1B
AAM              ;adjust product                02 07
ADD AX,3030h     ;make digits printable         32 37
PUSH AX          ;save AX                       32 37
MOV DL,AH        ;move first digit to DL        32 32
CALL DSPCHR      ;display digit (2)
POP DX           ;get second digit into DL      32 37
CALL DSPCHR      ;display it (7)
```

It might be of interest to know that AAM has exactly the same effect as dividing AX by 10 (0Ah) and exchanging the contents of AH and AL. Assume you have multiplied 09 by 09, and the product 81 (51h) is in AL. AH will contain only zeros. If you divide 51h by 10 (0Ah), the quotient in AL is 08 and the remainder in AH is 01. The instruction XCHG AH,AL produces the ASCII values 08 in AH and 01 in AL.

Longer BCD numbers can be multiplied and adjusted through use of loops with indexed addressing.

**AAD (ASCII Adjust before Division).**    Use *AAD* before division to cause the correct ASCII form of the quotient to be generated. The two unpacked ASCII digits of the dividend must be in AX, with the least significant in AL. AAD converts these two digits into a binary number in AL and sets AH to zero. When the division is performed, the remainder will be in AH and the quotient in AL, both in unpacked BCD form. Here is an example dividing 99 by 4 :

CONTENTS OF AX

```
MOV AX,09        ;move dividend (99) to AX      09 09
MOV BL,04        ;move divisor (4) to BL        09 09
AAD              ;adjust for division           00 63
DIV BL           ;divide (quotient = 24
                 ; rem. 3)                      03 18
AAM              ;adjust quotient to BCD        02 04
```

If you wish to adjust the remainder to BCD instead of the quotient, you could insert the instruction MOV AL,AH between the DIV and the AAM instructions. Note that the contents of AH are destroyed when AL is expanded to two bytes by the AAM instruction.

Like AAM, AAD does not perform any validity check on the contents of AX. The programmer is responsible for ensuring that valid BCD data is present when AAM or AAD is executed.

## Decimal Adjustments

Two instructions are available to adjust the results of addition or subtraction of packed BCD numbers. They both require no operands and do their work entirely in the AL register.

***DAA (Decimal Adjust for Addition).***    *DAA* is used to adjust the result of packed decimal addition. It normally follows an ADC instruction in a loop that operates on each byte in the packed BCD number. DAA considers both four-bit numbers in the AL register and the setting of the AF and CF flags. Where adjustment is necessary, 6 is added to either or both of the digits in AL, and the AF and CF flags are set accordingly.

Both the setting of the AF and CF flags by the preceding ADC instruction and the settings by the DAA itself are considered in making the adjustment.

The AF flag indicates a carry from bit 3 to bit 4, that is, a carry out of the rightmost digit. The CF flag indicates a carry out of the leftmost digit of AL. Here are several examples of binary addition and adjustment with DAA:

| FIRST NUMBER | SECOND NUMBER | SUM | FLAGS SET BY ADDITION | ADJUST-MENT | ADJUSTED SUM | FLAGS SET AFTER ADJ. |
|---|---|---|---|---|---|---|
| 23 | 49 | 6C | No | 6 | 72 | AF |
| 56 | 93 | E9 | No | 60 | 49 | CF |
| 99 | 99 | 32 | Both | 66 | 98 | Both |
| 09 | 98 | A1 | AF | 66 | 07 | Both |
| 09 | 09 | 12 | AF | 6 | 18 | AF |

In processing the rightmost digit in AL, 6 is added if the digit is greater than 9 or if the AF flag is already set. If adding 6 to that digit produces a carry, AF is set to 1.

In processing the leftmost digit in AL, 6 is added if that digit is greater than 9 or if the CF flag is already set to 1. The leftmost digit is incremented by 1 if adding 6 to the rightmost digit set AF to 1. Finally, CF is set to 1 if adding 6 to the leftmost digit caused a carry. If CF was already set to 1 before DAA was executed, it remains at 1.

You can create a useful subroutine called ADDDEC by making only one change in the ADDASC subroutine: replace the AAA instruction with DAA.

***DAS (Decimal Adjust for Subtraction).***    *DAS* works on the byte in AL after packed BCD subtraction. It adjusts the value by subtracting 6 from either or both digits in AL. It considers the settings of the AF and CF flags to determine whether to make the adjustment and whether to decrement the leftmost digit in AL to reflect a borrow.

A negative result after adjustment appears in 10s complement form, usually with one or more leading nines in the difference. Here are two examples:

| First number: | 05 52 89 36 | 00 98 76 54 |
|---|---|---|
| Second number: | 04 29 34 65 | 01 00 00 32 |
| Difference: | 01 23 54 71 | 99 98 76 22 |
| Result: | Valid | Invalid; 10s complement |

## PROGRAM 8: ARITHMETIC ON LONG NUMBERS

Our demonstration program for this chapter combines many of the subroutines we have illustrated so far. The DSPLINE subroutine displays two prompts each asking for the operator to enter a decimal number of up to 10 decimal digits. The MULTINDC subroutine receives the two numbers and converts them to five words at N1 and N2, respectively. Then DSPLINE displays column headings for decimal and hexadecimal results.

MULTIADD adds N1 and N2, storing the results at SUM. MULTISUB gets the difference between N1 and N2 and stores it at DIFF. Since no routines handle multiword negative numbers, the smaller of N1 or N2 is subtracted from the larger. MULTIMUL multiplies N1 by N2 and stores the result at PRODUCT. After each calculation, DSPLINE displays a message indicating the name of the result, and an internal subroutine DSPNBR displays the result in decimal and then in hex. After the last calculation, DSPLINE asks if the operator wishes to continue. INPCHR gets the response. The program continues until the response is 'N' or 'n'. Figure 8-8 shows program 8.

This program is typical of longer programs in that it makes extensive use of subroutines. We can simplify our programming and make it more accurate by making our subroutines external, assembling them separately, and linking the object modules to that of the main program.

Each subroutine demonstrated in this chapter is shown as an external subroutine. It is a procedure within a code segment. The name of the procedure is designated as PUBLIC. The subroutine is assembled separately, and its object module with filename extension of .OBJ is stored on the program disk. The simplest way to have DOS do this is to use a command line with the MASM statement. The general MASM command line format is:

```
MASM [options] sourcefile [,[objectfile] [,[listfile] [,
[crossreffile]]]] [;]
```

To create an object file and listing file for each module use:

```
A> B:
B> A:MASM sourcefile,,;
```

```
        PAGE 50,132
;-------------------------------------------------------------------------------
; Program name:  PROG8.ASM
;
; Author:   Alton R. Kindred
;
; This program reads in two decimal numbers with up to 10 digits each, adds
; them together, gets the difference, and multiplies them together.  Then
; it prints the results in decimal and hex.  It asks if the operator wishes
; to continue and does so until the response is 'N' or 'n'.
;-------------------------------------------------------------------------------
DATA        SEGMENT                     ;segment for data
PROMPT      DB 13,10,'Enter up to 10 decimal digits: $'
STRING      DB 25 DUP (?)
N1          DW 5 DUP (?)
N2          DW 5 DUP (?)
PRODUCT     DW 10 DUP (?)
SUM         DW 5 DUP (?)
DIFF        DW 5 DUP (?)
WORK        DW 5 DUP (?)
SPACE5      DB '     $'
CRLF        DB 13,10,'$'
HEADING     DB 13,10,'
            DB 'Decimal                Hex$'
SUMMSG      DB 13,10,'Sum:         $'
DIFFMSG     DB 13,10,'Difference:  $'
PRODMSG     DB 13,10,'Product:     $'
REQUEST     DB 13,10,'Do you wish to continue (Y/N)? $'
DATA        ENDS
;-------------------------------------------------------------------------------
STACK       SEGMENT STACK               ;stack segment
            DB 32 DUP ('STACK   ')
STACK       ENDS
;-------------------------------------------------------------------------------
CODE        SEGMENT                     ;segment for code
            ASSUME CS:CODE,DS:DATA,SS:STACK
            EXTRN DSPLINE:NEAR,MULTINDC:NEAR,MULTIADD:NEAR
            EXTRN MULTISUB:NEAR,MULTIMUL:NEAR,HEX5DEC:NEAR
            EXTRN INPCHR:NEAR,DSPHEX:NEAR,DSPCHR:NEAR,MULTICMP:NEAR
PROG8       PROC FAR
            MOV AX,DATA                 ;set up data segment in DS
            MOV DS,AX
REPEAT01:                               ;REPEAT
            LEA DX,PROMPT               ;  ask for number
            CALL DSPLINE
            LEA DI,STRING               ;  get in decimal number
            LEA SI,N1
            CALL MULTINDC
            LEA DX,PROMPT               ;  ask for another
            CALL DSPLINE
            LEA DI,STRING               ;  and get another
            LEA SI,N2
            CALL MULTINDC
```

**Figure 8-8    Source Listing of Program 8**

```
            LEA  DX,HEADING        ;  display heading
            CALL DSPLINE
            LEA  SI,N1             ;  add the two numbers
            LEA  DI,N2
            LEA  BX,SUM
            MOV  CX,5
            CALL MULTIADD
            LEA  DX,SUMMSG         ;  display the sum
            CALL DSPLINE
            LEA  SI,SUM
            CALL DSPNBR
            LEA  SI,N1+8           ;  find the larger number
            LEA  DI,N2+8
            MOV  CX,5
            CALL MULTICMP
IF01:       JL   ELSE01           ;  IF N1 > N2
THEN01:     LEA  SI,N1            ;     THEN subtract N2 from N1
            LEA  DI,N2
            JMP  ENDIF01
ELSE01:     LEA  SI,N2            ;  ELSE subtract N1 from N2
            LEA  DI,N1
ENDIF01:                         ;  ENDIF
            LEA  BX,DIFF
            MOV  CX,5
            CALL MULTISUB
            LEA  DX,DIFFMSG       ;  display the difference
            CALL DSPLINE
            LEA  SI,DIFF
            CALL DSPNBR
            LEA  SI,N1           ;  get the product
            LEA  DI,N2
            LEA  BX,PRODUCT
            CALL MULTIMUL
            LEA  DX,PRODMSG       ;  display the product
            CALL DSPLINE
            LEA  SI,PRODUCT
            CALL DSPNBR
            LEA  DX,REQUEST       ;  ask whether to continue
            CALL DSPLINE
            CALL INPCHR          ;  get response
            OR   AL,20h          ;  make response lowercase
            CMP  AL,'n'
            JE   UNTIL01
            JMP  REPEAT01
UNTIL01:                         ;UNTIL response = 'N' or 'n'
            MOV  AX,4C00h        ;return to DOS
            INT  21h
PROG8       ENDP                 ;end of procedure declaration
;----------------------------------------------------------------------
;                         DSPNBR Subroutine
;----------------------------------------------------------------------
; This subroutine displays a five-word number as a 25-digit decimal string,
; displays five spaces, and then displays the number as 20 hex digits.
```

**Figure 8-8**    *continued*

```
; At entry:   SI contains the address of the leftmost byte of the number.
;             All registers used are destroyed.
DSPNBR      PROC NEAR
            PUSH SI                     ;save address of number
            LEA DI,WORK                 ;set address of work area
            MOV CX,5                    ;set word counter to 5
REPEAT11:                               ;REPEAT
            MOV AX,[SI]                 ;   move word to work area
            MOV [DI],AX
            ADD SI,2                    ;   adjust word addresses
            ADD DI,2
            LOOP REPEAT11               ;   subtract 1 from word counter
UNTIL11:                                ;UNTIL word counter = 0
            LEA SI,WORK                 ;set LSW address of number
            LEA DI,STRING               ;set address of string
            CALL HEX5DEC                ;convert to string
            LEA SI,STRING               ;set string address
            MOV CX,25                   ;set byte count to 25
REPEAT12:                               ;REPEAT
            MOV DL,[SI]                 ;   display byte
            CALL DSPCHR
            INC SI                      ;   adjust byte address
            LOOP REPEAT12               ;   subtract 1 from byte count
UNTIL12:                                ;UNTIL byte count = 0
            LEA DX,SPACE5               ;display 5 spaces
            CALL DSPLINE
            POP SI                      ;restore address of number
            ADD SI,8                    ;set address to LSW of number
            MOV CX,5                    ;set word counter to 5
REPEAT13:                               ;REPEAT
            MOV DX,[SI]                 ;   move word to DX
            PUSH CX                     ;   save word counter
            MOV CX,4                    ;   display 4 hex digits
            CALL DSPHEX
            SUB SI,2                    ;   adjust address to next word
            POP CX                      ;   restore word counter
            LOOP REPEAT13               ;   subtract 1 from word counter
UNTIL13:                                ;UNTIL word counter = 0
            RET                         ;return
DSPNBR      ENDP
;------------------------------------------------------------------------
CODE        ENDS                        ;end of segment code declaration
            END PROG8                   ;end of program
```

**Figure 8-8**    *concluded*

where *sourcefile* is the name of the subroutine to be assembled. MASM looks for the ASM version of the source program and creates an OBJ version and ꞁ LST listing version with the same name, both on drive B. No CRF file is created. To create only the OBJ object module and no LST file, use:

```
B> A:MASM sourcefile,;
```

The subroutines may be combined with the main program by using a command line with the LINK statement as described in Chapter 6. However, it is more practical to add these subroutines to the subroutine library ASSEM.LIB that was created in Chapter 6, under the heading Creating an Object File Library. To do so, use the LIB utility program. The command line format is:

```
LIB oldlibrary [/PAGESIZE:number] [commands][,[listfile]
[,[newlibrary]]][;]
```

Since ASSEM.LIB already exists, we can add the new subroutines to it by writing these statements:

```
B> A:LIB ASSEM + MULTIADD + MULTISUB + MULTICMP +
   MULTIMUL, ASSEM.LST;
B> A:LIB ASSEM + HEX5DEC + MULTINHX + MULTINDC +
ADDASC,           ASSEM.LST;
```

The new updated file is named ASSEM.LIB, and the original created file is given the name ASSEM.BAK (for backup). The listing file is ASSEM.LST.

Where too many modules are named to fit on a single line, the command line can be extended by placing an ampersand (&) after the last module named on the line. LIB then will issue a prompt asking for the name of the remaining modules to be placed into the library. Or, as was done in this case, additional command lines can be given until all modules have been added to the library.

Any module that calls another module should be placed in the library ahead of the module it calls. Failure to do so will cause LINK to issue a fixup overflow message.

Figure 8-9 shows sample output from program 8.

## SUMMARY

To perform addition or subtraction on numbers longer than one word, we normally use a loop working on one pair of words at a time. Starting with the least significant words, we first clear the carry flag with the CLC instruction and then include the ADC (add carry) or the SBB (subtract borrow) instruction within a loop to add or subtract the successive words. CX normally is used as a counter for the number of words to be added or subtracted.

To compare two numbers having multiple words, compare first the most significant words of the pair. If the words are equal, then compare the next least significant words. Continue until a difference is found or the last words of the pair are found to be the same. Follow the compare routine with a conditional branch as usual.

A general routine is provided that multiplies two five-word numbers together and produces a 10-word product. The product is first cleared to zeros. Then the first word of the first number is multiplied in turn by each of the words in the second number, and the partial products are added, with

```
B>prog8

Enter up to 10 decimal digits: 98765432
Enter up to 10 decimal digits: 48509
                                Decimal                    Hex
Sum:                           98813941        00000000000005E3C7F5
Difference:                    98716923        00000000000005E24CFB
Product:                  4791012340888        00000000045B7E97B498
Do you wish to continue (Y/N)? y
Enter up to 10 decimal digits: 17
Enter up to 10 decimal digits: 55
                                Decimal                    Hex
Sum:                                72        00000000000000000048
Difference:                         38        00000000000000000026
Product:                           935        000000000000000003A7
Do you wish to continue (Y/N)? n
B>
```

**Output from Program 8**

carry, if any, into the product area. The process is repeated with each word of the first number until all partial products have been added.

Special subroutines are necessary to display large numbers in hex or decimal form. To display in decimal, each word of the number must be divided by 10 and the quotient saved. The remainder from the final division by 10 becomes the last (rightmost) digit to be displayed. Then the new quotient is divided by 10 and the next digit saved. The process continues until the quotient is zero. Digits then must be displayed in last-in, first-out order.

To display large hex numbers, each word can be displayed as four digits using the DSPHEX subroutine. The display must begin with the most significant word of the number.

Inputting large numbers as hex digits requires the MULTINHX subroutine. Each hex digit as it is entered must be verified as a valid hex digit. Then the hex character is converted to a one-word hex value and pushed on the stack. Words are counted until <ENTER> is pressed. Retrieve words from the stack and store them as a string of one-byte digits, with last-in as last-out, and padding with leading zeros, making a total of 20 digits. Retrieving the digits from left to right, add each digit into a word, and shift left in groups of four, converting each group of four digits into a hex word.

To enter large numbers as decimal digits, verify that each key contains a value between '0' and '9'. Convert it to a numeric value between 0 and 9 and push onto the stack. Continue until <ENTER> is pressed, counting the number of digits entered. Retrieve digits from the stack and put them into a string, working from the last byte downward and filling leading bytes with zeros. Then, multiply the five words by 10 and add the most significant digit. Continue this process 25 times, adding in the next least significant digit each time.

Two instructions are provided to double the length of signed numbers. The CBW instruction converts a byte in AL into a word in AX by copying the leftmost sign bit of AL into all bits of AH. The CWD instruction converts a word in AX into a doubleword with the leftmost sign bit in AX copied into all bits of DX.

Binary-coded decimal data may be unpacked or packed. Unpacked BCD data has one decimal digit in the rightmost four bits of a byte, and the leftmost four bits are always zeros. Packed BCD data has two decimal digits per byte, one in the leftmost four bits and another in the rightmost four bits. The programmer is responsible for correctly defining BCD data.

The DT (define tenword) directive may define a maximum of eighteen digits in the rightmost nine bytes of a 10-byte number. The leftmost byte contains the sign, 00h for positive and 80h for negative.

Four instructions are provided to adjust the results of arithmetic operations on unpacked BCD data. AAA (ASCII adjust for addition) is used after an ADD or ADC instruction. The AL and AH registers correctly reflect the results of unpacked addition. AAS (ASCII adjust for subtraction) adjusts the result of subtraction of unpacked BCD data in the AL and AH registers. AAM (ASCII adjust for multiplication) adjusts the multiplication of two ASCII digits into two unpacked digits, using only AL and AH registers. The AAD (ASCII adjust after division) is used before division to cause the correct ASCII form of the quotient to be generated. The most significant ASCII digit of the dividend must be in AH and the least significant digit in AL when this instruction is executed.

Two instructions adjust the result of packed decimal arithmetic. DAA (decimal adjust for addition) is used after an ADD or ADC instruction on packed BCD data. The contents of AL are adjusted and the AF and CF flags are set accordingly. The DAS (decimal adjust for subtraction) adjusts the byte in AL after packed BCD subtraction.

Subroutines may be written separately from the main program, assembled separately, and then have the object module linked with any other desired object module. This technique saves storage space for object modules on the disk, and saves time in that the subroutine needs to be assembled only once instead of every time it is used. The subroutine name must be declared with the PUBLIC statement in the subroutine to inform the linker program that special treatment is required. In the main program that calls the subroutine, the subroutine name must be declared in an EXTRN (external) statement.

Separately assembled subroutines may be linked to main modules in either of two ways. Each object module may be named in the LINK statement, with a space or plus sign separating the module names. The first module named becomes the name of the loan module. Or the separately assembled subroutines may be placed in a library from which LINK will extract those modules named in EXTRN statements. The LIB DOS program handles the creation and management of libraries of object modules. The fourth operand in the LINK statement names the library to be searched for any external modules.

## QUESTIONS

1.  Explain the use of the carry flag when addition is done on numbers containing more than one word.
2.  What is normally the position of the most significant word in numbers containing more than one word?
3.  How may the carry flag be saved so that it can be used with an ADC (add carry) instruction when other instructions within a loop also may set the carry flag?
4.  When is the carry flag set on a subtract instruction? What is it called in this instance?
5.  How does comparison of multiword numbers differ from addition or subtraction of multiword numbers?
6.  Explain the algorithm used in the MULTIMUL subroutine that permits two five-word numbers to be multiplied to produce a 10-word product.
7.  Describe the process by which a hex number may be displayed in decimal by repeatedly dividing the number by 10 and displaying the remainder.
8.  Explain how the DSPHEX subroutine may be used to display multiword numbers in hex form.
9.  Describe how the MULTINHX subroutine takes the hex digits entered and builds them into a 20-byte string containing leading zeros, if necessary.
10. How many decimal digits does it require to display a hex number containing five words? What is the largest hex number that can be contained in five words? What is its decimal equivalent?
11. How is the sign bit treated when the CBW instruction extends a byte into a word, or the CWD instruction extends a word into a doubleword?
12. Explain the difference between unpacked and packed BCD data. What other names are commonly used for each type of BCD numbers?
13. How is a subroutine defined in order to be assembled separately from a program that calls it? How must it be defined in the program that calls it?
14. Describe the steps to place a subroutine into a library and then tell the LINK program to link this subroutine into a desired load module.

## EXERCISES

1.  Write an external subroutine to add two multiword numbers. CX designates the number of words. Use MULTIADD subroutine as a model. Then write the necessary instructions in a main module to call the subroutine to add a 10-word number called N2 to a 10-word number called N1.
2.  Write an external subroutine to subtract two multiword numbers, with CX indicating the number of words. Then write the necessary instructions in a main

module to subtract a four-word number called N2 from a four-word number called N1.

3. Write instructions in a main module to use the MULTICMP subroutine to compare two six-word numbers called X1 and X2. If the numbers are equal, execute instructions at THEN; if X1 is larger, execute instructions at THEN2; if X2 is larger, execute instructions at ELSE2.

4. Write a tabulation showing partial products and final product of the steps in multiplying the number 30972 by the number 54321.

5. Write instructions in a main module to use the HEX5DEC to convert a five-word hex number into a 25-byte decimal string but display only the rightmost eight bytes of the string.

6. Write a loop that calls the DSPHEX subroutine to display a six-word number as 24 hex digits.

7. Write instructions to move the value 128 decimal to AL and then move the proper value to AH so that AX contains the value 128. Then do the same thing using MOV and CBW instructions.

8. Write DB directives to define the unpacked BCD numbers 76543 and 54321. Write a loop to add them together and adjust the sum to a correct unpacked BCD number.

9. Write instructions to divide the unpacked BCD number 85 by 7 and adjust the quotient to correct BCD form. Show the contents of AX following execution of each instruction.

10. Write necessary DOS statements to link the MULTIADD and MULTINDC subroutines to a main module named PROG8.

11. Write necessary DOS statements to create a library named SUBR.LIB, put MULTIADD and MULTINDC subroutines into the library, and then provide LINK with the name of the library from which to extract the subroutines and link them to PROG8.

## LAB PROBLEMS

1. Write a program that uses MULTINHX subroutine to enter one five-word number and MULTINDC to enter another. Then display each number side by side in hex and decimal form. Repeat for five pairs of numbers.

2. Write a program that accepts two decimal numbers up to 25 digits, converts the digits to unpacked BCD form, adds the two numbers together, and displays both numbers and their sum on three successive lines as decimal characters.

# STRING INSTRUCTIONS

# 9

## OBJECTIVES

After studying this chapter, you should be able to:

- Describe byte strings and word strings.
- Explain use of the direction flag in instructions that handle strings.
- Explain and illustrate the use of the REP prefixes with string handling instructions.
- Explain the uses of specific registers with the string handling instructions.
- Explain the use of the LODS instruction with bytes or words of a string.
- Describe the use of the PTR instruction to clarify the size of the string operand.
- Explain operation of the STOS instruction.
- Describe use of the SCAS instruction in searching strings for specific values.
- Describe operation of the MOVS instruction and explain how it differs from other string handling instructions.
- Describe operation of the CMPS instruction in comparing two strings.

## BYTE AND WORD STRINGS

The term *string* normally refers to an array or series of bytes. The 8088 and related chips provide a group of instructions for handling not only strings of bytes, but also strings of words. There are five powerful machine language instructions to manipulate strings: LODS (load string), STOS (store string), SCAS (scan string), MOVS (Move string), and CMPS (compare string). Each of these instructions performs several different operations and can be used to create loops to handle each of the bytes or words in a string automatically.

All of these string instructions use either the SI or DI register, or both, and automatically increment or decrement the register after the operation takes place. They therefore combine the execute and modify portions of a loop into a single instruction. As we will see, a single instruction can make a complete loop after the appropriate registers have been initialized.

Before considering each of these instructions separately, let us consider certain factors that relate to all of these instructions.

### DF Direction Flag

The DF (direction flag) determines whether strings are to be processed in ascending order or descending order of addresses. If strings are to be processed from the lowest address of the string to the highest, you must clear the direction flag (set it to zero) before performing the string instruction. Use the CLD (clear direction flag) instruction for this purpose.

If the string is to be processed from the highest address to the lowest, set the direction flag to 1 before the string instruction is executed. Use the STD (set direction flag) instruction to set this flag on.

Most strings are processed in order of ascending address, and you would use the CLD instruction to set the direction flag off.

### The REP (Repeat) Prefixes

Each of the string instructions is different from other instructions in that it can be repeated automatically. Place a number in CX to specify the number of times the operation is to be repeated. For example, the code:

```
MOV CX,100
REP MOVS
```

causes the MOVS instruction to be repeated 100 times. (Other parameters are actually needed.) The following sections will explain the detailed operation of each of the instructions.

*REP* has other forms of prefixes that are conditional on the setting of the zero flag. *REPE* (repeat if equal) and *REPZ* (repeat if zero) are identical and repeat if the zero flag indicates a zero result. *REPNE* and *REPNZ* (repeat if not equal/zero) repeats if the zero flag indicates a nonzero result.

Table 9-1 shows a summary of string instructions with the variations of REP and the register pairs used with each.

## THE STRING INSTRUCTIONS

The five string handling instructions are among the most powerful in the 8088 repertory. With their automatic modification of the SI and DI registers, and of CX when used with the REP option, single instructions provide the power of many subroutines in moving, scanning, and comparing strings of bytes and words.

The following sections give detailed explanations and examples of the LODS (load string), STOS (store string), SCAS (scan string), MOVS (move string), and CMPS (compare string) instructions.

Table 9-1
String Instruction Summary

| Instruction | Repeat Prefix | Source/Destination | Register Pair |
|---|---|---|---|
| LODS | None | Source | DS:SI |
| STOS | REP | Destination | ES:DI |
| SCAS | REPE/REPNE | Destination | ES:DI |
| MOVS | REP | Both | DS:SI, ES:DI |
| CMPS | REPE/REPNE | Both | DS:SI, ES:DI |
| INS | REP | Destination | ES:DI |
| OUTS | REP | Source | DS:SI |

## The LODS (Load String) Instruction

Like the other string instructions, *LODS* has two forms. *LODSB* operates on bytes and *LODSW* on words. Before LODSB is executed, you must place the address of the first byte of the string in the SI register. Each time LODSB is executed, the byte pointed to by SI is placed in AL, and SI is incremented or decremented by 1. As mentioned previously, the DF (direction flag) determines what adjustment is made to SI: incrementing if the flag is cleared (off or zero) and decrementing if the flag is set (on or 1). The CLD or STD instruction sets the direction flag off or on.

LODSW moves the word pointed to by SI to the AX register and adjusts SI to point to the next word by incrementing or decrementing SI by 2. DF determines whether SI is incremented of decremented.

The code below is equivalent to LODSB and LODSW when the direction flag is cleared:

```
LODSB = MOV AL,[SI]       LODSW = MOV AX,[SI]
        INC SI                    INC SI
                                  INC SI
```

There are no good reasons to use the REP prefix with the LODS instructions, since the effect would be simply to put one byte or word after another into AL or AX. Usually, the byte or word must be moved somewhere else or used in another instruction. The following sequence of instructions can be used to display a string of characters, including the carriage return and line feed, on the screen. Note that the string is terminated by a byte containing hex zeros.

```
PROMPT      DB 'This is any message to be displayed',13,10,0
            .
            LEA SI,PROMPT               ;load address of first byte
            CLD                         ;clear direction flag
            LODSB                       ;put one byte into AL
WHILE01:    CMP AL,0                    ;WHILE byte is not 0
```

```
                    JE WENDO1
                    MOV DL,AL                    ; transfer byte to DL for
                                                 ; output
                    CALL DSPCHR                  ; display byte
                    LODSB                        ; put next byte into AL
                    JMP WHILE01
WENDO1:                                          ;WEND
```

### The STOS (Store String) Instruction

The *STOS instruction* is the opposite of LODS — it takes the byte or word in AL or AX, stores it at the address specified by ES:DI, and adjusts the address in DI.

*STOSB* is used with byte strings and *STOSW* with word strings. The direction flag determines whether DI is incremented or decremented. Note that ES rather than DS always must be the segment register used with DI. In each of the following examples we assume that ES has the same address as DS. Immediate data and segment registers cannot be moved to segment registers. ES can be made equal to CS in this way at the start of the program:

```
          MOV AX,DATA
          MOV DS,AX
          MOV ES,AX
```

The following instructions move 80 hyphens to a byte string named HYPHENS:

```
          CLD                       ;clear direction flag
          MOV AL, '-'               ;move hyphen to AL
          MOV CX,80                 ;set counter to 80
          LEA DI,HYPHENS            ;set address of string
          REP STOSB                 ;move hyphens to string
```

The last instruction REP STOSB is actually repeated 80 times. It not only increments DI after moving the byte from AL to [DI] but also decrements CX. If you execute this segment of code one instruction at a time through DEBUG, you can see the change in the registers.

To set a string of 50 words at TABLE to values of 0, use:

```
          CLD                       ;clear direction flag
          MOV AX,0                  ;move zero to AX
          MOV CX,50                 ;set counter to 50
          LEA DI,TABLE              ;set address of TABLE
          REP STOSW                 ;move 50 words
```

The STOS instruction itself does not take an operand. If STOSB is used, the operand is presumed to be a byte; for STOSW, it is presumed to be a word. The PTR instruction also may be used with any of the string instructions to specify whether the operand is a byte or word, as in the following examples:

```
          LODS BYTE PTR DS:SI is equivalent to LODSB
```

```
        STOS WORD PTR ES:DI is equivalent to STOSW
```

Instead of using STOSB or STOSW (or any of the other specific string instructions) you may use the form

```
        STOS operand
```

where *operand* gives the name of the string. In the preceding examples, STOS HYPHENS would cause the assembler to produce a STOSB instruction, and STOS TABLE would produce a STOSW instruction.

## The SCAS (Scan String) Instruction

The *SCAS instruction* searches a string for a specific byte or word. ES:DI must always be used to address the string.

*SCASB* reads the byte at ES:DI and compares it with the byte in AL, and adjusts DI to the next byte, depending on the setting of the direction flag. *SCASW* reads the word at ES:DI and compares it with the word in AX and adjusts DI according to the setting of DF. DI is adjusted by 1 with SCASB and by 2 with SCASW.

SCAS often is used with REPE to continue the scan as long as the byte in the string is equal to that in the accumulator, or with REPNE to continue while not equal. It is important to note that the address in DI will be that of the byte or word following the one for which the scan was searching. The following routine finds the first word in a string of 100 words that contains a 0 value:

```
            CLD                 ;clear direction flag
            MOV CX,100          ;set counter for 100
            MOV AX,0            ;set accumulator to 0
            LEA DI,WORDS        ;set address of string of
                                ;words
            REPNE SCASW         ;scan while not equal to 0
IF01:       JCXZ ELSE01         ;IF zero word found
THEN01:     SUB DI,2            ; THEN back up to that word
            .                   ; process the zero word
            JMP END1F01
ELSE01:     .                   ;ELSE all words were nonzeros
END1F01:                        ;ENDIF
```

The SCAS instruction also can be used to scan a string for some special character, such as a comma, that indicates a delimiter or separator between fields or words in a character string. If INPUT is a buffer containing a string of characters entered from the keyboard and we wish to determine the number of characters before the first comma, this routine might be used:

```
            CLD                 ;clear direction flag
            LEA DI,INPUT+2      ;set address of string buffer
            MOV CL,INPUT+1      ;set number of characters
                                ;entered
            XOR CH,CH           ;convert byte in CL to word
                                ;in CX
```

```
              MOV AL, ','                  ;put comma in AL
              REPNE SCASB                  ;scan until comma found in
string
IF01:         JCXZ ELSE01                  ;IF comma is found
THEN01:       DEC DI                       ; THEN back DI up one byte
              .                            ; process the string
              JMP ENDIF01
ELSE01:       .                            ;ELSE no comma was present
ENDIF01:                                   ;ENDIF
```

## The MOVS (Move String) Instruction

The MOVS and CMPS instructions are among the very few that operate on two operands in main storage. *MOVS* is used to move a string of bytes or words from one memory location to another. *MOVSB* moves bytes and *MOVSW* moves words.

MOVSB moves a byte from the address contained in DS:SI to the address pointed to by ES:DI. Then both SI and DI are adjusted to point to the next byte. The setting of DF determines whether SI and DI are incremented or decremented. If DS is clear, they are incremented; if DF is set, they are decremented.

MOVSW works exactly like MOVSB except that a word instead of a byte is moved and the addresses in SI and DI are adjusted by 2 instead of by 1. Any segment override may be used for CS in pointing to the source string, but ES always must be used as the segment register with DI for the destination string.

MOVS may be used with the REP prefix to move long strings from one location to another. CX must contain the number of times the instruction is to be repeated. If you have two strings of 512 bytes called OLD and NEW, you can move OLD to NEW with this routine:

```
        CLD                     ;clear direction flag
        LEA SI,OLD              ;set source address
        LEA DI,NEW              ;set destination address
        MOV CX,512              ;set count to 512
        REP MOVSB               ;move 512 bytes
```

As an alternative to using MOVSB, you can use the format

```
MOVS destination,source
```

where *destination* and *source* must be the names of the two string areas. The last statement in the program segment above could be written as:

```
REP MOVS NEW,OLD
```

Both strings must be defined alike as either bytes or words. The assembler will generate MOVSB or MOVSW according to the way destination and source are defined.

If no operand is present so that the assembler can determine whether to move a byte or a word, you may use the PTR instruction. Its format is:

```
MOVS size PTR [DI],size PTR segment-register :[SI]
```

where *size* is either byte or word and *segment-register* may be CS, DS, ES, or SS. If size is not specified, the assembler assumes MOVSB. Recall that the segment register must be ES for the destination.

## The CMPS (Compare String) Instruction

The *CMPS instruction* compares two strings. As with other string instructions, *CMPSB* compares bytes and *CMPSW* compares words. CMPSB compares the byte pointed to by ES:DI with the byte pointed to by DS:SI and adjusts SI and DI to the next byte. DS:SI refers to the first operand and ES:DI to the second. If DF is clear, SI and DI are incremented; if DF is set, they are decremented.

CMPSW compares the words pointed to by ES:DI and DS:SI respectively and then adjusts SI and DI by 2. If DF is clear, SI and DI have 2 added; if DF is set, SI and DI have 2 subtracted.

Note that ES must be used with DI, but that a segment override may be made with the segment register used with SI.

The REPE or REPNE prefixes may be used with CMPS to continue comparison as long as the strings are equal or not equal. CX must contain the number of bytes or words to be compared. CMPS differs from SCAS in that any difference between the two strings will be recognized, while SCAS is looking only for one particular byte or word to match the one in the accumulator.

The following routine compares two 50-byte strings until it finds one byte different from its corresponding byte in the other string. After CMPS, SI and DI will point to the word after they differ.

```
CLD                          ;clear direction flag
MOV CX,50                    ;set counter to 50
LEA SI,STRING1               ;set address of first
                             ;string
LEA DI,STRING2               ;set address of second string
REPE CMPSB                   ;compare until byte is
                             ;different
```

Rather than using CMPSB or CMPSW, we can use the format

```
CMPS operandl,operand2
```

where *operand1* is the string pointed to by DS:SI and *operand2* is the string pointed to by ES:DI. The assembler will determine from how operandl and operand2 are defined whether to use CMPSB or CMPSW.

One special precaution must be taken when using a REP prefix and a segment override with a string instruction. The REP will not be completed if an interrupt occurs while such an instruction is being executed. Two things must be done to overcome this problem: (a) CX must be zero when the

REPeated instruction is completed, and (b) interrupts must be disabled while the string instruction is being executed and enabled afterwards.

## PROGRAM 9: BUBBLE SORT WITH STRING INSTRUCTIONS

Program 9 demonstrates a common *bubble sort technique*, using most of the string instructions covered in this chapter. Sometimes called an *exchange sort*, the bubble sort gets its name from the fact that numbers, or strings, in an array tend to move toward the end ("bubble up") as the items are compared.

The bubble sort involves comparing the first and second strings in an array, exchanging them if they are not in sequence, and continuing with the second and third strings until all adjacent pairs have been compared. This operation is called one *pass*.

Several options are possible with the bubble sort. One is to continue to make passes until no strings have to be exchanged. Then they are all in sequence. A second option is to reduce the number of pairs compared each pass until the final pass compares only one pair of strings.

Our technique counts the number of strings entered at the keyboard and put into the array. If we call this number *n*, then there will be a maximum of n-1 passes, with n-1 comparisons on the first pass. Each pass we reduce the number of comparisons by 1. We stop when the number of comparisons left is 0 or when a pass is made that requires no exchanges.

Program 9 makes use of a main module that is primarily a control module that calls six subroutines to perform the detail operations. The subroutines are internal, that is, included with and assembled with the main module. Four external subroutines, DSPLINE, DSPCHR, INPLINE, and IN-PCHR, are linked to program 9 from a subroutine library.

Figure 9-1 shows program 9. The data segment includes several prompts, each with its own line feeds and cursor returns. BUFFER is an area to hold a string of up to 20 characters input from the keyboard. One thousand bytes are provided in STRINGS to hold up to 50 strings of 20 bytes each. SAVESTR is a 20-byte area used in exchanging strings in the sorting process. SWAPFLAG is a switch that is set ON whenever an exchange is made during the sorting. If this flag remains OFF at the end of one pass, the sort is completed. Five words are provided to hold various counts and addresses needed during the program.

CLSTRNG subroutine uses the STOSB string instruction to move 1020 spaces into STRINGS and SAVESTR to blank out these string areas. CLRWORDS uses STOSW to move zeros to each of the five words in the data segment. MOVSTRNG determines the length of the string entered at the keyboard from BUFFER+1 and uses the MOVSB instruction to move that many bytes to the proper address in STRINGS specified by ES:DI. MOVSTRNG also increments STRNGCNT to count the number of strings entered and placed in the array.

```
        PAGE 50,132
;--------------------------------------------------------------------------
; Program name:  PROG9.ASM
;
; Author:   Alton R. Kindred
;
; This program uses string instructions to read in up to 50 20-byte strings,
; sort the strings into ascending sequence, and display the sorted strings on
; the screen.
; It makes extensive use of internal subroutines.
;--------------------------------------------------------------------------
DATA        SEGMENT                         ;segment for data
PROMPT1     DB 13,10,'Enter up to 50 20-byte strings'
            DB 13,10,'Press ENTER after each'
            DB 13,10,'Press ENTER alone to stop',13,10,'$'
PROMPT2     DB 13,10,'Do you wish to continue? (Y/N) $'
CRLF        DB 13,10,'$'
HEADING     DB 13,10,10,'           SORTED STRINGS',13,10,10,'$'
BUFFER      DB 20,?,20 DUP (?)
STRINGS     DB 1000 DUP (?)
SAVESTR     DB 20 DUP (?)
SWAPFLAG    DB ?
STRNGCNT    DW ?
PASSCNT     DW ?
COMPCNT     DW ?
STR1ADR     DW ?
STR2ADR     DW ?
DATA        ENDS
;--------------------------------------------------------------------------
STACK       SEGMENT STACK                   ;stack segment
            DB 32 DUP ('STACK   ')
STACK       ENDS
;--------------------------------------------------------------------------
CODE        SEGMENT                         ;segment for code
            ASSUME CS:CODE,DS:DATA,SS:STACK,ES:DATA
            EXTRN DSPLINE:NEAR,INPCHR:NEAR,INPLINE:NEAR,DSPCHR:NEAR
PROG9       PROC FAR                        ;for proper return to DOS
            MOV AX,DATA                     ;set up data segment in DS
            MOV DS,AX
            MOV ES,AX                        ;and in ES
REPEAT01:                                    ;REPEAT
            CALL CLRSTRNG                   ;   clear string area
            CALL CLRWORDS                   ;   set words to zero
            LEA DX,PROMPT1                  ;   issue prompt to enter strings
            CALL DSPLINE
            LEA DX,BUFFER                   ;   set buffer address
            CALL INPLINE                    ;   get string from keyboard
            LEA BP,STRINGS                  ;   set array address
WHILE01:    CMP BYTE PTR BUFFER+1,0         ;   WHILE string entered
            JE WEND01
            LEA DX,CRLF                     ;      return carriage and line feed
            CALL DSPLINE
            CALL MOVSTRNG                   ;      move string to array
            LEA DX,BUFFER                   ;      get another string
```

**Figure 9-1    Source Listing of Program 9**

```
                CALL INPLINE
                JMP WHILE01
WEND01:                              ;   WEND
                MOV AX,STRNGCNT      ;   set pass count to string count -1
                DEC AX
                MOV PASSCNT,AX
                MOV SWAPFLAG,'y'     ;   set swap flag ON
WHILE02:        CMP PASSCNT,0        ;   WHILE pass count > 0
                JNG WEND02
AND02:          CMP SWAPFLAG,'n'     ;   AND swap flag <> 'n'
                JE WEND02
                MOV AX,PASSCNT       ;     set compare count to pass count
                MOV COMPCNT,AX
                MOV SWAPFLAG,'n'     ;     set swap flag off
                LEA AX,STRINGS       ;     set address of first string
                MOV STR1ADR,AX
                ADD AX,20            ;     set address of second string
                MOV STR2ADR,AX
WHILE03:        CMP COMPCNT,0        ;       WHILE compare count > 0
                JNG WEND03
IF01:           CALL CMPSTRNG        ;         IF string1 > string2
                JNG ENDIF01
THEN01:         CALL SWAPSTR         ;           THEN exchange strings
ENDIF01:                             ;         ENDIF
                ADD STR1ADR,20       ;         modify string1 address
                ADD STR2ADR,20       ;         modify string2 address
                DEC COMPCNT          ;         subtract 1 from compare count
                JMP WHILE03
WEND03:                              ;       WEND
                DEC PASSCNT          ;       subtract 1 from pass count
                JMP WHILE02
WEND02:                              ;   WEND
                LEA DX,HEADING       ;   display heading for sorted records
                CALL DSPLINE
                CALL DSPSTRNG        ;   display sorted records
                LEA DX,PROMPT2       ;   display prompt whether to continue
                CALL DSPLINE
                CALL INPCHR          ;   get response
                OR AL,20h            ;   convert response to lowercase
                CMP AL,'n'
                JE UNTIL01
                JMP REPEAT01
UNTIL01:                             ;UNTIL response = 'n' or 'N'
                MOV AX,4C00h         ;return to DOS
                INT 21h
PROG9           ENDP                 ;end of main procedure declaration
;----------------------------------------------------------------------
CLRSTRNG        PROC NEAR
                MOV AL,' '           ;move space to accumulator
                LEA DI,STRINGS       ;set string address
                MOV CX,1020          ;set count for 1020 bytes
                REP STOSB            ;clear 1020 bytes
                RET                  ;return
CLRSTRNG        ENDP
;----------------------------------------------------------------------
CLRWORDS        PROC NEAR
                MOV AX,0             ;move zero to accumulator
```

**Figure 9-1**    *continued*

```
                LEA DI,STRNGCNT        ;set address of first word
                MOV CX,5               ;set word count to 5
                REP STOSW              ;move zeros to 5 words
                RET                    ;return
CLRWORDS        ENDP
;--------------------------------------------------------------------
MOVSTRNG        PROC NEAR
                MOV CL,BUFFER+1        ;get string length
                XOR CH,CH              ;make it a word in CX
                LEA SI,BUFFER+2        ;set source address
                MOV DI,BP              ;set destination address
                REP MOVSB              ;move string to array
                ADD BP,20             ;adjust address to next string
                INC STRNGCNT           ;add 1 to string count
                RET                    ;return
MOVSTRNG        ENDP
;--------------------------------------------------------------------
CMPSTRNG        PROC NEAR
                MOV SI,STR1ADR         ;set string1 address
                MOV DI,STR2ADR         ;set string2 address
                MOV CX,20              ;set string length to 20
                REPE CMPSB             ;compare until different
                RET                    ;return
CMPSTRNG        ENDP
;--------------------------------------------------------------------
SWAPSTR         PROC NEAR
                MOV SI,STR1ADR         ;set string1 address
                LEA DI,SAVESTR         ;set save area address
                MOV CX,20              ;set string length
                REP MOVSB              ;move string1 to save area
                MOV SI,STR2ADR         ;set string2 address
                MOV DI,STR1ADR         ;set string1 address
                MOV CX,20              ;set string length
                REP MOVSB              ;move string2 to string1
                LEA SI,SAVESTR         ;set save area address
                MOV DI,STR2ADR         ;set string2 address
                MOV CX,20              ;set string length
                REP MOVSB              ;move save area to string2
                MOV SWAPFLAG,'y'       ;set swap flag on
                RET                    ;return
SWAPSTR         ENDP
;--------------------------------------------------------------------
DSPSTRNG        PROC NEAR
                LEA BP,STRINGS         ;set address of first string
WHILE04:        CMP STRNGCNT,0         ;WHILE string count > 0
                JNG WEND04
                MOV SI,BP              ;  put string address in SI
                MOV CX,20              ;  set count for 20 bytes
WHILE05:        JCXZ WEND05            ;  WHILE byte count > 0
                LODSB                  ;    load byte into AL
                MOV DL,AL              ;    transfer byte to DL
                CALL DSPCHR            ;    display the byte
                DEC CX                 ;    subtract 1 from byte count
                JMP WHILE05
WEND05:                                ;  WEND
                ADD BP,20              ;  set address to next string
                DEC STRNGCNT           ;  subtract 1 from string count
```

**Figure 9-1**   *continued*

```
          LEA  DX,CRLF                ;   return cursor and line feed
          CALL DSPLINE
          JMP  WHILE04
WEND04:                               ;WEND
          RET                         ;return
DSPSTRNG  ENDP
;-----------------------------------------------------------------------
CODE      ENDS                        ;end of code segment declaration
          END  PROG9                  ;end of program
```

**Figure 9-1**    *concluded*

CMPSTRNG uses the CMPSB string instruction to compare the full 20 bytes (including trailing spaces) of the adjacent strings in the STRINGS array. Note that upon return from CMPSTRNG a regular conditional branch can be made to determine whether an exchange of strings is necessary. SWAPSTR uses the MOVSB string instruction three times whenever two adjacent strings need to be exchanged. The first string is moved to a save area, the second string is moved to the first, and the save area is moved to the second string. SWAPSTR also sets SWAPFLAG ON to indicate that an exchange was made.

The last internal subroutine, DSPSTRNG, is a loop that sets the address of the first string in STRINGS, uses a LODSB instruction to transfer each byte of the string to AL, where it is moved to DL to be displayed by the DSPCHR external subroutine. BP is used to contain the address of each string, and is incremented by 20 in each loop until each string has been displayed.

We will note that it is not possible to add directly to SI or DI to modify the address of the next string. SI and DI are incremented as the string instructions are executed. We therefore use address fields in main storage to keep track of the strings we are working on, and either move those fields into BP or directly to SI or DI as needed.

Figure 9-2 shows output from program 9.

## SUMMARY

The five string-handling instructions (LODS, STOS, SCAS, MOVS, and CMPS) have several similar features. They all refer to the address at DS:SI and/or ES:DI to determine the byte or word in the string to be processed. After performing the operation, SI or DI or both are adjusted to the address of the next byte or word in the string. If the DF (direction flag) is clear, the addresses are incremented; if the flag is set, the addresses are decremented. Each of the instructions may have the letter B or W (that is, LODSB or STOSW) attached to refer to a byte or word. If the operand is a byte, the address adjustment is 1; the operand is a word, the adjustment is 2.

The REP, REPE/REPZ, or REPNE/REPNZ prefix may be used with most of the string-handling instructions. In addition to other operations, the prefix

```
B>prog9

Enter up to 50 20-byte strings
Press ENTER after each
Press ENTER alone to stop
giraffe
raccoon
elephant
alligator
zebra
lion
          SORTED STRINGS
alligator
elephant
giraffe
lion
raccoon
zebra

Do you wish to continue? (Y/N) n

B>
```

**Figure 9-2    Output from Program 9**

causes the CX register to be decremented repeatedly until CX becomes 0 or until the stated condition (equal or not equal, zero or not zero) occurs when scanning or comparing strings.

Instead of using the B or W suffix with the instruction, the PTR instruction can be used with BYTE or WORD to specify the length of the string elements.

The LODS (load string) instruction loads the byte or word addressed by DS:SI into the AL register (if a byte) or the AX register (if a word). Then it adjusts the address in SI. There is no reason to repeat this instruction with the REP prefix, since it would only load one byte or word after another into the accumulator without acting further on them.

The STOS (store string) instruction stores the byte or word in AL or AX into the location specified by ES:DI and then adjusts the address in DI. STOS may be repeated to store the same byte or word into a succession of locations.

The SCAS (scan string) instruction compares the byte or word in AL or AX with the one at the location specified by ES:DI and adjusts the address in DI. Normally it is used with REPE or REPNE to continue comparing so long as the bytes are equal or not equal.

The MOVS (move string) instruction moves one byte or word at the location specified by DS:SI to another location specified by ES:DI and then adjusts both SI and DI. This is one of only two instructions for the 8088 family that operates on two operands in main storage.

The CMPS (compare string) instruction also works on two operands in main storage. It compares the byte or word specified by DS:SI with that specified by ES:DI, sets the condition code, and then adjusts both SI and DI. It is normally used with a form of the REP prefix to continue the comparison until the bytes are alike or different.

## QUESTIONS

1. Define the term *string* as it refers to string instructions in this chapter.
2. Name the common characteristics of the five string instructions described in this chapter.
3. Explain the effect of the DF (direction flag) on execution of the string instructions. What two instructions affect the direction flag?
4. Explain the effect of the REP prefix with string instructions. With which of the instructions is it not effective?
5. Explain operation of the LODS instruction. What determines whether it loads data into AL or AX?
6. Which of the string instructions may be used to put a single byte or word into an entire string?
7. Explain the operation of the SCAS instruction to locate a comma in a string of bytes. What address is in DI when the instruction is completed?
8. What register or registers hold the offset of the operand or operands in string instructions? Which segment registers can be used?
9. What characteristic of the MOVS and CMPS instructions does not apply to any other instructions of the 8088 processor?
10. Explain operation of the MOVS instruction.
11. Explain operation of the CMPS instruction to compare two strings.
12. What register must be initialized and used whenever the REP prefix appears with string instructions? Is it referred to specifically in the instruction?

## EXERCISES

1. Write instructions to move FFFFh to a string of 50 words starting with the last word. Use the STOS instruction.
2. You have just input a string of bytes into an area named BUFFER using the INPLINE subroutine. Write instructions to display each byte on the screen using the LODSB instruction and the DSPCHR subroutine.
3. Write a form of the LODS instruction with PTR that is equivalent to LODSB.
4. Write instructions that will scan an array of 100 words called TABLE and end with the address in ES:DI of the first word that contains all zeros.
5. Write instructions that copy an array of 25 bytes named FIRST into another array named SECOND. Use REP with the MOVSB instruction.
6. Rewrite the MOVSB instruction in exercise 5 to use only MOVS but name the operands to be moved.

7. Rewrite exercise 5 to use the LODSB and STOSB instructions. Do not use REP with either instruction.

8. Write a routine that will compare two strings of 25 bytes named INPUT and OUTPUT and display the first two bytes that differ (if any) and the number of their position within the strings.

## LAB PROBLEMS

1. Write a program in which you reserve space for an array with 10 strings of 25 characters each. Blank out this space. Then issue a prompt to enter up to 10 strings of up to 25 characters in length, key in the strings, and move them to the array, counting the number of strings entered. Then retrieve the strings in reverse order from that in which they were entered and display the strings on the screen. Repeat the operation until the operator responds 'N' or 'n' to a prompt.

2. Write a program in which, responding to a prompt, you enter a four-line name and address. Each line has a maximum of 25 bytes. Enter each line into a separate buffer area that is 80 bytes long and that previously has been set to blanks. Scan the string for the carriage return symbol at the end of the string and change it to a blank. Then copy the string starting at positions 27 and 54 of the buffer area and display the line. Repeat with the four lines of the name and address to display three address labels per line. Leave a blank link between labels. Continue until the operator keys nothing but the <ENTER> key in the name field.

# DISK FILE HANDLING, STRUCTURES, AND RECORDS

# 10

**OBJECTIVES**

After studying this chapter, you should be able to:

- Identify the DOS interrupts that pertain to disk file operations.
- Differentiate between file handling for DOS versions earlier than 2.00 and later than 2.00.
- Differentiate between creating a file and opening it.
- Explain the operation and purpose of closing a file.
- Open an existing disk file, read records from it, process them, and close the file.
- Create a new disk file, write records to it, and close the file.
- Delete or rename a disk file, or determine the free disk space.
- Differentiate between structures and records and create both.

## GENERAL PRINCIPLES OF DISK HANDLING

You have access to disk files through DOS interrupts. With them you are able to create files, open existing files, write records to disk, read them back from the disk into main storage, delete or rename files, determine free disk space, and close files. These are the most common operations with which application programmers are concerned.

Systems programmers and writers of disk drivers will need to refer to the DOS technical manuals, as well as machine manuals for specific disk units, for details about additional functions.

You reserve a buffer area in main storage in which to place data to be written to the disk or to receive data read from the disk. You must open a file before it can be read or written, and close it after use to ensure correct handling of the data and the disk directory.

There are three levels of disk handling available to the programmer:

1. DOS versions starting with 2.00 provide simplified interrupts for opening, creating, closing, reading, writing, deleting, and renaming disk files. With these interrupts, DOS assigns a file handle to each file as you open it, and you refer to the handle in later processing. The handle is a number between 0 and 65535. We cover only these interrupts in this text.

2. DOS version 1.10 required use of *file control blocks* (FCB), 37-byte areas in which you (or DOS) placed information to describe the name and characteristics of the file. The *program segment prefix* (PSP), a 256-byte area created by DOS just in front of any program that is loaded, contained space for two FCBs and a disk transfer area. This method of file handling is still supported by DOS, but it generally has been replaced by the method used by DOS version 2.00 and later versions. We therefore will omit further reference to it in this text.

3. INT 13h is the lowest level of disk access available through DOS. Instead of dealing with files or with sectors relative to the start of the file, this interrupt deals directly with the physical head, track, and sector on which to read or write. Normally this interrupt would be used only by systems programmers, and we will not discuss it further.

## DOS 2.00 AND LATER VERSIONS

Our old friend INT 21h, used previously for input and output to the screen and printer, also will handle disk operations. We place the appropriate hex code in AH and other data as appropriate in other registers before issuing the interrupt.

### Handles

DOS 2.00 and later versions keep track of all files that are open through a system of file handles. A *handle* is a unique number between 0 and 65535 assigned by DOS to each file that is created or opened for processing in a program. Once this is done, you refer to the handle to read, write, or close the file later.

The first five handle numbers are predefined by DOS to refer to standard input/output devices. These files do not have to be opened for use:

0 standard input device (normally the keyboard; can be redirected)
1 standard output device (normally the screen; can be redirected)
2 standard error output device (always the screen)
3 standard auxiliary device (the serial port or modem)
4 standard printer device (printer number 0)

Accordingly, the first file handle assigned to a disk file that you create or open normally will be 5, and each additional file will have the next higher handle number. Generally, DOS limits the number of files that can be open at one time to 15.

## ASCIIZ Strings

DOS 2.00 and later versions accept the filename to be created or opened in the form of a simple string, terminated with an ASCII 0. This is called an *ASCIIZ string*. The drive specifier, directory path, and extension may be included in the string along with the filename, if necessary. No spaces are allowed within the ASCIIZ string.

You may define a file name as an ASCIIZ string within a program as in:

```
FILENAME DB 'B:\MASMDIR\PROG10.ASM',0
```

Since you cannot enter an ASCII 0 directly from the keyboard, you will have to place the ASCII 0 at the end of the string by programming. The following statements indicate how you might input a filename from the keyboard and convert it to an ASCIIZ string:

```
PROMPT     DB 13,10,'Enter filename: $'
BUFFER     DB 20,?,20 DUP(?)
           .
           LEA DX,PROMPT              ;display prompt
           CALL DSPLINE
           LEA DX,BUFFER              ;get filename
           CALL INPLINE
           MOV AL,BUFFER+1            ;get length of filename
           CBW                        ;expand length to word
           MOV DI,AX                  ;put length in DI
           MOV BUFFER+2[DI],0         ;put 0 at end of filename
```

## Error Codes

Many of the disk handling functions return an *error code* if the disk operation is unsuccessful. Following these functions, the carry flag is set if an error has occurred, and AX holds the error code. No carry indicates a successful operation. Table 10-1 shows the possible error codes.

## Function 3Ch, Create a File

To create a new file with INT 21h, put the *function code 3Ch* in AH. DS:DX must point to the ASCIIZ string containing the filename, and CX contains the file attribute. Normally, CX is set to 0, but you may set one or more bits to 1. The meaning of the individual bits is as follows.

bit 0 read only file

Table 10-1.
Error Numbers for File-Handling Functions

1   invalid function number
2   file not found
3   path not found
4   too many files open (no handles available)
5   access denied (general error)
6   invalid handle
7   memory control blocks destroyed
8   insufficient memory
9   invalid memory block address
10  invalidenvironment
11  invalid format
12  invalid access code
13  invalid data
15  invalid drive specified
16  attempted to remove the current directory
17  not same device
18  no more files

bit 1 hidden file
bit 2 system file

DOS uses bit 3 to mark the volume name and bit 4 to specify a subdirectory.

On return from this function, AX holds the handle for the file if the file was created successfully or the error code if the carry flag is set. Possible error codes are 3 (path not found), 4 (too many files open), or 5 (access denied).

**Caution:**    If you use function 3Ch with an existing file, the file length is truncated to zero. This has the effect of wiping out the file in preparation for writing new data to it.

### Function 3Dh, Open a File

To open an existing file, place the *function code 3Dh* in AH and the address of an ASCIIZ string containing the filename in DS:DX. AL must contain the access code:

0 if file is opened for reading
1 if file is opened for writing
2 if file is opened for both reading and writing

If the open is successful, AX will contain the new handle for the file. This handle should be saved for use in further reading, writing, or closing. If the carry flag is set upon return, AX will hold error code 2 (file not found), 4 (too many files open), 5 (access denied), or 12 (invalid access code).

The following routine opens a file for reading. The filename is an ASCIIZ string at BUFFER+2:

```
                LEA DX,BUFFER+2          ;point to filename
                MOV AL,0                 ;set access code for reading
                MOV AH,3Dh               ;open the file
                INT 21h
IF01:           JC ELSE01                ;IF no error
THEN01:         MOV HANDLE,AX            ; THEN save the file handle
                .                        ; instructions to process the
                                         ; file
                JMP END1F01
ELSE01:         .                        ;ELSE error on open
                .                        ; error processing
                                         ; instructions
END1F01:                                 ;ENDIF
```

### Function 3Eh, Close a File

To close a file that has been opened previously, put the *function code 3Eh* into AH and the file handle in BX and call INT 21h. Closing an output file is necessary to write any data still remaining in the buffer. Closing an input file is good practice to avoid overloading DOS. If the carry flag is set after a close operation, AX will contain code 6, for invalid handle. This is the only possible error.

To close the file opened in the preceding section, use:

```
                MOV BX,HANDLE            ;supply file handle
                MOV AX,3Eh              ;close the file
                INT 21h
```

### Function 3Fh, Read from a File

To read from a file that has been created or opened, put the *function code 3Fh* into AH, the handle in BX, the address of the buffer to hold the data in DS:DX, and the number of bytes to be read in CX. If the read is successful, AX holds the number of bytes actually read. If AX is 0, you tried to read past the end of the file. If the carry flag is set, AX contains the error code, most likely 5 (access denied) or 6 (invalid handle).

This function can read from devices other than the disk. For example, if BX contains handle code 0, function 3Fh will read from the keyboard, much like input function 0Ah.

### Function 40H, Write to a File

To write to a disk file, use the same parameters as you do to read. AH contains the *function code 40h*, BX holds the handle, DS:DX contains the address of the output buffer, and CX indicates the number of bytes to write.

If the write is successful, AX will hold the number of bytes actually written. If AX and CX are not equal on return, perhaps because of a full disk, the carry flag is set and AX will hold the error code. Possible error codes are 5 (access denied) and 6 (invalid handle).

If BX contains a handle of 1 (for screen) or 4 (for printer), you can use this function to direct output to a standard output device instead of to the disk.

### Function 41h, Delete a File

To delete a file from the disk directory, put *function code 41h* into AH and the address of the ASCIIZ filename into DS:DX. Only one file per interrupt can be deleted, and wild card characters such as the asterisk (*) and question mark (?) are not allowed in the filename.

If the carry flag is set when the function is complete, AX may contain error code 2 (file not found) or 5 (access denied).

### Function 56h, Rename a File

To change the name of a file using *function code 56h* in AH, DS:DX must point to an ASCIIZ string containing the current name of the file, and ES:DI points to the new name. Both drives must be the same, but a different directory path may be specified for the new name.

Possible error codes returned in AX if the carry flag is set include 3 (path not found), 5 (access denied), and 17 (not same device).

### Function 36h, Get Free Disk Space

To request DOS to furnish the amount of free disk space, put *function code 36h* in AH and the desired drive in DL. Drive codes are 0 for default drive, 1 for drive A, 2 for drive B, and so forth. On return, if the specified drive was invalid, AX holds FFFFh. If the drive was valid, BX holds the number of available clusters, DX the total number of clusters on the disk, CX the number of bytes per sector, and AX the number of sectors per cluster. There are normally 512 bytes per sector and one or two sectors per cluster.

To get the total number of bytes remaining on the disk, multiply BX by AX and the product by CX.

## STRUCTURES AND RECORDS

We previously have discussed and worked with two kinds of data structures: strings and arrays. *Strings* are made up of consecutive bytes or consecutive words. In ordinary computer terminology a string refers only to bytes that are related, such as those making up a name, address, or item description. An *array* is a series of related data elements of the same type, such as group of numbers representing test scores or a group of strings of employee names. Ordinarily an array cannot contain different types of data. A structure where different types of data such as item number, description, quantity, and price are repeated is generally called a *table*.

MASM provides two additional ways of organizing data: structures and records. Both may contain multiple fields. Let us see how these terms in MASM may differ from their use in other contexts.

## Structures

A *structure variable* is a collection of separate data elements, or *fields*, that can be accessed individually or as a group. The fields may be of different types and sizes. There are three steps involved in using structure variables:

1. Declare the structure type.
2. Define one or more variables having the structure type.
3. Use structure operands to manipulate the data within the fields.

Structures may be useful in organizing data for storing on disk. Logically, related data about a single person, item, or subject is grouped and read from or written to disk as a single unit.

***Declaring Structure Types***    The STRUC and ENDS directives designate the start and end of a *structure type*. The assembler can tell from the syntax of the statements that ENDS in this instance is the end of a structure rather than the end of a segment. Between the two directives you place the field declarations, that is, the statements that define the fields making up the structure. Here is an example:

```
DATE      STRUC
MONTH     DB  ?
DAY       DB  ?
YEAR      DW  ?
DATE      ENDS
```

DATE is a structure type having three fields and four bytes. MONTH is one byte with an offset of 0 from the start of DATE. DAY is one byte with an offset of 1 from the start of DATE. YEAR is a word of two bytes with an offset of 2 from the start of DATE. In declaring fields, be sure to allocate enough space to hold the maximum value that is to be placed in each field; hence, you need a word to hold YEAR while a byte is large enough for MONTH and DAY.

Any number of fields may be declared within a structure type. Fields may be given initial values by defining constants as with other data definitions.

The structure type declaration does not actually place a structure in memory. It simply describes the format that the structure will have.

***Defining Structure Variables.***    You may define a *structure variable* of a declared type using the following syntax:

```
[name] structuretype <[initialvalue [,initialvalue...]]>
```

where items within the square brackets are optional. The *structuretype* must be the name previously declared with STRUC and ENDS directives. *Initialvalue* is the initial value assigned to one or more of the fields. We can define two structure variables in memory with type DATE as follows:

```
NEWYEAR    DATE    <1,1,1990>
INDPDAY    DATE    <7,4,1776>
```

The angle brackets <> are required even if you do not assign values to one or more of the fields. Any fields not having values remain undefined unless you give them a value when declaring the structure type. You also may use the DUP operator to initialize an array of structure variables, as in:

```
AUGUST    DATE    31 DUP <8>
```

This statement creates 31 four-byte structure variables with the first byte (MONTH) in each having a value of eight (for August) and the DAY and YEAR fields undefined.

You cannot initialize any structure fields that are given multiple values when the structure is declared. For example:

```
STURECD    STRUC
STUID      DW ?                           ;can override
STUNAME    DB "Last, First, Initial "    ;can override string
SCORES     DB 16 DUP (0)                  ;can't override multiple
                                          ;values
STURECD    ENDS
```

***Using Structure Operands***    Structure variables may be accessed by name. Fields within the structure also may be accessed individually by using this syntax:

```
variable.field
```

where *variable* is the name of a structure (or its address) and *field* is the name of a field within that structure. The following examples operate on fields defined in the preceding sections:

```
MOV AL,NEWYEAR.DAY      ;moves 1 to AL
MOV AX,INDPDAY.YEAR     ;moves 1776 to AX
LEA SI,NEWYEAR          ;gets address of NEWYEAR
MOV DL,[SI].MONTH       ;moves 1 to DL
```

The address of a field is found by adding together the offset of the structure variable and the offset of the field within the structure. Either offset may be placed in a base or index register.

## Records

A *record variable* is a byte or word containing fields made up of one or more bits. The major difference between records and structures is that the fields in records are made up of small groups of bits, while the fields in structures consist of groups of bytes or words.

Three steps are needed when working with records: declaring record types, defining record variables, and using record operands and record variables.

***Declaring Record Types.*** The *RECORD directive* declares the record type for an eight- or 16-bit record containing one or more bit fields. Its syntax is:

```
recordname RECORD field [,field...]
```

where *recordname* is the name of the record type to be used when defining the record. *Field* gives the name, width, and (optionally) the initial value for the field. A record declaration does not actually place a record in memory.

The syntax of each field operand is:

```
fieldname:width[=expression]
```

where *fieldname* is the name of a field within the record, *width* is the number of bits in the field, and *expression* is the optional initial value for the field. Field operands must be separated by commas, and the total widths for all fields must not exceed 16 bits.

If the total of all field widths is not greater than eight bits, the assembler assigns one byte for the record. If the total is between nine and 16 bits, the record is assigned two bytes. If the fields you declare do not total exactly eight or 16 bits, the entire record is shifted right to align the last bit of the last field in the rightmost byte of the record. Unused bits to the left of the record are set to 0. Examples include the following:

```
COLORS     RECORD    BLINK:1,BKGD:3,INTENSTY:1,FGD:3
                               ;8 bits, 1 byte
MISCREC    RECORD    F1:3=0,F2:4=7,F3:3=1,F4:6=2
                               ;16 bits, 2 bytes
SHORTREC   RECORD    A:1=1,B:2=1,C:3=1;6 bits, 1 byte
```

COLORS has four fields: BLINK occupies bit 7; BKGD bits 6-4; INTENSTY bit 3; and FGD bits 2-0. Each field has a default value of 0.

MISCREC also has four fields, with these characteristics:

| FIELD NAME | BIT POSITIONS | INITIAL VALUE | BIT SETTINGS |
|:---:|:---:|:---:|:---:|
| F1 | 15–13 | 0 | 000 |
| F2 | 12–9 | 7 | 0111 |
| F3 | 8–6 | 1 | 001 |
| F4 | 5–0 | 2 | 000010 |

SHORTREC has three fields totaling six bits. They are shifted to the right of the record. The record has these characteristics:

| FIELD NAME | BIT POSITIONS | INITIAL VALUE | BIT SETTINGS |
|---|---|---|---|
| None | 7-6 | 0 | 00 |
| A | 5 | 1 | 1 |
| B | 4-3 | 1 | 01 |
| C | 2-0 | 1 | 001 |

***Defining Record Variables.*** A *record variable* is an eight- or 16-bit variable whose bits are divided into one or more fields. You may define values for a record whose type has been declared by using the following syntax:

[name] recordtype <[initialvalue [,initialvalue...]]>

where *recordtype* has been previously declared with a RECORD statement, and *initialvalue* is optional. Initialvalues for the fields in the record must be separated by commas. The following examples define one record for each of the types previously declared:

```
COLORS    RECORD  BLINK:1,BKGD:3,INTENSTY:1,FGD:3
                            ;8 bits, 1 byte
COLOR1    COLORS  <1,3,0,4>
MISCREC   RECORD F1:3=0,F2:4=7,F3:3=1,F4:6=2
                            ;16 bits, 2 bytes
REC2      MISCREC <,,2,>
RECS      MISCREC 10 DUP (<2,2,2,2>)
```

The first example defines values for the four fields of COLOR1 as follows:

| FIELD NAME | BIT POSITIONS | VALUE | BIT VALUES |
|---|---|---|---|
| BLINK | 7 | 1 | 1 |
| BKGD | 6-4 | 3 | 011 |
| INTENSTY | 3 | 0 | 0 |
| FGD | 2-0 | 4 | 100 |

The second example sets the third field of REC2 (F3) to a value of 2 in bit positions 8-6. F1, F2, and F4 retain the default values of 0, 7, and 2, respectively.

The third example creates an array of 10 records named RECS and sets F1, F2, F3, and F4 in each record to an initial value of 2. When the DUP operator is used to initialize multiple record variables, only the angle brackets and initial values need to be enclosed in parentheses.

***Using Record Operands and Record Variables.*** A *record operand* is a constant that may be used with the following syntax:

recordtype < [[value],[value...]]>

where *recordtype* is the name of a record type declared within the source program and *value* is optional. If you use two or more values, separate them by commas. The angle brackets are required, even if no value is given. If no value for a field is given, the default value given in the record declaration is used. Examples of record operands include the following:

```
COLORS     RECORD   BLINK:1,BKGD:3,INTENSTY:1,FGD:3
                                  ;8 bits, 1 byte
MISCREC    RECORD   F1:3=0, F2:4=7,F3:3=1,F4:6=2
                                  ;16 bits, 2 bytes
           .
           MOV AL,COLORS <1,3,0,2>   ;value B2h (1 011 0 010)
           MOV AX,MISCREC <1,2,3,4>  ;value 24C4H (001 0010 011
                                     ;000100)
```

A *record variable* is a value stored in memory. The name of the variable may be used in instructions like other variable names.

```
COLORS     RECORD   BLINK:1,BKGD:3,INTENSTY:1,FGD:3
                                  ;8 bits, 1 byte
MISCREC    RECORD   F1:3=0,F2:4=7,F3:3=1,F4:6=2
                                  ;16 bits, 2 bytes
COLOR1     COLORS <1,3,0,4>
REC2       MISCREC <,,2,>
           .
           MOV BH,COLOR1            ;value as defined B4h (1 011
                                    ;0100)
           MOV DX,REC2              ;value OE82h (000 0111 010
                                    ;000010)
```

## Record Operators

Two operators, WIDTH and MASK, return constant values about previously declared records. They are used exclusively with records.

*WIDTH Operator.* The *WIDTH operator* returns the width in bits of a record or field within a record. Its syntax is:

```
WIDTH {fieldname | recordname}
```

where the braces indicate that either the name of a field or that of a record may be given. This operator usually is used with an EQU statement to assign the width to a named constant.

```
COLORS     RECORD   BLINK:1,BKGD:3,INTENSTY:1,FGD:3
                                  ;8 bits, 1 byte
MISCREC    RECORD   F1:3=0,F2:4=7,F3:3=1,F4:6=2
                                  ;16 bits, 2 bytes
WCOLORS    EQU      WIDTH COLORS   ;value of WCOLORS = 8
WBKGD      EQU      WIDTH BKGD     ;value of WBKGD = 3
WMISCREC   EQU      WIDTH MISCREC  ;value of WMISCREC = 16
WF4        EQU      WIDTH F4       ;value of WF4 = 6
```

*Mask Operator*     Closely related to WIDTH is the *MASK operator*, which returns a bit mask showing the bit positions in a record occupied by the specified record field. Bits in the mask corresponding to the position of the field contain is; all other positions contain 0s. The NOT operator can be used to reverse the bits in the mask.

The syntax of the MASK operator is

```
MASK {fieldname | record}
```

where the name of a field or a record may be used. Here are some masks:

```
COLORS     RECORD   BLINK:1,BKGD:3,INTENSTY:1,FGD:3
                                    ;8 bits, 1 byte
MISCREC    RECORD   F1:3=0,F2:4=7,F3:3=1,F4:6=2
                                    ;16 bits, 2 bytes
SHORTREC   RECORD   A:1=1,B:2=1,C:3=1 ;6 bits, 1 byte

           MOV AX,MASK F3           ;mask = 0000000111000000
           OR AX,MASK F1            ;mask = 1110000000000000
           AND AL,MASK INTENSTY     ;mask = 00001000
           MOV AH,NOT MASK B        ;mask = 11100111 (fields
                                    ;shifted 2 bits)
```

## PROGRAM 10: DISPLAY DISK FILE

Program 10 (see Figure 10-1) uses some of the interrupts discussed in this chapter to display the contents of any specified disk file. The format of the display is similar to that used by DEBUG. In the lefthand column is a hex number indicating the relative position in the file of the first byte in that column. Sixteen bytes are displayed on each line, first in two-digit hex code and then in character form. If the byte does not contain a printable character, it is converted to a period(.).

The program is organized into a main driver module that carries out the overall logic of the program. Most of the detail work is handled by eight internal subroutines. Several of the standard external input and output subroutines are attached by LINK.

The logic for the driver module sets an error flag OFF at the start and turns it ON and displays a message if any error is encountered on a disk operation. Whenever the flag is ON no further operations are attempted on that file.

The driver module opens by setting the error flag OFF and requesting the name of the file to be displayed. The filename entered is converted to an ASCIIZ string and the file is opened. If the open is successful, then the first sector of 512 bytes is read into a buffer. The byte number is set to 0 and shown on the first line of the display. Then the first 16 bytes are displayed in hex form, with a space between bytes. Then the cursor is set at column 55, and the bytes are displayed as ASCII characters, converting each notprintable byte to

```
          PAGE 50,132
;----------------------------------------------------------------------
;Program name: PROG10.ASM
;
;Author:  Alton R. Kindred
;----------------------------------------------------------------------
;Allows examination of a file in hex code ASCII printable characters.
;16 bytes are displayed in hex and then in character form on each line.
;Periods replace unprintable ASCII characters.
;----------------------------------------------------------------------
DATA      SEGMENT
PROMPT    DB   13,10,'Enter filename (Press <ENTER> alone to quit): $'
PROMPT2   DB   13,10,'Press any key to continue; ESC to stop $'
FILENAME  DB   20,?,20 DUP (?)
BYTENBR   DW   ?                     ;byte counter for file
RECLEN    DW   ?                     ;number of bytes read
HANDLE    DW   ?                     ;handle number for input
NOOPEN    DB   13,10,'The file could not be opened.$'
NOREAD    DB   13,10,'Error while reading a data sector.$'
DONE      DB   13,10,'BDOS code on exit: $'
BUFFER    DB   64 DUP ('BUFFER  ')
BUFFLEN   EQU  $-BUFFER
ERRFLAG   DB   ?
CRLF      DB   13,10,'$'
DATA      ENDS
;----------------------------------------------------------------------
STACK     SEGMENT STACK
          DB   32 DUP ('STACK   ')
STACK     ENDS
;----------------------------------------------------------------------
CODE      SEGMENT
          ASSUME CS:CODE,SS:STACK,DS:DATA
          EXTRN INPLINE:NEAR,DSPLINE:NEAR,DSPHEX:NEAR,INPCHR:NEAR
          EXTRN DSPCHR:NEAR,CLRSCN:NEAR
PROG10    PROC FAR                 ;driver procedure
          MOV AX,DATA              ;set up data segment in DS
          MOV DS,AX
          MOV ERRFLAG,0            ;set error flag OFF
          CALL GETNAME             ;ask for filename
WHILE01:  MOV AL,FILENAME+1        ;WHILE filename entered
          CMP AL,0
          JNE DO01
          JMP WEND01
DO01:     CALL OPENFILE            ;  DO open the file
IF01:     CMP ERRFLAG,0            ;  IF error flag OFF
          JNZ ENDIF01
THEN01:   MOV RECLEN,BUFFLEN       ;    THEN set buffer length
          MOV BYTENBR,0            ;    clear byte counter
          CALL READNX              ;    read first record
ENDIF01:                          ;  ENDIF
WHILE02:  CMP ERRFLAG,0            ;  WHILE no flags set
          JNE WEND02
          MOV RECLEN,AX            ;    save number of bytes read
```

**Figure 10-1    Source Listing of Program 10**

```
                MOV BX,0                 ;       reset buffer-pointer
WHILE03:        CMP BX,RECLEN            ;       WHILE more data in this record
                JE WEND03
AND03:          CMP ERRFLAG,0            ;       AND no error flag set
                JNZ WEND03
                CALL PRTLINE             ;         print the line
                JMP WHILE03
WEND03:                                  ;       WEND
                CALL READNX              ;       read next record
                JMP WHILE02
WEND02:                                  ;   WEND
                MOV DX,OFFSET DONE       ;   print "final BDOS code:"
                CALL DSPLINE
                MOV CX,4
                MOV DX,AX
                CALL DSPHEX
                MOV BX,HANDLE            ;   close file
                MOV AH,3Eh
                INT 21h
                MOV ERRFLAG,0            ;   clear error flag
                CALL GETNAME             ;   get another filename
                JMP WHILE01
WEND01:                                  ;WEND
                MOV AX,4C00h             ;back to DOS or DEBUG
                INT 21h
PROG10          ENDP                     ;end of driver procedure
;-----------------------------------------------------------------------
SUBS            PROC NEAR
;
;                          GET FILENAME subroutine
;
; Gets filename and converts to ASCIIZ string
;
GETNAME:        MOV DX,OFFSET PROMPT     ;prompt for filename
                CALL DSPLINE
                MOV DX,OFFSET FILENAME   ;get filename
                CALL INPLINE
                MOV DL,10                ;line feed
                CALL DSPCHR
                MOV AL,FILENAME+1        ;get length of filename
                XOR AH,AH
                MOV SI,AX                ;change filename to ASCIIZ string
                XOR AL,AL
                MOV FILENAME+2[SI],AL
                RET
;-----------------------------------------------------------------------
;                          OPEN FILE subroutine
;
OPENFILE:       MOV AH,3Dh               ;code for open
                MOV AL,0
                LEA DX,FILENAME+2        ;point to filename
                INT 21h
IF41:           JNC ELSE41               ;IF error on open
THEN41:         MOV DX,OFFSET NOOPEN     ;   THEN print error message
                CALL DSPLINE
                OR ERRFLAG,01h           ;   set open error flag ON
```

**Figure 10-1**   *continued*

```
                JMP ENDIF41
ELSE41:                             ;ELSE
        MOV HANDLE,AX               ;  save handle
ENDIF41:                            ;ENDIF
        RET                         ;return
;--------------------------------------------------------------------------
;                       READ NEXT SECTOR subroutine
;
;   return z=0 if no more data
;   if c=1, AL holds the error number and z=?
;   otherwise, return number of bytes in new sector in AX
;
READNX:   PUSH CX
          PUSH BX
          MOV AH,03FH               ;read next sector
          MOV BX,HANDLE
          MOV CX,BUFFLEN
          LEA DX,BUFFER
          INT 21h
          POP BX
          POP CX
          MOV RECLEN,AX             ;save number read
IF51:     JNC ELSE51                ;IF read error (c=1)
THEN51:   OR ERRFLAG,02h            ;  THEN set read error flag ON
          LEA DX,NOREAD             ;  print error message
          CALL DSPLINE
          JMP ENDIF51
ELSE51:                             ;ELSE
IF61:     CMP AX,0                  ;  IF end of file
          JNE ENDIF61
THEN61:   OR ERRFLAG,04h            ;     THEN set EOF flag ON
ENDIF61:                            ;  ENDIF
ENDIF51:                            ;ENDIF
          RET                       ;return
;--------------------------------------------------------------------------
;                       PRINT LINE Subroutine
; Displays byte number, displays 16 bytes in hex, then 16 bytes as characters.
;
PRTLINE:  CALL NEWLINE
IF31:     CMP ERRFLAG,0             ;IF no error flag (ESC)
          JNZ ENDIF31
THEN31:   CALL PRTHEX               ;  THEN display line
          CALL CHARS
ENDIF31:                            ;ENDIF
          RET
;--------------------------------------------------------------------------
;                       PRINT HEX CHARACTERS Subroutine
;
PRTHEX:
REPEAT41:                           ;REPEAT
          MOV DL,' '                ;  print a space
          CALL DSPCHR
          MOV DH,BUFFER [BX]        ;  display character in hex
          PUSH CX
          MOV CX,2
          CALL DSPHEX
```

**Figure 10-1** *continued*

```
          POP CX
          INC BX                      ;  increment buffer pointer
          CMP BX,RECLEN               ;  test for early end
          JE UNTIL41
          TEST BX,000Fh               ;  test for 16 bytes displayed
          JNZ REPEAT41
UNTIL41:                              ;UNTIL no more data in this record
                                      ;OR 16 lines finished
          RET                         ;return
;-----------------------------------------------------------------------
;                      PRINT CHARACTERS subroutine
;
; Prints 16 characters in ASCII code.  Converts codes  20h or  7Fh to
; periods.

CHARS:    CALL TAB                    ;place cursor at column 55
          DEC BX                      ;go back to start of line
          AND BX,0FFF0h
REPT51:                               ;REPEAT
          MOV DL,BUFFER[BX]           ;  get value
IF52:     CMP DL,32                   ;  IF less than 32
          JB THEN52                   ;
          CMP DL,128                  ;  OR greater than 127
          JB ENDIF52
THEN52:   MOV DL,'.'                  ;    THEN set character to a period
ENDIF52:                              ;  ENDIF
          CALL DSPCHR                 ;  display the character
          INC BX
          CMP BX,RECLEN               ;  test for early end
          JE UNTIL51
          TEST BX,000Fh               ;  test for 16 bytes displayed
          JNZ REPT51
UNTIL51:                              ;UNTIL end of file or 16 bytes displayed
          RET                         ;return
;-----------------------------------------------------------------------
;                   TAB cursor to column 55 subroutine
;
; Places cursor at column 55, saves BX & CX
;
TAB:      PUSH BX                     ;save BX and CX
          PUSH CX                     ;
          MOV AH,15                   ;get active page
          INT 10h
          MOV AH,3                    ;get cursor row & column
          INT 10h                     ;place in DH, DL
          MOV DL,55                   ;set column = 55
          MOV AH,2                    ;set cursor
          INT 10h
          POP CX                      ;restore CX and BX
          POP BX
          RET
;-----------------------------------------------------------------------
;                        NEWLINE subroutine
;
; Returns to cursor to left margin and displays the count of characters in hex
; form.
```

**Figure 10-1**    *continued*

```
;
NEWLINE:
IF53:      TEST BYTENBR,00FFh     ;IF 256 bytes displayed
           JNZ ENDIF53
AND53:     CMP BYTENBR,0          ;AND byte number <> 0
           JE ENDIF53
THEN53:    LEA DX,PROMPT2         ;   THEN ask to press any key
           CALL DSPLINE
           MOV AH,8               ;   wait for response
           INT 21h
           PUSH AX
           CALL CLRSCN            ;   clear screen
           POP AX
ENDIF53:                          ;ENDIF
IF54:      CMP AL,1Bh             ;IF ESC pressed
           JNE ELSE54
THEN54:    OR ERRFLAG,08h         ;   THEN set ESC flag ON
           JMP ENDIF54
ELSE54:                          ;ELSE
           LEA DX,CRLF            ;   return cursor
           CALL DSPLINE
           MOV DX,BYTENBR         ;   print the count
           PUSH CX
           MOV CX,4
           CALL DSPHEX
           POP CX
           MOV DL,' '             ;   extra space
           CALL DSPCHR
           ADD BYTENBR,16
ENDIF54:                          ;ENDIF
           RET
;----------------------------------------------------------------------
SUBS       ENDP                   ;end of procedures
CODE       ENDS                   ;end of code segment
           END PROG10             ;end of program
```

**Figure 10-1**   *concluded*

a period. The byte number is incremented by 16, and the process is continued until all 512 bytes have been displayed.

We pause the display at the end of each 256 bytes to give the operator a chance to view it and discontinue the display by pressing the ESC key. A new sector is read after the 512 bytes have been displayed. After each read operation, the number of bytes actually read is recorded so that the display can be stopped when the end of the file is reached. Then the operator is given a chance to enter a new filename to be displayed or press <ENTER> alone to terminate the program.

Subroutines are used extensively so that the driver module can concentrate on the overall logic. Three levels of subroutines are used: the driver calls PRTLINE, which calls NEWLINE, PRTHEX, and CHARS. Each of these subroutines calls one or more of the external standard subroutines.

Figure 10-2 shows a portion of the output from program 10.

```
B> prog10

Enter filename (Press <ENTER> alone to quit): prog10.asm

0000   20 20 20 20 20 20 20 20 20 20 50 41 47 45 20 35            PAGE 5
0010   30 2C 31 33 32 0D 0A 20 20 20 20 20 20 20 20 20   0,132..
0020   20 20 20 20 20 20 20 20 20 20 20 20 20 20 20 20
0030   20 20 20 20 3B 2D 2D 2D 2D 2D 2D 2D 2D 2D 2D 2D      ;————
0040   2D 2D 2D 2D 2D 2D 2D 2D 2D 2D 2D 2D 2D 2D 2D 2D   ————
0050   2D 2D 2D 2D 2D 2D 2D 2D 2D 2D 2D 2D 2D 2D 2D 2D   ————
0060   2D 2D 2D 2D 2D 2D 2D 2D 2D 2D 2D 2D 2D 2D 2D 2D   ————
0070   2D 2D 2D 2D 2D 2D 2D 2D 2D 2D 2D 2D 2D 2D 2D 2D   ————
0080   0D 0A 3B 50 72 6F 67 72 61 6D 20 6E 61 6D 65 3A   ..;Program name:
0090   20 50 52 4F 47 31 30 2E 41 53 4D 0D 0A 3B 0D 0A    PROG10.ASM..;..
00A0   3B 41 75 74 68 6F 72 3A 20 20 41 6C 74 6F 6E 20   ;Author:  Alton
00B0   52 2E 20 4B 69 6E 64 72 65 64 0D 0A 3B 2D 2D 2D   R. Kindred..;——
00C0   2D 2D 2D 2D 2D 2D 2D 2D 2D 2D 2D 2D 2D 2D 2D 2D   ————
00D0   2D 2D 2D 2D 2D 2D 2D 2D 2D 2D 2D 2D 2D 2D 2D 2D   ————
00E0   2D 2D 2D 2D 2D 2D 2D 2D 2D 2D 2D 2D 2D 2D 2D 2D   ————
00F0   2D 2D 2D 2D 2D 2D 2D 2D 2D 2D 2D 2D 2D 2D 2D 2D   ————
Press any key to continue; ESC to stop
.
.
.
2900   4E 44 20 50 52 4F 47 31 30 20 20 20 20 20 20 20   ND PROG10
2910   20 20 20 20 20 20 20 20 3B 65 6E 64 20 6F 66 20            ;end of
2920   70 72 6F 67 72 61 6D 0D 0A 0D 0A 0D 0A 0D 0A 0D   program........
2930   0A 0D 0A 20 0D 0A 1A                              .. ...
BDOS code on exit: 0000
Enter filename (Press ENTER along to quit):  <ENTER>

B>
```

**Figure 10-2    Portion of Output from Program 10**

## SUMMARY

Disk files are accessed through DOS interrupts. Each of the file handling interrupts uses DOS INT 21h. Function codes are placed into AH to indicate the type of operation. Other specifications, such as the address of a file buffer, the number of bytes to be read or written, and other parameters, are placed in other registers.

DOS 2.00 and later versions use a system of file handles to simplify reference to the file. The handle is a number assigned when a file is created and opened. Thereafter, the handle is used to specify the file to be read, written, or closed.

The filename must be specified in the form of an ASCIIZ string, a character string with binary 0 in the last byte.

If an error occurs during file processing, the carry flag is set and a code indicating the type of error is placed by DOS into AX.

Structures are a form of data organization declared by use of the STRUC and ENDS directives. Fields defined between STRUC and ENDS show the format for the structure type. Each field has an offset based on its distance from the start of the structure. Fields may be assigned initial values when the structure is declared.

A structure variable is define by giving it a name, followed by the name of the structure type previously declared. New values may be assigned to one or more of the fields by placing the values in angle brackets separated by commas, or the default values may be used.

Structure fields are used as operands by naming the structure variable followed by a period and the name of the field.

Records are made up of one or two bytes in which groups of individual bits make up the fields. Records are declared as to type by giving a name, followed by the RECORD directive and the description of each field in the record. The field name is followed by a colon and the number of bits in the field and, optionally, an equal sign and the initial value to be placed in that filed. If the total bits in the record are eight or fewer, the record occupies one byte. For bits between 9 and 16, two bytes are assigned. If the bits do not total exactly 8 or 16, fields are shifted to be right justified within the record.

Record variables are defined by specifying the name, the name of the record type previously declared, and (optionally) the values to be assigned to any of the fields enclosed within angle brackets and separated by commas.

Record operands are constants consisting of the name of the record type followed by values enclosed in angle brackets and separated by commas. Record variables are values stored in memory.

The WIDTH operator returns a number equal to the number of bits in a record field. The MASK operator returns a bit mask showing 1s in the record positions where the field is located, with 0s in all other record positions. The NOT operator reverses the setting of the bits in the mask.

## QUESTIONS

1. What is a major difference between file handling interrupts for DOS versions earlier than 2.00 and those since?
2. What is a file handle? What usually is the handle assigned to the first file created or opened in a program?
3. What devices other than disk files may be accessed through handles?
4. Describe the appearance and use of an ASCIIZ string in disk file operations.
5. How are errors indicated if a file operation is unsuccessful? What register contains an error code?
6. What function code creates a new file? What other data must be supplied? What happens if the name file already exists?
7. How is an existing file opened? What parameters must be furnished?

8.  What happens when a file is closed? Why is closing the file especially important with an output file?

9.  Name the parameters that must be furnished to read from a disk file. How do they differ from those needed to write to a disk file?

10. How is a disk file deleted? How many files can be deleted with a single interrupt?

11. State the parameters to rename a disk file.

12. What parameters are needed to request the amount of free disk space on a drive? How is the data returned?

13. What is the difference between a structure and a record.

14. How is a structure declared? How many fields can be placed within one structure? What is placed in memory by a structure declaration?

15. How are structure variables defined? In what kinds of fields may we not assign new initial values.

16. How is a field within a structure named as an operand?

17. What is the maximum length a record may have? What determines the length the assembler assigns to a record?

18. How is a record variable defined? Can initial values be set in this definition?

19. What is the difference between a record operand and a record variable?

20. What does the WIDTH operator return? How is it normally used?

21. Explain the use of the MASK operator. What is the effect of the NOT operator with the MASK?

# EXERCISES

1.  Write statements to input from the keyboard a filename and convert it to an ASCIIZ string.

2.  Write statements to define a filename as a constant and refer to it to create a new disk file. Test that the file was successfully created.

3.  Write statements to open the file you created in exercise 2 for reading. If opened OK, save the handle. If not, display an error message.

4.  Write statements to read records from the file opened in exercise 3. Display an error message if not successfully opened.

5.  Write statements to rename the file created in exercise 2. Provide an error routine if the operation is not successful.

6.  Write statements to delete the file you renamed in exercise 5.

7.  Write statements to determine the free disk space on drive B. Display the number of bytes available in the form "B: Bytes Available NNNNNN", where NNNNNN is a decimal number.

8.  Define a structure variable named BIRTHDAY to fit the declaration for DATE as described in this chapter. Give it the values for your birthday.

9.  Declare a structure type named ADDRESS, containing fields called NAMEX, STREET, CITY, STATE, and ZIP. Each of the first three fields is 20 bytes long. STATE contains two bytes, and ZIP is one word. Assign your own data as initial default values.

10. Declare a record type containing fields having 3, 4, 2, and 1 bits respectively. Assign your own names. What bit positions within the record does each field occupy?

11. Define a record variable for the record type declared in exercise 10. Assign new initial values.

12. Write a statement to EQUate the width of the first field in the record you defined in exercise 11 to a variable with the name W*xxx*, where *xxx* is the name of the first field in your record.

13. Write a statement to OR register AX (or AL) with the MASK of the second field in the record type you declared in exercise 11.

## LAB PROBLEMS

1. Define a structure type called BOOK with four fields:

   IDNO      20 bytes
   AUTHOR  30 bytes
   TITLE     50 bytes
   PUBLISH  24 bytes
   YEAR     4 bytes

   Create one structure variable of this type. Create a disk file called MYLIB. Enter data from the keyboard for five or six of your books and place in the structure fields. Use the MOVSB instruction. Use the structure variable as the disk buffer and write each 128-byte structure to the disk. Stop entering data by pressing <ENTER> alone for IDNO. When finished, close the file.

   Test that each disk operation is successful. Display an error message and terminate the program if an error occurs.

2. Open the MYLIB file created in lab problem 1. Read each structure of 128 bytes from the disk. Display each field as a separate line on the screen. Double space between structures. Provide for error messages and terminate the program if any error occurs.

# MACRO DEFINITIONS AND CONDITIONAL ASSEMBLY

# 11

---

**OBJECTIVES**

After studying this chapter, you should be able to:

- Identify the parts of a macro definition.
- Distinguish between defining and invoking a macro.
- Explain ways of supplying parameters to macros.
- Explain the form and use of LOCAL parameters.
- Concatenate parameters with strings and other parameters.
- Create a library of macro definitions and include the library with a source module.
- Use control statements to cause listing or suppression of macro expansions.
- Name and explain three types of equate directives.
- Use the repeat commands both within and outside of macro definitions.
- Use conditional statements both within and outside of macro definitions.

---

## PURPOSE OF THE MACRO DEFINITION

A *macro* is a single statement that you use, or invoke, in a program at assembly time that is expanded into a group of source statements previously listed in a *macro definition*. *Macro expansion* is a text-processing function that takes place during pass 1 of the assembler. When MASM encounters the name of the macro in the text of the source code, it inserts the statements that have been defined previously.

By wise use of macros, you can greatly shorten programming time and increase accuracy. The macro definition may appear in your source program before the macro is invoked, or it may be placed into a macro library and brought into the source program with an INCLUDE statement.

The purpose of a macro is similar to that of a subroutine, which is to use a single statement to cause many statements to be executed. But macros and subroutines have a number of crucial differences. The code for a subroutine appears only once in a program. You CALL the subroutine from whatever points in the program you need it. As you recall from Chapter 6, control actually passes to the subroutine when CALL places the appropriate addresses in CS and IP and returns to the calling program when RET again uses CS and IP. Data or addresses needed by the subroutine must be passed to it by one of the methods described in Chapter 6.

The macro expansion appears directly in the source code every time the macro is invoked. This expansion takes place at assembly time. You may vary the statements produced when a macro is invoked by using certain parameters and conditional statements in the macro definition. These terms are defined and described in the following sections.

## FORMAT OF THE MACRO DEFINITION

If you wish to use a macro only within a single program, place the macro definition anywhere in the source code before the macro is invoked. To use a macro within many programs, you may wish to place the definition in a library on disk. Such a file is typically called MACRO.LIB. Macros defined within the library may be made available to the assembler by using the statement INCLUDE MACRO.LIB (see Figure 11-1).

The macro definition consists of three parts:

1.   The MACRO directive.
2.   The body of the macro definition.
3.   The ENDM directive.

### The MACRO Directive

The first statement in a macro definition is the *MACRO directive*. Its format is:

```
macroname MACRO [parameters]
```

where *macroname* is the name by which the macro is to be invoked and the *parameters* are optional. As many parameters may be used as will fit on a single line, and they must be separated by commas.

### Body of the Macro

The *body of the macro* consists of the statements you want the assembler to supply when you invoke the macro. These statements can be machine instructions, data definitions, directives, calls, interrupts, and even other macros. They also may contain conditional statements and repeat statements to provide for complex logic within the macro expansion.

```
          PAGE 50,132
;-------------------------------------------------------------------------------
; Program name:  MACRO.LIB
;
; Author:   Alton R. Kindred
;
; This is a library of commonly used macros that can be included with each
; program.
;-------------------------------------------------------------------------------
DSP_CHR    MACRO  CHARACTER
           IFB HARACTER
           MOV DL,' '
           ELSE
           MOV DL,CHARACTER
           ENDIF
           MOV AH,2
           INT 21h
           ENDM
;-------------------------------------------------------------------------------
DSP_STRING  MACRO STRING
           LEA DX,STRING
           MOV AH,9
           INT 21h
           ENDM
;-------------------------------------------------------------------------------
INP_CHR_ECHO MACRO
           MOV AH,1
           INT 21h
           ENDM
;-------------------------------------------------------------------------------
INP_CHR_NOECHO MACRO
           MOV AH,8
           INT 21h
           ENDM
;-------------------------------------------------------------------------------
INP_STRING MACRO LIMIT,STRING
           LEA DX,STRING
           MOV STRING,LIMIT
           MOV AH,10
           INT 21h
           ENDM
;-------------------------------------------------------------------------------
PRT_CHR    MACRO CHARACTER
           MOV DL,CHARACTER
           MOV AH,5
           INT 21h
           ENDM
;-------------------------------------------------------------------------------
CR         MACRO
           MOV DL,13
           MOV AH,2
           INT 21h
           ENDM
```

**Figure 11-1    Useful Macros**

```
;----------------------------------------------------------------------------
LF        MACRO
          MOV DL,10
          MOV AH,2
          INT 21h
          ENDM
;----------------------------------------------------------------------------
CR_LF     MACRO
          CR
          LF
          ENDM
;----------------------------------------------------------------------------
DOS_RET   MACRO
          MOV AX,4C00h
          INT 21h
          ENDM
;----------------------------------------------------------------------------
CLS       MACRO
          MOV AL,0
          MOV AH,6
          MOV BH,7
          MOV CX,0
          MOV DL,79
          MOV DH,24
          INT 10h
          ENDM
;----------------------------------------------------------------------------
SET_CURSOR MACRO ROW,COLUMN
          MOV BH,0
          MOV DH,ROW
          MOV DL,COLUMN
          MOV AH,2
          INT 10h
          ENDM
;----------------------------------------------------------------------------
GET_CURSOR MACRO
          MOV BH,0
          MOV AH,3
          INT 10h
          ENDM
;----------------------------------------------------------------------------
SET_VIDEO_MODE MACRO MODE
          MOV AH,0
          MOV AL,MODE
          INT 10h
          ENDM
;----------------------------------------------------------------------------
READ_ATTRIB_AND_CHAR MACRO
          MOV AH,8
          INT 10h
          ENDM
;----------------------------------------------------------------------------
WRITE_ATTRIB_AND_CHAR MACRO CHAR,ATTRIB,COUNT
          MOV AH,9
          MOV AL,CHAR
```

**Figure 11-1**    *continued*

```
            MOV BL,ATTRIB
            MOV CX,COUNT
            INT 10h
            ENDM
;-------------------------------------------------------------------------
CREATE_FILE MACRO FILENAME
            LEA DX,FILENAME
            MOV AH,3Ch
            INT 21h
            ENDM
;-------------------------------------------------------------------------
OPEN_FILE MACRO FILENAME,MODE
            LEA DX,FILENAME
            MOV AL,MODE
            MOV AH,3Dh
            INT 21h
            ENDM
;-------------------------------------------------------------------------
CLOSE_FILE MACRO HANDLE
            MOV BX,HANDLE
            MOV AH,3Eh
            INT 21h
            ENDM
;-------------------------------------------------------------------------
READ_FILE MACRO HANDLE,BUFFER,LENGTH
            MOV AH,3Fh
            MOV BX,HANDLE
            MOV CX,LENGTH
            LEA DX,BUFFER
            INT 21h
            ENDM
;-------------------------------------------------------------------------
WRITE_FILE MACRO HANDLE,BUFFER,LENGTH
            MOV AH,40h
            MOV BX,HANDLE
            MOV CX,LENGTH
            LEA DX,BUFFER
            INT 21h
            ENDM
;-------------------------------------------------------------------------
RENAME_FILE MACRO OLDNAME,NEWNAME
            PUSH ES
            PUSH DS
            POP ES
            MOV AH,56h
            LEA DX,OLDNAME
            LEA DI,NEWNAME
            INT 21h
            POP ES
            ENDM
;-------------------------------------------------------------------------
DELETE_FILE MACRO FILENAME
            MOV AH,41h
            LEA DX,FILENAME
            INT 21h
```

**Figure 11-1**    *continued*

```
            ENDM
;-----------------------------------------------------------------------
GET_DISK_SPACE MACRO DRIVE
            MOV AH,36h
            MOV DL,DRIVE
            INT 21h
            ENDM
```

**Figure 11-1** *concluded*

### The ENDM Directive

The last statement in the macro definition is the *ENDM directive*. ENDM, unlike ENDS and ENDP, does not require the name field. Nor does it need any operands. One and only one ENDM statement must appear in each definition to match the MACRO header.

Here is a macro that defines a complete stack segment:

```
STACKSEG    MACRO
STACK       SEGMENT STACK
            DB 32 DUP ('STACK +2')
STACK       ENDS
            ENDM
```

To invoke the macro, just write

```
    STACKSEG
```

in your source code. The three statements creating the 256-byte stack will be expanded by the assembler.

### Parameters

You may supply additional information to the assembler in a macro definition by placing operands on the first line following the MACRO statement. These operands are called *parameters* (or *dummy parameters*), and must be separated by commas. You may use as many as will fit on a single line.

The parameters are names that appear in statements in the body of the macro definition. When you invoke the macro, you supply names or numbers, called *arguments*, to replace the parameters in the body statements. You may thus specify a different filename to be opened, prompt to be displayed, or op code to be used each time you invoke a macro. Consider this example:

```
DSPMSG      MACRO       MESSAGE
            LEA         DX,MESSAGE
            MOV         AH,9
            INT         21h
            ENDM
```

MESSAGE is a parameter used in the LEA statement. If you invoke the macro with the statement

```
    DSPMSG PROMPT1
```

the assembler will substitute the argument PROMPT1 for the parameter MESSAGE and generate the statements in the body to read

```
        LEA     DX,PROMPT1
        MOV     AH,9
        INT     21h
```

Parameters are especially useful with the interrupts provided through DOS. Instead of having to remember which function code to place in the AH register, you can write one macro definition for each major function. You can use a parameter for anything that varies, such as filename, name of string, or location of input buffer.

Parameters also can be used for op codes, registers, or other parts of the statements in the body. Here is an example of specifying registers as dummy parameters to add numbers in two registers together and place the sum in the third register:

```
ADDREG      MACRO R1,R2,R3
            MOV R3,R1
            ADD R3,R2
            ENDM
```

If you invoke the macro with

```
    ADDREG SI,AX,DI
```

to indicate the registers you wish to use, the assembler produces the statements

```
        MOV DI,SI
        ADD DI,AX
```

## The LOCAL Directive

If a statement in the body of a macro definition contains a label and you invoke the macro more than once in a program, the label will be duplicated and flagged by the assembler as an error. To avoid this problem, you may use the *LOCAL directive*. Its syntax is:

```
    LOCAL localname[,localname]...
```

where at least one *localname* must be given. The LOCAL directive must precede all other statements within the body of the macro definition. Instead of using the local name when the macro is expanded, the assembler creates a new name in the form of ??nnnn, where nnnn is a hex number within the range of 0000 through FFFFh. Each time a local name is encountered, the assembler increments nnnn by 1. Thus the symbol will always be unique. Here is an example:

```
LARGE       MACRO P1,P2,LARGER
LOCAL       IF99,THEN99,ELSE99,ENDIF99
            MOV AX,P1
            MOV BX,P2
```

```
IF99:      CMP AX,BX
           JNA ELSE99
THEN99:    MOV LARGER,AX
           JMP ENDIF99
ELSE99:    MOV LARGER,BX
ENDIF99:
           ENDM
```

The following tabulation shows in the left column the code the first time the macro is invoked, while the right column shows the code from the second time.

| The statement | The statement |
|---|---|
| LARGE M1,M2,LARGEM | LARGE ONE,TWO,BIGGER |
| is expanded to | is expanded to |

```
          MOV AX,M1                      MOV AX,ONE
          MOV BX,M2                      MOV BX,TWO
??0000:   CMP AX,BX            ??0004:   CMP AX,BX
          JNA ??0002                     JNA ??0006
??0001:   MOV LARGEM,AX        ??0005:   MOV BIGGER,AX
          JMP ??0003                     JMP ??0007
??0002:   MOV LARGEM,BX        ??0006:   MOV BIGGER,BX
??0003:                        ??0007:
```

You will note that the body statements CMP, AX,BX and MOV LARGER,AX do not actually require labels. They are labeled to be consistent with the structured form used throughout this text.

## MACRO LISTING CONTROL DIRECTIVES

The assembler always lists in full all macro definitions appearing in a program. However, you may list or suppress listing of macro expansions by use of the .LALL, .XALL, and .SALL directives. Each of these directives can appear anywhere in your source code and is effective until replaced by either of the other directives.

### .LALL

The *.LALL directive* causes the assembler to list all statements, including comments and conditional statements, in macro and repeat expansions. Macro comments, indicated by two successive semicolons (;;) are not listed. The character 1, or sometimes 2, 3, or 4, appears to the left of each of the expanded statements.

### .XALL

The *.XALL directive* causes the assembler to list only the source statements in a macro expansion that generate code or data. Other statements, such as comments, segment definitions, and equates, are not listed. .XALL is the default option when MASM is loaded.

### .SALL

The *.SALL directive* causes the assembler to suppress the listing of all statements in the macro expansion. Only the statement that invokes the macro is listed.

## EQUATES

The *equate directives* allow you to assign values to symbols that can be used in statements throughout your source code. The equates, like macros, are processed at assembly time. They may be used both inside and outside macro definitions. They are of three kinds:

1. Redefinable numeric equates.
2. Nonredefinable numeric equates.
3. String (or text) equates.

### Redefinable Numeric Equates

*Redefinable numeric equates* assign a numeric constant to a symbol. No storage is allocated for the symbol. A different value may be assigned to the symbol at any point during assembly time. The values do not change at run time. The syntax is:

<u>name = expression</u>

where *name* is the symbol to which the value produced by *expression* is assigned. The name can be used as an immediate value in any subsequent statement. Expression can be an integer, a constant expression, a string constant of one or two characters, or an expression that produces an address. The name must be unique, but can be redefined in a later equate statement. Here are some examples:

```
VALUE     = 0                ;VALUE is now 0
VALUE     = VALUE + 2         ;VALUE is now 2
VALUE     = VALUE * 3         ;VALUE is now 6
SIX       DB (VALUE)          ;SIX has value of 6
```

### Nonredefinable Numeric Equates

*Nonredefinable numeric equates* assign a numeric constant to a symbol. No storage is allocated to the symbol. The value of the symbol cannot be redefined. A common use of this equate is to assign a number or address to a symbol that is referenced throughout the source code. Later, only the one equate statement must be changed if the program is revised rather than finding and changing every occurrence of the symbol. The syntax is:

```
name        EQU expression
```

where *name* is the symbol and *expression* must evaluate to a numeric constant. Here are some examples:

```
LINES      EQU 66                    ;Numeric value 66
ROWS       EQU 25                    ;Numeric value 25
COLUMNS    EQU 80                    ;Numeric value 80
SCREEN     EQU ROWS * COLUMNS        ;Numeric value 2000
DISPLAY    EQU SCREEN                ;Alias for SCREEN
```

### String Equates

*String equates* (also called *text macros*) are used to assign a string constant to a symbol. They may be used to define string constants and aliases. An *alias* is another name that may be used for the string. The syntax is:

```
name        EQU [<[string]>]
```

where *name* is the symbol to which the *string* enclosed in the angle brackets is assigned. The symbol may be redefined with a new string. The angle brackets distinguish the string equate from the nonredefinable numeric equate, which also uses the EQU directive. Definitions examples include the following:

```
PROMPT     EQU <'Enter date: '>
ARG2       EQU <[BP+6]>
AUTHOR     EQU <'Alton R. Kindred'>
```

Uses of string equates include the following:

```
HEAD1      DB AUTHOR                 ;HEAD1 contains 'Alton R.
                                     ;Kindred'
MSG        DB PROMPT                 ;MSG contains 'Enter date: '
MOV        SI,ARG2                   ;ARG2 contains [BP+6]
```

## MACRO OPERATORS

Five macro operators are useful in macro and conditional directives. They include the following:

    &   Substitute and concatenation operator
    < > Literal-text operator
    !   Literal-character operator
    %   Expression operator
    ;;  Macro comment

Each of these operators has its own special control function.

### Substitute and Concatenation Operator (&)

The *ampersand (&)* is a substitute operator that forces the assembler to replace a parameter with the actual value of the corresponding argument. One common use is to *concatenate* (or join together) parameters with other text. When you place an ampersand in front of a parameter in a body statement, you tell the assembler to create a new string containing the argument that replaced the parameter with any other text shown. You may use concatenation with names, op codes, or operands in the body statements. Here is a macro that defines an array. When invoking the macro, you can replace the parameter TYPE with a letter to define an array of bytes, words, tenwords, or other types. You can also specify the number of elements in the array (NUMBER).

```
DEFARRAY   MACRO TYPE,NUMBER
           D&TYPE NUMBER DUP (0)
           ENDM
```

The tabulation below shows two statements that invoke the macro to create an array of 50 words and one of 20 bytes, together with the expanded statements. Notice that the TYPE argument (W or B) is concatenated to the letter D to define the desired type of data.

```
           DEFARRAY W,50          DEFARRAY B,20
           DW 50 DUP (0)          DB 20 DUP (0)
```

You may wish to call a subroutine depending upon a certain condition. The condition was tested before invoking the macro. This macro demonstrates not only concatenation, but also two LOCAL variables:

```
CALLSUB    MACRO COND,SUBROUTINE
           LOCAL IF99,THEN99,ENDIF99
IF99:      J&COND THEN99
           JMP ENDIF99
THEN99:    CALL SUBROUTINE
ENDIF99:
           ENDM
```

Here are two different ways to invoke the macro, with the resulting expansion. In the first example, you wish to call the DSPCHR subroutine if the condition just tested in less than or equal (LE). In the second, you wish to call MULTIDIV if the condition is not zero.

```
           CALLSUB LE,DSPCHR          CALLSUB NZ,MULTIDIV
??0000:    JLE ??0001          ??0003: JNZ ??0004
           JMP ??0002                  JMP ??0005
??0001:    CALL DSPCHR         ??0004: CALL MULTIDIV
??0002:                        ??0005:
```

### Literal-Text Operator (< >)

*Angle brackets (< >)* are the literal-text operator that tells MASM that the enclosed list is a single string rather than separate arguments. Any enclosed commas, spaces, or tabs are merely characters in the string rather than delimiters. Special characters, such as the semicolon or ampersand when enclosed in angle brackets, are processed as characters only, not as indicators for comments or concatenation.

Suppose you define a macro as:

```
LIST        MACRO P1,P2,P3
            DB P1,P2,P3
            ENDM
```

If you invoke the macro with

```
        LIST 1,2,3
```

LIST receives three arguments: 1 for P1, 2 for P2, and 3 for P3.
If you use

```
        LIST <1,2,3>
```

LIST receives the string 1,2,3 for P1, and P2 and P3 are set to zeros by default.

### Literal-Character Operator (!)

The *exclamation point (!)* preceding a character tells MASM to treat the character literally rather than as a special symbol, such as a comment or arithmetic operator. It has the same effect as enclosing a single character within angle brackets, that is !; is the same as <;>. This operator normally is used when supplying an argument to a macro.

The following macro definition demonstrates both the literal-character operator and concatenation:

```
MAKEMSG     MACRO CODE,TEXT
MSG&CODE    DB 'Note &CODE: &TEXT'
            ENDM
```

If you invoke the macro with

```
        MAKEMSG 13,  <Line number !> 25>
```

the statement generated is

```
MSG13       DB 'Note 13:  Line number > 25'
```

Without the literal-character operator (!) the assembler would assume the first > indicated the end of the string and would show a syntax error for the extra characters.

### Expression Operator (%)

The *percent sign (%)* preceding any text is an expression operator. It normally is used to supply an argument to a macro. It tells MASM to compute the *value* of the expression and replace the text with the result. The expression can be either a numeric expression or a text equate. Here is an example:

```
DISP      MACRO EXPR,VALUE
          DB    '&EXPR = &VALUE'
          ENDM
N1        EQU 25
N2        EQU 50
```

If you invoke the macro with

```
          DISP <N1 + N2>,%(N1 + N2)
```

the generated statement will read

```
          DB 'N1 + N2 = 75'
```

## Macro Comments

Ordinary comments when placed in macro definitions and preceded by a semicolon appear in the expanded statements if the .LALL option is in effect. If you wish to write comments for the definition alone and not have them expanded, use two semicolons (;;) instead of one.

; This comment appears in the macro expansion following .LALL.
;; This comment appears only in the macro definition.

# REPEAT DIRECTIVES

There are three *repeat directives* — REPT, IRP, and IRPC — that permit you to create blocks of repeated statements. They may be used both inside and outside macro definitions. Like macros, they can have parameters that are replaced with actual arguments during assembly and are terminated with the ENDM directive. Unlike macros, they are not named and thus cannot be invoked.

Do not confuse these directives with the REP instruction, used in Chapter 9 with string instructions. These directives are processed at assembly time. REP is effective at run time.

## The REPT Directive

With the *REPT directive*, you create the number of repeat blocks that you specify with a numeric argument. The syntax is:

```
REPT expression
statements
ENDM
```

where *expression* must result in a 16-bit unsigned constant specifying the number of repetitions, and *statements* may be any valid assembler statements. The statements

```
REPT 4
INC AX
ENDM
```

produce

```
INC AX
INC AX
INC AX
INC AX
```

## The IRP Directive

The *IRP directive* specifies the number of repetitions for repeat blocks, as well as the parameters for each repetition. Its format is:

```
IRP parameter, <argument[,argument]...>
statements
ENDM
```

where *parameter* is replaced by the argument supplied, *argument* specifies a value to be used during one repetition, and *statements* are repeated once for each argument in the list. The arguments must be enclosed by angle brackets (< >) and separated by commas.
The statements

```
IRP NUMBER,<0,1,2,3,4,5,6,7,8,9,0>
DB    NUMBER
DB    '&NUMBER'
ENDM
```

are repeated 10 times to create statements defining 20 bytes. The first is the number 0, followed by the character 0, then the number 1, the character 1, on up to the number 9 and the character 9.

## The IRPC Directive

The *IRPC directive* is used to create blocks with the number of repetitions as well as the value for each repetition specified in a string. The syntax is:

```
IRPC parameter,string
statements
ENDM
```

where *parameter* is the name replaced by the current value in *string*. If the string contains any spaces, commas, or other delimiters, it should be enclosed in angle brackets (< >). Parameter can be used as often as desired in the statements. The statements

```
IRPC  x,54321
DB    x DUP (x * 2)
ENDM
```

create the following byte definitions:

```
DB    5 DUP (10)
DB    4 DUP (8)
DB    3 DUP (6)
DB    2 DUP (4)
DB    1 DUP (2)
```

# CONDITIONAL ASSEMBLY

MASM provides two kinds of conditional directives. Conditional-assembly directives assemble a block of statements only if a specified condition is true. Conditional-error directives generate an assembly error if the specified condition is true. Both kinds of directives are effective at assembly time. They may be used either inside or outside of macro definitions.

## Conditional-Assembly Directives

The *conditional-assembly directives* include a number of variations on the IF statement, together with ENDIF and an optional ELSE. The syntax is:

```
IF condition
statements if true
[ELSE
statements if false]
ENDIF
```

where *condition* is one of the directives in the following paragraph, *statements* can be any valid statements, and the ELSE with its statements are optional. The ENDIF ends the conditional block.

There are two forms of the IF for each condition stated, one of which is the counterpart of the other. Here are the pairs of IF that may be used:

| IF    | IFE   | Expression is true or false        |
|-------|-------|------------------------------------|
| IF1   | IF2   | Assembler is making pass 1 or 2    |
| IFB   | IFNB  | Argument is blank or not blank     |
| IFDEF | IFNDEF| Name is defined or not defined     |
| IFIDN | IFDIF | Arguments are identical or different |

IF statements can be nested up to 255 levels. Each IF can have no more than one ELSE, and each conditional-assembly block must end with an ENDIF.

***IF and IFE.***    These directives test the value of an expression and assemble the following statements based on the result. The syntax is:

```
IF expression
IFE expression
```

The *IF directive* allows assembly if expression is true (1, or nonzero), to a constant value and may refer only to names previously defined. The expression must use one of the following relational operators:

| | | |
|---|---|---|
| EQ = equal | GT = greater than | GE = greater than or equal |
| NE = not equal | LT = less than | LE = less than or equal |

The operators = <> > < => and <= are not effective with IF directives. For example:

```
SET_LINE   MACRO LINE
           IF LINE GT 25         ;;IF line > 25
           .LALL                 ;; THEN generate error comment
                                 ;Line number exceeds 25
           .XALL
           ELSE                  ;;ELSE
           MOV AH,2              ;; Set code to set cursor
           MOV DL,0              ;; Specify start of line
           MOV DH,LINE           ;; Specify line number
           INT 10h
           ENDIF                 ;;ENDIF
           ENDM
```

**IF1 and IF2.**   These directives test which pass the assembler is making and permit the block of statements to be assembled only on the pass specified. No other argument is required. IF1 is commonly used with macro definitions or with INCLUDE statements naming macro libraries. For example:

```
IF1
INCLUDE MACRO.LIB
ENDIF
```

**IFB and IFNB.**   These directives are used only inside a macro definition to test whether an argument was passed to the macro and to grant assembly accordingly. If the argument was passed, it is not blank; if not passed, it is blank. The syntax is:

```
IFB <argument>
IFNB <argument>
```

where the angle brackets are required and *argument* can be any name, number, or expression.

```
MOVCHAR    MACRO CHAR,BYTES,DEST
           IFNB  <CHAR>          ;IF character is present
           MOV AL,CHAR           ;THEN move character to
                                 ;AL
           ELSE                  ;ELSE
           MOV AL, ' '           ; move space to AL
```

```
        ENDIF                   ;ENDIF
        MOV CX,BYTES            ;set length
        LEA DI,DEST             ;set destination address
        STOSB                   ;move character in AL to
                                ;destination

        ENDM
```

Any one-byte argument you write to replace CHAR when invoking the macro will appear in BYTES positions in DEST. If you omit the first argument, the macro will move spaces to the specified number of bytes in DEST.

*IFDEF and IFNDEF.*    These directives grant assembly depending on whether the named symbol has been defined. The syntax is:

```
        IFDEF name
        IFNDEF name
```

where *name* is a label, variable, or symbol. IFDEF grants assembly if name is defined, and IFNDEF if it is not. For example:

```
        IFDEF BUFFLEN
BUFFER  DB BUFFLEN DUP (' ')
        ENDIF
```

If BUFFLEN has been previously specified, a buffer that long is defined; otherwise, no buffer is created.

*IFIDN and IFDIF.*    These directives compare two macro arguments and grant assembly based on the result. They are used only within macro definitions. The syntax is:

```
        IFIDN[I] <argument1>,<argument2>
        IFDIF[I] <argument1>,<argument2>
```

where *argument1* and *argument2* are tested to see if they are identical or different. Arguments must be enclosed in angle brackets, and they are separated by a comma. IFIDN grants assembly if the arguments are identical, and IFDIF if they are different.

The optional *I* indicates case insensitive; that is, upper- and lowercase letters are considered equal. If the I is omitted, upper- and lowercase are considered different. The I is not enclosed in brackets in the IF statement. For example:

```
SWAPWDS MACRO WORD1,WORD2
        IFDIF  <WORD1>,<WORD2>  ;;IF arguments are
                                ;;different
        PUSH WORD1              ;;THEN swap words
        PUSH WORD2
        POP WORD1
        POP WORD2
        ENDIF                   ;;ENDIF
        ENDM
```

The SWAPWDS macro first tests the two arguments WORD1 and WORD2. If they are different, the four statements to exchange them are assembled. If the arguments are the same, nothing is done. The statement SWAP AX<AX assembles the PUSH and POP statements, while SWAPWDS ax,AX does not. With the optional *I* in the IFIDNI statement, ax and AX are considered identical.

### Conditional-Error Directives

*Conditional-error directives* may be inserted at key points in a program to check for assembly-time errors and display error messages. These directives test the same conditions as the conditional-assembly statements discussed in the preceding sections, but they force an error and display an appropriate error message. Error messages are shown in the form A20nn, where nn represents an error number.

Table 11-1 lists the conditional-error directives, their numbers, and the message that each displays.

**.ERR, .ERR1, and .ERR2.**  These three directives force an error when they occur in the source file. They usually are placed within conditional-assembly blocks to control the condition under which the error message will be displayed.

*.ERR* forces an error whenever it is encountered. *.ERR1* is effective only on pass 1 and *.ERR2* only on pass 2. Each statement is used with no other parameters.

**.ERRE and .ERRNZ.**  The directives generate an error based on the result of the value of an expression. *.ERRE* generates an error if the expression is false, or 0. *.ERRNZ* generates an error if the expression is true, or nonzero. The syntax is:

```
.ERRE  expression
.ERRNZ expression
```

where *expression* must use the logical operators EQ, NE, GT, LT, GE, or LE; must resolve to a constant value; and must not contain forward references. For example, the statement

```
.ERRE LINE LE 25
```

in a macro definition would produce an error message if it were not true that LINE were less than or equal to 25.

**.ERRB and .ERRNB.**  These directives test whether or not an argument has been passed to a macro. *.ERRB* displays an error message if an argument has not been passed (blank), while *.ERRNB* displays the error message if the argument is not blank. The syntax is:

Table 11-1.
Conditional-Error Directives and Error Messages

| Directive | Error Number | Error Message |
|---|---|---|
| .ERR1 | 87 | Forced error - pass 1 |
| .ERR2 | 88 | Forced error - pass 2 |
| .ERR | 89 | Forced error |
| .ERRE | 90 | Forced error - expression true (1) |
| .ERRNZ | 91 | Forced error - expression false (0) |
| .ERRNDEF | 92 | Forced error - symbol not defined |
| .ERRDEF | 93 | Forced error - symbol defined |
| .ERRB | 94 | Forced error - string blank |
| .ERRNB | 95 | Forced error - string not blank |
| .ERRIDN[I] | 96 | Forced error - strings identical |
| .ERRDIF[I] | 97 | Forced error - strings different |

I indicates case insensitive; omit brackets [ ]

```
.ERRB <argument>
.ERRNB <argument>
```

where argument can be any name, number, or expression. Then angle brackets (< >) are required.

*.ERRDEF and .ERRNDEF.*   These directives display an error message based on whether or not a symbol has been defined. *.ERRDEF* displays the message if the symbol has been defined, and *.ERRNDEF* if it has not. The format is:

```
.ERRDEF name
.ERRNDEF name
```

where *name* must be a label, variable, or symbol.

If name is a forward reference, it will be undefined on pass 1 but defined on pass 2 of the assembler.

*.ERRIDN and .ERRDIF.*   These directives compare two arguments and generate an error message based on the result. *.ERRIDN* generates the error message if the arguments are identical, and *.ERRDIF* does so if they are different. The format is:

```
.ERRIDN[I] <argument1>,<argument2>
.ERRDIF[I] <argument1>,<argument2>
```

where the *arguments* can be names, numbers, or expressions and must be enclosed in angle brackets. The optional *I* specifies that arguments should be insensitive to case, that is, upper- and lowercase are considered identical.

### The EXITM Directive

Some conditions in macro definitions require that expansion of the macro cannot be completed. For example, if a macro to open a file does not receive an argument giving the filename, it is necessary to exit from the macro. The *EXITM directive* tells the assembler to abandon the macro expansion and proceed to the next source statement. The EXITM directive almost always follows one of the conditional-assembly statements.

## RECURSION, NESTING, AND REDEFINITION OF MACROS

MASM allows four advanced features in macro definitions that allow macros to be complex and flexible. They are recursion, nesting of macro definitions, nesting of macro call, and redefining macros.

### Recursion

Macro definitions may call themselves to repeat tasks until some condition is met. The following macro calls itself to add up to six words specified as parameters to AX register until no words are left to add. It also tests that AX is not one of the specified words.

```
ADDEM      MACRO P1, P2, P3, P4, P5, P6
           IFNB <P1>
           .ERRE <P1> EQ <AX>
           ADD AX, P1
           ADDEM P2, P3, P4, P5, P6
           ENDIF
           ENDM
```

If you invoke the macro with

```
ADDEM BX,CX,DX,WORD1
```

the assembler will produce

```
ADD AX,BX
ADD AX,CX
ADD AX,DX
ADD AX,WORD1
```

Writing

```
ADDEM N1,N2
```

will produce

```
ADD AX,N1
ADD AX,N2
```

## Nesting of Macro Definitions

You may use one macro to define another. This technique is useful when you wish to define a number of similar macros. Any time you wish to modify the macros, you have only to modify the original definition that created the others.

The macro that defines the other is called the *outer macro*, while the one that is defined is the *inner macro*. Macros may be nested to any depth. The outer macro must be called at least once before the inner macros may be called.

For example:

```
ADDSUBM    MACRO OP
OP&M       MACRO LOC1,LOC2,NBR
DISP       = 0
           CLC
           REPT NBR
           MOV AX,LOC1+DISP
           OP AX,LOC2+DISP
           MOV LOC1+DISP,AX
DISP       = DISP + 2
           ENDM
           ENDM
           ENDM
```

The outer macro (ADDSUBM) can be used with parameters ADD, ADC, SUB, or SBB to create inner macros named ADDM, ADCM, SUBM, or SBBM. The inner macro contains statements to add or subtract multiple words in memory starting at parameters LOC1 and LOC2 respectively. NBR is the number of words to be processed. Nested inside the inner macro is a REPT block that adds or subtracts two words at DISP and then adds 2 to DISP for the next repetition.

Writing the macro

```
ADDSUBM ADC
```

creates an inner macro definition

```
ADCM    MACRO LOC1,LOC2,NBR
```

Then writing the macro

```
ADCM         FIRST,SECOND,2
```

produces these source statements:

```
CLC
MOV AX,FIRST+DISP          ;DISP = 0
ADC AX,SECOND+DISP         ;DISP = 0
MOV FIRST+DISP,AX          ;DISP = 0
MOV AX,FIRST+DISP          ;DISP = 2
ADC AX,SECOND+DISP         ;DISP = 2
MOV FIRST+DISP,AX          ;DISP = 2
```

Writing the macro

```
ADCM ANYWD,OTHERWD,50
```

would generate a macro expansion of 150 instructions to add 50 words starting at OTHERWD to 50 other words starting at ANYWD.

## Nesting of Macro Calls

One macro definition may contain calls to other macros. The inner call is expanded only when the outer macro is called. For example:

```
LF        MACRO
          MOV DL,10
          MOV AH,1
          INT 21h
          ENDM
FEEDM     MACRO LINES
          REPT LINES
          LF
          ENDM
          ENDM
```

Writing the macro

```
FEEDM 5
```

causes the LF macro to be expanded five times to move the cursor down five lines.

## Redefining Macros

A macro may *redefine* itself. The first time it is expanded it uses one group of defined statements; on subsequent calls it expands other statements. The following nested macro definition ACCUMWDS initially clears the destination where the sum will be accumulated and adds in the specified word. Then ACCUMWDS is redefined so that each following call will bypass the first two instructions that clear the sum and will only add in the specified word.

```
ACCUMWDS   MACRO SUM,WORD
           XOR AX,AX
           MOV SUM,AX
           MOV AX,WORD
           ADD SUM,AX
ACCUMWDS   MACRO
           MOV AX,WORD
           ADD SUM,AX
           ENDM
           ENDM
```

Writing the macro

```
ACCUMWDS TOTAL,X
```

generates

```
XOR AX,AX
MOV TOTAL,AX
MOV AX,X
ADD TOTAL,AX
```

Another macro call such as

```
ACCUMWDS TOTAL,25
```

generates only

```
MOV AX,25
ADD TOTAL,AX
```

## PROGRAM 11: INSERTION SORT WITH MACROS

This program (Figure 11-2) demonstrates the insertion sort, which arranges words into ascending sequence in an array as they are entered at the keyboard. The program first clears the screen using the CLS macro and then positions the cursor at column 29 of line 0 with macro SET_CURSOR to center the first heading line. The macro DSP_STRING displays the heading and prompt. An internal subroutine GETNBR gets up to five decimal digits, converts them to a word, and returns the cursor.

The insertion sort routine places each number entered into the proper position in the array. After the first number is placed in the first element location (ARRAY + 0), BP is set to point to the second word, and the second number is entered.

The loop at WHILE01-WEND01 continues to receive additional numbers until <ENTER> alone is pressed, so that DX = 0. The loop at WHILE02-WEND02 is the heart of the sorting technique. BP points to the next available location in the array, while SI points to the last element placed in the array. If the new word in DX is lower than the last element currently in the array, that element is shifted up one position and SI is reduced by 2 to point to the next lower word. As the loop continues, each number in the array higher than the new word is shifted up one position until eventually the new word in DX is equal to or higher than the word compared. Then the new word is inserted into the position vacated by the last shift.

As SI is being decremented while searching for the position to insert the new word, it must be tested at WHILE02 to see that it is not less than zero, indicating a location lower than the first element in the array. Each time a new word is inserted into the array, BP is incremented by 2 to show the next available location.

After all numbers are inserted into the array, the loop at WHILE03-WEND03 sets SI back to the first element of the array and displays the numbers, 10 per line, incrementing SI for each number, until SI reaches BP, indicating all numbers have been displayed.

```
          PAGE 50,132
;----------------------------------------------------------------------
; Program name:   PROG11.ASM
;
; Author:   Alton R. Kindred
;
; This program accepts up to 100 five-digit decimal numbers, converts them
; to 16-bit words, and inserts them in ascending sequence into an array.
; Input is terminated when <ENTER> alone is entered.
; After the last number is entered, the array is displayed in ascending
; sequence on the screen with 10 values per line.
;----------------------------------------------------------------------
DATA       SEGMENT                    ;segment for data
MSG        DB 'Insertion Sort Routine',13,10,10
           DB 'Enter up to 100 five-digit decimal integers (0-65535)',13,10
           DB 'Press <ENTER> alone to stop',13,10,'$'
ARRAY      DW 100 DUP (?)
DATA       ENDS
;----------------------------------------------------------------------
STACK      SEGMENT STACK              ;stack segment
           DB 32 DUP ('STACK   ')
STACK      ENDS
;----------------------------------------------------------------------
           IF1
           INCLUDE MACRO.LIB
           ENDIF
CODE       SEGMENT                    ;segment for code
PROG11     PROC FAR
           ASSUME CS:CODE,DS:DATA,SS:STACK
           EXTRN INPHEX:NEAR,DSPDEC:NEAR,INPDEC:NEAR
           MOV AX,DATA                ;set up data segment in DS
           MOV DS,AX
           CLS                        ;clear screen
           SET_CURSOR 0,29            ;line = 0; column = 29
           DSP_STRING MSG             ;issue prompt
           CALL GETNBR                ;get decimal number into DX
           MOV ARRAY,DX               ;move it to array(1)
           XOR CX,CX                  ;set counter to zero
           MOV BP,2                   ;point BP at array(2)
           CALL GETNBR                ;get another number
WHILE:     CMP DX,0                   ;WHILE more numbers entered
           JE WEND
           MOV SI,BP                  ;  point SI at word below BP
           SUB SI,2
WHILE2:    CMP SI,0                   ;  WHILE not at first word
           JL WEND2
AND2:      CMP DX,ARRAY[SI]           ;  and new word < array word
           JA WEND2
           MOV AX,ARRAY[SI]           ;    shift array word upward
           MOV ARRAY[SI+2],AX
           SUB SI,2                   ;    point to next lower word
           JMP WHILE2
WEND2:                                ;  WEND
           MOV ARRAY[SI+2],DX         ;  insert new word into array
```

**Figure 11-2    Program 11. Insertion sort with macros**

```
            INC CX                      ;   add 1 to counter
            ADD BP,2                    ;   point BP at next element
            CALL GETNBR                 ;   get next number
            JMP WHILE
WEND:                                   ;WEND
            MOV SI,0                    ;set SI at first word
            MOV CX,10                   ;set count to 10
WHILE3:     CMP SI,BP                   ;WHILE more words in array
            JNB WEND3
            MOV DX,ARRAY[SI]            ;   print the word
            CALL DSPDEC
            REPT 2
            DSP_CHR                     ;   space twice
            ENDM
            ADD SI,2                    ;   increment pointer in SI
            LOOP WHILE3                 ;   IF 10 words printed
            CR_LF                       ;      space down
            MOV CX,10                   ;      reset counter to 10
            JMP WHILE3                  ;   ENDIF
WEND3:                                  ;WEND
            DOS_RET                     ;return to DOS
;
PROG11      ENDP                        ;end of procedure declaration
;----------------------------------------------------------------------
GETNBR      PROC NEAR
            CALL INPDEC                 ;get decimal number
            PUSH DX
            CR_LF                       ;return cursor and line feed
            POP DX
            RET
GETNBR      ENDP
CODE        ENDS                        ;end of code segment
            END PROG11                  ;end of program
```

**Figure 11-2    *concluded***

This program uses the CLS, SET_CURSOR, DSP_STRING, DSP_CHR, and CR_LF macros from MACRO.LIB, shown in Figure 11-1. It also uses the external subroutines INPHEX, DSPDEC, and INPDEC shown in earlier chapters.

Figure 11-3 shows the assembler listing of program 11. This listing shows the macro expansions under the standard .XALL option preceded with a code 1 or 2. The listing of symbols gives the name and number of lines of each macro examined by the assembler. Only those called in the program are expanded.

Figure 11-4 shows a sample of output from program 11.

# SUMMARY

A macro definition is a group of source statements that may be copied into a source program when the macro is invoked, or called. Wise use of

```
Microsoft (R) Macro Assembler Version 5.00                1/17/90 14:27:59
                                                          Page    1-1


             PAGE 50,132
;----------------------------------------------------------------------------
; Program name:   PROG11.ASM
;
; Author:   Alton R. Kindred
;
; This program accepts up to 100 five-digit decimal numbers, converts them
; to 16-bit words, and inserts them in ascending sequence into an array.
; Input is terminated when <ENTER> alone is entered.
; After the last number is entered, the array is displayed in ascending
; sequence on the screen with 10 values per line.
;----------------------------------------------------------------------------
 0000                          DATA    SEGMENT              ;segment for data
 0000  49 6E 73 65 72 74 69 MSG      DB 'Insertion Sort Routine',13,10,10
       6F 6E 20 53 6F 72 74
       20 52 6F 75 74 69 6E
       65 0D 0A 0A
 0019  45 6E 74 65 72 20 75           DB 'Enter up to 100 five-digit decimal
       70 20 74 6F 20 31 30               integers (0-65535)',13,10
       30 20 66 69 76 65 2D
       64 69 67 69 74 20 64
       65 63 69 6D 61 6C 20
       69 6E 74 65 67 65 72
       73 20 28 30 2D 36 35
       35 33 35 29 0D 0A
 0050  50 72 65 73 73 20 3C           DB 'Press <ENTER> alone to stop',13,10,'$'
       45 4E 54 45 52 3E 20
       61 6C 6F 6E 65 20 74
       6F 20 73 74 6F 70 0D
       0A 24
 006E  0064[                  ARRAY    DW 100 DUP (?)
  ????
  ]

 0136                          DATA    ENDS
;----------------------------------------------------------------------------
 0000                          STACK   SEGMENT STACK        ;stack segment
 0000  0020[                           DB 32 DUP ('STACK   ')
  53 54 41 43 4B
  20 20 20
  ]

 0100                          STACK       ENDS
;----------------------------------------------------------------------------
                               ENDIF
 0000                          CODE    SEGMENT              ;segment for code
      Microsoft (R) Macro Assembler Version 5.00            1/17/90 14:27:59
                                                            Page    1-2
```

**Figure 11-3    Assembler Listing of Program 11**

```
0000                              PROG11    PROC FAR
                                            ASSUME CS:CODE,DS:DATA,SS:STACK
                                            EXTRN INPHEX:NEAR,DSPDEC:NEAR,INPDEC:NEAR
0000  B8 ---- R                   MOV AX,DATA                ;set up data segment
0003  8E D8                       MOV DS,AX
                                  CLS                        ;clear screen
0005  B0 00              1        MOV AL,0
0007  B4 06              1        MOV AH,6
0009  B7 07              1        MOV BH,7
000B  B9 0000            1        MOV CX,0
000E  B2 4F              1        MOV DL,79
0010  B6 18              1        MOV DH,24
0012  CD 10              1        INT 10h
                                  SET_CURSOR 0,29           ;line = 0; column = 29
0014  B7 00              1        MOV BH,0
0016  B6 00              1        MOV DH,0
0018  B2 1D              1        MOV DL,29
001A  B4 02              1        MOV AH,2
001C  CD 10              1        INT 10h
                                  DSP_STRING MSG            ;issue prompt
001E  8D 16 0000 R       1        LEA DX,MSG
0022  B4 09              1        MOV AH,9
0024  CD 21              1        INT 21h
0026  E8 009C R                   CALL GETNBR               ;get decimal number
0029  89 16 006E R                MOV ARRAY,DX              ;move it to array(1)
002D  33 C9                       XOR CX,CX                 ;set counter to zero
002F  DD 0002                     MOV BP,2                  ;point BP at array(2)
0032  E8 009C R                   CALL GETNBR               ;get another number
0035  83 FA 00           WHILE:   CMP DX,0                  ;WHILE more numbers
0038  74 2A                       JE WEND
003A  8B F5                       MOV SI,BP                 ;  point SI at word
003C  83 EE 02                    SUB SI,2
003F  83 FE 00           WHILE2:  CMP SI,0                  ;   WHILE not at first
0042  7C 13                       JL WEND2
0044  3B 94 006E R  AND2:         CMP DX,ARRAY[SI]          ;   and new word < arr
0048  77 0D                       JA WEND2
004A  8B 84 006E R                MOV AX,ARRAY[SI]          ;     shift array word
004E  89 84 0070 R                MOV ARRAY[SI+2],AX
0052  83 EE 02                    SUB SI,2                  ;     point to next
0055  EB E8                       JMP WHILE2
0057                    WEND2:                              ;   WEND
0057  89 94 0070 R                MOV ARRAY[SI+2],DX        ;   insert new word
005B  41                          INC CX                    ;   add 1 to counter
005C  83 C5 02                    ADD BP,2                  ;   point BP at next
005F  E8 009C R                   CALL GETNBR               ;   get next number
0062  EB D1                       JMP WHILE
      Microsoft (R) Macro Assembler Version 5.00             1/17/90 14:27:59
                                                             Page     1-3


0064                    WEND:                               ;WEND
0064  BE 0000                     MOV SI,0                  ;set SI at first word
0067  B9 000A                     MOV CX,10                 ;set count to 10
006A  3B F5              WHILE3:  CMP SI,BP                 ;WHILE more words in
006C  73 29                       JNB WEND3
```

**Figure 11-3**    *continued*

```
006E  8B 94 006E R                  MOV DX,ARRAY[SI]      ;  print the word
0072  E8 0000 E                     CALL DSPDEC
                                    REPT 2
                                    DSP_CHR               ;  space twice
                                    ENDM
0075  B2 20             2           MOV DL,' '
0077  B4 02             2           MOV AH,2
0079  CD 21             2           INT 21h
007B  B2 20             2           MOV DL,' '
007D  B4 02             2           MOV AH,2
007F  CD 21             2           INT 21h
0081  83 C6 02                      ADD SI,2              ;  increment pointer
0084  E2 E4                         LOOP WHILE3           ;  IF 10 words printed
                                    CR_LF                 ;     space down
0086  B2 0D             2           MOV DL,13
0088  B4 02             2           MOV AH,2
008A  CD 21             2           INT 21h
008C  B2 0A             2           MOV DL,10
008E  B4 02             2           MOV AH,2
0090  CD 21             2           INT 21h
0092  B9 000A                       MOV CX,10             ;     reset counter
0095  EB D3                         JMP WHILE3            ;  ENDIF
0097                    WEND3:                            ;WEND
                                    DOS_RET               ;return to DOS
0097  B8 4C00           1           MOV AX,4C00h
009A  CD 21             1           INT 21h
;
009C                    PROG11      ENDP                  ;end of procedure
declaration
;---------------------------------------------------------------------------
009C                    GETNBR      PROC NEAR
009C  E8 0000 E                     CALL INPDEC           ;get decimal number
009F  52                            PUSH DX
                                    CR_LF                 ;return cursor and
00A0  B2 0D             2           MOV DL,13
00A2  B4 02             2           MOV AH,2
00A4  CD 21             2           INT 21h
00A6  B2 0A             2           MOV DL,10
00A8  B4 02             2           MOV AH,2
00AA  CD 21             2           INT 21h
00AC  5A                            POP DX
00AD  C3                            RET
```

Microsoft (R) Macro Assembler Version 5.00                    1/17/90 14:27:59
                                                              Page     1-4

```
00AE                    GETNBR      ENDP
00AE                    CODE        ENDS                  ;end of code segment
                                    END PROG11            ;end of program
```

Microsoft (R) Macro Assembler Version 5.00                    1/17/90 14:27:59
                                                              Symbols-1

Macros:

**Figure 11-3**    *continued*

```
     N a m e   Lines

CLOSE_FILE . . . . . . . . . . .      3
CLS  . . . . . . . . . . . . .        7
CR . . . . . . . . . . . . . .        3
CREATE_FILE . . . . . . . . .         3
CR_LF . . . . . . . . . . . .         2
DELETE_FILE . . . . . . . . .         3
DOS_RET . . . . . . . . . . .         2
DSP_CHR . . . . . . . . . . .         7
DSP_STRING . . . . . . . . . .        3
GET_CURSOR . . . . . . . . . .        3
GET_DISK_SPACE . . . . . . . .        3
INP_CHR_ECHO . . . . . . . . .        2
INP_STRING . . . . . . . . . .        4
INT_CHR_NOECHO . . . . . . . .        2
LF . . . . . . . . . . . . . .        3
OPEN_FILE  . . . . . . . . . .        4
PRT_CHR  . . . . . . . . . . .        3
READ_ATTRIB_AND_CHAR . . . . .        2
READ_FILE  . . . . . . . . . .        5
RENAME_FILE  . . . . . . . . .        8
SET_CURSOR . . . . . . . . . .        5
SET_VIDEO_MODE . . . . . . . .        3
WRITE_ATTRIB_AND_CHAR . . . . .       5
WRITE_FILE . . . . . . . . . .        5

Segments and Groups:

                N a m e         Length  Align Combine Class

CODE . . . . . . . . . . . . . .      00AE PARA NONE
DATA . . . . . . . . . . . . . .      0136 PARA NONE
STACK  . . . . . . . . . . . . .      0100 PARA STACK

Symbols:

                N a m e        Type  Value  Attr

AND2 . . . . . . . . . . . . . .     L NEAR 0044 CODE
ARRAY  . . . . . . . . . . . . .     L WORD 006E DATA Length = 0064

DSPDEC . . . . . . . . . . . . .     L NEAR 0000 CODE External

    Microsoft (R) Macro Assembler Version 5.00              1/17/90 14:27:59
                                                            Symbols-2


GETNBR . . . . . . . . . . . . .     N PROC 009C CODE Length = 0012

INPDEC . . . . . . . . . . . . .     L NEAR 0000 CODE External
INPHEX . . . . . . . . . . . . .     L NEAR 0000 CODE External

MSG  . . . . . . . . . . . . . .     L BYTE 0000 DATA

PROG11 . . . . . . . . . . . . .     F PROC 0000 CODE Length = 009C
```

**Figure 11-3**    *continued*

```
WEND . . . . . . . . . . . . . .    L NEAR 0064 CODE
WEND2 . . . . . . . . . . . . . .   L NEAR 0057 CODE
WEND3 . . . . . . . . . . . . . .   L NEAR 0097 CODE
WHILE . . . . . . . . . . . . . .   L NEAR 0035 CODE
WHILE2 . . . . . . . . . . . . . .  L NEAR 003F CODE
WHILE3 . . . . . . . . . . . . . .  L NEAR 006A CODE

. . . . . . . .    TEXT  prog11


    87 Source  Lines
   136 Total   Lines
    43 Symbols

 51022 + 389298 Bytes symbol space free

     0 Warning Errors
     0 Severe  Errors
```

**Figure 11-3**    *concluded*

macros can shorten programming time and improve accuracy. Macro definitions can be written directly into the source program or placed into a library and copied by an INCLUDE statement in the source program.

The MACRO directive starts the macro definition. Its name field gives the name by which the macro will be invoked, and its operand field contains parameters that will be replaced by arguments to be used at the time the macro is invoked. The ENDM directive ends the macro definition.

The body of the macro definition between the MACRO and ENDM directives may contain almost any statement used in assembler language. Conditional and repeat statements often are used to create loops that assemble certain statements repeatedly or selection structures that assemble one block of statements if a condition is true and another block if the condition is false. Arguments that replace parameters when the macro is invoked also replace those parameters in the body statements wherever they occur.

The LOCAL directive identifies labels within the body of the macro definition. These labels are changed to the form ??nnnn in the macro expansion, where nnnn starts at 0000 and is incremented by 1 each time a LOCAL label is used. This technique ensures that labels are not duplicated if the macro is used more than once in a program.

Statements in a macro expansion may be listed under three options: .LALL lists all statements in the expansion, .XALL lists only the executable statements, and .SALL suppresses all statements in the expansion.

Three types of equate statements can be used both inside and outside macro definitions. Redefinable numeric equates assign the value of the expansion to the right of an equal sign (=) to the symbol to the left of the sign. Nonredefinable numeric equates assign the value of a constant to the right of

```
Insertion Sort Routine
Enter up to 100 five-digit decimal integers (0-65535)
Press <ENTER> alone to stop
4327
155
20000
9
43
689
223
5280
1846
65535
22
890
4
3239

00004   00009   00022   00043   00155   00223   00689   00890   01846   03239
04327   05280   20000   65535
B>
```

**Figure 11-4    Output from Program 11**

EQU directive to the symbol to the left of the EQU. This value cannot be changed later in the source program. String equates assign the value of a string enclosed in angle brackets (< >) to the right of an EQU directive to the symbol to the left of the EQU. String equates may be redefined later with a new string.

Five macro operators are useful in macro and conditional statements. The ampersand (&) permits parameters to be concatenated, or joined, together to form a single string. Angle brackets (< >) enclose a string of literal text. The exclamation point (!) identifies a character to be used literally rather than assigned its special meaning in assembler language. The percent sign (%) tells the assembler to compute the value of an expression and replace the text in the expression with the result. Two semicolons (;;) designate a macro comment that appears in the definition but not in the macro expansion.

The three repeat directives, REPT, IRP, and IRPC, permit blocks of statements to be repeated. The repeat block may appear inside or outside of macro definitions and must be ended with the ENDM directive. The REPT directive repeats the block the number of times specified in the expression that follows it. The IRP directive, followed by a parameter and list of arguments enclosed in angle brackets (< >) and separated by commas, repeats the block once for each item in the list. The parameter takes on the value of the next item on the list during each successive repetition. The IRPC directive, followed by a parameter and a string, repeats the block with the parameter having the value of one character of the string until each character has been used. If the string contains spaces, commas, or other delimiters, it should be enclosed in angle brackets.

Conditional-assembly directives assemble a block of statements only if a specified condition is true and may, optionally, assemble another block if the condition is false. The IF directive, in its various forms, specifies the condition to be tested and is followed by the block of statements to be assembled if the condition is true. The optional ELSE directive is followed by statements to be assembled if the condition is false. The ENDIF directive terminates the entire conditional-assembly block. IF statements may be nested.

Conditional-error directives test a specified condition and force an error and display a message if an error occurs. Conditional-error directives begin with .ERR and have a number of forms somewhat similar to the IF directives.

Powerful variations on macros may be made through recursion, nesting of macro definitions, nesting of macro calls, and redefining macros.

## QUESTIONS

1. What are some advantages of defining and using macros?
2. How does a macro definition differ from a macro call?
3. How and where are macro definitions placed into a source program?
4. Describe the parts of the MACRO directive. How can different arguments be supplied to the macro each time it is called?
5. What two kinds of statements are ended with the ENDM directive? Which kinds may be used only inside the macro definition and which may be used either inside or outside it?
6. Describe the nature and purpose of a LOCAL directive.
7. Name and describe the operation of the three macro listing control directives.
8. Name and describe the three types of equates.
9. What is meant by concatenation? Which operator performs it?
10. What is the difference between a macro comment and an ordinary comment? Under which condition will each be listed?
11. Name the three repeat directives and describe their operation.
12. What is the purpose of conditional-assembly directives? At what point in the assembly and execution process do they test the specified conditions?
13. How do relational operators used in conditional-assembly statements differ from those used in operands for machine instructions?
14. Which IF statements determine if an argument has or has not been passed to a macro?
15. What is the difference between a conditional-assembly statement and a conditional-error statement? In what respect are they similar?

## EXERCISES

1. Write a macro definition that defines a stack segment and permits you to specify how many times the constant 'STACK    ' will be repeated in the stack.

2.  Write a definition for a macro named MYNAME that creates DB statements to define you name and mailing address. Include a cursor return and line feed after each line but the dollar sign only after the last line.

3.  Write a definition called UPCASE that contains LOCAL directives to create an IF-THEN structure to test if AL contains a character 'a' through 'z' and if so, change it to 'A' through 'Z' by using the statement AND AL,11011111b. Do not change any other characters.

4.  Use redefinable numeric equates and repeat block within a macro definition to define five words having values of 100, 200, 300, 400, and 500.

5.  Using the concatenation operator (&), write a definition of a macro named DEFARRAY so that you can specify the name, type, size, and initial value of each element of the array. The type of data is concatenated to the word ARRAY to make the name of the array. Two examples of the expansion might be ARRAYW DW 50 DUP (?) or ARRAYB DB 10 DUP ('-').

6.  Use the IRP directive to create 10 bytes having values of the cube of the numbers from 1 through 10.

7.  Write a macro definition to swap contents of two registers or words in storage named as arguments if both names are not the same.

8.  Write a macro definition that will take two unpacked BCD digits in AX and pack them together into AL. Hint: Use shift or rotate instructions.

## LAB PROBLEMS

1.  Modify program 11 to permit input of up to 50 strings of up to 20 characters each. As each string is entered, insert it into the correct position of the array. Each array element must be 20 characters, padded with blanks if necessary. Write macro definitions that use the string handling instructions to compare two strings, to move a string from one location to another, and to print out the sorted strings. Write any other macros you find helpful to define segments, data, or groups of instructions.

# ADVANCED ASSEMBLER CONTROL

# 12

## OBJECTIVES

After studying this chapter, you should be able to:

- Identify and use MASM options.
- Explain the various memory models.
- Explain and use simplified segment definitions.
- Define full segments and combine them into groups.
- Use special MASM listing directives.
- Use many special MASM directives and operators.

## MASM OPTIONS

*MASM* provides a number of options that may be specified in the command line when MASM is loaded for execution. Recall that the format for the MASM command line is:

```
MASM [options] sourcefile
     [,[objectfile][,[listfile][,[crossreffile]]]][;]
```

The codes for options consist of a slash (/), followed by a one- or two-letter command, followed in several cases with other operands. Table 12-1 shows the options used with version 5.0 of MASM.

Each option specified remains in effect unless it is modified by a directive in the source program. Default options may be set as described in the section headed Environment Variables.

### Specifying Segment Order

Segments may be arranged in alphabetic order or in the sequence they are written in the source code. The /A *option* specifies alphabetic order, while the /S *option* specifies source-code order. The default is /S. To arrange segments in alpha order and to create object and list files for PROG1, use the command line:

TABLE 12-1.  MASM Options

| OPTION | ACTION |
| --- | --- |
| /A | Write segments in alphabetical order |
| /Bnumber | Set buffer size |
| /C | Specify cross-reference file |
| /D | Create pass 1 listing |
| /Dsymbol[=value] | Define assembler symbol |
| /E | Create code for emulated floating-point instructions |
| /H | List command-line syntax and all assembler options |
| /Ipath | Set include-file search path |
| /L | Specify an assembly-listing file |
| /ML | Make names case sensitive |
| /MU | Convert names to uppercase |
| /MX | Make public and external names case sensitive |
| /N | Suppress tables in listing file |
| /P | Check for impure code |
| /S | Write segments in source-code order |
| /T | Suppress messages for successful assembly |
| /V | Display extra statistics to screen |
| /W{0\|1\|2} | Set error-display level |
| /X | Include false conditional blocks in listings |
| /Z | Display error lines on screen |
| /ZD | Put line-number information in object file |
| /ZI | Put symbolic and line-number information in object file |

```
B> A:MASM /A PROG1,,;
```

The .ALPHA directive in the source code also causes MASM to arrange the segments in alphabetic order, while the .SEQ directive specifies that segments are to be in the sequence shown in source code. The directive, if used, will override the command line.

## Setting File-Buffer Size

The /B option sets the file-buffer size used by MASM for the source file. If the buffer is larger than the source file, the entire assembly may be done in memory, faster than using disk swapping. The default buffer size is 32K, but may be set at any number from 1K to 63K.

The format for the command is:

```
MASM /Bnumber
```

where *number* can be 1 through 63. For example,

```
B> A:MASM /B63
```

makes the buffer its maximum size of 63K and gives the greatest assembly speed. You normally would reduce the buffer size only if your computer has insufficient memory or you are using too many resident programs.

### Creating Pass 1 Listing

The */D option* adds a pass 1 listing if you specify an assembly listing file and displays error messages for both pass 1 and pass 2 even if no assembly listing is created. The pass 1 listing helps to identify errors in assembler assumptions that are not valid during pass 2. For example:

```
B> A:MASM /D PROG1,,;
```

### Defining Assembler Symbols

The */D option, followed by the name of a symbol,* has the same effect as defining a text equate in the source file. In addition, the symbol can be given a value. If no value is given, the symbol is a null string. More than one symbol can be defined in a command line. For example:

```
B> A:MASM /Dscreen=2000 /Dnumber PROG1,,;
```

In this example, SCREEN is a string with value of 2000, while NUMBER is a null string.

### Creating Code for Floating-Point Emulator

The */E option* tells the assembler to produce data and code in the format expected by the 8087, 80287, or 80387 coprocessors. This permits you to use emulator libraries in conjunction with high-level languages such as C, BASIC, FORTRAN, and Pascal. This option cannot be used in stand-alone assembler programs unless you write your own assembler library.

### Getting Command Line Help

The */H option* displays all MASM options and command-line syntax on the screen. Do not use any file names or other options with the /H option. For example:

```
B> A:MASM /H
```

### Setting Search Paths for Include Files

The */I option* sets a search path for include files. As many as 10 paths may be set in one command line. Each path requires a separate /I option. The paths are searched in the order they appear in the command line. For example:

```
B> A:MASM /I\a:macro /I\b:subs
```

This line tells the assembler to search for any file specified in an IN-CLUDE statement, first in the MACRO directory on drive A, and then in the SUBS library in drive B. You should not give path names in your INCLUDE statement in the source program if you use the /I option in the command line.

### Specifying Listing and Cross-Reference Files

The /L *option* tells the assembler to create a listing file. The /C *option* tells it to create a cross-reference file. These files will have the same name as the source file with extensions of .LST or .CRF, respectively.

These options are effective even if no listing or cross-reference file is named in the command line or in response to a prompt. The following lines both produce read a file named PROG1.ASM and create three output files: PROG1.OBJ, PROG1.LST, and PROG1.CRF:

```
B> A:MASM /L /C PROG1;
B> A:MASM PROG1,,,;
```

### Specifying Case Sensitivity

The /MU, /ML, and /MX options tell the assembler how to treat letters in names that might be uppercase or lowercase in source code. By default, MASM converts all names into uppercase letters.

The /MU option (default) tells the assembler to make names into upper-case letters. The /ML *option* makes all names case sensitive, i.e. preserves the case shown in the source code. The /MX *option* makes only public and exter-nal names case sensitive. Even if two names are spelled alike, they are considered different if some or all of the letters in the names have different cases.

Case sensitivity is important if object modules are to be linked with modules created by other compilers, such as that for Microsoft C.

### Suppressing Listing File Tables

The /N *option* directs MASM to omit all tables from the end of the listing file. Normally, the assembler will include tables of symbols, macros, struc-tures, records, segments, and groups.

### Checking for Impure Code

The /P *option* tells MASM to check for impure code when in 80286 or 80386 privileged mode. The use of the CS:override when moving data into memory is valid in real mode, but will generate an error in protected mode.

This feature is compatible with XENIX and with anticipated developments in OS/2.

## Controlling Display of Assembly Statistics

The /V and /T options affect the amount of information displayed on the screen at the end of assembly. If no option is given, the assembler displays a line stating the amount of symbol space free and the number of warnings and errors.

The /V *option* (verbose) causes MASM, at the end of assembly, to report on the screen the number of lines and symbols processed. The /T *option* (terse) tells MASM not to output anything on the screen unless errors are encountered.

Messages about any errors encountered will be displayed whether or not the /V or /T options appear.

## Setting the Warning Level

The /W *option* sets the level at which MASM is to report warning messages. The three warning levels are:

| LEVEL | TYPE | DESCRIPTION |
|---|---|---|
| 0 | Severe errors | Illegal statements |
| 1 | Serious warnings | Ambiguous statements or poor programming practice |
| 2 | Advisory warnings | Inefficient use of statements |

The default warning level is 1. Each higher warning level includes the lower levels. No object file is produced if there are any severe errors.

Examples include the following:

```
MASM /W0 PROG1,,;        ;list only severe errors
MASM /W1 PROG1,,;        ;list severe errors and
                         ;serious warnings
MASM /W2 PROG1,,;        ;list severe errors,
                         ;serious warnings, and
                         ;advisory warnings
```

## Listing False Conditionals

The /X *option* tells MASM to show on the assembly listing all statements in conditional-assembly blocks whose condition is false. It has no effect unless you have requested a listing file. Without this option, MASM suppresses the false statements, since they do not generate code.

Three directives in source code can override the effect of the /X option: .LFCOND lists false-conditional blocks, .SFCOND suppresses the false-conditional listing, and .TFCOND toggles the false-conditional listing. If the /X option is used, the .TFCOND reverses the effect so that the first conditional block would not be listed, the second would be, the third would not, and so forth.

### Displaying Error Lines on the Screen

The /Z *option* directs the assembler to display lines containing errors, as well as the corresponding error message, on the screen. Without this option, only the error message is displayed. Assembly is slightly slower with the /Z option in effect, but the convenience of seeing the line in error may well offset the additional time.

### Writing Symbolic Information to the Object File

The /ZI and /ZD options direct MASM to write symbolic information to the object file. /ZI causes both line-number data and symbolic data to the object file; /ZD writes only line-number data.

Advanced debuggers require this symbolic information. The /ZI option is preferred for EXE programs to be debugged with CodeView (supplied with MASM version 5.0). Debugging information is removed from programs prepared in the COM format. The /ZD option is sufficient for programs to be debugged with SYMDEB (supplied with version 4.0). Neither option is required for use of DEBUG.

## ENVIRONMENT VARIABLES

DOS provides seven *environment variables* that may be used to set default options or specify directories used by certain programs. Use of these environment variables can reduce the length of command lines when these programs are executed.

The names and descriptions of the environment variables are shown in Table 12-2. The INCLUDE and MASM variables are of particular interest to users of MASM.

### INCLUDE Environment Variable

The *INCLUDE environment variable* can give the name of the directory where include files are stored. Include files are source statements such as macros brought into the source statement by use of the INCLUDE directive. It often is efficient to keep all include files in the same directory. This need not be the same directory where the source file is kept.

If the assembler knows where to look for the file specified in the INCLUDE directive, you need not give the full directory path along with the file name in the INCLUDE statement in the source statement.

TABLE 12-2.  Environment Variables

| VARIABLE | DESCRIPTION |
|---|---|
| PATH | Specify directories for DOS executable files. Language developers often use \BIN as the directory for executable files. |
| LIB | Specify directory for LINK library and object files. \LIB is often named for this directory. |
| INCLUDE | Specify directory for MASM include files. \INCLUDE is a commonly used name for this directory. |
| MASM | Specify default options to be used when MASM is executed. |
| LINK | Specify default options to be used when LINK is executed. |
| TMP | Specify directory where LINK places temporary files it may need to create. |
| INIT | Specify directory where MAKE looks for the file TOOLS.INI that contains inference tools. Used in connection with Microsoft CodeView. |

The DOS SET command is used to define the INCLUDE environment variable. The following example specifies that INCLUDE files will be in a directory named INCLLIB on drive B:

```
A>SET INCLUDE=B:\INCLLIB
```

If a source program contains an INCLUDE directive, MASM first looks at the directory specified by the /I option, as discussed in the section titled Setting Search Paths for Include Files. If no /I option was used, or if the file is not found in that directory, then MASM looks in the current directory. If the file is still not found, MASM looks in the directories named in the INCLUDE environment variable in the order specified.

## MASM Environment Variable

You may put default assembler options in the *MASM environment variable.* Then you need not set those options in the MASM command line or (in some cases) through directives in the source program.

The DOS SET command places the specified options into the MASM environment variable. For example:

```
A>SET MASM=/A/L/C
```

will set the three default options to arrange segments alphabetically, to produce an assembly listing file, and to create a cross-reference file. These default options can be overridden in the MASM command line. For example,

```
B> A:MASM /S PROG1;
```

causes segments in PROG1 to be arranged in source-code sequence, but the defaults for the listing and cross-reference files still remain in effect.

When you execute MASM, it first reads the options in the environment variable and then any in the command line. If the options conflict, then the last one read takes effect. Any assembler directives always will override any related options.

# SIMPLIFIED SEGMENT DEFINITIONS

Up to this point in the text, full segment definitions have been used as required by MASM 4.0 and earlier versions. MASM 5.0 provides several new directives that shorten and simplify the definition of segments. However, the simplified definitions may not cover all possible instances, so that full definitions often may be necessary or desirable.

Figure 12-1 shows a short program defined with the simplified method. Each of its features is discussed in the following sections.

## Specifying DOS Segment Order

The DOSSEG directive causes segments to be placed in the DOS segment-order convention consistent with that used by Microsoft high-level language compilers. Then you actually may write the segments in any order you wish.

Although segment order can depend on a number of factors, it probably is good practice to use the DOSSEG directive consistently. You should be aware that when the DOSSEG directive (or the /DOSSEG linker option) is used, the linker generates symbols called *_end* and *_edata*. You should not use these names in your program.

## Defining the Memory Model

The *memory model* controls the default size of data and code in a program. There are six memory models described in Table 12-3. Note that the *tiny* model programs must be written in COM format and that simplified segment directives cannot be used. Any of the other five models may be specified in the simplified format.

The .MODEL directive should appear in the source code before any segment directive. It usually follows immediately after the DOSSEG directive. Its format is:

```
.MODEL memorymodel
```

where *memorymodel* can be SMALL, MEDIUM, COMPACT, LARGE, or HUGE. A stand-alone assembler program can use any model, although

```
Microsoft (R) Macro Assembler Version 5.00          5/2/89 15:05:03
                                                    Page    1-1


          PAGE 50,132
      ;-------------------------------------------------------------------
      ; Program Name: SIMPLE.ASM
      ;
      ; Author:       Alton R. Kindred
      ;
      ; This program prints out a four-line name and address as a single
      ; constant.  It demonstrates simplified segment definitions.
      ;-------------------------------------------------------------------
                                     DOSSEG
                                     .MODEL SMALL
0000                                 .DATA
0000  41 6C 74 6F 6E 20 52 MYNAME    DB 'Alton R. Kindred',13,10
      2E 20 4B 69 6E 64 72
      65 64 0D 0A
0012  4D 61 6E 61 74 65 65           DB 'Manatee Community College',13,10
      20 43 6F 6D 6D 75 6E
      69 74 79 20 43 6F 6C
      6C 65 67 65 0D 0A
002D  35 38 34 30 20 32 36           DB '5840 26th Street West',13,10
      74 68 20 53 74 72 65
      65 74 20 57 65 73 74
      0D 0A
0044  42 72 61 64 65 6E 74           DB 'Bradenton, FL 34209',13,10,'$'
      6F 6E 2C 20 46 4C 20
      33 34 32 30 39 0D 0A
      24
0100                                 .STACK 256
0000                                 .CODE
0000                        SIMPLE   PROC NEAR
0000  B8 ---- R                      MOV AX,@DATA
0003  8E D8                          MOV DS,AX
0005  8D 16 0000 R                   LEA DX,MYNAME
0009  E8 0011 R                      CALL DSPLINE
000C  B8 4C00                        MOV AX,4C00h
000F  CD 21                          INT 21h
0011                        SIMPLE   ENDP
      ;-------------------------------------------------------------------
0011                        DSPLINE  PROC NEAR
0011  B4 09                          MOV AH,9
0013  CD 21                          INT 21h
0015  C3                             RET
0016                        DSPLINE  ENDP
0016                                 END SIMPLE


                                                    5/2/89 15:05:03
    Microsoft (R) Macro Assembler Version 5.00      Symbols-1
  Segments and Groups:
```

**Figure 12-1    Program with Simplified Segment Definitions**

```
                  N a m e              Length  Align Combine Class

DGROUP . . . . . . . . . . . . . .    GROUP
  _DATA  . . . . . . . . . . . . .    005A WORD PUBLIC 'DATA'
  STACK  . . . . . . . . . . . . .    0100 PARA STACK 'STACK'
-TEXT  . . . . . . . . . . . . . .    0016 WORD PUBLIC 'CODE'

Symbols:

                  N a m e              Type  Value  Attr

DSPLINE  . . . . . . . . . . . . .    N PROC 0011 _TEXT Length = 0005

MYNAME   . . . . . . . . . . . .      L BYTE 0000 _DATA

SIMPLE   . . . . . . . . . . . .      N PROC 0000 _TEXT Length = 0011

@CODE    . . . . . . . . . . . . .    TEXT  _TEXT
@CODESIZE . . . . . . . . . . . .     TEXT  0
@DATASIZE . . . . . . . . . . . .     TEXT  0
@FILENAME . . . . . . . . . . . .     TEXT  SIMPLE

    33 Source  Lines
    33 Total   Lines
    17 Symbols

  51186 + 406254 Bytes symbol space free

    0 Warning Errors
    0 Severe   Errors
```

**Figure 12-1**   *concluded*

SMALL is usually the best choice. When writing an assembler routine for a high-level language, use the same memory model used by the compiler or interpreter for that language.

The .MODEL directive defines default segments for the memory model specified and creates the ASSUME and GROUP statements used by that model. For small and compact models, the linker starts the first byte of the code segment at an offset of 16 bytes (10h) from the address in CS to be consistent with executable files created with Microsoft compilers.

### Defining Simplified Segments

Seven directives indicate the start of a segment. These directives are .CODE, .STACK, .DATA, .DATA?, .FARDATA, .FARDATA?, and .CONST. Each one also ends any segment defined earlier that is still open. The END directive closes the last open segment in the source file.

*Code Segment.* The *code segment* is defined by the .CODE directive. Its format is:

TABLE 12-3.  Memory Models

| MODEL | DESCRIPTION |
|---|---|
| Tiny | All data and code must fit within a single segment and be written in COM format. Microsoft high-level languages do not use this format. Simplified segment directives may not be used. |
| Small | All data must fit within a single 64K segment, and all code must also fit within a 64K segment. Most stand-alone assembler programs can use this model. Microsoft C supports the small model. |
| Medium | All data must fit within a single 64K segment, but code may be greater than 64K. Most Microsoft languages support this model. |
| Compact | The total amount of data may exceed 64K, but all code must fit within a single 64K segment. No array can exceed 64K. Microsoft C is the only language that supports the compact model. |
| Large | Both data and code may exceed 64K, although no array may exceed 64K. All Microsoft languages support this model. |
| Huge | Both data and code may exceed 64K, and arrays may also exceed 64K. Both code and data, as well as pointers to arrays, must be FAR. Most recent version of Microsoft languages support this model. Segments are alike for large and huge models. |

        .CODE [name]

where *name* is the optional segment name. Normally only one code segment is defined in the source module. The name can be specified only for medium and large or huge models, which allow multiple segments. Name will be ignored if shown for small or compact models.

**Stack Segment.**  The *stack segment* is defined by the .STACK directive. Its format is

        .STACK [size]

where the optional *size* is the number of bytes allocated to the stack. The default size is 1K.

**Data Segments.**  Any variable having the DUP operator and the indeterminate symbol (?) is considered to be *uninitialized*. For routines to be called from Microsoft high-level languages, use .DATA? or .FARDATA? to define segments of uninitialized data and .DATA or .FARDATA for segments of initialized data. For stand-alone assembler programs, you may place uninitialized data in any segment.

The .CONST directive defines a constant-data segment. Constant data consists of strings, real numbers, and other constant data that must be allocated in routines called from high-level languages. Such data may not be changed at run time. This segment is optional with stand-alone assembler programs.

Segments defined with the .STACK, .DATA, .DATA?, and .CONST directives are placed in a group named DGROUP. The value of DGROUP rather than that of the segment name should be loaded into DS register at the start of the code section.

### Default Segment Names and Types

Segments defined with simplified segment directives automatically are assigned default names and types by MASM. You may wish to know these names if you mix simplified and full segment definitions. Table 12-4 shows segment directives that may be used with each memory model and the default names and types that are assigned.

By using the optional name operand in the .CODE, .FARDATA, and .FARDATA? directives, you can override the default name. Note that the name operand is valid with the .CODE directive only with medium and large or huge models and that .FARDATA and .FARDATA? directives may be used only with compact and large or huge models.

### Simplified Segment Defaults

Defaults assigned by simplified segment directives are different from those assigned by full segment definitions. The default size for the PROC directive is always NEAR with full segment definitions. With the .MODEL directive, the default size for PROC is NEAR for small and compact models and FAR for medium, large, or huge models.

With full segment definitions, the data segment address in the DS register is the address from which OFFSET addresses are calculated. With simplified definitions, the base address for OFFSET addresses is that of DGROUP for .DATA, .DATA? or STACK segments..CODE, .FARDATA, and .FARDATA? segments have their own base addresses and are not part of DGROUP.

### Using Predefined Equates

Several equates have been predefined by MASM 5.0. These names may be used in your code. You should not use these names in your own EQU statements.

The name *@curseg* refers to the name of the current segment. It can be used in ASSUME statements, segment overrides, or with the ENDS directive to end the current segment. The @curseg equate also may be used with full segment definitions.

TABLE 12-4.   Default Names and Types of Segments

| DIRECTIVE | MODEL | NAME | ALIGN | COMBINE | CLASS | GROUP |
|---|---|---|---|---|---|---|
| .CODE | Small or compact | _TEXT | WORD | PUBLIC | 'CODE' | |
| | Medium, large, or huge | name_TEXT | WORD | PUBLIC | 'CODE' | |
| .DATA | All | _DATA | WORD | PUBLIC | 'DATA' | DGROUP |
| .CONST | All | CONST | WORD | PUBLIC | 'CONST' | DGROUP |
| .DATA? | All | _BSS | WORD | PUBLIC | 'BSS' | DGROUP |
| .FARDATA | Compact, large or huge | FAR_DATA | PARA | private | 'FAR_DATA' | |
| .FARDATA? | Compact, large or huge | FAR_BSS | PARA | private | 'FAR_BSS' | |
| .STACK | All | STACK | PARA | STACK | 'STACK' | DGROUP |

The name *@filename* stands for the name of the current source file. It may be used to assign this name to a procedure or other purpose. The @filename equate also may be used with full segment definitions.

The name *@codesize* has value of 0 for small and compact models or 1 for medium, large, or huge models. The name *@datasize* has value of 0 for small and medium models, 1 for compact and large models, and 2 for huge models. These names may be used in conditional-assembly statements.

Each segment directive has a corresponding equate consisting of the at sign (@) followed by the segment directive. For example, *@code* stands for the name defined by the .CODE directive and *@fardata* and *@fardata?* for the names of the .FARDATA and .FARDATA? segments respectively. But the name *@data* refers to the group name that applies to all near data segments. @data can be used for the base address for the .DATA, .DATA?, .CONST, and .STACK segments, all of which are grouped in DGROUP. For example, if NEAR data in the .DATA segment is to be addressed by DS and FAR data in .FARDATA segment by ES, the following statements may be used:

```
ASSUME ES:@FARDATA        ;ASSUME for DS is handled by
                          ;.MODEL
MOV AX,@FARDATA           ;initialize ES
MOV ES,AX
MOV AX,@DATA              ;initialize DS
MOV DS,AX
```

## FULL SEGMENT DEFINITIONS

Although we have used full segment definitions throughout this text, we have not yet considered all of the options and variations that are available. Only with full segment definitions is it possible to take full advantage of the main ways in which segments may be sequenced, organized, and combined.

### Setting the Segment-Order Method

As mentioned earlier under MASM options, segments may be written to the object file in either sequential or alphabetical order. The default is sequential, i.e., the order in which segments are defined in source code.

You may specify sequential order by using the .SEQ directive or the /S option, or alphabetical order by using the .ALPHA directive or the /A option. The directive will always override the option if there is a conflict.

The DOSSEG directive and the segment class type (to be discussed shortly) also can affect the final order of the segments in memory.

### Defining Full Segments

Full segments are defined by placing a SEGMENT directive at the beginning and an ENDS directive at the end. The syntax is:

```
segname SEGMENT [align] [combine] [use] ['class']

statements within the segment

segname ENDS
```

where *segname* defines the name of the segment and the type operands in brackets all are optional. Segments having the same name in one program are treated as the same segment. Type operands should be specified in order, but no operands need to be specified for any segment.

*Align Type.*   The *align type* tells the assembler and linker how to select the starting address for the segment. Any of the following types may be used:

| ALIGN TYPE | START SEGMENT AT | MULTIPLE OF |
|---|---|---|
| BYTE | Next available byte address | 1 |
| WORD | Next available word address | 2 |
| DWORD | Next available doubleword address | 4 |
| PARA | Next available paragraph address | 16 |
| PAGE | Next available page address | 256 |

PARA is the default except for the 80386 processor if no align type is given. The 80386 normally uses the DWORD align type with 32-bit segments.

**Note:**  The PAGE align type is different from the PAGE directive that sets the width and length of the page of the assembler listing file. The PAGE align type appears only with a SEGMENT directive.

*Combine Type.*  The *combine type* states how to combine segments with the same name. Five types are possible, as illustrated in Table 12-5:

*Use Type.*  The *use type* sets the segment word size for the 80386 processor only. If you have used the .386 directive to enable 80386 instructions and addressing modes, you may specify USE16 or USE32 to specify 16-bit or 32-bit segment word size. A 16-bit word size can address 65536 bytes, while a 32-bit word size can address 4,294,967,296 bytes. When the .386 directive is used but no use type is specified, the default segment word size is 32 bits.

Present versions of DOS limit segment word size to 16 bits.

*Class Type.*  The *class type* allows you to associate segments having different names but similar purposes. The class name must be enclosed in single quotation marks ('). The name is case sensitive only if the /ML or /MX options have been specified in the MASM command line.

All segments belong to a class. If no name is specified, segments have a null class name. There is no limit on the number of segments or their size in a class.

LINK expects the class name CODE or a name containing the suffix CODE to be used for the segment containing program code. The CodeView debug program also expects this name.

Class type determines the final order of segments in the executable file. Segments of the same class type are loaded into memory together, regardless of their sequence in the object file. LINK processes modules in the order they are received in the command line. If you have a problem getting segments from separate modules into the proper sequence, you can define dummy segments in an include file in the order you want them. Then you can write the actual segments in any order you wish.

## Defining Segment Groups

The GROUP statement permits you to associate a collection of segments with the same starting address. It has this syntax:

```
name GROUP segment [,segment]...
```

where *name* is the symbol assigned to the starting address of the group. All addresses within the segments in the group are relative to this same starting address, rather than relative to the start of the segments in which they are defined. *Segment* can be any previously defined segment.

Beginning with MASM version 5.0, you may add segments to a group one at a time. In earlier versions of MASM, you had to name all segments in a GROUP statement at one time.

TABLE 12-5.   Segment Combine Types

| COMBINE TYPE | MEANING |
|---|---|
| PUBLIC | Join all segments having the same name into a single, contiguous segment. All addresses are relative to a single segment register. |
| STACK | Join all segments having the same name into a single, contiguous segment with all addresses relative to the SS segment register. SP is initialized to the length of the segment. Any EXE program should define at least one STACK segment. |
| COMMON | Create overlapping segments by starting all segments having the same name at the same address. All segments have the same base address. The most recently initialized data replace any previously initialized data. |
| MEMORY | Join all segments having the same name into a single, contiguous segment. Similar to PUBLIC segments. LINK does not recognize MEMORY type, but other linkers do. |
| AT address | Cause all addresses defined in the segment to be relative to *address*. An AT segment typically represents an area in memory such as a screen buffer and contains no code or initialized data. |

The GROUP directive does not affect the order in which segments are loaded. LINK loads segments according to class or in the order the object modules are presented for linking.

Segments that do not belong to a group may be loaded between segments that do. But the total distance between the first byte of the first segment in the group and the last byte of the last segment in the group cannot exceed 65535 bytes.

Group names may be used in ASSUME directives and as an operand prefix with the segment-override operator.

## Nesting Segments

You may nest one segment within another. When MASM encounters the inner segment, it suspends assembly of the outer segment and begins to assemble the inner one. When MASM reaches the end of the inner segment, it then resumes assembly of the outer one. It is possible to mix simplified and full segment definitions in this fashion.

One possible use of nested segments is to nest a data segment inside the code segment within a macro that uses the data. Figure 12-2 shows an example.

In this example, the first call of the macro DSPMSG assembles the DATA segment with the message 'Make menu selection: ' and then assembles the code to display the message. Later, another DATA segment is assembled with the message 'Continue (Y/N)?'. As each string is assembled, it is placed in the data space with any other data defined in the DATA segment.

```
DSPMSG    MACRO MESSAGE
          LOCAL STRING
DATA      SEGMENT WORD PUBLIC 'DATA'
STRING    DB &MESSAGE
          DB 13,10,'$'
DATA      ENDS
          MOV AH,9
          LEA DX,STRING
          INT 21h
          ENDM
CODE      SEGMENT BYTE PUBLIC 'CODE'
          .
          DSPMSG 'Make menu selection: '
          .
          DSPMSG 'Continue (Y/N)? '
          .
CODE      ENDS
```

**Figure 12-2    Nested Segments**

## LISTING DIRECTIVES

Directives that control assembler listings fall into two major groups: those that control page format and those that control the content of the listings.

### Controlling Page Format

Three directives have an effect on the page format of the program listing file. They are PAGE, TITLE, and SUBTTL.

***PAGE.*** The *PAGE directive* has been used at the start of each sample program to designate the line length and width for the program listing. It may also be used to increment the section and section number or to cause a page break in the listing. Its format is:

```
PAGE [length][,width]
PAGE +
```

where *length* and *width* specify the maximum number of lines per page and maximum number of characters per line, respectively. Length can be from 10 to 255 lines, with a default of 50. Width must be from 60 to 132 characters, with a default of 80. If length is omitted, a comma must precede width.

If a plus sign (+) is used, a page break occurs, the section number is incremented, and the page number is reset to 1. The module is divided into sections, and the section into pages. Pages are numbered with the section and page numbers separated by a hyphen.

If PAGE is used with no argument, it starts a new page and generates new title and subtitle lines.

***TITLE.*** The *TITLE directive* specifies a heading to appear on each page of assembly listings. Its format is:

```
TITLE text
```

where *text* can be any string of characters with a maximum length of 60. Only one TITLE directive per module may appear. The title appears on the second line of the page justified left.

***SUBTTL.*** The *SUBTTL directive* specifies the subtitle to appear on each page of assembly listings. Its format is:

```
SUBTTL text
```

where *text* can be any string of characters with a maximum length of 60. The subtitle appears on the third line of the page justified left.

Any number of SUBTTL directives can appear in a program. Each new directive replaces the text of the preceding directive. A SUBTTL directive often is placed ahead of a PAGE + directive to create a page break and a new heading.

## Controlling the Contents of Listings

Eight directives control the text that is to be shown in listings. They are .LIST, .XLIST, .LFCOND, .SFCOND, .TFCOND, .LALL, .SALL, and .XALL.

***.LIST and .XLIST.*** The *.XLIST directive* suppresses listing of source lines that follow it. The *.LIST directive* restores copying. When used in pairs, they can suppress listing of a portion of the source program. .XLIST overrides other directives such as .SFCOND, .LFCOND, and .LALL that cause listing of certain statements.

***.SFCOND, .LFCOND, and .TFCOND.*** These three directives control whether false-conditional blocks should be listed. False-conditional blocks are those statements following an IF or ELSE directive that are not true at assembly time.

The *.SFCOND directive* suppresses listing of any following false-conditional blocks. The *.LFCOND directive* restores listing of these blocks. They can be used as a pair to suppress listing of false-conditional blocks for only a portion of a program.

The *.TFCOND directive* toggles (alternates) the false-conditional setting. Ordinarily, when .TFCOND is used, the first false-conditional block is listed, the second is not, and so forth. However, if the /X MASM option is used, the effect of .TFCOND is opposite. The first false-conditional block is not listed, the second one is listed, and so forth.

***.LALL, .XALL, and .SALL.*** These three directives control the listing of macro expansions. Macro definitions are always listed.

*.LALL* lists all source statements in a macro expansion except macro comments preceded by a double semicolon.

*.XALL* causes listing of only macro statements that generate code or data. Comments, equates, and segment definitions are suppressed. .XALL is the default option when assembly begins.

*.SALL* suppresses listing of all macro expansions. The macro call itself is listed, but not the generated statements.

## OTHER DIRECTIVES AND OPERATORS

Many directives and operators have been discussed in appropriate sections of the preceding chapters. In this section we present some that have not been treated earlier or that have additional features not covered earlier.

### .RADIX Directive

The *.RADIX directive* allows you to set any number base from 2 through 16 as the default for integer constants. Ordinarily base 10, or decimal, is the default. The format is:

```
.RADIX expression
```

where *expression* must evaluate to an integer in the range of 2 through 16. Numbers in expression are considered to be decimal.

A number base other than the default is indicated by the letters B for binary, D for decimal, H for hex, or Q or O for octal following the number. However, B or D always is considered a radix specifier. Even if .RADIX 16 has set the default radix to hex, the number 001B would be considered to be 1 binary, while ABCD would be considered to be the illegal decimal number ABC.

### LABEL Directive

The *LABEL directive* permits you to define a second entry point into a procedure. It has the syntax

```
name LABEL distance
```

where *name* is the label name and *distance* is NEAR, FAR, or PROC. PROC is either NEAR or FAR, depending upon the memory model specified by the .MODEL directive. For example:

```
           PUBLIC SUB,SUB2
SUB        PROC NEAR                    ;main procedure starts here
             .
SUB2       LABEL NEAR                   ;this is secondary entry point
             .
           RET
SUB        ENDP
```

## Arithmetic Operators

*Arithmetic operators* work with integer constants or memory values at assembly time to produce values used as operands. They differ from instructions, which perform arithmetic at run time. The arithmetic operators are:

| OPERATOR | SYNTAX | MEANING |
|---|---|---|
| + | +expression | Positive (unary) |
| − | -expression | Negative (unary) |
| + | expression1+expression2 | Addition |
| − | expression1-expression2 | Subtraction |
| * | expression1*expression2 | Multiplication |
| / | expression1/expression2 | Division (integer quotient) |
| MOD | expression1MODexpression2 | Remainder (modulus) |

Examples include the following:

```
A       DW  -5          ;unary negative value (FFFBh)
B       DB  -3+7        ;negative 3 plus 7 = 4 (04h)
C       EQU B*3         ;4*3=12
D       EQU C/6         ;12/6=2
E       EQU C MOD 7     ;12/7=1, remainder (MOD) 5
```

A period between the name of a structure and the name of a field within that structure indicates addition. Thus, STRUC1.FLD3 indicates that the offset of STRUC1 is added to the offset of FLD3 within the structure to refer to the address of FLD3.

We have seen in Chapter 7 that the index operator [] also indicates addition. The operand TABLE[BX][DI] forms the effective address by adding together the address of TABLE, the contents of BX, and the contents of DI.

## Logical Operators

The logical operators, NOT, AND, OR, and XOR, perform operations on individual bits, as do the logical instructions having the same names. The operators take effect on operands at assembly time, while the instructions are executed at run time. To review the logical operations, refer to chapter 5. The logical operators are summarized below:

| OPERATOR | SYNTAX | MEANING |
|---|---|---|
| NOT | NOT expression | Form ones complement |
| AND | expression1 AND expression2 | AND the two expressions |
| OR | expression1 OR expression2 | OR the two expressions |
| XOR | expression1 XOR expression2 | XOR the two expressions |

Results of NOT are 16 bits, while results of AND, OR, and XOR are 32 bits. However, operand lengths will be adjusted according to the rules of assembler language. Examples include the following:

```
MOV AX,NOT 00001111b       ;result = 1111111111110000b
MOV AL,NOT 00001111b       ;result = 11110000b
MOV AH,01010101b AND 10101010b;result = 00000000b
MOV AH,01010101b OR 11110000b ;result = 11110101b
MOV AH,01010101b XOR 1111000b ;result = 10100101b
```

## Shift Operators

The *shift operators*, SHR and SHL, perform logical shifts by moving all bits in constant values to the right or left, respectively, and filling in the vacated bit positions with zeros. These operators are effective only at assembly time and may not refer to the contents of registers or memory locations. The syntax is:

```
expression SHR count
expression SHL count
```

where *expression* is a constant and *count* gives the number of bits to be shifted. Bits shifted off either end of expression are lost. For example:

```
MOV AX,11001100b SHL 3   ;result = 0000011001100000b
MOV AH,11110000b SHR 2   ;result = 00111100b
```

## Relational Operators

*Relational operators* compare two expressions at assembly time and set the result to -1 if the condition specified by the operator is true and to 0 if it is not true. The syntax and value returned by each relational operator is shown below:

| OPERATOR | SYNTAX | VALUE RETURNED |
|---|---|---|
| EQ | expression1 EQ expression2 | True if expressions are equal |
| NE | expression1 NE expression2 | True if expressions are not equal |
| LT | expression1 LT expression2 | True if left expression < right |
| LE | expression1 LE expression2 | True if left expression <= right |
| GT | expression1 GT expression2 | True if left expression > right |
| GE | expression1 GE expression2 | True if left expression >= right |

Expressions are treated as 32-bit numbers for EQ and NE. LT, LE, GT, and GE treat the expressions as 33-bit numbers, with the 33rd bit specifying the sign. For this purpose 0FFFFFFFFh is equal to 4,294,967,295 and not -1.

Examples:

```
MOV AH,00000101b EQ 4    ;result = false (0)
MOV AH,5 GT 3            ;result = true (-1)
MOV AX,0FFFFFFFFh EQ -1   ;result = false (0)
MOV AX,6 LT 1000b        ;result = true (-1)
```

## Type Operators

The *type operators* specify or analyze types of memory operands and other expressions. They include PTR, SHORT, THIS, HIGH, LOW, SEG, OFF-

SET, .TYPE, TYPE, LENGTH, and SIZE. Some of these operators have been described in earlier chapters but are reviewed here for completeness.

**PTR, FAR, and SHORT.** The *PTR operator* specifies the data type of a variable or the distance type of a label. It has this syntax:

    type PTR expression

where *type* can be BYTE, WORD, DWORD, FWORD, QWORD, or TBYTE for variables or NEAR, FAR, or PROC for labels. *Expression* usually is a variable or label but it may be indexed, as in TABLE[SI].

The PTR operator is required for far calls and forward jumps to labels that have not yet been defined. Far references require two bytes for the segment address and two bytes for the offset. PTR also allows you to refer to part of data that may be defined in a different way. Examples include the following:

```
JMP FAR PTR SUB2          ;jump to far label in another
                          ;segment
MOV BL,BYTE PTR WORD2     ;move first byte of WORD2
                          ;into BL
MOV AX,WORD PTR TABLE     ;move first two bytes of a
                          ;byte table
```

The *SHORT operator* can be used whenever a JMP instruction goes less than 128 bytes. It is most useful with forward jumps. The assembler on its first pass must make certain assumptions about a forward jump to a symbol that has not yet been defined. It normally assumes a near jump and allocates two bytes for the destination address. If on the second pass, it turns out that the jump is short, the second byte becomes a NOP (no-op); but, if on the first pass MASM is informed that the jump will be short, it allocates only one byte for the distance of the short jump. The length of the jump is computed from the location of the instruction following the jump. Assume in the following examples that the JMP instruction is at offset 000100h and ENDIF01 is at 000160h:

| INSTRUCTION | OBJECT CODE | REMARKS |
|---|---|---|
| JMP ENDIF01 | E9 5D 90 | ;160-103=5D; NOP = 90 |
| JMP SHORT ENDIF01 | EB 5E | ;160-102=5E distance of short<br>;jump |

**THIS.** The *THIS operator* creates an operand having the offset and segment values of the current location counter value and the type as specified. Its format is:

    THIS type

where *type* can be BYTE, WORD, DWORD, FWORD, QWORD, or TBYTE for memory operands or NEAR, FAR, or PROC for labels. It is usually used with

EQU or = equates. It works much like the LABEL directive, discussed earlier in this chapter. Examples include the following:

```
VAR1      EQU      THIS BYTE          ;VAR1 and VAR2 refer to same
                                      ;byte
VAR2      DB       ?
LOC1      EQU      THIS NEAR          ;LOC1, LOC2, LOC3, and LOC4
                                      ;all
LOC2      LABEL    NEAR               ;refer to same address
LOC3:
LOC4      PROC     NEAR
LOC4      ENDP
```

**HIGH and LOW.**   The *HIGH operator* returns the high-order byte and the *LOW* operator the low-order byte of an expression at assembly time. The syntax is:

```
HIGH expression
LOW expression
```

where *expression* must evaluate to a 16-bit constant. HIGH and LOW cannot be used with the contents of registers or memory operands whose contents may change at run time. Examples include:

```
MOV AH,LOW 1275h             ;moves 75h
MOV AL,HIGH 0BEEFh           ;moves BEh
```

**SEG and OFFSET.**   The *SEG operator* returns the segment address of an expression. Its syntax is:

```
SEG expression
```

where *expression* can be any label, variable, segment name, group name, or other memory operand, but not a constant expression. The return 16-bit value can be used as a memory operand. Examples include the following:

```
          .DATA
BYTE1     DB ?
          .CODE
          MOV AX,SEG .DATA           ;both .DATA and BYTE1 have
                                     ;the
          MOV BX,SEG BYTE1           ;same segment address
```

The *OFFSET operator* returns the offset address of an expression. Its syntax is:

```
OFFSET expression
```

where *expression* can be a label, variable, or other direct memory operand. Constant expressions cannot be used. The value returned is an immediate operand.

The offset value varies according to the way in which the segment is defined. With full segment definitions, the returned value is the number of bytes between the item and the beginning of the segment in which it is defined. With simplified segment definitions, the returned value for a near data segment is the number of bytes between the item and the beginning of its group; for a far segment, the returned value is the number of bytes between the item and the beginning of its segment.

The segment-override operator can be used to force OFFSET to return the number of bytes between the item and the start of its group. Examples include:

```
            .DATA
MESSAGE     DB 'Any message'
            .FARDATA
TABLE       DB 100 DUP (0)
            .CODE
            ASSUME ES:@FARDATA
            MOV AX,@DATA
            MOV DS,AX                ;DS = address of DGROUP
            MOV AX,@FARDATA
            MOV ES,AX                ;ES = address of FARDATA
            MOV DX,OFFSET MESSAGE    ;offset=0 from DGROUP
            MOV SI,OFFSET TABLE      ;offset=0 from FARDATA
```

**.TYPE and TYPE.** The *.TYPE operator* returns a byte containing a code that describes the mode and scope of an expression. Its syntax is:

```
.TYPE expression
```

where *expression* usually refers to a symbol in a macro, where different statements are generated for different types of data. If expression is not valid, .TYPE returns 0. If it is valid, .TYPE returns a byte with bits 0, 1, 5, or 7 set as follows, and bits 2, 3, 4, and 6 set always to 0.

| BIT POSITION | IF BIT = 0 | IF BIT = 1 |
|---|---|---|
| 0 | Not program related | Program related (code segment) |
| 1 | Not data related | Data related |
| 5 | Not defined | Defined |
| 7 | Local or public | External |

Figure 12-3 shows some examples of .TYPE operands.

The *TYPE operator* returns a number that describes the type of an expression. Its syntax is:

```
TYPE expression
```

where *expression* may evaluate to a variable, a structure or structure variable, a label, or a constant. If expression is a variable, TYPE returns the number of bytes in each data object in the variable, 1 for strings or bytes, 2 for words, 4 for doublewords, and so forth. If expression is a structure or structure variable, TYPE returns the number of bytes in the structure. If expression is a label, TYPE returns 0FFFFh for a NEAR label or 0FFFEh for a FAR label. If expression is a constant, TYPE returns 0. Examples include:

```
0000                .data
0000    ????        word1 dw ?
0002    0014[??}    string db 20 dup (?)
0016    2710        word2 dw 10000
0000                .code
                    extrn exsub:near,exdata:near
0000                tsttype proc far
                                    ;Bit Positions
                                    ;76543210
0000    B0 22       mov al,.type string   ;00100010  Defined, data related
0002    B0 22       mov al,.type word1    ;00100010  Defined, data related
0004    B0 00       mov al,.type word3    ;00000000  Not defined
0006    B0 A1       mov al,.type exsub    ;10100001  External, defined, program
                                          ;          related
0008    B0 21       mov al,.type tsttype  ;00100001  Local or public, defined,
                                          ;          program related
000A                tsttype endp
000A                end tsttype
```

**Figure 12-3    .TYPE Operands**

```
WORD      DW ?                    ;TYPE word = 2
STRING    DB 'Here is a string.'  ;TYPE string = 1 (strings
                                  ;always 1)
ARRAY     DD 20 DUP (0)           ;TYPE array = 4
PROC1     PROC NEAR               ;TYPE proc1 = 0FFFFh
PROC2     PROC FAR                ;TYPE proc2 = 0FFFEh
          54321                   ;TYPE 54321 = 0
```

**LENGTH and SIZE.** The *LENGTH* operator returns the number of data elements in a variable defined with the DUP operator. Its syntax is:

```
LENGTH variable
```

If *variable* was defined with nested DUP operators, only the number for the outer DUP is returned. If the variable definition contained no DUP, the value returned is 1. Examples include the following:

```
STRING    DB 'Here is a string."  ;LENGTH string = 1 (no DUP)
WORD      DW ?                     ;LENGTH word = 1
ARRAY     DW 20 DUP (0)            ;LENGTH array = 20
TABLE     DW 10 DUP (5 DUP (0))    ;LENGTH table = 10 (outer DUP
                                   ;only)
```

The *SIZE operator* returns a value equal to the product of the LENGTH variable and the TYPE variable. Its syntax is:

```
SIZE variable
```

If *variable* contains nested DUP operators, the value of the outer DUP is used for LENGTH. If the variable contains no DUP operator, SIZE is the same as the TYPE value. Examples include:

```
STRING      DB 'Here is a string."    ;SIZE string = 1 (no DUP)
WORD        DW ?                       ;SIZE word = 2
ARRAY       DW 20 DUP (0)              ;SIZE array = 40
TABLE       DW 10 DUP (5 DUP (0))      ;SIZE table = 20 (outer DUP
                                       ;only)
```

## OPERATOR PRIORITY

There is a definite order in which operators are processed in expressions. This order is shown in Table 12-6.

Expressions are evaluated according to these rules:

1.  Operators with the highest priority are processed first.
2.  Operators of equal priority are processed left to right.
3.  Operators within parentheses are processed by rules 1 and 2 before operators outside parentheses.

Here are some examples of priority:

```
A         EQU 6 / 3 * 2            ;value = 4
B         EQU 6 / (3 * 2)          ;value = 1
C         EQU 6 + 3 * 2            ;value = 12
D         EQU (6 + 3) * 2          ;value + 18
E         EQU 2 or 4 and 8         ;value = 2
F         EQU (2 OR 4) AND 8       ;value = 0
```

## CROSS-REFERENCE LISTING FILE

MASM receives one input file (.ASM) and creates an output object file (.OBJ) and two optional output files, a listing file (.LST) and a cross-reference file (.CRF). We have so far been ignoring the cross-reference file as there has been no particular need for it.

We can request MASM to produce this file through the command line as the fourth operand, with the assembler option /C, or through the MASM prompt. The simplest way to produce all three output files is through the command line. We could use the following command line to produce all output files for SIMPLE.ASM, as depicted in Figure 12-1.

```
B> A:MASM SIMPLE,,,;
```

This command line causes MASM to read in SIMPLE.ASM and create SIMPLE.OBJ, SIMPLE.LST, and SIMPLE.CRF, all on drive B.

CRF files are in a binary format that cannot be displayed in meaningful form on the screen or printer. The DOS utility program CREF converts a CRF file into a cross-reference listing file with the default extension REF. The command line is:

TABLE 12-6.   Operator Priorities

| PRIORITY | OPERATORS |
|---|---|
| (Highest) | |
| 1 | LENGTH, SIZE, WIDTH, MASK, (), [], <> |
| 2 | . (structure-field-name operator) |
| 3 | : (segment-override operator) |
| 4 | PTR, OFFSET, SEG, TYPE, THIS |
| 5 | HIGH, LOW |
| 6 | +, - (unary) |
| 7 | *, /, MOD, SHR, SHL |
| 8 | +, - (addition and subtraction) |
| 9 | EQ, NE, LT, LE, GT, GE |
| 10 | NOT |
| 11 | AND |
| 12 | OR, XOR |
| 13 | SHORT, .TYPE |
| (Lowest) | |

```
B> A:CREF SIMPLE,;
```

Figure 12-4 shows the listing of SIMPLE.REF. This listing, together with the symbol tables from LST files, helps you to debug long programs. It shows an alphabetical listing of each symbol in the program, together with each line number that refers to that symbol. The number sign (#) designates the line in which the symbol is defined.

## PROGRAM 12: SHELL SORT

Program 12 asks the operator to enter up to 100 four-digit hex numbers from the keyboard, prints them in their original order, calls a subroutine to sort them into ascending order using a Shell sort, and prints them again in their new sequence. It continues as long as the operator wishes.

This program uses simplified segment definitions. It defines and uses three macros. CRLF provides a cursor return and line feed, SPACE displays a blank space, and DSPMSG displays any string named as a parameter when the macro is called. DSPMSG uses nested segments. Each time the macro is called, it adds a string constant to the data segment and a group of three statements to the code segment.

The Shell sort is considerably faster than the bubble sort demonstrated in program 9. Instead of comparing adjacent pairs of words, the Shell sort

```
Microsoft Cross-Reference  Version 5.00      Tue May 02 17: 35:57 1989

   Symbol Cross-Reference    (# definition, + modification) Cref-1

CODE . . . . . . . . . . . . .   29

DATA . . . . . . . . . . . . .   12
DGROUP . . . . . . . . . . . .   31
DSPLINE. . . . . . . . . . . .   34       39#       43

MYNAME . . . . . . . . . . . .   13#      33

SIMPLE . . . . . . . . . . . .   30#      37        44
STACK  . . . . . . . . . . . .   28#      28


_DATA. . . . . . . . . . . . .   12#
_TEXT. . . . . . . . . . . . .   29#

 9 Symbols
```

**Figure 12-4    Cross-reference Listing**

compares words separated by a gap. The gap starts out as half the number of items in the array. Words are compared at this gap and exchanged if necessary. The pass is repeated until no exchanges are necessary. Then the gap is cut in half, and the process continues until the gap is 0.

The use of the gap in the Shell sort technique moves low numbers toward the low end of the array and high numbers toward the high end of the array more quickly than the bubble sort, which moves numbers downward in the array only one position in a pass.

Figure 12-5 shows the assembler listing of program 12. The .LALL directive causes statements generated by the macros DSPMSG twice and CRLF the first time to be listed. Then the .XALL directive suppresses listing of the other macro expansions.

Figure 12-5 also shows the symbol table. Notice that segments named _DATA, _BSS, and STACK are all combined under DGROUP. The several parts of the code segment named _TEXT have all been combined into a single segment.

Figure 12-6 shows the subroutine SHELSORT.ASM. It was assembled separately from PROG12.ASM. It makes use of the .FARDATA segment and the @FARDATA address to separate the subroutine's data from that of the main program. The ES segment register points to the data in the subroutine.

The object program of SHELSORT was not placed in ASSEM.LIB with other more commonly-used subroutines. Therefore, this command line was used to link all necessary object modules:

```
B> A:LINK PROG12 + SHELSORT,,,ASSEM;
```

```
Microsoft (R) Macro Assembler Version 5.00                5/22/90 11:15:51
                                                          Page    1-1


          PAGE 50,132
;------------------------------------------------------------------------------
; Program name:  B:PROG12.ASM
;
; Author:  Alton R. Kindred
;
;This program enters up to 100 four-digit hexadecimal numbers from the keyboard,
;prints them in their original number, calls a subroutine to sort them into
;ascending order using a Shell sort, and prints them again in their new
;sequence.  It then asks if the operator wishes to continue.  It uses the
;simplified segment definitions and two macros.
;------------------------------------------------------------------------------
CRLF      MACRO
          PUSH DX
          PUSH AX
          MOV DL,13
          MOV AH,2
          INT 21h
          MOV DL,10
          MOV AH,2
          INT 21h
          POP AX
          POP DX
          ENDM
SPACE     MACRO
          PUSH DX
          PUSH AX
          MOV DL,' '
          MOV AH,2
          INT 21h
          POP AX
          POP DX
          ENDM
DSPMSG    MACRO TEXT
          LOCAL SYMBOL
          .DATA
SYMBOL    DB &TEXT
          DB 13,10,'$'
          .CODE
          MOV AH,9
          LEA DX,SYMBOL
          INT 21h
          ENDM
;------------------------------------------------------------------------------
                              DOSSEG
                             .MODEL SMALL
Microsoft (R) Macro Assembler Version 5.00                5/22/90 11:15:51
                                                          Page    1-2
```

**Figure 12-5    Assembler Listing of PROG12.LST**

```
                                       .ALPHA          ;put segments in alphabetic
0000                                   .DATA
0000   45 6E 74 65 72 20 75  MSG1      DB 'Enter up to 100 four-digit hex
   numbers.',13,10
       70 20 74 6F 20 31 30
       30 20 66 6F 75 72 2D
       64 69 67 69 74 20 68
       65 78 20 6E 75 6D 62
       65 72 73 2E 0D 0A
0029   50 72 65 73 73 20 3C            DB 'Press <ENTER> alone to stop: $'
       45 4E 54 45 52 3E 20
       61 6C 6F 6E 65 20 74
       6F 20 73 74 6F 70 3A
       20 24
0047   4E 75 6D 62 65 72 73  MSG2      DB 'Numbers in original order:$'
       20 69 6E 20 6F 72 69
       67 69 6E 61 6C 20 6F
       72 64 65 72 3A 24
0062   53 6F 72 74 65 64 20  MSG3      DB 'Sorted numbers:$'
       6E 75 6D 62 65 72 73
       3A 24
0072   44 6F 20 79 6F 75 20  MSG4      DB 'Do you wish to continue (Y/N)?  $'
       77 69 73 68 20 74 6F
       20 63 6F 6E 74 69 6E
       75 65 20 28 59 2F 4E
       29 3F 20 24
;---------------------------------------------------------------------------
0000                                   .DATA?          ;segment for uninitialized
0000   0064[                 ARRAY     DW 100 DUP (?)
   ????
   ]
00C8   ????                  WORDCNT   DW ?
;---------------------------------------------------------------------------
0100                                   .STACK 100h
;---------------------------------------------------------------------------
0000                                   .CODE
0000                         PROG12    PROC FAR
                                       EXTRN DSPLINE:NEAR,DSPHEX:NEAR,INPHEX:NEAR,
                                       EXTRN CLRSCN:NEAR,INPCHR:NEAR,SHELWORT:NEAR
0000   B8 ---- R                       MOV AX,DGROUP   ;set up data segment in DS
0003   8E D8                           MOV DS,AX
0005   E8 0000 E                       CALL CLR SCN    ;clear screen
                                       .LALL           ;list macro-generated
                                       DSPMSG 'Alton R. Kindred, Shell Sort
0092                         1         .DATA
0092   41 6C 74 6F 6E 20 52  1 ??0000  DB 'Alton R. Kindred, Shell Sort
   Microsoft (R) Macro Assembler Version 5.00                5/22/90 11:15:51
                                                        Page    1-3


       2E 20 4B 69 6E 64 72  1
       65 64 2C 20 53 68 65  1
       6C 6C 20 53 6F 72 74  1
       20 44 65 6D 6F 6E 73  1
       74 72 61 74 69 6F 6E  1
00BC   0D 0A 24              1         DB 13,10,'$'
0008                         1         .CODE
```

**Figure 12-5**    *continued*

```
0008  B4 09                     1        MOV AH,9
000A  8D 16 0092 R              1        LEA DX,??0000
000E  CD 21                     1        INT 21h
                                         DSPMSG 'Sorts up to 100 numbers into
00BF                            1        .DATA
00BF  53 6F 72 74 73 20 75      1 ??0001 DB 'Sorts up to 100 numbers into ascending
      70 20 74 6F 20 31 30      1
      30 20 6E 75 6D 62 65      1
      72 73 20 69 6E 74 6F      1
      20 61 73 63 65 6E 64      1
      69 6E 67 20 6F 72 64      1
      65 72 2E                  1
00EC  0D 0A 24                  1        DB 13,10,'$'
0010                            1        .CODE
0010  B4 09                     1        MOV AH,9
0012  8D 16 00BF R              1        LEA DX,??0001
0016  CD 21                     1        INT 21h
0018                  REPEAT1:                ;REPEAT
0018  8D 16 0000 R              LEA DX,MSG1    ;   display prompt
001C  E8 0000 E                 CALL DSPLINE
                                CRLF           ;   return cursor
001F  52                    1   PUSH DX
0020  50                    1   PUSH AX
0021  B2 0D                 1   MOV DL,13
0023  B4 02                 1   MOV AH,2
0025  CD 21                 1   INT 21h
0027  B2 0A                 1   MOV DL,10
0029  B4 02                 1   MOV AH,2
002B  CD 21                 1   INT 21h
002D  58                    1   POP AX
002E  5A                    1   POP DX
                                .SALL          ;   (suppress macro listing)
002F  B9 0000                   MOV CX,0       ;   set word counter to 0
0032  8D 36 0000 R              LEA SI,ARRAY   ;   set array address
0036  E8 0000 E                 CALL INPHEX    ;   get a hex number
0039  83 FA 00          WHILE01: CMP DX,0      ;   WHILE number <> 0
003C  74 1A                     JE WEND01
                                CRLF           ;      return cursor
004E  89 14                     MOV [SI],DX    ;      put number into array
      Microsoft (R) Macro Assembler Version 5.00          5/22/90 11:15:51
                                                     Page     1-4


0050  46                        INC SI         ;      set to next element
0052  41                        INC CX         ;      add 1 to word counter
0053  E8 0000 E                 CALL INPHEX    ;      get a hex number
0056  EB E1                     JMP WHILE01
0058                  WEND01:                  ;   WEND
0058  8D 16 0047 R              LEA DX,MSG2    ;   print title original
005C  E8 0000 E                 CALL DSPLINE
                                CRLF           ;   return cursor
006F  89 0E 00C8 R              MOV WORDCNT,CX ;   save word count
0073  8D 36 0000 R              LEA SI,ARRAY   ;   set array address
0077                  REPEAT3:                 ;   REPEAT
0077  8B 14                     MOV DX,[SI]    ;      get number from array
0079  51                        PUSH CX        ;      save word counter
```

**Figure 12-5**   *continued*

```
007A  B9 0004                        MOV CX,4          ;    print number in hex
007D  E8 0000 E                      CALL DSPHEX
                                     SPACE             ;    space cursor
008A  46                             INC SI            ;    set address to next
008B  46                             INC SI
008C  59                             POP CX            ;    restore word counter
008D  E2 E8                          LOOP REPEAT3      ;    subtract 1 from word
008F                   UNTIL3:                         ;  UNTIL word counter = 0
                                     CRLF              ;  return cursor
009F  8D 16 0000 R                   LEA DX,ARRAY      ;  set array address
00A3  8B 0E 00C8 R                   MOV CX,WORDCNT    ;  set word counter
00A7  E8 0000 E                      CALL SHELSORT     ;  sort the numbers
00AA  8D 16 0062 R                   LEA DX,MSG3       ;  print title for sorted
00AE  E8 0000 E                      CALL DSPLINE
                                     CRLF              ;  return cursor
00C1  8D 36 0000 R                   LEA SI,ARRAY      ;  set array address
00C5  8B 0E 00C8 R                   MOV CX,WORDCNT    ;  set word counter
00C9               REPEAT4:                            ;  REPEAT
00C9  8B 14                          MOV DX,[SI]       ;    get sorted number
00CB  51                             PUSH CX           ;    save word counter
00CC  B9 0004                        MOV CX,4          ;    display number in hex
00CF  E8 0000 E                      CALL DSPHEX
                                     SPACE             ;    space cursor
00DC  59                             POP CX            ;    restore word counter
00DD  46                             INC SI            ;    set address to next
00DE  46                             INC SI
00DF  E2 E8                          LOOP REPEAT4      ;    subtract 1 from word
00E1                   UNTIL4:                         ;  UNTIL word counter = 0
                                     CRLF              ;  return cursor
00F1  8D 16 0072 R                   LEA DX,MSG4       ;  ask whether to continue
00F5  E8 0000 E                      CALL DSPLINE
00F8  E8 0000 E                      CALL INPCHR       ;  get response
```

        Microsoft (R) Macro Assembler Version 5.00                     5/22/90 11:15:51
                                                                       Page      1-5

```
                                     CRLF              ;  return cursor
010B  0C 20                          OR AL,20h         ;  make response lowercase
010D  3C 6E                          CMP AL,'n'        ;  test for 'N' or 'n'
010F  74 03                          JE UNTIL1
0111  E9 0018 R                      JMP REPEAT1
0114                   UNTIL1:                         ;UNTIL response = 'N' or 'n'
0114  B8 4C00                        MOV AX,4C00h      ;return to DOS
0117  CD 21                          INT 21h
0119                   PROG12        ENDP              ;end of procedure
0119                                 END              ;end of program
```

        Microsoft (R) Macro Assembler Version 5.00                     5/22/90 11:15:51
                                                                       Symbols-1


Macros:

  N a m e    Lines

CRLF . . . . . . . . . . . . . .    10


**Figure 12-5**    *continued*

```
DSPMSG . . . . . . . . . . . . .        7
SPACE  . . . . . . . . . . . . .        7
```

Segments and Groups:

```
                  N a m e           Length  Align Combine Class

DGROUP . . . . . . . . . . . . .  GROUP
  _DATA . . . . . . . . . . . .   00EF WORD PUBLIC 'DATA'
  _BSS  . . . . . . . . . . . .   00CA WORD PUBLIC 'DATA'
  STACK . . . . . . . . . . . .   0100 PARA STACK 'STACK'
_TEXT . . . . . . . . . . . . .   0119 WORD PUBLIC 'CODE'
```

Symbols:

```
                  N a m e           Type  Value  Attr

ARRAY . . . . . . . . . . . . .   L WORD 0000 _BSS Length = 0064

CLRSCN . . . . . . . . . . . . .  L NEAR 0000 _TEXT External

DSPHEX . . . . . . . . . . . . .  L NEAR 0000 _TEXT External
DSPLINE . . . . . . . . . . . .   L NEAR 0000 _TEXT External

INPCHR . . . . . . . . . . . . .  L NEAR 0000 _TEXT External
INPHEX . . . . . . . . . . . . .  L NEAR 0000 _TEXT External

MSG1 . . . . . . . . . . . . . .  L BYTE 0000 _DATA
MSG2 . . . . . . . . . . . . . .  L BYTE 0047 _DATA
MSG3 . . . . . . . . . . . . . .  L BYTE 0062 _DATA
MSG4 . . . . . . . . . . . . . .  L BYTE 0072 _DATA

PROG12 . . . . . . . . . . . . .  F PROC 0000 _TEXT Length = 0119

REPEAT1 . . . . . . . . . . . .   L NEAR 0018 _TEXT
REPEAT3 . . . . . . . . . . . .   L NEAR 0077 _TEXT
REPEAT4 . . . . . . . . . . . .   L NEAR 00C9 _TEXT

SHELSORT . . . . . . . . . . .    L NEAR 0000 _TEXT External

UNTIL1 . . . . . . . . . . . . .  L NEAR 0114 _TEXT
```

Microsoft (R) Macro Assembler Version 5.00              5/22/90 11:15:51
                                                        Symbols-2

```
UNTIL3 . . . . . . . . . . . . .  L NEAR 008F _TEXT
UNTIL4 . . . . . . . . . . . . .  L NEAR 00E1 _TEXT

WEND01 . . . . . . . . . . . . .  L NEAR 0058 _TEXT
WHILE01 . . . . . . . . . . . .   L NEAR 0039 _TEXT
WORDCNT . . . . . . . . . . . .   L WORD 00C8 _BSS

??0000 . . . . . . . . . . . . .  L BYTE 0092 _DATA
??0001 . . . . . . . . . . . . .  L BYTE 00BF _DATA
. . . . . . . . . .  TEXT _TEXT
. . . . . . . . .  TEXT  0
```

**Figure 12-5   continued**

```
. . . . . . . . .    TEXT   0
. . . . . . . . .    TEXT   prog12


   138 Source  Lines
   236 Total   Lines
    41 Symbols

 50580 + 389740 Bytes symbol space free

     0 Warning Errors
     0 Severe  Errors
```

**Figure 12-5**    *concluded*

```
        PAGE 50,132
;------------------------------------------------------------------------------
; Program name:  SHELSORT.ASM
;
; Author:  Alton R. Kindred
;
; This routine sorts an array of up to 100 16-bit words into ascending order
; using the Shell sort.
; Upon entry:  DS:DX points to the array
;              CX has number of words to be sorted
;------------------------------------------------------------------------------
          DOSSEG
          .MODEL LARGE
          .FARDATA
GAP       DW ?
EXCH      DB ?
ARRAYADR  DW ?
NITEMS    DW ?
;------------------------------------------------------------------------------
          .CODE
          ASSUME ES:@FARDATA
SHELSORT  PROC NEAR
          PUBLIC SHELSORT
          PUSH AX                ;save registers
          PUSH BX
          PUSH CX
          PUSH DX
          PUSH BP
          PUSH SI
          PUSH ES
          MOV AX,@FARDATA        ;point ES to data segment
          MOV ES,AX
          MOV ES:NITEMS,CX       ;save array counter
          MOV ES:ARRAYADR,DX     ;save array address
          SHR CX,1               ;set gap to n/2
          MOV ES:GAP,CX          ;save gap
          MOV ES:EXCH,0          ;set exchange switch OFF
```

**Figure 12-6    Source Statements of Shell Sort Procedure**

```
WHILE01:   MOV AX,ES:GAP              ;WHILE gap > 0
           CMP AX,0
           JNG WEND01
           MOV BX,ES:GAP             ;   convert gap to word offset
           SHL BX,1
           MOV SI,0
           MOV AX,ES:NITEMS          ;   compute n - gap
           SUB AX,ES:GAP
           MOV BP,AX
           SHL BP,1                  ;   convert n - gap to word offset
           ADD SI,ES:ARRAYADR
           ADD BP,ES:ARRAYADR
WHILE02:   CMP SI,BP                 ;   WHILE SI < BP
           JNB WEND02
IF01:      MOV AX,[SI]               ;      IF x(i) > x(i+gap)
           CMP AX,[SI+BX]
           JBE ENDIF01
THEN01:    MOV DX,[SI+BX]            ;         THEN exchange
           MOV [SI],DX
           MOV [SI+BX],AX
           MOV ES:EXCH,0FFh          ;         set exchange flag ON
ENDIF01:                            ;         ENDIF
           ADD SI,2                  ;         increment SI
           JMP WHILE02
WEND02:                              ;      WEND
IF02:      MOV AL,ES:EXCH            ;   IF exchange flag OFF
           CMP AL,0
           JNE ENDIF02
THEN02:    SHR ES:GAP,1              ;      THEN divide gap by 2
ENDIF02:                             ;   ENDIF
           XOR AX,AX                 ;   clear exchange flag
           MOV ES:EXCH,AL
           JMP WHILE01
WEND01:                              ;WEND
           POP ES                    ;restore registers
           POP SI
           POP BP
           POP DX
           POP CX
           POP BX
           POP AX
           RET
SHELSORT   ENDP                      ;end of procedure declaration
           END                       ;end of program
```

**Figure 12-6    *concluded***

Figure 12-7 shows the linkage editor map PROG12.MAP. Note the arrangement of the segments. The five parts of the code segment starting at 001COH through 00264H are subroutines linked from ASSEM.LIB.

Figure 12-8 shows output from program 12.

```
Start   Stop    Length  Name                    Class
00000H  00128H  00129H  _TEXT                   CODE
0012AH  001AEH  00085H  SHELSORT_TEXT           CODE
001B0H  001B6H  00007H  FAR_DATA                FAR_DATA
001C0H  001C4H  00005H  CODE
001D0H  001EEH  0001FH  CODE
001F0H  001F6H  00007H  CODE
00200H  00220H  00021H  CODE
00230H  00264H  00035H  CODE
00266H  0032FH  000CAH  _BSS                    DATA
00330H  0041BH  000ECH  _DATA                   DATA
00420H  0051FH  00100H  STACK                   STACK


Origin   Group
0026:0   DGROUP
```

**Figure 12-7    Linkage Editor Map of PROG12**

## SUMMARY

This chapter shows a number of advanced features of the MASM 5.0 assembler. Options consisting of a slash followed by a one- or two-letter command and, in several instances, additional operands are used in the command line along with the names of the various files to be processed. The options may override default options assumed by MASM, but they in turn may be overridden by directives in the source program.

Environment variables also may be used to set default options for DOS or to specify directories used by certain programs. The INCLUDE environment variable can give the name of a directory where include files are stored. The MASM environment variable allows you to set certain MASM options so that they need not be given in the command line. The DOS SET command places the specified options to the environment variables.

MASM version 5.0 provides a method of simplified segment definitions not available in earlier version. The DOSSEG directive precedes other directives to cause segments to be placed in an order consistent with that used in Microsoft high-level language compilers. The .MODEL directive controls the default size of data and code in a program. The six models are TINY, SMALL, MEDIUM, COMPACT, LARGE, and HUGE.

The directives .CODE, .STACK. .DATA, .DATA?, .FARDATA, .FARDATA?, and .CONST indicate the start of a segment and also indicate the close of a previously defined segment that is still open. The END directive closes the last open segment. No ASSUME statement is require for the .CODE, .STACK, and .DATA segments.

With full segment definitions, each segment may be given one or more of four types: align, combine, use, and 'class'. The align type can cause the

```
Alton R Kindred, Shell Sort Demonstration
Sorts up to 100 numbers into ascending order.
Enter up to 100 four-digit hex numbers.
Press <ENTER> alone to stop:
abcd
9823
4966
0A94
7777
000c
000C
Numbers in original order:
ABCD 9823 4966 0A94 7777 000C 000C
Sorted numbers:
000C 000C 0A94 4966 7777 9823 ABCD
Do you wish to continue (Y/N)? n

B>
```

**Figure 12-8    Output from Program 12**

segment starting address to be the next available byte, word, doubleword, paragraph, or page. The combine type groups together segments with the same name. The use type sets the default word size for the 80386 processor only to use 16- or 32-bit word size for addresses. The 'class' type permits grouping of segments having different names but similar purposes.

The GROUP directive permits grouping the named segments so that they all are relative to the same starting address.

Segments may be nested. This technique is used most commonly within macros that may want to have some data and some code each time the macro is called.

The PAGE, TITLE, and SUBTTL directives control the listing of source programs. PAGE gives the number of lines per page and the number of characters per line and also can specify the point to skip to a new page. TITLE and SUBTTL can give headings to appear on each page of the assembler listing. Other directives control the listing of the entire program, of conditional statements, or of macro expansions within the program.

The .RADIX directive permits hex, binary, octal, or some other number base other than decimal to be set as the default for source programs. The LABEL directive assigns the specified name to the current value of the location counter.

A large number of operators allow arithmetic, logical, shifting, relational, and type operations to be performed by MASM on source statements. These operations are performed in a prescribed priority sequence.

MASM can create an optional cross-reference file having the extension .CRF. The DOS utility program CREF can convert CRF files to listing files having the extension REF. REF files show each symbol in alphabetical order, together with each line number that refers to that symbol.

Program 12 uses simplified segment definitions and other features described in this chapter. It has a subroutine using the Shell sort technique to sort up to 100 words entered by the operator in hex notation and prints them out in the original and sorted sequences.

# QUESTIONS

1. Where may MASM options be placed in the command Line? What special character precedes each command?
2. What is the default file-buffer size used by MASM? What are the minimum and maximum sizes?
3. Which MASM option displays all options and command-line syntax on the screen? Can this option be used with file names or other options?
4. What is meant by an environment variable? Which two are especially useful to MASM?
5. What is the function of the DOSSEG directive? Where should it appear in the source program?
6. Name and explain the six memory models supported by MASM.
7. Name the segment directives that are valid with simplified segment definitions. What two types of directives may be omitted when they are used?
8. What is meant by an align type? How many such types are there?
9. What three directives control page format? Describe the function of each.
10. What directives suppress and restore the listing of source statement lines? Where may they appear in the program?
11. Explain the differences among the .SFCOND, .LFCOND, and .TFCOND directives?
12. Explain the difference between the SHL and SHR operators and the instructions having the same names.
13. Explain the differences in the values returned by the .TYPE and TYPE operators.
14. What must be done to a cross-reference listing file created by MASM to make it printable? What extension does the listing file have?

# EXERCISES

1. Write MASM command line options to set the file-buffer to maximum size, create a pass 1 listing, create listing and cross-reference files, report the number of lines and symbols processed, and list false-conditional blocks.
2. Write a SET statement to name SOURCE on drive B as the directory where INCLUDE files are stored.
3. Write simplified segment definitions for a data segment containing two strings of your own choice, a stack segment of 256 bytes, and a code segment that displays the two strings on the screen.

4. Write the default name used with each of these directives for simplified segment definitions:

   `.CODE  .DATA  .DATA?  .STACK  .FARDATA  .FARDATA?`

5. Show values for @codesize and @datasize for each memory model below:

   |  | @CODESIZE | @DATASIZE |
   |---|---|---|
   | Small | _____ | _____ |
   | Medium | _____ | _____ |
   | Compact | _____ | _____ |
   | Large | _____ | _____ |
   | Huge | _____ | _____ |

6. Write the names of all the segments automatically grouped in DGROUP when simplified segment definitions are used.

7. Write a full segment definition for a code segment to be aligned on a paragraph, with PUBLIC combined type, and class type 'CODE'.

8. Write statements to suppress the listing of all macro expansions, then list a macro named CRLF, then suppress the remaining macro expansions.

9. Write THIS, LABEL, and EQU statements to permit the same label to be called A, B, C, or D.

10. Write the value of each of the following expressions if A = -5 and B = 3:
    a. `A + B`
    b. `A MOD B`
    c. `NOT B`
    d. `A AND B`
    e. `A XOR B`
    f. `A SHL 2`
    g. `B SHR 2`
    h. `A GT B`
    i. `6 EQ B SHL 1`

11. Write instructions to move the segment address of a field named PROMPT to SEGADDR and the offset of PROMPT to OFFSTADDR.

12. WORD1 contains the value 3456h. Write instructions to move its leftmost byte to AL. and its rightmost byte to BL. Use LOW and HIGH operators.

13. ARRAY is defined by DW 25 DUP (0). Write the value of each of the following expressions:
    a. `.TYPE ARRAY`
    b. `TYPE ARRAY`
    c. `LENGTH ARRAY`
    d. `SIZE ARRAY`

## LAB PROBLEMS

1. Write a program using simplified segment definitions and a small memory model. Use .DATA for initialized data and .DATA? for uninitialized data. Write

a macro definition that includes nested segments for data and code to input a string of characters. The macro is invoked with the statement

```
INPSTRNG N,BUFFER
```

where *N* is the maximum number of characters to be input and *BUFFER* is the name of the input area. The value of N appears at BUFFER, BUFFER+1 is a byte to contain the number of bytes actually input, and BUFFER+2 starts the input string.

# LINKING ASSEMBLER LANGUAGE TO OTHER LANGUAGES

# 13

---

**OBJECTIVES**

After studying this chapter, you should be able to:

- Describe conventions used by Microsoft compilers to call procedures written in assembler language.
- Use the stack for passing near and far parameters.
- Use the stack to provide work space for data needed by an assembler subroutine.
- Explain the difference between functions and procedures in high-level languages.
- Adapt assembler subroutines to specific requirements of different compilers.
- Explain and demonstrate how to place machine code of assembler subroutines directly into interpretive BASIC.

---

## MIXED-LANGUAGE CONVENTIONS

The term *mixed-language programming* refers to any situation where a program written in one programming language calls a routine written in another language. There generally are two types of calls: those that return a value and those that do not. We shall use the general term *routine* to refer to whatever is called. Table 13-1 shows terms used by the high-level languages to specify whether or not a value is to be returned by the routine.

Certain mixed-language conventions have been adopted by Microsoft for its principal languages to facilitate calls to or from those languages. MASM is the principal assembler distributed by Microsoft for the 8088, 80286, and 80386 microprocessors. Microsoft has produced compilers for BASIC, C, FORTRAN, and Pascal. BASIC also is available in several versions using an interpreter rather than a compiler. Other software companies have compilers for these languages that may or may not follow the same conventions.

The *Mixed-Language Programming Guide*, distributed with MASM, contains a full discussion of calling programs and subroutines in each language.

Table 13-1.  Comparison of Languages for Calling Routines

| Language | Return Value | No Return Value |
|---|---|---|
| BASIC | FUNCTION<br>procedure | subprogram |
| C | function | (void)function |
| FORTRAN | function | subroutine |
| Pascal | function | procedure |
| Assembler | procedure | procedure |

We will consider only calls from BASIC, C, FORTRAN, and Pascal to procedures written in assembler language.

The assembler routine first must be written and assembled to produce an object file on disk. Then the calling program is written in the appropriate high-level language. Some compilers combine the functions of editor, compiler, and linker to produce an EXE file including the assembler routine. Others produce an object file which LINK combines with one or more object files to produce the EXE load module.

All high-level languages have standard routines, either in the compiler or in separate libraries, that also must be linked to the calling program along with the assembler routine. You often may need to swap disks during the compiling and linking process if the libraries are too extensive to be held on the same disks with the system software.

## Naming Conventions

The way the compiler handles the name of a routine determines whether LINK can correctly find and combine routines in different languages. The object file contains not only machine code but also names of routines and variables to be accessed publicly.

BASIC, FORTRAN, and Pascal translate each letter of a name to uppercase. BASIC type declarations (%, &, !, #, and $) are dropped from the names. But FORTRAN recognizes only the first 6 characters of a name, Pascal the first 8, and BASIC the first 40.

C does not change any letters to uppercase, but it inserts an underscore (_) in front of the name of each called routine and recognizes only the first 8 characters. The name of the object file of the called routine must begin with an underscore.

## Calling Conventions

*Parameters* are actual data or the addresses of data that are sent to the routine for processing. The four Microsoft compilers mentioned all pass parameters to the called routine by pushing them on the stack before the return address is pushed. BASIC, FORTRAN, and Pascal push the parameters in the order in which they appear in the source statement. For example, the statement CALL SUB1(A,B) would push A, then B, then the return address. However, C pushes the parameters in reverse order; that is, the last parameter named is pushed first and the first parameter named is pushed last before the return address.

BASIC, FORTRAN, and Pascal expect the called routine to remove the extra parameters from the stack with the statement RET $n$, where $n$ is the number of bytes to be removed. The C compiler expects a standard RET statement and adjusts the stack in the calling program upon return from the called routine.

The Microsoft compilers provide three ways to pass a parameter:

1. *By near reference.* Only the offset address of the parameter is pushed on the stack. One word for each parameter is pushed. Any change to the parameter by the routine will change the data in the calling program.

2. *By far reference.* Both the segment and the offset address of the parameter are pushed on the stack. Two words for each parameter are pushed. Far processing allows data to be outside the default data segment, but it is somewhat slower than near processing.

3. *By value.* The actual value, and not the address, of the parameter is pushed on the stack. Changes made to the variable by the routine have no effect on the original data in the calling program.

Table 13-2 shows the parameter-passing defaults for the four Microsoft high-level languages. There are keywords or other language features that allow you to override the defaults for passing parameters.

### Compiling and Linking

Apart from the parameters that are pushed on the stack, the return address of the calling program may be either far or near, depending upon the model used in compiling the high-level program. By default, BASIC, FORTRAN, and Pascal use far code addresses. C uses far calls with medium, large, or huge models, but near calls with small or compact models. The far call pushes both the segment and offset of the return address on the stack as two words, while the near call pushes only the offset of the return address as a single word.

The assembler routine must match the calling program exactly, not only in defining the procedure as far or near, but also in retrieving the parameters from the stack.

## WRITING THE ASSEMBLER ROUTINE

The interface conventions used by Microsoft compilers for BASIC, C, FORTRAN, and Pascal generally are the same. To write an assembler routine to be called by any of these languages, you must carry out these steps:

Table 13-2.   Parameter-Passing Defaults

| Language | Near Reference | Far Reference | By Value |
|----------|----------------|---------------|----------|
| BASIC | all | | |
| C | near arrays | far arrays | nonarrays |
| FORTRAN | | all | all (1) |
| Pascal | VAR,CONST | VARS, CONSTS | other paramaters |

(1) FORTRAN passes by value if the Pascal or C attribute is specified

1.   Define the procedure.
2.   Enter the procedure.
3.   Allocate local data, if required.
4.   Save register values.
5.   Access parameters.
6.   Return a value, if required.
7.   Return from the procedure.

## Defining the Procedure

Your procedure will be either near or far. It can be defined in any of several ways to match the form expected by the high-level calling program. For MASM versions earlier than 5.0, you should declare the procedure far for every program except C that is defined as a small or compact model. For version 5.0 MASM, you may use .MODEL LARGE for Pascal or FORTRAN, .MODEL MEDIUM for BASIC, and the .MODEL form for C corresponding with that used in the C program.

With MASM version 5.0, you should use the simplified segment directives .CODE and .DATA (if needed) to combine these segments with those of the calling program.

As usual, declare the procedure label as PUBLIC, as well as any data to be made available to other modules. If the assembler uses any external routines they must be named in EXTRN directives.

## Entering the Procedure

The assembler routine begins with the two instructions

```
PUSH BP
MOV BP,SP
```

These instructions save the contents of BP on the stack and then replace them with the address where BP is stored. Recall that BP refers to addresses in the stack by default. Addresses in the stack higher than BP were pushed by the calling program. Addresses in the stack lower than BP may be used by the assembler routine.

## Allocating Local Data

It often is convenient to use the stack for storing variables needed by the assembler routine, rather than defining a data segment. If, for example, you need eight bytes for local data, you may reserve space for it by simply subtracting eight from the stack pointer SP. The following instructions enter the procedure and reserve eight bytes for local data:

```
PUSH BP
MOV BP,SP
SUB SP,8
```

Assume that the high-level language issued CALL SUBA(PARAM1, PARAM2) where both parameters and the SUBA routine are far. The stack then appears as in Figure 13-1. The segment address for PARAM1 is at SS:BP+12 and its offset is at SS:BP+10. The addresses for PARAM2 are at SS:BP+8 and SS:BP+6. The return segment address is at SS:BP+4 and the offset is at SS:BP+2. The eight bytes from SS:BP-1 through SS:BP-8 are available to store local data.

The use of local data can be further simplified by generous use of EQU statements. For example:

```
PARAM1     EQU WORD PTR [BP-2]
PARAM2     EQU WORD PTR [BP-4]
ERRFLAG    EQU BYTE PTR [BP-5]
SAVEWORD   EQU WORD PTR [BP-7]
```

Unlike PUSH and POP operations, which can put only words on the stack, local data can be moved as either bytes or words. For example, the instruction

```
MOV ERRFLAG,0
```

in the example above is equivalent to the statement

```
MOV BYTE PTR [BP-5],0
```

and moves only a single byte to the local area of the stack.

## Saving Register Values

PUSH registers that you plan to use in the assembler routine to preserve values that they might contain from the calling program. Then at the end of the routine, POP these registers in the reverse order to restore the values for the calling program.

## Accessing Parameters

The next step is to gain access to the parameters passed to the routine by the calling program. In the example of Figure 13-1, parameters are passed by far reference. You may place the actual data for PARAM1 and PARAM2 in the local data area of the stack by using these instructions:

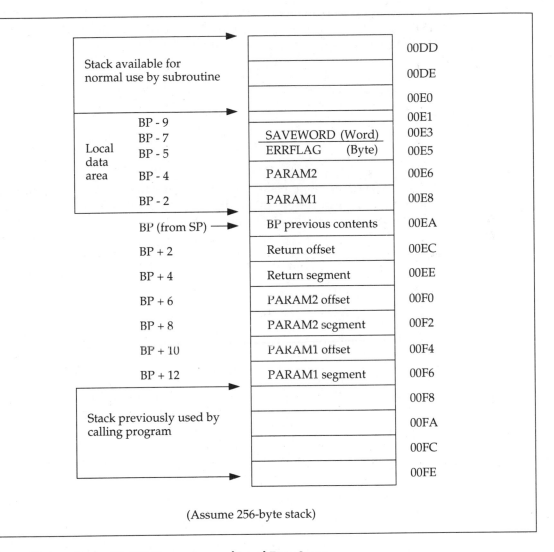

| | |
|---|---|
| Stack available for normal use by subroutine | 00DD |
| | 00DE |
| | 00E0 |
| BP - 9 | 00E1 |
| BP - 7 | SAVEWORD (Word) | 00E3 |
| BP - 5 | ERRFLAG (Byte) | 00E5 |
| BP - 4 | PARAM2 | 00E6 |
| BP - 2 | PARAM1 | 00E8 |
| BP (from SP) → | BP previous contents | 00EA |
| BP + 2 | Return offset | 00EC |
| BP + 4 | Return segment | 00EE |
| BP + 6 | PARAM2 offset | 00F0 |
| BP + 8 | PARAM2 segment | 00F2 |
| BP + 10 | PARAM1 offset | 00F4 |
| BP + 12 | PARAM1 segment | 00F6 |
| Stack previously used by calling program | 00F8 |
| | 00FA |
| | 00FC |
| | 00FE |

(Assume 256-byte stack)

**Figure 13-1    Stack with FAR Parameters and Local Data Space**

```
LDS SI,[BP+10]          ;get address of PARAM1 into
                        ;DS:SI
MOV AX,[SI]             ;mov PARAM1 into AX
MOV PARAM1,AX           ;and store in local data area
LES SI,[BP+6]           ;get address of PARAM2 into
                        ;ES:SI
MOV AX,ES:[SI]          ;mov PARAM2 into AX; note ES
                        ;override
MOV PARAM2,AX           ;and store in local data area
```

If the routine and all parameters were defined as near, only three words on the stack above BP would be required for the offset addresses of PARAM1, PARAM2, and the return address. Figure 13-2 shows the stack with two near parameters, a near return address, and eight bytes of local data space.

The parameters could be accessed in this way:

```
MOV SI,[BP+6]          ;get offset of PARAM1 into SI
MOV AX,[SI]            ;move PARAM1 into AX
MOV PARAM1,AX          ;and store in local data area
MOV SI,[BP+4]          ;get offset of PARAM2 into SI
MOV AX,[SI]            ;move PARAM2 into AX
MOV PARAM2,AX          ;and store in local data area
```

If the parameters are passed by value rather than by address, you need not use SI. You can merely move the parameter value from the stack to a register and then to the local data area in this way:

```
MOV AX,[BP+6]          ;move value of PARAM1 to AX
MOV PARAM1,AX          ;and store in local data area
MOV AX,[BP+4]          ;move value of PARAM2 to AX
MOV PARAM2,AX          ;and store in local data area
```

## Returning a Value

If the calling program expects a value to be returned by the assembler routine, the Microsoft compilers use this convention:

1. A value of the size of one byte is to be returned in AL register.
2. A value two bytes in size is to be returned in AX register.
3. A value of four bytes should contain the high-order portion in DX and the low-order portion in AX.
4. If the return value is larger than four bytes, the assembler routine must place the segment address of this value in DX and the offset in AX before returning to the calling program.

When the calling program is written in BASIC or C, the assembler routine must declare space in a data segment for the return value greater than four bytes and then put the segment/offset address of that space in DX:AX.

If the calling program is in FORTRAN or Pascal, the calling program takes these actions before making the CALL:

1. Creates space somewhere in the stack segment for the actual return value.
2. Names one extra parameter in the CALL statement whose offset is pushed on the stack just before the return address. This offset always will be found at BP+6 when the far return segment address is at BP+4 and the return offset is at BP+2.
3. Puts the segment address of the return value in both SS and DS.

Your assembler routine before return must put the return value at the location pointed to by the offset at BP+6. Then copy this same value into AX and copy SS into DX. Thus DX:AX will point to the return value as expected.

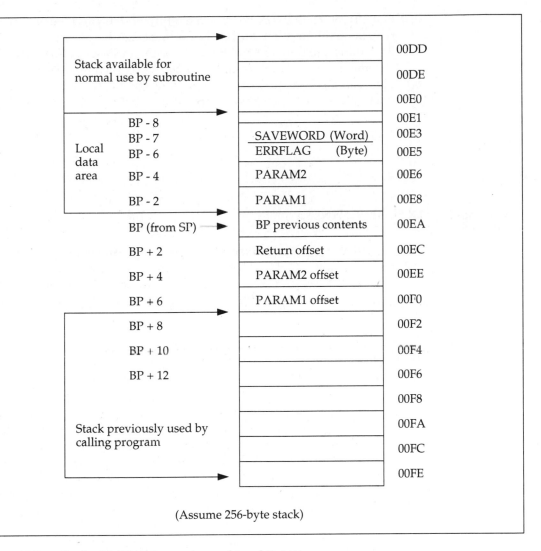

| | | |
|---|---|---|
| Stack available for normal use by subroutine | | 00DD |
| | | 00DE |
| | | 00E0 |
| | | 00E1 |
| BP - 8 | | |
| BP - 7 | SAVEWORD (Word) | 00E3 |
| BP - 6 | ERRFLAG      (Byte) | 00E5 |
| BP - 4 | PARAM2 | 00E6 |
| BP - 2 | PARAM1 | 00E8 |
| BP (from SP) | BP previous contents | 00EA |
| BP + 2 | Return offset | 00EC |
| BP + 4 | PARAM2 offset | 00EE |
| BP + 6 | PARAM1 offset | 00F0 |
| BP + 8 | | 00F2 |
| BP + 10 | | 00F4 |
| BP + 12 | | 00F6 |
| | | 00F8 |
| Stack previously used by calling program | | 00FA |
| | | 00FC |
| | | 00FE |

(Assume 256-byte stack)

**Figure 13-2     Stack with NEAR Parameters and Local Data Space**

### Exiting the Procedure

To return to the calling program, your assembler routine must do these steps:

1. POP any registers in reverse order that were saved when the routine was entered.
2. If local data space was reserved in the stack, restore SP by issuing either MOV SP,BP or ADD SP,8 (or whatever value was subtracted to create local data space).

3.   POP BP. When this is done, only the return address and the parameters remain on the stack relating to the routine call.

4.   For calling programs in BASIC, FORTRAN, or Pascal, issue the RET *n* statement, where *n* is the number of bytes occupied by the parameters. This statement, in addition to removing the return address from the stack, adds *n* to the stack pointer SP to restore the stack to the condition it was in before the CALL was issued. For calling programs in C, issue only a normal RET. The C compiler adjusts the stack upon return from the call.

## TWO ASSEMBLER SUBROUTINES

We shall use two assembler subroutines to demonstrate calling from programs in BASIC, C, FORTRAN, and Pascal. The first routine, named PAUS, causes a delay of *n* seconds, where *n* is the parameter passed by the calling routine. The second routine is a modification of the Shell sort routine used in Chapter 12.

### The PAUS Routine

The name for PAUS has the format PAUS*pr[C]* to reflect several versions. The letter *p* is replaced by F, N, or V to specify if the number of seconds is passed by far or near address or by value. The letter *r* is replaced by F or N to specify a far or near return. The final *C* is used only with the routine to be called by C, which handles the stack differently from other languages.

Figure 13-3 shows PAUSVF, which we will call from programs in FORTRAN and Pascal that pass parameters by value and a far return address. We use the fact that the internal clock on the 8088 chip ticks approximately 18.2 times per second. After pushing BP and saving work registers, we get the number of seconds from the stack and place the value in CX. Then we multiply the number in CX by 182 to get 10 times the number of ticks to pause, divide this number by 10, and put into BX the resulting number of ticks to pause.

Then we call INT 1Ah to get in DX the number of ticks since midnight and add DX to BX to set the tick count at the end of the pause period. We then loop and repeatedly get the tick count in DX until it reaches the number in BX.

In PAUSVF we need no local data area on the stack. The far return address is at SS:BP+2 and SS:BP+4. The value for number of seconds is moved directly to CX by the statement

```
MOV CX, [BP+6]
```

The statement RET 2 removes the two-byte parameter value from the stack along with the far return address.

```
;--------------------------------------------------------------
;Program name:  PAUSVF Subroutine
;Author:        Alton R. Kindred
;
;This routine is to be called from BASIC,FORTRAN, or Pascal to pause a
;specified number of seconds.  It expects a far call with the
;number of seconds to be passed by value.
;
;At entry:  BP+2 = return address
;           BP+6 = number of seconds
;--------------------------------------------------------------
COPE      SEGMENT
          ASSUME CS:CODE
          PUBLIC PAUSVF
PAUSVF    PROC FAR
          PUSH BP
          MOV BP,SP
          PUSH AX
          PUSH BX
          PUSH CX
          PUSH DX
          MOV CX, [BP+6]          ;CX = n seconds
          MOV AX,182              ;multiply by ticks in 10 seconds
          MUL CX
          MOV BX,10               ;divide by 10
          DIV BX
          MOV DX,AX               ;BX = ticks in n seconds
          MOV AH,0                ;get current tick count
          INT 1Ah
          ADD BX,DX               ;BX = future tick cnt. after n secs.
WHILE01:  CMP BX,DX               ;WHILE tick count <> future tick count
          JE WEND01
          MOV AH,0                ;  get next tick count
          INT 1Ah
          JMP WHILE01
WEND01:                          ;WEND
          POP DX
          POP CX
          POP BX
          POP AX
          POP BP
          RET 2                  ;return
PAUSVF    ENDP
CODE      ENDS
          END
```

**Figure 13-3    PAUSVF Subroutine**

## The SHEL Routine

SHEL is a modification of the SHELSORT routine presented in Chapter 12. The SHEL routine also has several versions named SHEL*pr[C]*, where *p* can be F, N, or V for the method of passing parameters and *r* can be F or N to indicate far or near return.

The name *SHELFF* implies that parameters will be passed by far reference and the return also will be far. All of the Microsoft languages can use this subroutine except C. A different version _SHELFFC (note underscore preceding name) accommodates the C convention of passing parameter addresses in reverse order and using a standard RET.

Instead of having FARDATA section as we used in SHELSORT in Chapter 12, in SHELFF we reserve eight bytes of local data area on the stack. Whereas in SHELSORT we passed the array address in DX and the number of items to sort in CX, in SHELFF we retrieve these parameters from far addresses on the stack. Figure 13-4 shows the stack organization for SHELFF.

Figure 13-5 shows the SHELFF subroutine. To accommodate the possibility that the array and the number of elements are in different data segments, we use DS to point to the array and ES segment override to point to the number of elements. The array address is retrieved from the stack and its offset is placed in ARRAYADR with the statements

```
LDS BX,[BP+10]          ;get address of array in DS
                        ;and BX
MOV ARRAYADR,BX         ;store offset in ARRAYADR
```

The number of elements to sort is placed in NITEMS with

```
LES BX,[BP+6]           ;get address of count in ES
                        ;and BX
MOV NITEMS,ES:[BX]      ;move count to NITEMS
```

After completion of the sort, SHELFF removes the eight bytes containing the two far addresses for the stack with RET 8.

## LINKING TO PASCAL

In this section we demonstrate not only linking to Microsoft Pascal, but also the widely used Turbo Pascal, written by Borland International.

### Microsoft Pascal

Microsoft Pascal by default expects the called procedure to be far and parameters to be passed by value. The far assembler routine PAUSVF is designed for any routine that passes a value representing the number of seconds to pause. The Pascal program PAS13A.PAS (Figure 13-6) calls PAUSVF. The procedure declaration

```
PROCEDURE PAUSVF (SECONDS:INTEGER); EXTERN;
```

names PAUSVF as the external procedure and names SECONDS as the argument to be passed by value. If the number of seconds were to be passed by reference, the form would be

```
PROCEDURE PAUSNF(VAR SECONDS:INTEGER); EXTERN;
```

| | | |
|---|---|---|
| Stack available for normal use by subroutine | | 00DD |
| | | 00DE |
| | | 00E0 |
| | | 00E1 |
| BP - 9 | | |
| BP - 7 | NITEMS          (Word) | 00E3 |
| Local data area    BP - 5 | ARRAYADR (WORD) | 00E5 |
| BP - 3 | EXCH          (Byte) | 00E7 |
| BP - 2 | GAP | 00E8 |
| BP (from SP) ⟶ | BP previous contents | 00EA |
| BP + 2 | Return offset | 00EC |
| BP + 4 | Return segment | 00EE |
| BP + 6 | NITEMS offset | 00F0 |
| BP + 8 | NITEMS segment | 00F2 |
| BP + 10 | Array offset | 00F4 |
| BP + 12 | Array segment | 00F6 |
| Stack previously used by calling program | | 00F8 |
| | | 00FA |
| | | 00FC |
| | | 00FE |

(Assume 256-byte stack)

**Figure 13-4     Stack Used by SHELFF Subroutine**

for near reference and

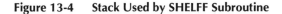

```
PROCEDURE PAUSFF(VARS SECONDS:INTEGER); EXTERN;
```

for far reference. Where only the name of the parameter SECONDS is given, its value is placed on the stack. Where the name is preceded by VAR, only the offset address is passed; where preceded by VARS, both the segment and the offset addresses are passed. The keyword VAR or VARS precedes each individual parameter.

```
          PAGE 50,132
;------------------------------------------------------------------------
; Program name:  SHELFF.ASM
;
; Author:  Alton R. Kindred
;
; This routine sorts an array of 16-bit words into ascending order using the
; Shell sort.  It is intended to link to a calling program that passes
; far references to data and a far return address.
; Upon entry:  BP + 2 = return address offset
;              BP + 4 = return address segment
;              BP + 6 = offset of count of items
;              BP + 8 = segment of count of items
;              BP + 10 = offset of array
;              BP + 12 = segment of array
;------------------------------------------------------------------------
GAP        EQU  [BP-2]
EXCH       EQU  [BP-3]
ARRAYADR   EQU  [BP-5]
NITEMS     EQU  [BP-7]
;------------------------------------------------------------------------
CODE       SEGMENT
           ASSUME CS:CODE
           PUBLIC SHELFF
SHELFF     PROC FAR
START:     PUSH BP                    ;mark BP
           MOV BP,SP
           SUB SP,8                   ;reserve local data space on stack
           IRP REGISTER,<AX,BX,CX,DX,DI,SI,ES,DS>
           PUSH REGISTER
           ENDM
           LDS DX,[BP+10]             ;get address of array into DS:DX
           MOV ARRAYADR,DX            ;and save it in arrayadr
           LES SI,[BP+6]              ;get address of count N into ES:SI
           MOV DX,ES:[SI]             ;move count N into DX
           MOV NITEMS,DX              ;and then into nitems
           MOV CX,NITEMS
           SHR CX,1                   ;set gap to N/2
           MOV GAP,CX                 ;save gap
           MOV BYTE PTR EXCH,0        ;set exchange flag OFF
WHILE:     MOV AX,GAP                 ;WHILE gap > 0
           CMP AX,0
           JNG WEND
           MOV BX,GAP                 ;   convert gap to word offset
           SHL BX,1
           MOV SI,0
           MOV AX,NITEMS              ;   compute nitems - gap
           SUB AX,GAP
           MOV DI,AX
           SHL DI,1                   ;   convert n-g to word offset
           ADD SI,ARRAYADR
           ADD DI,ARRAYADR
WHILE2:    CMP SI,DI                  ;   WHILE SI < DI
           JNB WEND2
```

**Figure 13-5    SHELFF Subroutine**

```
IFA:        MOV AX,[SI]                 ;     IF x(i) > x(i+g)
            CMP AX,[SI+BX]
            JBE ENDIFA
THENA:      MOV DX,[SI+BX]              ;        THEN exchange
            MOV [SI],DX
            MOV [SI+BX],AX
            MOV BYTE PTR EXCH,0FFh      ;        set exchange flag ON
ENDIFA:                                 ;     ENDIF
            ADD SI,2                    ;     increment SI
            JMP WHILE2
WEND2:                                  ;   WEND
IFB1:       MOV AL,EXCH                 ;   IF exchange flag OFF
            CMP AL,0
            JNE ENDIFB1
THENB1:     SHR WORD PTR GAP,1          ;     THEN divide gap by 2
ENDIFB1:                                ;   ENDIF
            XOR AX,AX                   ;   clear exchange flag
            MOV EXCH,AL
            JMP WHILE
WEND:                                   ;WEND
            IRP REGISTER,<DS,ES,SI,DI,DX,CX,BX,AX>
            POP REGISTER
            ENDM
            ADD SP,8                    ;reset stack pointer
            POP BP
            RET 8                       ;return and clear parameters
;----------------------------------------------------------------------
SHELFF      ENDP
CODE        ENDS
            END                         ;end of program
```

---

```
(* Program name:   PAS13A.PAS *)
(* Author:         Alton R. Kindred *)
(* This Pascal program calls a far assembler routine to pause for the *)
(* specified number of seconds.  The number of seconds is passed by value. *)
(*--------------------------------------------------------------------*)

PROGRAM PAS13A;

VAR SECONDS: INTEGER;

PROCEDURE PAUSVF(SECONDS: INTEGER); EXTERN;

BEGIN
     WRITE ('How many seconds to pause? ');
     READLN (SECONDS);
     IF SECONDS > 0 THEN BEGIN
       PAUSVF(SECONDS);
       WRITELN ('Paused for ', SECONDS, ' seconds');
     END;
```

**Figure 13-6    Program PAS13A**

PAS13A displays a message asking how long to pause, gets the number of seconds, passes the value to the assembler routine, waits that length of time, and then prints a message indicating the elapsed seconds.

This program must be compiled and the object program placed on disk. Then LINK can combine PAS13A.OBJ with PAUSVF.OBJ to create the executable module PAS13A.EXE. Sample output from program PAS13A looks like this:

```
How many seconds to pause? 5
Paused for 5 seconds
```

Figure 13-7 shows Microsoft Pascal program PAS13B to create an array of a specified number of random integers, having value between 0 and 255. The program calls SHELFF to sort the numbers. We pass two parameters: the far address of the routine and the far address of the number of elements to sort.

The procedure declaration

```
PROCEDURE SHELFF(VARS LIST2:ARAY, VARS COUNT:INTEGER);
EXTERN;
```

says that SHELFF will have a far call by default. The VARS keyword determines that the parameters LIST2 and COUNT will have far addresses. SHELFF is actually called in the main program with the statement

```
SHELFF(LIST2,COUNT);
```

After the numbers are sorted, we print the unsorted array and the sorted array side by side. We continue as long as the operator responds 'Y' or 'y' to a question whether to continue.

Figure 13-8 shows the output from program PAS13B.

## Turbo Pascal

Turbo Pascal has somewhat different conventions from those used by Microsoft. The Turbo compiler, in addition to providing an editor for source code, can compile the Pascal program and link to the external procedures named.

When using Turbo Pascal, you first must write the assembler routine, assemble it, and place the object file on disk. Then you write the Pascal program, naming in it the assembler object file to be linked. The Turbo compiler then compiles the Pascal program, links the assembler routine, and, if requested, places the EXE file on disk, where it can be executed from DOS like any other EXE program.

The Turbo Pascal program TUR13A calls PAUSVF to pause the specified number of seconds. TUR13A is identical to PAS13A except for the procedure declaration of PAUSVF. We write three statements as follows:

```
{$F+}
PROCEDURE PAUSVF(SECONDS:INTEGER); EXTERNAL;
{$L B:PAUSVF.OBJ}
```

```
(* Program name:  PAS13B.PAS *);
(* Author:        Alton R. Kindred *)
(* This Pascal program creates an array of random integers with values *)
(* between decimal 0 and 255.  It then calls an assembler language *)
(* subroutine to sort the numbers.  Finally, it prints the original *)
(* numbers and sorted side by side.  This version uses far references *)
(* and a far call. *)
(*-------------------------------------------------------------------*)
PROGRAM PAS13B;
TYPE ARAY = ARRAY[1..100] OF INTEGER;


VAR
  SEED: REAL;
  I, COUNT:    INTEGER;
  CONTINUE: CHAR;
  LIST1, LIST2: ARAY;

PROCEDURE SHELFF(VAR LIST2:ARAY; VAR COUNT:INTEGER); EXTERN;

FUNCTION RAND(N: INTEGER): INTEGER;
BEGIN
  SEED := SQR(SEED + 3.1415927);
  SEED := SEED - TRUNC(SEED);
  RAND := TRUNC(N * SEED)
END; (* rand *)

BEGIN (* main program *)
  REPEAT
    WRITE('Enter seed for RNG between 0 and 1 (form 0.999): ');
    READLN(SEED);
    WRITE('How many numbers to sort (1-100)? ');
    READLN(COUNT);
    FOR I := 1 TO COUNT DO
      BEGIN
        LIST1[I] := RAND(255);
        LIST2[I] := LIST1[I];
      END;
    SHELFF(LIST2,COUNT)      (* sort the array *);

    WRITELN('Original Numbers    Sorted Numbers');
    FOR I := 1 TO COUNT DO
      BEGIN
        WRITE(LIST1[I]:12);
        WRITELN(LIST2[I]:20);
      END;
    WRITE('Sort another set (Y/N)? ');
    READ(CONTINUE);
    WRITELN;
  UNTIL (CONTINUE <> 'Y') AND (CONTINUE <> 'y')
END.
```

**Figure 13-7    Program PAS13B**

```
Enter seed for RNG between 0 and 1 (form 0.999): 0.577
How many numbers to sort (1-100)? 8
Original Numbers      Sorted Numbers
          211               42
          193               50
           50              120
           42              134
          240              170
          170              193
          134              211
          120              240
Sort another set (Y/N)? n
```

**Figure 13-8    Output from Program PAS13B**

The directive {$F+} is necessary to enable a far call, because the default call for Turbo is near. The use of the parameter SECONDS without VAR or VARS indicates that SECONDS will be passed by value. Turbo uses the term EX-TERNAL instead of the shorter form EXTERN. The directive {$L B:PAUSVF.OBJ} names the assembler procedure on disk to be linked to TUR13A.

TUR13B is the Turbo Pascal program to create an array of random integers to be sorted and then printed out in both sorted and unsorted form. It is identical to the Microsoft Pascal program PAS13B in Figure 13-7 except for the following procedure declaration:

```
{$F+}
PROCEDURE SHELFF (VAR LIST2:ARAY; VAR COUNT:INTEGER);
EXTERNAL;
{$L B:SHELFF:OBJ}
```

The Turbo directive {$F+} must be given to permit a far call. Turbo uses VAR instead of VARS to indicate a far reference for parameters and the term EXTERNAL instead of EXTERN. The SHELFF object file must be named in the linker directive {$L B:SHELLTNF.OBJ}.

The output from TUR13B is identical to that in Figure 13-8.

## LINKING TO FORTRAN

All calls from Microsoft FORTRAN are far by default. Parameter addresses are far where the FORTRAN program is compiled in large or huge memory models and near in medium memory models. FORTRAN will pass parameters by value when the keyword VALUE is used.

We shall use a medium memory model in FOR13A to pause the requested number of seconds. The value of the number of seconds is at BP+6, while the far return address is at BP+2 and BP+4. Figure 13-9 shows program FOR13A.

```
C      Program name:  FOR13A.FOR
C      Author:         Alton R. Kindred
C      This FORTRAN program calls a far assembler routine to pause for the
C      specified number of seconds.  Seconds are passed by value.
C---------------------------------------------------------------------------

       INTERFACE TO SUBROUTINE PAUSVF (N)
       EXTERNAL PAUSVF FAR
       INTEGER*2 N [VALUE]
       END

       PROGRAM FOR13A

       INTEGER*2 NSECS

       WRITE(*,*) 'How many seconds to pause? '
       READ(*,11) NSECS
11     FORMAT (I3)
       IF (NSECS .GT. 0) THEN
         CALL PAUSVF (NSECS)
       ENDIF
       WRITE (*,12) NSECS
12     FORMAT (' Paused for ', I4, ' seconds')
       END
```

**Figure 13-9    Program FOR13A**

The external far procedure PAUSVF is defined in an INTERFACE section. This section shows that the call to PAUSVF will use one parameter, an integer of two bytes, that will be passed by value.

Only the first six bytes of external names are recognized by the FORTRAN compiler unless the ALIAS attribute is used with this syntax:

```
ALIAS:'aliasname'
```

where *aliasname* is the full file name of the object file to be linked. If the name of the external procedure were PAUSEVF, for example, the INTERFACE statement should read:

```
INTERFACE TO SUBROUTINE PAUSEVF [ALIAS: 'PAUSEVF'] (N)
```

Otherwise, the compiler would assume the subroutine name was PAUSEV, limited to six bytes.

FOR13B is the FORTRAN program that creates an array of up to 100 random numbers and calls SHELFF to sort it. A complete INTERFACE statement is not required. The statement

```
EXTERNAL SHELFF [FAR]
```

is sufficient because FOR13B uses far parameter addresses by default. Figure 13-10 shows program FOR13B.

```
C      Program name:  FOR13B.FOR
C      Author:  Alton R. Kindred
C      This FORTRAN program creates an array of random integers with values
C      beween decimal 0 and 255.  It then calls the assembler language
C      subroutine SHELFF to sort the numbers.  Finally, it prints the original
C      numbers side by side.
C      The program uses far references and a far call.
C-----------------------------------------------------------------------

       PROGRAM FOR13B

       REAL*4 SEED, X
       CHARACTER RESP
       INTEGER*2 LIST1, LIST2, N, I
       DIMENSION  LIST1(100),LIST2(100)

       EXTERNAL SHELFF [FAR]

1      WRITE(*,*) 'Enter seed for RNG between 0 and 1 (form 0.999): '
       READ(*,10) SEED
10     FORMAT (F5.3)
       WRITE(*,*) 'How many numbers to sort (1-100)? '
       READ(*,11) N
11     FORMAT (I3)
       IF (N .GT. 0) THEN
         X = 255.0
         DO 101 I = 1, N
           LIST1(I) = RAND(X, SEED)
           LIST2(I) = LIST(I)
101      CONTINUE
       ENDIF
       CALL SHELFF(LIST2, N)
       WRITE(*,*) 'Original Numbers   Sorted Numbers'
       DO 102 I = 1, N
         WRITE (*,12) LIST1(I), LIST2(I)
12       FORMAT (1H , 8X, I4, 12X, I4)
102    CONTINUE
       WRITE (*,*) 'Sort another set (Y/N)? '
       READ (*,13) RESP
13     FORMAT (A1)
       IF (RESP .EQ. 'Y') GO TO 1
       IF (RESP .EQ. 'y') GO TO 1
       END
       FUNCTION RAND(X,SEED)
         SEED = (SEED+3.1415927)**2
         SEED = SEED - INT(SEED)
         RAND = INT(X * SEED)
       END
```

**Figure 13-10    Program FOR13B**

# LINKING TO BASIC

BASIC has traditionally been included with DOS with almost all micro-computers. BASIC usually is processed through an interpreter, which stores source statements, translates them one at a time, and executes each statement as it is translated. No object file or executable file is produced.

Because interpreted BASIC runs slowly, several BASIC compiler versions are now available. The compiler provides an object file that can be linked to other modules in BASIC or other languages to produce an EXE file.

## Interpretive BASIC

With no object file and no use of LINK, interpretive BASIC poses a problem as to how to connect an assembler routine to the BASIC program. Several techniques are available, but we shall demonstrate how to use the POKE statement to place the object code of the assembler routine directly into the BASIC program, where it can be executed by use the CALL or CALLS statement.

By default, BASIC passes parameters by near reference and uses a far call. The PAUSNF routine provides these attributes. It is just like the PAUSVF routine in Figure 13-3 except that BP+6 contains the offset address of the number of seconds instead of the actual value. The statements

```
MOV SI,[BP+6] ;put offset of SECONDS into SI
MOV CX,[SI]   ;put value of SECONDS into CX
```

will place the value of SECONDS into CX.

We assemble the PAUSNF routine, creating OBJ and LST files. Then we copy the object code of 48 bytes shown on the LST file into DATA statements in program INT13A.BAS. The statement CLEAR ,64511 instructs BASIC to clear only 64511 (0FBFFh) bytes. We assign the name PAUSNF to location 64512 (0FC00h). Then we read the object code, byte by byte, from the DATA statements and POKE it into the area starting at PAUSNF. The CALL statement by default uses a near reference to SECONDS and a far call. Figure 13-11 shows INT13A.BAS.

To run INT13A.BAS follow these steps:

1. After booting DOS, insert disk containing BASIC in drive A and data disk in drive B.
2. Type B: <ENTER> At B> prompt type A:BASIC to load the BASIC interpreter.
3. At the prompt ok, type in the INT13A.BAS program.
4. When finished, type RUN.
5. If program runs OK, type SAVE "B:INT13A" to save source statements on drive B. BASIC supplies the extension .BAS by default.
6. From then on, load BASIC and run the program by typing

```
100 'Program name:    INT13A.BAS
110 'Author:          Alton R. Kindred
120 'This interpretive BASIC program pauses for a specified number of seconds.
130 'BASIC sends the near address of the number of seconds and sends a far
140 'call to the assembler subroutine PAUSNF.  The object code of the
150 'subroutine is poked into storage starting at location 64512.
160 '------------------------------------------------------------------------
170 CLEAR ,64511!
180 PAUSNF = 64512!
190 READ PROGLEN
200 FOR I = 1 TO PROGLEN
210    READ HEXCODE$
220    POKE 64511 + I, VAL("&H" + HEXCODE$)
230 NEXT I
240 INPUT "How many seconds to pause? ", SECONDS%
250 IF SECONDS% > 0 THEN CALL PAUSNF(SECONDS%)
260 PRINT "Paused for "; SECONDS%; "seconds"
270 END
500 '        Number of bytes in PAUSNF subroutine
510 DATA 48
520 '        Object code for PAUSNF subroutine
530 DATA 55,8B,EC,50,53,51,52,8B,5E,06,8B,0F,B8,B6,00,F7
540 DATA E1,BB,0A,00,F7,F3,8B,D8,B4,00,CD,1A,03,DA,3B,DA
550 DATA 74,06,B4,00,CD,1A,EB,F6,5A,59,5B,58,5D,CA,02,00
```

**Figure 13-11    Program INT13A.BAS**

```
B> A:BASIC INT13A
```

BASIC supplies the extension .BAS by default.

A similar procedure is used in program INT13B.BAS to store and call the assembler SHELFF routine. The CALLS statement generates far references to the first element of LIST2 and to NITEMS.

The RANDOMIZE statement in BASIC generates a request to enter a seed for the random number generator. The RND function produces a random value between .000000 and 0.999999. The integer (INT) portion of RND * 255 produces a random number between 0 and 255.

Figure 13-12 shows program INT13B.BAS.

## Compiler BASIC

QuickBASIC is a Microsoft compiler version using generally the same statements and syntax as interpretive BASIC. With compiler BASIC you need not show the object code for assembler subroutines in DATA statements. The compiled BASIC object code can be linked to the assembler object code to produce the EXE program.

QuickBASIC versions 4.0 and later provide a DECLARE statement to name a subroutine to be called. The DECLARE statement has the syntax:

```
DECLARE SUB name (parameter-list)
```

```
100 'Program name:   INT13B.BAS
110 'Author:         Alton R. Kindred
120 'This interpretive BASIC program creates an array of up to 100
130 'random integers between 0 and 255 and then calls the assembler
140 'routine SHELFF to sort them using the Shell sort technique.
150 'Then, it prints out the original array and the sorted array in
160 'parallel columns.  Last, it asks if the operator wishes to continue
170 'and does so until the response is not 'Y' or 'y'.
180 'The program creates far references for parameters and a far call.
190 '-------------------------------------------------------------------
200 CLEAR ,64511!
210 SHELFF = 64512!
220 READ PROGLEN
230 FOR I = 1 TO PROGLEN
240   READ HEXCODE$
250   POKE 64511! + I,VAL("&H" + HEXCODE$)
260 NEXT I
270 DIM LIST1%(100), LIST2%(100)
280 RESPONSE$ = "Y"
290 WHILE RESPONSE$ = "Y" OR RESPONSE$ = "y"
300   RANDOMIZE
310   INPUT "How many numbers to sort (0-100)? "; NITEMS%
320   FOR I = 1 TO NITEMS%
330     LIST1%(I) = INT (RND * 255)
340     LIST2%(I) = LIST1%(I)
350   NEXT I
360   CALLS SHELFF(LIST2%(1), NITEMS%)
370   PRINT "Unsorted Numbers     Sorted Numbers"
380   FOR I = 1 TO NITEMS%
390     PRINT TAB(10) LIST1%(I); TAB(29) LIST2%(I)
400   NEXT I
410   INPUT "Sort another set (Y/N)? ", RESPONSE$
420 WEND
430 END
500 '          Length of SHELFF subroutine
510 DATA 130
520 '          Object code for SHELFF subroutine
530 DATA 55,8B,EC,83,EC,08,50,53,51,52
540 DATA 57,56,06,1E,C5,56,0A,89,56,FB
550 DATA C4,76,06,26,8B,14,89,56,F9,8B
560 DATA 4E,F9,D1,E9,89,4E,FE,C6,46,FD
570 DATA 00,8B,46,FE,3D,00,00,7E,42,8B
580 DATA 5E,FE,D1,E3,BE,00,00,8B,46,F9
590 DATA 2B,46,FE,8B,F8,D1,E7,03,76,FB
600 DATA 03,7E,FB,3B,F7,73,15,8B,04,3B
610 DATA 00,76,0A,8B,10,89,14,89,00,C6
620 DATA 46,FD,FF,83,C6,02,EB,E7,8A,46
630 DATA FD,3C,00,75,03,D1,6E,FE,33,C0
640 DATA 88,46,FD,EB,B6,1F,07,5E,5F,5A
650 DATA 59,5B,58,83,C4,08,5D,CA,08,00
```

**Figure 13-12    Program INT13B.BAS**

where *name* is the name of the assembler procedure and *parameter-list* names the variables to be passed. Parameter-list has the syntax:

```
[BYVAL|SEG] variable [AS type]...,
```

where *BYVAL* indicates passing the variable by value, *SEG* indicates a far reference, and neither BYVAL nor SEG indicate a near reference. The *AS type* clause can specify a valid BASIC type such as INTEGER, LONG, SINGLE, DOUBLE, or STRING.

You can omit the DECLARE statement and use BYVAL or SEG preceding any arguments in the parameter list with the CALL or CALLS statement. When this is done, however, neither the type nor the number of parameters is checked as would be the case with a DECLARE statement.

BAS13A.BAS is a compiler BASIC program that calls PAUSNF to pause the specified number of seconds. Omitting the routine to define DATA statements and load the subroutine, it is like INT13A.BAS:

```
240 INPUT "How many seconds to pause? "; SECONDS%
250 IF SECONDS% > 0 THEN CALL PAUSNF(SECONDS%)
260 PRINT " Paused for "; SECONDS%; "seconds"
270 END
```

BAS13B.BAS is the compiler BASIC program that creates an array and calls the SHELFF assembler routine to sort the array. It consists of statements 270 through 430 of INT13B.BAS as shown in Figure 13-12. The CALLS statement 360 ensures that addresses will be by far reference.

## LINKING TO C

Microsoft C differs from other languages discussed in this chapter in five respects:

1.  C modules can be compiled in small or compact models to cause near returns or medium, large, or huge models to cause far returns.
2.  The C compiler pushes data and values on the stack in reverse order from the way variables are named in the parameter list of the calling statement.
3.  The C calling program removes extra parameters from the stack upon return from the called subroutine. The subroutine uses only a normal RET statement.
4.  C is case-sensitive. If keywords such as IF, INT, or SCANF are written with capital letters, C assumes they are variable names. We have used lowercase letters in C programs to avoid possible confusion.
5.  C expects every external name to be preceded by an underscore (_); however, the underscore is not used in the C program itself.

We have written special C versions of our two assembler subroutines to adjust to these differences. _PAUSVNC.ASM expects a near call and the number of seconds to be passed by value. It also uses RET instead of RET 2, because the C compiler causes the calling program to remove parameters from the stack after return from _PAUSVNC. Figure 13-13 shows the _PAUSVNC subroutine.

Figure 13-14 shows Program C13A.C, which calls _PAUSVNC. As shown in the program description, it uses a near call and passes the number of seconds by value. The statement

```
#include <a:\include\stdio.h>
```

directs the C compiler to extract the standard input/output routines from the stdio.h library in subdirectory \include\ on drive A and include them in the source code. The statement

```
extern void pausvnc near (int);
```

defines _PAUSVNC as an external routine with a near call. The term *void* means that no return value is expected. One integer parameter will be furnished.

Assembler routine _SHELFFC, shown in Figure 13-15, accommodates the C convention of passing the far references to the parameters in reverse order. It also uses the normal RET statement.

Figure 13-16 shows program C13B.C to create two arrays of up to 100 random integers and call _SHELFFC to sort them. It includes three libraries from which the C compiler will extract standard routines.

The statement

```
extern void far shelffc (int far *, int far *)
```

declares that _SHELFFC is a far external routine that returns no value. Two integer parameters will be listed by far reference.

_SHELFFC is actually called by the statement

```
shelffc(&list2[1],&nitems)
```

The & prefix before list2[1] and nitems tells the C compiler to send the parameter addresses rather than the values.

## SUMMARY

Mixed-language programming occurs when a program written in one language calls a function or procedure written in another language. To be successful, mixed-language programming requires that certain conventions be observed in naming, calling, compiling, and linking the procedures. Microsoft compilers for BASIC, C, FORTRAN, and Pascal have adopted certain standard conventions, but differ on others.

BASIC, FORTRAN, and Pascal translate each letter of names to uppercase. C does not, but inserts a leading underscore in front of each name.

```
;----------------------------------------------------------------
;Program name:  _PAUSVNC Subroutine
;Author:        Alton R. Kindred
;
;This routine is to be called from C to pause a specified number of seconds.
;It expects a NEAR call and the number of seconds to be passed by
;value.  It uses an ordinary RET because C has built-in instructions to
;remove passed parameters from the stack.
;
;At entry:  BP+2 = return address
;           BP+4 = number of seconds by value
;----------------------------------------------------------------
            PUBLIC _PAUSVNC
            CODE   SEGMENT
            ASSUME CS:CODE
_PAUSVNC    PROC NEAR
            PUSH BP                 ;save BP
            MOV BP,SP               ;set BP as stack pointer
            PUSH AX                 ;save registers
            PUSH BX
            PUSH CX
            PUSH DX
            MOV CX,[BP+4]           ;CX = n seconds
            MOV AX,182              ;multiply by ticks in 10 seconds
            MUL CX
            MOV BX,10               ;divide by 10
            DIV BX
            MOV BX,AX               ;BX = ticks in n seconds
            MOV AH,0                ;get current tick count
            INT 1Ah
            ADD BX,DX               ;BX = future tick cnt. after n secs.
WHILE01:    CMP BX,DX               ;WHILE tick count <> future tick count
            JE WEND01
            MOV AH,0                ;  get next tick count
            INT 1Ah
            JMP WHILE01
WEND01:                             ;WEND
            POP DX                  ;restore registers
            POP CX
            POP BX
            POP AX
            POP BP
            RET                     ;return
_PAUSVNC    ENDP
CODE        ENDS
            END
```

**Figure 13-13   _PAUSVNC Subroutine**

BASIC recognizes the first 40 characters of names, Pascal and C the first eight, and FORTRAN the first six.

All four languages pass parameters and return addresses to the called procedure by pushing them on the stack. Parameters may be passed by near

```
/* PROGRAM NAME:  C13A.C */
/* AUTHOR:        ALTON R. KINDRED */
/* This C program calls the PAUSVNC assembler routine to pause for the */
/* specified number of seconds.  It uses a near call and passes the */
/* number of seconds by value.  */
/*---------------------------------------------------------------------*/

#include <a:\include\stdio.h>

extern void near pausvnc (int);
int seconds;

main ()
{
  printf ("How many seconds to pause? ");
  scanf ("%d", &seconds);
  if (seconds > 0)
    { pausvnc (seconds);
    }
  printf ("Paused for %d seconds", seconds);
}
```

**Figure 13-14    Program C13A.C**

reference, by far reference, or by value. Special keywords in the calling program designate how parameters are passed. BASIC, FORTRAN, and Pascal push the parameters on the stack in the order they are named in the CALL statement. C pushes parameters in reverse order of naming.

By default, BASIC, FORTRAN, and Pascal pass far return addresses. C passes near return address for small or compact models and far addresses for medium, large, or huge models.

The assembly routine uses seven steps to interface with the calling program: (a) setting up the procedure, (b) entering the procedure, (c) optionally allocating local data, (d) preserving register values, (e) accessing parameters, (f) optionally returning a value, and (g) exiting the procedure.

The assembly routine normally begins by pushing BP on the stack and moving SP to BP. Addresses immediately above BP in the stack are the return address and the parameters. Optionally, a local data area in the stack may be provided by subtracting the desired number of bytes from SP. The local data area is addressed as BP-$n$, where $n$ points to a specific word or byte. It is crucial that the calling program and the subroutine agree on the form of the parameters and return address on the stack to process the data correctly.

The called procedure normally exits by adding to SP any amount subtracted to allocate local data space, popping BP, and using RET $n$, where $n$ is the number of bytes occupied by the parameters. For C, only RET is used, since C restores the stack upon return to the calling program.

We have provided two assembler routines to be called by each language. The first one pauses for a specified number of seconds. The second sorts an array of 1 to 100 integers using the Shell sort technique. We have illustrated

```
          page 50,132
;------------------------------------------------------------------------
; Program name:  _SHELFFC.ASM
;
; Author:  Alton R. Kindred
;
; This routine sorts an array of 16-bit words into ascending order using the
; Shell sort.  It is intended to link to a C calling program that passes
; far references to data and a far return address.
; C passes parameters in reverse order of listing.
; Upon entry:  BP+2 = return offset
;              BP+4 = return segment
;              BP+6 = array offset
;              BP+8 = array segment
;              BP+10 = number of items offset
;              BP+12 = number of items segment
;------------------------------------------------------------------------
GAP        EQU [BP-2]
EXCH       EQU [BP-3]
ARRAYADR   EQU [BP-5]
NITEMS     EQU [BP-7]
;------------------------------------------------------------------------
CODE       SEGMENT                    ;segment for code
           ASSUME CS:CODE
_SHELFFC   PROC FAR
           PUBLIC _SHELFFC
START:     PUSH BP
           MOV BP,SP
           SUB SP,8
           IRP REGISTER,<AX,BX,CX,DX,DI,SI,ES,DS>
           PUSH REGISTER
           ENDM
           LDS DX,[BP+6]              ;get address of array into DS:DX
           MOV ARRAYADR,DX           ;and save it in ARRAYADR
           LES SI,[BP+10]            ;get address of count into DS:SI
           MOV DX,ES:[SI]            ;move count into DX
           MOV NITEMS,DX             ;and then into NITEMS
           MOV CX,NITEMS
           SHR CX,1                  ;set gap to N/2
           MOV GAP,CX                ;save gap
           MOV BYTE PTR EXCH,0       ;set exchange flag OFF
WHILE:     MOV AX,GAP                ;WHILE gap > 0
           CMP AX,0
           JNG WEND
           MOV BX,GAP                ;  convert gap to word offset
           SHL BX,1
           MOV SI,0
           MOV AX,NITEMS             ;  compute nitems - gap
           SUB AX,GAP
           MOV DI,AX
           SHL DI,1                  ;  convert n-g to word offset
           ADD SI,ARRAYADR
           ADD DI,ARRAYADR
```

**Figure 13-15     _SHELFFC Subroutine**

```
WHILE2:     CMP SI,DI                 ;   WHILE SI < DI
            JNB WEND2
IFA:        MOV AX,[SI]               ;     IF x(i) > x(i+g)
            CMP AX,[SI+BX]
            JBE ENDIFA
THENA:      MOV DX,[SI+BX]            ;        THEN exchange
            MOV [SI],DX
            MOV [SI+BX],AX
            MOV BYTE PTR EXCH,0FFh    ;        set exchange flag ON
ENDIFA:                               ;        ENDIF
            ADD SI,2                  ;        increment SI
            JMP WHILE2
WEND2:                                ;     WEND
IFB1:       MOV AL,EXCH               ;     IF exchange flag OFF
            CMP AL,0
            JNE ENDIFB1
THENB1:     SHR WORD PTR GAP,1        ;        THEN divide gap by 2
ENDIFB1:                              ;     ENDIF
            XOR AX,AX                 ;     clear exchange flag
            MOV EXCH,AL
            JMP WHILE
WEND:                                 ;WEND
            IRP REGISTER,<DS,ES,SI,DI,DX,CX,BX,AX>
            POP REGISTER
            ENDM
            ADD SP,8
            POP BP
            RET
;-----------------------------------------------------------------------
_SHELFFC    ENDP
CODE        ENDS                      ;end of code segment declaration
            END                       ;end of program
```

**Figure 13-15**   *concluded*

calling programs for each routine in each of the four languages. In addition, calling programs in interpretive BASIC and Turbo C have been shown.

## QUESTIONS

1. What is meant by mixed-language programming?
2. Why does the number of characters recognized in names by the various compilers have some effect on mixed-language programming?
3. In what two respects does C differ from BASIC, FORTRAN and Pascal in its treatment of names?
4. How are parameters and return addresses passed by the Microsoft high-level languages to a called routine?
5. Name two types of return addresses and three types of parameter-passing conventions.

```
/* Program name:  C13B.C */
/* Author:        Alton R. Kindred */
/* This C program creates an array of random integers with values */
/* between decimal 0 and 255.  It then calls the _SHELFFC assembler */
/* subroutine to sort the numbers.  Finally, it prints the original */
/* numbers side by side.  This version uses far references and a far call. */
/* ------------------------------------------------------------------------*/

#include <a:\include\stdio.h>
#include <a:\include\stdlib.h>
#include <a:\include\math.h>

extern void far shelffc (int far *, int far*);

main () /* main program */
{
  char response;
  double seed;
  int list1[100], list2[100], i, nitems, x, rng;

  response = 'Y';
  while (response == 'Y' || response == 'y') {
    printf("Enter seed for RNG between 0 and 1 (form 0.999): ");
    scanf("%f",&seed);
    printf("How many numbers to sort (1-100)? ");
    scanf("%d",&nitems);
    x = 255;
    for (i = 1; i <= nitems; i++) {
      seed = (seed + 3.14159) * (seed + 3.14159);
      seed = seed - floor(seed);
      rng = floor(seed * x);
      list1[i] = rng;
      list2[i] = list1[i];
      }
    shelffc(&list2[1],&nitems)     /* sort the array */ ;

    printf("Original Numbers     Sorted Numbers\n");
    for (i = 1; i <=  nitems; i++) {
      printf("%12d%19d\n",list1[i], list2[i]);
      }
    printf("Sort another set (Y/N)? ");
    scanf("%1s",&response);
  }
}
```

Figure 13-16      Program C13B.C

6. Name the seven steps the assembler routine must perform when called by a high-level language.

7. What register is used in the assembler routine as a pointer to both the parameters and the local data space? How is it placed?

8. How does C differ from BASIC, FORTRAN, and Pascal in the way it passes parameters and adjusts the stack after calling a routine?

9.  If a called routine returns a one-byte value to the calling program, where is it placed? A two-byte value? A four-byte value? A value longer than four bytes?

10. What are ticks in the PAUS routine in this chapter? How many are there in a second?

11. How does interpretive BASIC differ from compiled BASIC in the way it handles a called routine?

12. What directives are required by Turbo Pascal to identify and call a far routine that are not required by Microsoft Pascal?

13. What is the purpose of the ALIAS statement in BASIC or FORTRAN?

# EXERCISES

1.  Write assembler statements to push BP on the stack and create 10 bytes of local data space.

2.  A Pascal program has passed two word parameters by value when making a far call to an assembler routine. Write statements to move the first named parameter to the first available word in the local data space and the second parameter to CX.

3.  Assume that the parameters in exercise 2 were passed by near reference. Write statements to put the values of the parameters where they were moved in exercise 2.

4.  A BASIC program has the statement CALLS SUB1(A,B,C). Write the necessary statements in SUB1 to put the values for A, B, and C into the first three words of the local data area.

5.  Write necessary Microsoft Pascal statements to call a far subroutine named SUBX and pass far references for parameters X, Y, and Z.

6.  Write a BASIC routine to poke 48 bytes of object code defined in DATA statements into a subroutine named MYSUB located at address F000h. Do not define the actual object code.

7.  Write a FORTRAN INTERFACE statement for a subroutine named ASSEMSUB to show parameters N1 and N2 to be passed by near reference. You will need an ALIAS clause, since the name ASSEMSUB is longer than 6 bytes.

8.  Write a C routine that makes a far call to an assembler subroutine to display in binary form a 16-bit integer passed by value.

9.  Adapt the DSPBIN routine from Chapter 6 to display a 16-bit word in binary form. Write it to be called by the C program you wrote for exercise 8.

# LAB PROBLEMS

1.  Write a far assembler routine that returns the function 3A - B as a 32-bit value integer. A and B are 16-bit integers passed by far reference. Write a calling routine in any of the languages discussed in this chapter to assign values to A and B, call the assembler routine, and print out A, B, and the function value.

2.  Change the assembler routine in problem 1 to receive the values for A and B by value. Write the calling routine in a different language from the one in which you wrote problem 1.

# VIDEO MEMORY AND GRAPHICS

# 14

---

**OBJECTIVES**

After studying this chapter, you should be able to:

- Describe the method of dividing video memory into pages.
- Explain and use attributes for characters displayed on the screen.
- Identify the principal display adapters.
- Explain the use of I/O ports by the Motorola 6845 Cathode Ray Tube Controller.
- Demonstrate color graphics.
- Interpret special keys through use of scan codes.

---

In Chapter 3, we saw how BIOS and DOS interrupts can be used to display characters on the video screen, to move the cursor, and to perform other necessary operations.

In this chapter, we shall review this subject in more depth and see how the screen display is physically represented by an area of main memory, called a *video buffer*, that contains not only one byte for each of the 2000 character positions (25 x 80) that appear on the screen, but also an attribute byte for each character that specifies its color and whether or not it blinks. Thus, the video buffer occupies a total of 4000 bytes for an 80-column screen.

## FUNDAMENTAL DISPLAY CONCEPTS

As we have seen through the text, the terms *display, monitor, screen,* and *video* are used rather interchangeably. The display is not a part of the 8088 microcomputer chip, but a separate device, often manufactured by a different company from the one that makes the microcomputer. The screen requires a *display adapter* to act as an interface between the character and attribute in storage and the way the output actually appears on the screen. Some adapters process text only and some both text and graphics. Some handle only monochrome (single color) and some handle 4, 16, 64, or more colors.

Some adapters allow more than one *page* to be used. Each page represents an area of 4000 bytes in memory where the data and the attribute bytes can be moved. Only one page is active, that is, displayed on the screen at any one time.

The display adapter requires a *controller chip* and an *interrupt controller* that make the hardware interface between main memory and the screen.

The screen can be different *modes*, which determine what colors can be used, how many characters appear on a line, and the number of pixels (graphics picture elements) that may appear.

The display can be set up by moving data and attribute bytes, often through string-handling instructions, directly to one of the video buffers representing one page. When that page is made active, the display is instantly visible. BIOS interrupts are prewritten routines that service the screen in a variety of ways. The interrupts are somewhat slower than moving data directly to the video buffers, but are convenient and, in some instances, necessary.

## DISPLAY ADAPTERS

A *display adapter* is a hardware device that takes the data (and attributes) in the active page and converts it into the proper form for display on the screen. The number of pages that may be used depends upon the type of adapter in use.

Six of the most popular adapters include the following:

1. MDA — monochrome (single color) display adapter.
2. CGA — color/graphics adapter.
3. PCjr —IBM PCjr system board video controller.
4. EGA — enhanced graphics adapter.
5. MCGA — multi-color graphics array (PS/2 models 25 and 30).
6. VGA — video graphics array (PS/2 models 50 and above).

Other adapters are always under development that may incorporate many of the same features as these named but also may have additional features not presently available.

The monochrome display adapter (MDA), although called a single-color adapter, actually has one background color for the screen and a foreground color for the character. Foreground and background colors may be reversed. The colors may be black and white on certain monitors and green and white or gray and amber on others.

The MDA offers a resolution of 9 x 14 picture elements (pixels) for each character position, a total of 720 x 350, or 252,000 pixels on the entire screen.

The color/graphics adapter (CGA) can operate in either the text mode or the graphics mode. The CGA offers a high resolution of 8 x 8 pixels per character position, making 640 x 200, or 128,000, pixels per screen. Sixteen colors are available.

The PCjr video controller has more extensive features than some of the other boards. It alone can operate in modes 8, 9, and 10.

The enhanced graphics adapter (EGA) allows 16 or 64 colors as well as higher resolution and more display models than the CGA. The EGA has a maximum of 8 x 14 pixels per character, 640 x 480, or 307,200, pixels on the entire screen. It has 256 colors available at a resolution of 320 x 200 pixels.

The VGA provides 16 colors in high resolution of up to 8 x 20 pixels per character. This makes a total of 640 x 480, or 307,200 pixels on the entire screen. In 320 x 200 mode the VGA provides 256 colors.

## BIOS FUNCTION INTERRUPTS

In Chapter 3 we presented a brief introduction to the Basic Input/Output System (BIOS) routines placed in ROM (ready-only memory). They usually are written by a software company other than Microsoft and are specific to the machine that contains the ROM.

These BIOS routines may provide for keyboard input, screen output, and other screen-handling routines. As with the DOS interrupts, you must place a function code in AH and other values in different registers according to the nature of the function.

INT 10h through INT 1Fh are available to BIOS, although not all are currently used. INT 10h is the most common interrupt.

### Video Mode Setting Function

The term *video mode* refers to the colors available, the number of characters per line, and the number of graphics pixels per page that apply to the various video adapters.

***Function 0, Set Video Mode.*** When AH = 00h, AL may contain any one of many different codes to determine screen size, graphic density, or number of colors. Certain codes pertain only to special machines or monitors. Any mode entered in AL not acceptable to the monitor is ignored. Acceptable values for AL are shown in Table 14-1.

The following sequence sets the display mode for 80 x 25 black-and-white text:

```
MOV AH,00h
MOV AL,02h
INT 10h
```

**Note:** This function also clears the screen and resets the cursor at the upper left corner of the screen.

TABLE 14-1. Video Modes

| TEXT MODES | ADAPTERS | | | | | |
|---|---|---|---|---|---|---|
| | MDA | CGA | PCir | EGA | MCGA | VGA |
| 00h 40 x 25 black-and white text, color adapter | | x | x | x | x | x |
| 01h 40 x 25 color text | | x | x | x | x | x |
| 02h 80 x 25 black-and-white text | | x | x | x | x | x |
| 03h 80 x 25 color text | | x | x | x | x | x |
| GRAPHICS MODES | | | | | | |
| 04h 320 x 200 4-color graphics | | x | x | x | x | x |
| 05h 320 x 200 4-color graphics, color burst off | | x | x | x | x | x |
| 06h 640 x 200 2-color graphics | | x | x | x | x | x |
| 07h monochrome adapter text display | x | | | x | | x |
| EXTENDED GRAPHICS MODES | | | | | | |
| 08h 160 x 200 16-color graphics | | | x | | | |
| 09h 320 x 200 16-color graphics | | | x | | | |
| 0Ah 640 x 200 4-color graphics | | | x | | | |
| 0Bh reserved | | | | | | |
| 0Ch reserved | | | | | | |
| 0Dh 320 x 200 16-color graphics | | | | x | | x |
| 0Eh 640 x 200 16-color graphics | | | | x | | x |
| 0Fh 640 x 350 monochrome graphics | | | | x | | x |
| 10h 640 x 350 4-color or 16-color graphics (depending on RAM available) | | | | x | | x |
| 11h 640 x 480 2-color graphics | | | | | x | x |
| 12h 640 x 480 16-color graphics | | | | | | x |
| 13h 320 x 200 256-color graphics | | | | | x | x |

## Cursor Handling Functions

Three *cursor handling functions* are provided by BIOS to set the cursor size, to set its position, and to read its present position.

***Function 1, Set Cursor Size.*** The cursor size may vary in size from a thin line to a block covering the entire character position. The top of the cursor position is line 0 and the bottom of the cursor character is line 7 or 12, depending on the type of adapter in use.

When AH = 01h, INT 10h selects the starting and ending lines for the cursor. CH must contain the starting (top) line number for the cursor and CL the ending (bottom) line number. In text modes (AL = 00h through 03h), the cursor automatically blinks, and starting and ending lines are set to 6 and 7 by default. For monochrome mode 07h, starting and ending lines are 11 and 12 by default. The maximum legal starting and ending lines depend upon the type of display adapter in use. Placing the value 20h in CH will turn off the cursor entirely.

The table below shows some possible settings of the cursor:

| MODE | CH | CL | LOCATION AND SIZE OF CURSOR |
|------|-----|-----|------------------------------|
| 07h | 0Bh | 0Ch | Narrow line at bottom of character position |
| 07h | 00h | 01h | Narrow line at top of character position |
| 07h | 00h | 0Ch | Tall block the height of a full character |
| 03h | 06h | 07h | Thin line at bottom of character position |
| 03h | 20h | xxh | No cursor; contents of CL irrelevant |

*Function 2, Set Cursor Position.* When AH = 02h, the cursor is positioned according to page number, row, and column. BH contains the page number, which must be zero in graphics mode. DH contains the row (*y* coordinate). DL contains the column (*x* coordinate). Coordinates are usually expressed as (*x,y*). (0,0) indicates the leftmost position of the top line on the screen. (79,24) indicates the last position of the bottom line.

The following routine places the cursor on page 0 at the leftmost position of line 10:

```
MOV AH,02h
MOV BH,00h          ;set page
MOV DL,00h          ;set column (0-79)
MOV DH,0Ah          ;set row (0-23)
INT 10h
```

*Function 3, Read Cursor Position.* When AH = 03h and BH = page number, INT 10h obtains the current size and position of the cursor in *x* and *y* coordinates. This function returns in CH the starting line for the cursor, in CL the ending line for the cursor, in DH the *y* row coordinate, and in DL the *x* column coordinate.

### Display Handling Routines

Certain BIOS interrupts provide *display handling routines*, such as those that read the light pen position, select the active display page, scroll the page up or down, and get the current display mode.

*Function 4, Read Light Pen Position.* (Not valid on MDA). When AH = 04h and a light pen is installed, on output this interrupt returns the following information:

AH = 0 if light pen switch is not triggered.

AH = 1 if valid light pen values are in registers below.

BX = pixel column (graphics *x* coordinate) if AH = 1.

CH = pixel row (graphics *y* coordinate, modes 04h-06h) if AH = 1.

CL = pixel row (graphics *y* coordinate, modes 0Dh-10h) if AH = 1.

DH,DL = character row, column if AH = 1.

***Function 5, Select Active Display Page.*** (Not valid for MDA). Placing 05h in AH requires the standard color/graphics adapter. For 40-column displays, page numbers of 0 through 7 may be placed in AL; for 80-column displays, page numbers of 0 through 3 may be specified in AL.

To select page 3, write:

```
MOV AH,5
MOV AL,3
INT 10h
```

***Functions 6, 7, Scroll Page Up or Down.*** Placing 06h in AH allows any part of the current active page to be scrolled up; 07h in AH allows scrolling down. A portion of the page is called a *window*. On input, CH,CL must contain the row and column of the upper left corner of the window, while DH,DL contains the row and column of the lower right corner. AL must specify the number of lines to scroll up or down, and BH the attribute to be used on blank lines. If AL = 0, the entire window is blanked out and set to the attribute in BH.

A common use of this function is to blank the entire screen, using these instructions:

```
MOV AH,6          ;scroll up
MOV BH,07h        ;standard black-on-white
                  ;attribute
MOV CX,0          ;CL and CH = 0 for upper left
                  ;of screen
MOV DL,79         ;for 80 columns; use 39 for
                  ;40 columns
MOV DH,24         ;bottom line
MOV AL,0          ;option to clear entire screen
INT 10h
```

The following instructions scroll the right half of the screen up 12 rows and set foreground color to black (0h) and background color to red (4h) in the vacated positions:

```
MOV AH,6          ;scroll up
MOV AL,12         ;number of lines to scroll
MOV BH,40h        ;set color to black on red
MOV CH,0          ;upper left at row 0
MOV CL,40         ;upper left at column 40
MOV DH,24         ;lower right at bottom line
MOV DL,79         ;lower right at column 79
INT 10h
```

Table 14-2 shows the format of the attribute byte and the available foreground and background colors.

*Function 15, Get Current Display Mode.* When AH contains OFh, this function returns in AL the current display mode of the active video controller and in BH the active display page. The display modes 00h through 10h are listed previously under Function 0, Set Video Mode.

## Character Handling Routines

Several BIOS functions used with INT 10h provide *character handling routines* to read or write characters, with or without their corresponding attributes, at the current cursor location.

*Function 8, Read Attribute and Character at Cursor.* For this function, AH must contain 08h and BH any desired page (not just the active page). Upon return, AH contains the attribute of the byte at the cursor, and AL contains the ASCII code for the character. This function often is preceded by use of function 2 to set the cursor position at the desired position to be read.

Because this function can read any desired page, you may use it to work on, say, page 2 while page 0 is still displayed on the screen.

*Function 9, Write Attribute and Character at Cursor.* This function writes a character with its attribute one or more times at the cursor location on any page. Upon entry, AH must contain 09h, AL the ASCII character code, BH the page number, BL the attribute, and CX the number of times the character and attribute are to be written. The results are unpredictable if the character count is greater than the remaining columns in the current line. Control characters, such as cursor return and linefeed, do not affect the cursor position. Use Function 2 to set the cursor if desired before using Function 9. This function does not automatically advance the cursor.

You may use this function to move data and attributes to any page while another page is still displayed on the screen.

*Function 10, Write Character Only at Cursor.* This function is similar to Function 9 but does not change the attribute of the character at the cursor. Upon entry, AH must contain 0Ah, AL the ASCII character code, BH any page, and CX the number of times the character is to be written. This function does not automatically advance the cursor.

*Function 14, Write Text in Teletype Mode.* When 0Eh is in AH, this function writes an ASCII character to the video display and then moves the cursor position appropriately. AL must contain the ASCII character code, BH the page, and BL the foreground color if in graphics modes.

TABLE 14-2.  Format of Attribute Byte and Colors Available

| 7 | 6 | 5 | 4 | 3 | 2 | 1 | 0 |
|---|---|---|---|---|---|---|---|
| B | background | | | I | foreground | | |

### VIDEO DISPLAY MODE 7

B = blink          0 = no blink; 1 = blink
I = intensity      0 = low, 1 = high

| Background | Foreground | Display |
|------------|------------|---------|
| 000 | 000 | No display (black on black) |
| 111 | 111 | No display (white on white) |
| 000 | 001 | Underline |
| 000 | 111 | Normal display; white on black |
| 111 | 000 | Reverse display; black on white |

### VIDEO DISPLAY MODES 0–3

B = blink or background intensity (default = blink)
I = foreground intensity or character select (default = intensity)

| Background Colors | Foreground Colors |
|-------------------|-------------------|
| 000 (0) - Black | 0000 (0) - Black |
| 001 (1) - Blue | 0001 (1) - Blue |
| 010 (2) - Green | 0010 (2) - Green |
| 011 (3) - Cyan | 0011 (3) - Cyan |
| 100 (4) - Red | 0100 (4) - Red |
| 101 (5) - Magenta | 0101 (5) - Magenta |
| 110 (6) - Brown | 0110 (6) - Brown |
| 111 (7) - White | 0111 (7) - White |
| | 1000 (8) - Gray |
| | 1001 (9) - Light blue |
| | 1010 (10 - Light green |
| | 1011 (11) - Light cyan |
| | 1100 (12) - Light red |
| | 1101 (13) - Light magenta |
| | 1110 (14) - Yellow |
| | 1111 (15) - Intense white |

The ASCII codes for bell, backspace, cursor return, and linefeed are recognized and the appropriate action is taken. All other characters are written to the display, and the cursor position is incremented by one.

## Other BIOS Routines

Other INT 10h routines are listed here as information. Details may be obtained from the current technical manuals.

*Function 11, Set Color Palette.* Selects a palette, background, or border color. Call with AH = 0Bh, BH = color palette ID, and BL = color value to be used.

If BH = 00h, this function sets the background color and border color for graphics modes or the border color only for text modes. The background color in text mode is controlled by the attribute byte for each individual character. BL contains the desired color (see Table 14-2).

If BH = 01h, this function selects a palette in 320 x 200 4-color graphics modes. BL must contain either 00h or 01h to give a choice of colors to be used when writing or reading pixels with Functions 12 or 13 (0Ch or 0Dh). The choices of palettes are:

| PALETTE | PIXEL VALUE | COLOR |
|---------|-------------|-------|
| 0 | 0 | Same as background |
| | 1 | Green |
| | 2 | Red |
| | 3 | Brown or yellow |
| 1 | 0 | Same as background |
| | 1 | Cyan |
| | 2 | Magenta |
| | 3 | White |

*Function 12, Write Graphics Pixel.* Plots a point on the video display at the specified *x* and *y* graphics coordinates. Call with AH = 0Ch, AL = pixel value, CX = column number (*x* coordinate), and DX = row number (*y* coordinate). The pixel value to be chosen depends upon the palette selected in Function 11, described in the preceding section.

The following routine presumes a CGA adapter. It sets mode 4 (320 x 200 graphics mode) selects a background color of white, chooses palette 0 (red, green, or brown or yellow), and writes a red pixel at the center of the screen.

```
MOV AH,0            ;set graphics mode 4
MOV AL,4
INT 10h
MOV AH,0Bh          ;select background and border
                    ;color
MOV BH,0
MOV BL,7            ; color = 7 (white)
INT 10h
```

```
        MOV AH,0Bh                    ;select palette
        MOV BH,1
        MOV BL,0                      ; palette 0 = green, red,
                                      ; brown or yellow
        INT 10h
        MOV AH,0Ch                    ;write pixel
        MOV AL,2                      ; make pixel red
        MOV BH,0                      ; make page 0
        MOV CX,160                    ; pixel column = 160
        MOV DX,100                    ; pixel row = 100
        INT 10h
```

***Function 13, Read Graphics Pixel.***   Obtains the current value of the pixel on the video display. Call with AH = 0Dh, BX = any desired page, CX = column number (*x* coordinate), and DX = row number (*y* coordinate). Upon return, AL = pixel value. The actual color represented by the pixel depends on whether the palette is 0 or 1 (see Function 11 above).

## USING VIDEO MEMORY DIRECTLY

As mentioned under Fundamental Display Concepts earlier in this chapter, a portion of main memory is normally used by BIOS as the *video buffer*. Any data placed in this buffer is displayed instantly on the screen. A single buffer for the monochrome display adapter starts at one location in storage, while multiple buffers for the color adapters start at different locations.

Only one video buffer can be displayed on the screen at a time, but it is possible to move data at any time to any other buffer and to switch buffers to change the screen display almost instantly. This approach is much faster than using the standard I/O interrupts to clear the screen, to locate the cursor, and to display the data in the desired locations.

### Monochrome Display Adapter

The MDA can use only one buffer. It occupies 4,000 bytes in 80 x 25 text mode starting at B000:0000h and ending at B000:0F9F. Each character display position occupies two bytes in the buffer. The first byte (even-numbered address) contains the ASCII code of the character to be displayed. The second byte (odd-numbered address) is called the *attribute byte*. Attributes include such features as blinking, highlighting, and reverse video (reversing the color of the characters and the background).

The byte at B000:0000 is the character that appears at row 0, column 0 and B000:0001 holds its attribute. The character and attribute for row 24, column 79, are at B000:0F9E and B000:0F9F. In 40 x 25 text mode, the buffer is only 2,000 bytes, from B000:0000h through B000:07CFh.

The string-handling instructions discussed in Chapter 9 are especially useful in moving the characters and attributes to or from the monochrome buffer. This routine clears the entire screen and sets the attribute for each position to 07h (black background with white characters):

```
MOV  AX,0B000h              ;establish ES with buffer
                            ;address
MOV  ES,AX
MOV  DI,0                   ;set offset at start of buffer
MOV  CX,2000                ;set counter for 2000 words
MOV  AH,07h                 ;set attribute to white on
                            ;black
MOV  AL,' '                 ;make character blank
REP  STOSW                  ;move 2000 characters and
                            ;attributes
```

Merely change the third statement from the end to read MOV AH,70h to make the attribute for each position black characters on a white background.

We place the character in AL and the attribute in AH because the least significant byte in AL will be stored ahead of the most significant byte in AH when the word in AX is stored in memory.

The proper offset in memory for each row and column of the screen can be calculated from the formula:

```
(row * 80 + column) * 2
```

Remember that rows are numbered from 0 through 24 and that columns are numbered from 0 through 79 in 80-column mode and from 0 through 39 in 40-column mode. You even can let the assembler do the calculations for you, as in

```
MOV DI,(12*80+40)*2 or LEA DI,(12*80+40)*2
```

To reverse the attributes of the first 10 characters of line 7, use this routine:

```
         MOV  AX,0B000h              ;set ES to screen buffer
         MOV  ES,AX
         MOV  SI,(7*80+0)*2          ;set offset to line 7, column
                                     ;0
         MOV  CX,10                  ;set counter to 10
REPEAT01:                            ;REPEAT
         MOV  AX,ES:[SI]             ; get character in AL and
                                     ; attribute in AH
         XOR  AH,01110111b           ; reverse colors
         MOV  ES:[SI],AX             ; replace character and
                                     ; attribute
         ADD  SI,2                   ; increment SI
         LOOP REPEAT01               ; subtract 1 from counter
UNTIL01:                             ;UNTIL counter = 0
```

## Program 14A: Fill Screen

Program 14A (Figure 14-1) demonstrates direct use of video memory. When a key is pressed, the ASCII character is received in AL. The attribute

```
          PAGE 50,132
;-----------------------------------------------------------------
;Program name:  PROG14A.ASM
;
;Author:        Alton R. Kindred
;
;This program displays any character pressed on the keyboard on
;the entire screen by moving it directly to all 2000 bytes of
;video memory.  This version assumed the monochrome display adapter
;(MDA) with video memory starting at 0B800:0000.
;-----------------------------------------------------------------
          DOSSEG
          .MODEL SMALL
          .DATA
          .STACK 256
;-----------------------------------------------------------------
          .CODE
          EXTRN INPCHR:NEAR
PROG14A   PROC
          MOV AX,@DATA
          MOV DS,AX
          CALL INPCHR            ;input a key into AL
WHILE01:  CMP AL,13              ;WHILE <ENTER> not pressed
          JE WEND01
          MOV AH,07             ;   set normal white on black
          MOV BX,0B000h         ;   set monochrome address in ES
          MOV ES,BX
          MOV CX,2000           ;   set counter to 2000
          MOV DI,0              ;   set offset to 0
          REP STOSW             ;   move 2000 bytes and attributes
          CALL INPCHR           ;   input another key into AL
          JMP WHILE01
WEND01:                         ;WEND
          MOV AX,4C00h          ;return to DOS
          INT 21h
PROG14A   ENDP
          END PROG14A
```

**Figure 14-1    Program 14A**

07h (white on black) is placed in AH. Then, using the STOSW operation repeated 2000 times, the character and attribute are moved directly to the monochrome screen buffer area starting at B000h.

Many of the special function keys display some character, while a few do not enter any displayable code. The program is terminated when <ENTER> is pressed.

### Color/Graphics Adapter

For the color/graphics adapter, video memory starts at B800:0000h. As with the monochrome adapter, each buffer requires 4000 bytes for 80 x 25 mode and 2000 bytes for 40 x 25 mode. The number of pages available varies from four to eight according to the type of adapter. The table below summarizes the starting addresses of the buffers for color/graphics adapters. The offsets are always 0000-0F9Fh for 80 x 25 mode and 0000-07CFh for 40 x 25 mode.

| PAGE | STARTING ADDRESS |
|------|------------------|
| 0 | B800:0000 |
| 1 | B900:0000 |
| 2 | BA00:0000 |
| 3 | BB00:0000 |
| 4 | BC00:0000 |
| 5 | BD00:0000 |
| 6 | BE00:0000 |
| 7 | BF00:0000 |

We can address any row or column in any page by either of these methods:

1.  Put the correct page address in either segment register (DS or ES — usually ES) and calculate the offset with the formula shown under the section titled Monochrome Display Adapter above:

    ```
    (row * 80 + column) * 2
    ```

2.  Put the address B800h in the segment register and use the offset formula:

    ```
    (page * 4096 + (line * 80 + column) * 2)
    ```

For example, page 3, line 10, column 30, produces the offset

```
(3 * 4096 + (10 * 80 + 30) * 2) = 13848, or 367Ch
```

The address B800:367Ch is identical to BB00:067Ch, the correct address in page 3. Thus, we can change from one page to another by modifying either the segment address or the offset address.

### Program 14B: Four-Page Colors

In program 14B (Figure 14-2) we work with both video memory and the BIOS interrupts to create four pages in different colors. We require one of the color/graphics adapters.

First, we select mode 3 (80 x 25 16-color text). In the first loop at REPEATO1 we move a blank and color attribute to each of the 2000 character positions on each page. We move to the next page by adding 4096 (1000h) to the offset address in DI. We change colors by adding 11h to the attribute byte in AH. Colors used on each page are:

```
          PAGE 50,132
;-------------------------------------------------------------------------
;Program name:  PROG14B.ASM
;
;Author:         Alton R. Kindred
;
;This program clears pages 0-4 of the CGA screen and sets attributes
;for the following colors:
;     Page 0 - magenta on blue
;     Page 1 - white on green
;     Page 2 - gray on cyan
;     Page 3 - light blue on red
;Then it puts a black and white prompt at the bottom of each page
;and allows you to press any key to change from one page to the
;next.  You exit by pressing <BREAK>.
;-------------------------------------------------------------------------
          DOSSEG
          .MODEL SMALL
          .DATA
PROMPT    DB 'Press any key to see next page.  '
          DB 'Press <ESC> to end.'
LPROMPT   DW $-PROMPT
;----    -----------------------------------------------------------------
          .STACK 100
;-------------------------------------------------------------------------
          .CODE
PROG14B   PROC
          MOV AX,@DATA
          MOV DS,AX
          MOV AH,0                 ;set mode to 80 x 25 text
          MOV AL,3
          INT 10h
          MOV AH,5                 ;set to page 0
          MOV AL,0
          INT 10h
          CLD                      ;clear direction flag
          MOV AX,0B800h            ;set ES to page 0
          MOV ES,AX
          MOV DI,0                 ;set offset to page 0
          MOV AH,16h               ;set color magenta on blue
          MOV AL,' '               ;set character to space
          MOV CX,4                 ;set page counter to 4
REPEAT01:                          ;REPEAT
          PUSH CX                  ;    save page counter
          MOV CX,2000              ;    set character counter to 2000
          REP STOSW                ;    move 2000 characters and attributes
          AND DI,0F000h            ;    zap row and column offset
          ADD DI,1000h             ;    set DI to next page
          ADD AH,11h               ;    set colors for next page
          POP CX                   ;    restore page counter
          LOOP REPEAT01            ;    subtract 1 from page counter
UNTIL01:                           ;UNTIL page counter = 0
          MOV CX,4                 ;set page counter to 4
```

**Figure 14-2    Program 14B**

```
                MOV DI,0                  ;set DI to first page
    REPEAT02:                             ;REPEAT
                PUSH CX                   ;   save page counter
                ADD DI,(24*80+0)*2        ;   set DI to line 24, column 0
                LEA SI,PROMPT             ;   set SI to prompt
                MOV CX,LPROMPT            ;   set cx to length of prompt
                MOV AH,70h                ;   set black on white
    REPEAT03:                             ;   REPEAT
                MOV AL,[SI]               ;      move byte of prompt to AL
                STOSW                     ;      store byte and attribute
                INC SI                    ;      add 1 to prompt address
                LOOP REPEAT03             ;      subtract 1 from length
    UNTIL03:                              ;   UNTIL length = 0
                AND DI,0F000h             ;   clear row and column address
                ADD DI,1000h              ;   set DI to next page
                POP CX                    ;   restore page counter
                LOOP REPEAT02             ;   subtract 1 from page counter
    UNTIL02:                              ;UNTIL page counter = 0
                MOV AH,5                  ;select page 0
                MOV AL,0
                PUSH AX                   ;save page indicator
                INT 10h
                MOV AH,8                  ;get key without echo
                INT 21h
    WHILE01:    CMP AL,1Bh                ;WHILE key <> <ESC>
                JE WEND01
                POP AX                    ;   restore page indicator
                ADD AL,1                  ;   add 1 to page indicator
    IF01:       CMP AL,03                 ;   IF page indicator > 3
                JBE ENDIF01
    THEN01:     MOV AL,0                  ;      THEN set page indicator to 0
    ENDIF01:                              ;   ENDIF
                PUSH AX                   ;   save page indicator
                INT 10h                   ;   select next page
                MOV AH,8                  ;   get key without echo
                INT 21h
                JMP WHILE01
    WEND01:                               ;WEND
                POP AX                    ;restore page indicator
                MOV DI,0                  ;set page 0 to black & white
                MOV CX,2000
                MOV AH,07h
                MOV AL,' '
                REP STOSW
                MOV AH,5                  ;select page 0
                MOV AL,0
                INT 10h
                MOV AX,4C00h              ;return to DOS
                INT 21h
    PROG14B     ENDP
                END PROG14B
```

**Figure 14-2** *concluded*

| PAGE | BACKGROUND COLOR | FOREGROUND COLOR |
|------|------------------|-------------------|
| 0 | Blue (1h) | Magenta (6h) |
| 1 | Green (2h) | White (7h) |
| 2 | Cyan (3h) | Gray (8h) |
| 3 | Red (4h) | Light blue (9h) |

In the loop at REPEAT02 we put the prompt 'Press any key to see next page. Press <ESC> to end.' on the bottom line of each page, with black characters on a white background.

In the loop at WHILE01 we display each page in turn when any key is pressed and end if <ESC> is pressed. Finally, we select page 0 and clear its video buffer and set the color to white on black to exit the program.

# SPECIAL MEMORY LOCATIONS

In addition to the video display adapters mentioned in the previous sections, several other hardware devices play important roles in handling the screen and other I/O components. The Motorola 6845 CRT Controller chip is used with the CGA and, somewhat modified, with the EGA. The 8259 Interrupt Controller assigns priorities to as many as eight interrupts. The 8253 timer chip provides three independent timer channels and six operation modes. The 8255 Programmable Peripheral Interface (PPI) controls the keyboard, the speaker, and the configuration switches.

Certain memory locations are reserved to pass vital information back and forth between the various hardware devices and the 8088 processor. The exact locations may change according to the specific hardware in use. The ROM BIOS communication area is in main memory, while the I/O ports are segregated from main memory only by the presence of a signal on a control line.

## ROM BIOS Communication Area

Recall that the first 1,024 (400h) bytes of main memory hold the interrupt vectors, and four bytes hold the segment and offset address of the routine to service each of the 256 possible interrupts. Immediately above the interrupt vectors is the ROM BIOS communication area, in locations 400h through 4FFh. The allocation of this area is shown below:

400-416h — configuration data.
417-417h — keyboard data.
43E-442h — disk data.
449-466h — video data.
467-46Bh — cassette data.
46C-4FFh — miscellaneous data.

These locations are used by the various functions of INT 10h discussed in this chapter. They may be viewed through DEBUG with the command

```
D 0:400
```

We shall look briefly at the equipment flags in the configuration data and several locations in the video data area.

**Equipment Flags**    Locations 410h and 411h contain equipment flags 1 and 2. They may be accessed through INT 11h or directly through MOV instructions. INT 11h places the contents of location 411h into AH and those of location 410h into AL. Location 411h is not relevant to video operations. The content of location 410h is as follows:

Bits 7-6: number of disks present (if bit 0 = 1)
　　00=1　　01=2　　10=3　　11=4
Bits 5-4: initial video mode
　　00=none (or enhanced video adapter)
　　01=40 x 25 color
　　10=80 x 25 color
　　11=80 x 25 monochrome
Bits 3-2: system board RAM
　　00=64K　　01=128K　　10=192K　　11=256K
Bit 1: not used
Bit 0: 1=disk drive installed

When writing software for general distribution, you might use the following routine to determine what type of monitor is installed so that the correct video buffer address can be placed into ES:

```
          MOV BX,40h              ;set ES to BIOS data areas
          MOV ES,BX
          MOV AL,ES:10h           ;move equipment flag 1 to AL
          MOV BX,0B800h           ;put color buffer address in
                                  ;BX
          AND AL,30h              ;clear all bits in flag but
                                  ;5-4
IF01:     CMP AL,30h              ;IF bits 5-4=11 (monochrome)
          JNE ENDIF01
THENO1:   MOV BX,0B000h           ;THEN put monochrome address
                                  ;in BX
ENDIF01:                          ;  ENDIF
          MOV ES,BX               ;put correct buffer address
                                  ;in ES
```

This routine moves only byte 410h to AL. Byte 411h could be moved to AH at the same time if desired by changing the third instruction above to be

```
          MOV AX,ES:10h
```

The first three instructions also could be replaced by INT 11h, which puts 410h in AL and 411h in AH.

*Video Data Area*. Memory locations 449h through 466h contain data used by BIOS INT 10h, INT 1Dh, and INT 1Fh. Table 14-3 lists the locations and names of various bytes and words in this area.

You can have access to any of these addresses through ES using this technique:

```
MOV BX,40h
MOV ES,BX
MOV AL,ES:nnh or MOV AX,ES:nnh
```

where AL is used for a byte and AX for a word, and nn is the offset from the video data area 400h.

Location 463h contains the active 6845 display index register port address. This address is:

```
3B4h    for the monochrome adapter
3D4h    for the color adapter
```

We shall use these port addresses in the next section.

## Video Controller Ports

A type of special memory makes up the I/O port address space in the 8088 microcomputer. Because only 10 bits can be used in addressing each port, the address space is limited to 1024 (400h) bytes, numbered from 000h through 3FFh.

Most of these ports are used for functions beyond the scope of this book, such as communications, printer and disk control, timer, and other system features. Ports 3B0-3BBh are reserved for the monochrome monitor adapter, but only ports 3B4h, 3B5h, 3B8h and 3BAh are actually used. Ports 3D0-3DBh are reserved for the color/graphics adapter, but only ports 3D4h, 3D5h, 3D8h, 3D9h, and 3DAh are actually used.

As mentioned in the preceding section, location 463h contains either port address 3B4h, if a monochrome monitor is used, or 3D4h, if a color/graphics monitor is used.

Ports may be accessed only through the use of the IN and OUT instructions. IN loads a byte into AL or a word into AX from the specified port. OUT stores a byte from AL or a word from AX into the specified port. If the port address is 255 or less, it may be specified as an immediate operand. Since each address of a video port is higher than 255, the address must be placed in DX. For example:

```
MOV DX,3BAh          MOV AL,10h
IN AL,DX             MOV DX,3B4h
                     OUT DX,AL
```

TABLE 14-3. BIOS Video Data Areas

**449h: CRT Mode**. Set by INT 10h, Function 0. Read by INT 10h, Function 0Fh. (See Table 14-1 for mode settings and meanings.)

**44Ah: CRT Columns.** Set by INT 10h, Function 0, Read by INT 10h, Function 0Fh.

28h = 40 columns          50h = 80 columns

**44C-44Dh: CRT Buffer Length**. Set by INT 10h, Function 0.

| LENGTH | USE | SCREEN WIDTH | MODE | PAGES |
|---|---|---|---|---|
| 800h | Color text | 40 | 0 | 8 |
| 1000h | Color text | 80 | 2/3 | 4 |
| 4000h | Color graphics | 40,80 | 4/6 | 1 |
| 1000h | Monochrome | 40,80 | 7 | 1 |

**44E-44Fh: CRT Start.** Set by INT 10h, Function 5h. Read by INT 10h, Function 0Fh. Shows offset of the starting byte of the active page in the display buffer.

**450-45Fh: Cursor Position.** Set by INT 10h, Function 2. Read by INT 10h, Function 3. Shows cursor location for each of up to eight pages. First byte of pair shows the column, the second byte the row.

| | | | |
|---|---|---|---|
| 450-451h | page 0 | 458-459h | page 4 |
| 452-453h | page 1 | 45A-45Bh | page 5 |
| 454-455h | page 2 | 45C-45Dh | page 6 |
| 456-457h | page 3 | 45E-45Fh | page 7 |

**460-461h: Cursor Size**. Set by INT 10h, Function 1.4
    **460h**   **Cursor end line**
        0Ch monochrome default     07h color default
    461h   Cursor start line
        bits 7-6 unused
        bit 5       0 = cursor displayed
                    1 = not displayed
        bits 4-0 cursor start line
        0Bh monochrome default     06h color default

**462h: Active Page.** Set by INT 10h, Function 5. Read by INT 10h, Function 0Fh.

**463-464h: Address of Active 6845 Port**
    3B4h for monochrome
    3D4h for color

**465h: CRT Mode Setting**. Set by INT 10h, Function 0. Read by INT 10h, Function 0Fh. Gives current setting of the active 6845 mode register (port 3B8h or 3D8h). This is different from CRT mode 449h.

| bits 7-6 | unused | bit: | 543210 | |
|---|---|---|---|---|
| bit 5 | background intensity | | 101100 | 40 x 25 b/w |
| | bit becomes blink | | 101000 | 40 x 25 16-color |
| bit 4 | 640 x 200 pixels | | 101101 | 80 x 25 b/w |
| bit 3 | enable video signal | | 101001 | 80 x 25 16-color |
| bit 2 | select b/w mode | | 001110 | 320 x 200 b/w |
| bit 1 | select graphics mode | | 001010 | 320 x 200 4-color |
| bit 0 | 80 x 25 text mode | | 011110 | 640 x 200 b/w |

**466h Color Palette.** Set by INT 10h, Function 0Bh. Contains current palette mask from port 3D9h.

Text Modes

|  | bits 7-5 | unused |
|---|---|---|
| | bit 4 | intensity of background |
| | bits 3-0 | screen/border intensity, red, green, blue (IRGB) |

Graphics Modes

|  | bits 7-6 | unused |
|---|---|---|
| | bit 5 | 0 = green, red, and brown palette |
| | | 1 = cyan, magenta, and white palette |
| | bit 4 | unused |
| | bits 3-0 | IRBG of background |

Default Contents

|  | 3Fh | 640 x 200 b/w |
|---|---|---|
| | 30h | all other modes |

Table 14-4 shows the contents of the video ports. The exact bit arrangements may vary according to the type of video adapter in use. The IBM PCjr microcomputer differs a widely from other models of the PC in its handling of the video display.

The video ports for the monochrome adapter correspond to those for the color adapter except that the middle digit of the port address is B while that for the color adapter is D. 3B4h is the monochrome index register, while 3D4h is the color index register.

The index register is output only. Its value cannot be read. A value between 0 and 17 (11h) must be placed there to refer to one of the 18 registers listed under port 3B5h. Most of these registers are write-only. Only registers 12, 13, 14, and 15 can be read with an IN instruction. The following routine would be necessary to read the contents of register 12:

```
MOV DX,3B4h          ;set index register port
                     ;address
MOV AL,12            ;select register 12 in port
                     ;3B5h
OUT DX,AL
```

TABLE 14-4.   Display Adapter Ports

## MONOCHROME MONITOR ADAPTER

**3B4h: 6845 Index Register.** Used to select register to be accessed through port 3B5h. Memory location 463h points here if monochrome adapter is active. Not readable; use OUT only.

**3B5h: 6845 Data Area.** Receives data to be placed in the register selected through port 3B4h. All registers, but 0C-0Fh, are write-only.

| Register | Use | Contents |
|---|---|---|
| 0 | Horizontal total characters -1 | 61h |
| 1 | Horz displayed characters/line | 50h |
| 2 | Horz synch position | 52h |
| 3 | Horz synch width in chracters | 0Fh |
| 4 | Vertical total lines -1 | 19h |
| 5 | Vert total lines -1 fraction | 06h |
| 6 | Vert displayed rows | 19h |
| 7 | Vert synch position | 19h |
| 8 | Interlace mode | 02h |
| 9 | Maximun scan line address | 0Dh |
| 10 | Cursor starting scan line | 0Bh |
|  | bit 7 unused | |
|  | bit 6 blink rate unused | |
|  | bit 5 = 0 display; 1 no display | |
|  | bits 4-0 starting scan line | |
|  | 0 = top; 0Dh = bottom | |
| 11 | Cursor ending scan line | 0Ch |
|  | bits 7-5 unused | |
|  | bits 4-0 ending scan line | |
|  | 0 = top; 0Dh = bottom | |
| 12 | Memory address MSB | 00h |
|  | bits 7-6 unused | |
|  | bits 5-0 half the offset for top left byte | |
| 13 | Memory address LSB | 00h |
|  | half the offset for top left byte | |
| 14 | Cursor address MSB | 00h |
|  | bits 7-6 unused | |
|  | bits 5-0 half the offset for top left byte, plus cursor offset | |
| 15 | Cursor address LSB | 00h |
|  | half the offset for top left byte, plus cursor offset | |
| 16 | Reserved for light pen | 00h |
| 17 | Reserved for light pen | 00h |

**3B8h: 6845 Mode Control Register**
      bit 5 enable blink
      bit 3 enable video signal
      bit 0 80 x 25 text

**3BAh: Status Register (read only)**
      bit 3   1 = vertical retrace
      bit 0   0 = video enabled
                1 = horizontal retrace

**3BAh: Status Register (read only)**
      bit 3   1 = vertical retrace
      bit 0   0 = video enabled
                1 = horizontal retrace

**3BBh: Reserved for light pen strobe reset.**

---

## COLOR/GRAPHICS MONITOR ADAPTER

---

**3D4h:** Same as 3B4h except used with color/graphics adapter.

**3D5h:** Same as 3B5h except that contents vary according to mode.

**3D8h: Control Register**
      bit 5   1 = background intensity means blink
                0 = background intensity for 16 colors
      bit 4   640 x 200 mode
      bit 3   enable video signal
      bit 2   select black and white mode
      bit 1   select graphics
      bit 0   80 x 25 text

**3D9h: Color Select Register**
      For text modes:
             bits 7-5     unused
             bit 4        intensity of background
             bits 3-0     screen /border color
      For graphics modes:
             bits 7-6     unused
             bit 5        0  = 1 green, red, and brown palette
                            1 = cyan, magenta, and white palette
             bit 4        unused
             bits 3-0     background

**3DAh: Status Register**
             bits 7-4     unused
             bit 3        vertical retrace
             bit 2        light pen switch

bit 1         light pen trigger set
bit 0         display enabled

**3DBh: Clear light pen latch by any write.**

**3DCh: Preset light pen latch.**

```
INC DX                          ;set data register port
                                ;address (3B5h)
IN AL,DX                        ;read register 12, port 3B5h
```

The following routine turns off the cursor by setting on bit 5 of register 10 at port 3B5h:

```
MOV DX,3B4h                     ;select index register port
MOV AL,10                       ;select register 10
OUT DX,AL
INC DX                          ;set to data register 3B5h
MOV AL,00100000b                ;set bit 5 to 1 to turn off
                                ;cursor
OUT DX,AL                       ;send code to register 10
```

To turn the cursor back on and set the cursor back to its normal starting scan line value of 11 (0Bh), reselect register 10 if necessary and then use:

```
MOV AL,00001011b                ;set bit 5 to 0 and cursor
                                ;line to 11
OUT DX,AL                       ;send code to register 10
```

## KEYBOARD SCAN CODES

We have used various forms of INT 21h to receive data keyed in from the keyboard, with or without echoing it on the screen. Actually, when a key is pressed, two separate codes are made available, the *ASCII character* and the keyboard *scan code*. The interrupt routines use tables to analyze the characters and scan codes to display the characters or to cause the various keyboard functions.

The scan code for the typewriter keys is a serial number giving the position of the key, starting with 01 the <ESC> key at the upper left of the keyboard, 02 for the "1" key next to it, 03 for the "2" key, and so forth. The scan code or the ASCII character, or both, are changed when the key is pressed in combination with the <SHIFT>, <CTRL>, or <ALT> key. The tabulation below shows the first six keys on the number row when pressed alone, then with the <SHIFT> key, then with the <CTRL> key, and finally with the <ALT> key. The character displayed is in AL unless AL contained 00, in which case the scan code in AH is displayed. Each column shows the character if it is printable, the two hex digits of the scan code, and the two hex digits of the ASCII code:

| KEY | LOWERCASE | UPPERCASE | \<CTRL\> + KEY | \<ALT\> + KEY |
|-----|-----------|-----------|----------------|---------------|
| ESC | 011B | 011B | 011B | 8B00 |
| 1 | 1 0231 | ! 0221 | E100 | x 7800 |
| 2 | 2 0332 | @ 0340 | 0300 | y 7900 |
| 3 | 3 0433 | # 0423 | E300 | z 7A00 |
| 4 | 4 0534 | $ 0524 | E400 | { 7B00 |
| 5 | 5 0635 | % 0625 | E500 | \| 7C00 |

### BIOS Scan Code Functions

BIOS INT 16h, Function 0, reads these two codes whenever a key, or a combination of certain keys, is pressed and puts the keyboard scan code in AH and the ASCII character in AL. There the codes can be analyzed and used in any way we wish.

It is useful to be able to view the various scan codes or to display the characters without having them perform their usual functions, such as tabbing or moving the cursor. INT 10h, Function 10, displays a character in AL on the screen at the current cursor position. BH must contain the page, and CX contains a count of characters to write. The cursor is not advanced by this interrupt, and you must move it explicitly to the next position. INT 10h, Function 9, writes both the character in AL and the attribute in BL at the current cursor location. As with Function 10, BH contains the page and CX the count of characters to write.

### Program 14C: Scan Codes and ASCII Codes

Program 14C (Figure 14-3) permits you to examine the codes produced by any key on the keyboard, alone and in combination with the \<SHIFT\>, \<CTRL\>, or \<ALT\> keys. A few of the keys do not send any scan or ASCII code: \<SHIFT\> alone, \<CTRL\> alone, \<ALT\> alone, \<CAPS\> lock, \<NUM LOCK\>, and \<HOLD\> or \<SCROLL LOCK\>. The program uses INT 16h, Function 0, to input from each key or combination and INT 10h, Function 10, to display AL or AH. Where AL contained an ASCII code of 00, the contents of the scan code in AH are displayed.

Figure 14-4 shows the output from program 14C. A few of the keys are not active in combination with \<CTRL\> or \<ALT\>. This output is from the Tandy 1000 TX keyboard. It is likely that different keyboards will produce different codes for some of the keys.

## SUMMARY

In this chapter we have examined some of the fundamental concepts behind the display screen. The screen is not directly controlled by the 8088 processor, but requires additional hardware interfaces.

```
            PAGE 50,132
;------------------------------------------------------------------------
; Program name:  PROG14C.ASM
;
; Author:        Alton R. Kindred
;
; This program scans each key on the keyboard in turn and displays
; the results obtained in AX.  Each key is pressed four times:  alone,
; with the <SHIFT> key, with the <CTRL> key, and with the <ALT> key.
; Each ASCII character returned in AL is displayed on the screen.
; If AL contains 00, the contents of AH are displayed.  INT 10h,
; function 0Ah, is used to display the character so that control
; functions such as cursor return or tab will be ignored.  The
; program terminates when <BREAK> is pressed, entering 0000 in AX.
;------------------------------------------------------------------------
SPACE       MACRO
            MOV DL,' '
            CALL DSPCHR
            ENDM
;
TAB         MACRO
            MOV DL,9
            CALL DSPCHR
            ENDM
;
CRLF        MACRO
            MOV DL,13
            CALL DSPCHR
            MOV DL,10
            CALL DSPCHR
            ENDM
;------------------------------------------------------------------------
            DOSSEG
            .MODEL SMALL
            .DATA
HDG1        DB 13,10,9,9,'Keyboard Scan Codes '
            DB 13,10,10,'Key Alone',9 DUP (' ')
            DB 'SHIFT + Key',8 DUP (' ')
            DB 'CTRL + Key',8 DUP (' ')
            DB 'ALT + Key',13,10,10,'$'
;------------------------------------------------------------------
            .STACK 256
;------------------------------------------------------------------
            .CODE
            EXTRN DSPCHR:NEAR, DSPLINE:NEAR, DSPHEX:NEAR
PROG14C     PROC
            MOV AX,@DATA
            MOV DS,AX
            LEA DX,HDG1             ;display headings
            CALL DSPLINE
            MOV AH,0               ;get character and scan code
            INT 16h
WHILE01:    CMP AX,0              ;WHILE not <BREAK> key
            JE WEND01
```

**Program 14-3    Program 14C**

```
              MOV CX,4                ;   set counter to 4
REPEAT01:                             ;   REPEAT
              PUSH CX                 ;     save counter
              PUSH AX                 ;     save AX
IF01:         CMP AL,0                ;     IF character = 0
              JNE ENDIF01
THEN01:       MOV AL,AH               ;        THEN put AH in AL
ENDIF01:                             ;     ENDIF
              MOV AH,0Ah              ;     display byte in AL
              MOV BH,0
              MOV CX,1
              INT 10h
              MOV AH,03               ;     get cursor position
              MOV BH,0
              INT 10h
              INC DL                  ;     advance cursor two bytes
              INC DL
              MOV AH,02               ;     reset cursor
              INT 10h
              POP AX                  ;     restore AX
              MOV DH,AH               ;     display AX in hex
              MOV DL,AL
              MOV CX,4
              CALL DSPHEX
              TAB                     ;     tab twice
              TAB
              POP CX
IF02:         CMP CX,1                ;     IF counter = 1
              JNE ENDIF02
THEN02:       CRLF                    ;        THEN return cursor and line feed
ENDIF02:                             ;     ENDIF
              MOV AH,0                ;     get character and scan code
              INT 16h
              CMP AX,0                ;     test for <BREAK> code
              JE UNTIL01
              LOOP REPEAT01           ;     subtract 1 from counter
UNTIL01:                             ;   UNTIL counter = 0 OR <BREAK> pressed
              JMP WHILE01
WEND01:                              ;WEND
              MOV AX,4C00h            ;return to DOS
              INT 21h
PROG14C       ENDP
              END   PROG14C
```

**Figure 14-3**   *concluded*

The monochrome display adapter (MDA) works with the monochrome screen, while the CGA, EGA, PCjr, MCGA, and VGA are adapters for color/graphics screens. The Motorola 6845 CRT Controller and the Intel 8253 Timer, 8255 Programmable Peripheral Interface, and the 8259 Interrupt Controller are other hardware devices serving the screen and other I/O devices.

BIOS provides a number of interrupts that set video modes, handle the cursor and the display screen, display characters, and control foreground and background colors.

```
                    Keyboard Scan Codes

    Key Alone          SHIFT + Key      CTRL + Key      ALT + Key

    1 0231             !  0221          E100            x 7800
    2 0332             @  0340          0300            y 7900
    3 0433             #  0423          E300            z 7A00
    4 0534             $  0524          E400            { 7B00
    5 0635             %  0625          E500            | 7C00
    6 0736             ^  075E          071E            } 7D00
    7 0837             &  0826          E700            ~ 7E00
    8 0938             *  092A          E800              7F00
    9 0A39             (  0A28          E900            à 8000
    0 0B30             )  0B29          E000              8100
    - 0C2D             _  0C5F          0C1F              8200
    = 0D3D             +  0D2B          F500              8300
    q 1071             Q  1051          1011              1000
    w 1177             W  1157          1117              1100
    e 1265             E  1245          1205              1200
    r 1372             R  1352          1312              1300
    t 1474             T  1454          1414              1400
    y 1579             Y  1559          1519              1500
    u 1675             U  1655          1615              1600
    i 1769             I  1749          1709              1700
```

**Figure 14-4    Output from Program C**

Video memory is a portion of memory that reflects upon the screen any characters and attributes placed there. For monochrome adapters, video memory is 4000 bytes starting at B000:0000. For color adapters, video memory consists of up to eight pages of 4000 bytes each, starting at B800:0000. The even-numbered byte in video memory contains the character to be displayed, while the odd-numbered byte immediately following is the attribute for that character.

The BIOS communication area is in main memory at location 400-4FFh. This area holds data about equipment currently installed and the operational modes. Locations 410-411h contain two equipment flags. Locations 449-466h are the video data area.

I/O ports are numbered locations, separate from main memory, used to pass data between the processor and the I/O hardware devices. Ports are numbered from 000h through 3FFh. Monochrome ports are 3B0-3BBh, while color ports are 3D0-3DCh. Ports are read or written by the IN or OUT instruction when the address is placed in DX.

Keyboard scan codes are sent to the input buffer along with the ASCII characters when keys are pressed. The scan code for upper- and lowercase is usually a number indicating the position on the keyboard. For keys pressed in combination with <CTRL> or <ALT>, the scan code often is 00h. INT 16h, Function 0, inputs the scan code in AH and the ASCII character in AL. INT

10h, Function 10, displays a character on the screen without carrying out its normal control function.

## QUESTIONS

1. What is the difference between a video buffer and video memory? What causes the size of the video buffer to vary?
2. Name some of the hardware devices that act as an interface between the 8088 memory and the display screen.
3. What is meant by a page? Why might more than one page be desirable?
4. What is the format of the attribute byte? Where does it appear in the video buffer?
5. What is meant by video mode? What factors can vary from one mode to the next?
6. How can data be displayed on the screen without using DOS or BIOS interrupts?
7. What is the address of the video buffer for the monochrome adapter? For page 3 of the color/graphics adapter?
8. Describe the content of the equipment flags in the BIOS communication area.
9. What addresses contain the video data area? What instructions give access to this data area?
10. What and where are the video controller ports? What instructions give access to these ports? Can you address main memory with these instructions?
11. What is meant by a keyboard scan code? What BIOS interrupt and function gives access to the scan code?
12. What BIOS interrupt and function allows a control code to be displayed on the screen as a character without using its control function?

## EXERCISES

1. Write string instructions to clear the screen for the monochrome adapter and to set the attribute to black foreground and white background.
2. Use BIOS Interrupt 10h, Function 6, to do the same thing you did in exercise 1.
3. Write string instructions to move your name to the left of line 12 of page 2 of the color/graphics adapter to display yellow foreground against a brown background. Then select page 2 for display.
4. Calculate the video memory addresses for page 3, line 4, column 20 of an 80 x 25 color text display.
5. Write instructions to set mode to 640 x 200 color and to display a line of 20 pixels centered on the screen.
6. Write instructions to examine the equipment flags in the BIOS communication area to see what kind of adapter is installed. If monochrome, move B000h to a field called VIDEO_MEMORY; if color, move B800h to VIDEO_MEMORY. In either event, move the contents of location 463h to a field called REG_PORT.
7. Write instructions to change the attribute byte so that the bottom line of the monochrome screen blinks.

8.  Write to register ports 10 and 11 at port 3B5h to set the cursor starting scan line to 0 and the bottom scan line to 7.

9.  Write instructions to set the control register at 3D8h to 640 x 200 color graphics mode.

## LAB PROBLEMS

1.  Write a program that divides a color display screen into four quarters. Make the attributes as follows:

| QUARTER | FOREGROUND | BACKGROUND |
|---|---|---|
| Upper left | White | Blue |
| Upper right | Black | Red |
| Lower left | Yellow | Brown |
| Lower right | Bright white | Green |

Then position the cursor in turn at the upper left of each quarter and display your name. Return color to white on black before leaving the program.

2.  Using the monochrome vide buffer directly, write a routine that causes whatever you type to appear on the bottom four lines of the screen. When you reach the end of the bottom line, or press <ENTER>, start the display again on the fourth line from the bottom.

# 8088 INSTRUCTION SUMMARY

Notes and conventions:

- Items in capital letters must be used exactly as shown.
- <> indicates operands supplied by the programmer.
- [ ] indicates optional operands.
- Unless stated otherwise, <destination> and <source> must be the same size; i.e., both must be bytes or both must be words.
- In general, <destination> can be a general register or a memory location. <Source> can be a general register, memory location, or immediate value. However, both <destination> and <source> cannot be memory locations.
- All instructions may be preceded by a label and followed by comments, which are not shown in the Format section to save space. The label when used must be followed by a colon (:), and comments must be preceded by a semicolon (;). a full format for the MOV statement, for example, would be:

    Format: [<label:>] MOV <destination>,<source> [;comments]
- On conditional jump instructions, <short label> is the label of an instruction within -128 to 127 bytes from instruction following the conditional jump instruction.
- The effect that each instruction has on the flags register appears in Appendix I.
-

**AAA (ASCII Adjust for Add)  Format: AAA**

After addition of two unpacked BCD digits, adjust sum in AL. If AL <= 09, clear carry flag. If AL is 0A through 0F, add 6 to AL, increment AH by 1, and set the carry flag.

**AAD (ASCII Adjust for Division)  Format: AAD**

Before division of two unpacked BCD digits in one such digit, adjust two-digit BCD number in AX by multiplying AH by 10, adding AL to the product, placing the result in AL, and clearing AH.

**AAM (ASCII Adjust for Multiplication)  Format: AAM**

After multiplication of two unpacked BCD digits, divide AH by 10, place quotient in AH and remainder in AL.

**AAS (ASCII Adjust for Subtraction)  Format: AAS**

After subtraction of one unpacked BCD digit from another, adjust difference in AL. If AL <= 09, clear carry flag. If AL = 0A through 0F, subtract 6 from AL, increment AH, and set carry flag.

**ADC (Add with Carry)  Format: ADC <destination>, <source>**

Add source and carry flag to destination and place sum at destination.

**ADD (Add)  Format: ADD <destination>, <source>**

Add source to destination and place sum at destination.

**AND (AND)  Format: AND <destination>, <source>**

Modify each bit in destination according to corresponding bit in source. If corresponding bits are both 1, result is 1; otherwise, result is 0.

**CALL (CALL)  Format: CALL <procedure>**

Push address of next instruction on stack and branch to address of procedure. If procedure is NEAR, push only IP and put offset of procedure into IP; if procedure is FAR, push CS and IP and replace with segment and offset addresses of procedure.

**CBW (Convert Byte to Word)  Format: CBW**

Expand 8-bit integer in AL to 16-bit integer in AX by copying sign bit from AL into all bits of AH.

**CLC (Clear Carry Flag)  Format: CLC**

Set carry flag to zero.

**CLD (Clear Direction Flag)  Format: CLD**

Set direction flag to zero to cause DI and/or SI to be incremented during string operations.

**CLI (Clear Interrupt Flag)  Format: CLI**

Set interrupt flag to zero to disable external interrupts.

**CMC (Complement Carry Flag)  Format: CMC**

Reverse setting of carry flag.

**CMP (Compare)  Format: CMP <destination>,<source>**

Compare destination to source and set flags accordingly. In effect, subtract source from destination without changing destination.

**CMPS/CMPSB/CMPSW (Compare String)  Format: CMPS <source>,<destination> or CMPSB or CMPSW**

Compare byte or word of source string identified by DS:SI with byte or word of destination string identified by ES:DI and set flags accordingly. If direction flag = 0, increment SI and DI; if direction flag = 1, decrement SI and DI.

**CWD (Convert Word to Doubleword)  Format: CWD**

Convert signed 16-bit integer in AX to signed 32-bit integer in DX:AX pair by extending sign bit of AX into all bits of DX.

**DAA (Decimal Adjust for Addition)   Format: DAA**

Adjust result of previous addition to two packed BCD digits in AL. If bits 3-0 of AL > 9 or AF = 1, add 6 to AL and set AF to 1. If bits 7- 4 of AL > 9 or CF = 1, add 60h to AL and set CF to 1.

**DAS (Decimal Adjust for Subtraction)   Format: DAS**

Adjust result of previous subtraction of two packed BCD digits in Al. If bits 3-0 of AL > 9 or AF = 1, subtract 6 from AL and set AF to 1. If bits 7-4 of AL > 9 or CF = 1, subtract 60h from AL and set CF to 1.

**DEC (Decrement)   Format: DEC <destination>**

Subtract 1 from destination register or memory location.

**DIV (Divide, Unsigned)   Format: DIV <source>**

If source is a byte, divide AX by source, leaving quotient in AL and remainder in AH; if source is a word, divide DX:AX pair by source, leaving quotient in AX and remainder in DX. Use only with unsigned numbers.

**ESC(Escape)   Format: ESC**

Escape to external device, usually an 8087 coprocessor.

**HLT (Halt)   Format: HLT**

Halt processor until interrupt is received.

**IDIV (Integer Divide, Signed)   Format: IDIV <source>**

If source is a byte, divide AX by source, leaving quotient in AL and remainder in AH. If source is a word, divide DX:AX pair by source, leaving quotient in AX and remainder in DX. Use with signed numbers.

**IMUL (Integer Multiply, Signed)   Format: IMUL <source>**

If source is a byte, multiply AL by source, leaving signed product in AH. If source is a word, multiply AX by source, leaving signed product in DX:AX pair.

**IN (Input from Port)   Format: AL, <port> or AX, <port>**

Transfer byte to  AL or word to AX from specified port. Port can be an immediate value from 0-255 or DX register.

**INC (Increment)   Format: INC<destination>**

Add 1 to destination register or memory location.

**INT (Interrupt)   Format: INT <interrupt-type>**

Push flags register, CS, and IP onto stack; clear trap and interrupt flags; multiply interrupt-type by 4 to get interrupt address; put first word at interrupt address into IP and next word into CS; and jump to interrupt routine. Interrupt type must be an immediate value 0-255.

**INTO (Interrupt on Overflow)   Format: INTO**

If overflow flag is set, push flags register, CS, and IP onto stack; clear trap and interrupt flags; load word at address 0000:0010 into IP and next word into CS; and jump to interrupt routine. If overflow flag is not set, do nothing.

**IRET (Interrupt Return)   Format: IRET**
Pop top three words from stack into IP, CS, and flags register, respectively.

**JB/JNAE (Jump if Below/Not Above or Equal)   Format: Jxxx <short label>**
Jump to short label if CF = 0 and ZF = 0.

**JBE/JNA (Jump if Below or Equal/Not Above)   Format: Jxxx <short label>**
Jump to short label if CF = 0.

**JCXZ (Jump if CX = 0)   Format: JCXZ <short label>**
Jump to short label if CX register = 0.

**JE/JZ (Jump if Equal/Zero)   Format: Jxxx <short label>**
Jump to short label if ZF = 1.

**JL/JNGE (Jump if Low/Not Greater or Equal)   Format: Jxxx <short label>**
Jump to short label if SF <> OF.

**JLE/JNG (Jump if Low or Equal/Not Greater)   Format: Jxxx <short label>**
Jump to short label if ZF = 1 or SF <> OF.

**JMP (Jump)   Format: JMP <address>**
Jump unconditionally to specified address. Address may be a near or far label or a register. If a near label, distance to address from instruction following JMP is added to IP. If a far label, segment and offset values of address replace CS:IP. If a register, register contents replace IP.

**JNB/JAE (Jump if Not Below/Above or Equal)   Format: Jxxx <short label>**
Jump to short label if CF = 0.

**JNBE/JA (Jump if Not Below or Equal/Above)   Format: Jxxx <short label>**
Jump to short label if CF = 0 and ZF = 0

**JNE/JNZ (Jump if Not Equal/Not Zero)   Format: Jxxx <short label>**
Jump to short label if ZF =0.

**JNL/JGE (Jump if Not Low/Greater or Equal)   Format: Jxxx <short label>**
Jump to short label if SF = OF.

**JNLE/JG (Jump if Not Low or Equal/Greater)   Format: Jxxx <short label>**
Jump  to short label if ZF = 0 and SF = OF.

**JNO (Jump if Not Overflow)   Format: JNO <short label>**
Jump to short label if OF = 0.

**JNP/JPO (Jump if Parity Odd)   Format: Jxxx <short label>**
Jump to short label if PF = 0.

**JNS (Jump if NONnegative Sign)   Format: JNS <short label>**
Jump to short label if SF = 0.

**JO (Jump on Overflow)   Format: JO <short label>**
Jump to short label if OF = 1.

**JP/JPE (Jump if Parity Even)   Format: Jxxx <short label>**
Jump to short label if PF = 1.

**JS (Jump if Negative Sign)   Format: JS <short label>**
Jump to short label if SF = 1

**LAHF (Load AH Register from Flags)   Format: LAHF**
Copy bits 7-0 of flags register into AH register.

**LDS (Load Pointer with Data Segment)   Format: LDS <register>,<source>**
Load specified 16-bit register with first word at source and DS with following word at source.

**LEA (Load Effective Address)   Format: LEA <register>,<source>**
Load specified 16-bit register with offset of source. Offset may be computed from use of base or index registers.

**LES (Load Pointer with Extra Segment)   Format: LES <register>,<source>**
Load specified 16-bit register with first word at source and ES with following word at source.

**LOCK (Lock)   Format: LOCK**
Lock out other processors until the instruction preceded by LOCK has finished execution.

**LODS/LODSB/LODSW (Load String)   Format: LODS <source> or LODSB or LODSW**
Load AL with byte or AX with word at source addressed by DS:SI. If direction flag is 0, add 1 for byte or 2 for word to SI; if direction flag is 1, subtract 1 for byte or 2 for word from SI.

**LOOP (Loop)   Format: LOOP <short label>**
Subtract 1 from CX. If result is not zero, jump to short label; if result is zero, proceed to instruction following LOOP.

**LOOPE/LOOPZ (Loop if Equal/Zero)   Format: LOOPx <short label>**
Subtract 1 from CX. If result is not zero and ZF = 1, jump to short label; otherwise, proceed to next instruction.

**LOOPNE/LOOPNZ (Loop if Not Equal/Not Zero)   Format: LOOPxx <short label>**
Subtract 1 from CX. If result is not zero and ZF = 0, jump to short label; otherwise, proceed to next instruction.

**MOV (Move)   Format: MOV <destination>,<source>**
Replace byte or word at destination with copy of value of same size at source. Destination may be general register, segment register, or memory location. Source may be any of these or immediate operand. Both oper-

ands cannot be segment registers or memory locations. Immediate values cannot be moved to segment registers.

**MOVS/MOVSB/MOVSW (Move String)  Format: MOVS <destination>, <source> or MOVSB or MOVSW**

Replace byte or word at destination addressed by ES:DI with byte or word at source addressed by DS:SI. If direction flag = 0, increment SI and DI by 1 for bytes or 2 for words; if direction flag = 1, decrement SI and DI by 1 for bytes or 2 for words.

**MUL (Multiply)  Format: MUL <source>**

If source is a byte, multiply unsigned integer in AL by source, placing product in AX. If source is a word, multiply AX by source, placing product in DX:AX register pair.

**NEG (Negate)  Format: NEG <destination>**

Replace value at destination with its twos complement.

**NOP (No Operation)  Format: NOP**

Delay machine operation for 3 clock cycles by exchanging AX with itself.

**NOT (Logical NOT)  Format: NOT <destination>**

Replace value at destination with its ones complement.

**OR (Logical OR)  Format: OR <destination>, <source>**

Perform OR operation on each bit at destination with corresponding bit at source. If either bit of corresponding pair is 1, result bit is 1; if both bits are 0, result is 0.

**OUT (Output Byte or Word to Port)  Format: OUT <port>,AL or OUT <port>,AX**

Transfer byte from AL or word from AX to specified port, which must be an immediate value 0-255 or DX register.

**POP (Pop)  Format: POP <destination>**

Replace destination with word on stack pointed to by SS:SP and increment SP by 2.

**POPF (Pop Flags)  Format: POPF**

Replace flags register with word on stack pointed to by SS:SP and increment SP by 2.

**PUSH (Push)  Format: PUSH <source>**

Decrement SP by 2 and store copy of 16-bit source on stack at SS:SP.

**PUSHF (Push Flags)  Format: PUSHF**

Decrement SP by 2 and store flags register on stack at SS:SP.

**RCL (Rotate through Carry Left)  Format: RCL <destination>,1 or RCL <destination>,CL**

Shift each in destination left one position (or number specified in CL); shift leftmost bit into carry flag and carry flag into rightmost bit of destination.

**RCR (Rotate through Carry Right)   Format: RCR <destination>,1 or RCR
<destination>,CL**

Shift each bit in destination to the right one position or the number
specified in CL; shift rightmost bit of destination into carry flag, and
carry flag into leftmost bit of destination.

**REP (Repeat)   Format: REP <string-op> <operands>**

Create a loop to execute the following string operation (<string-op>) and
decrement CX until CX = 0. String-op should be one of the forms of
MOVS, LODS, or STOS instructions. Operands is the list of operands, if
any, needed by the string instruction.

**REPE/REPZ (Repeat on Equal/Zero)   Format: REPx <string-op>
<operands>**

Create a loop to execute the string operation (<string-op>) and decrement CX until CX = 0 or ZF = 0. Use with forms of CMPS or SCAS string
instructions.

**REPNE/REPNZ (Repeat on Not Equal/Not Zero)   Format: REPxx
<string-op> <operands>**

Create a loop to execute the string operation (<string-op>) and decrement CX until CX = 0 or ZF = 1. Use with forms of CMPS or SCAS string
instructions.

**RET (Return)   Format: RET [<number>]**

Pop return address from top of stack and return to that address. For
NEAR return, pop word at SS:SP into IP and increment SP by 2. For FAR
return, pop word at SS:SP into IP, increment SP by 2, pop next word into
CS, and increment SP again by 2. If number is present, increment SP by
that number to discard values previously pushed on the stack. Number
should always be even number.

**ROL (Rotate Left)   Format: ROL <destination>,1 or ROL
<destination>,CL**

Rotate each bit in byte or word at destination to the left one position or
the number of bit positions specified in CL. The leftmost bit in destination is shifted to the carry flag and also to bit 0 at the right of destination.

**ROR (Rotate Right)   Format: ROR <destination>,1 or ROR
<destination>,CL**

Rotate each bit in byte or word at destination ;to the right one position or
the number of bit positions specified in CL. Bit 0 of destination is shifted
to the carry flag and also to the leftmost bit of destination.

**SAHF (Store AH Register into Flags)   Format: SAHF**

Store a copy of AH register into bits 7-0 of the flag register.

**SAL (Shift Arithmetic Left)  Format: SAL <destination>,1 or SAL <destination>,CL**

Shift all bits in destination left one bit position or the number or bits specified in CL. Shift the leftmost bit into the carry flag. Fill vacated bits in bit 0 of destination with 0s.

**SAR (Shift Arithmetic Right)  Format: SAR <destination>,1 or SAR <destination>, CL**

Shift all bits in destination right one bit position or the number of bits specified in CL. Shift the rightmost bit into the carry flag. Copy the sign bit into the bit position to its right.

**SBB (Subtract with Borrow)  Format: SBB <destination>,<source>**

Subtract source and carry (borrow) flag from destination and place difference at destination.

**SCAS/SCASB/SCASW (Scan String)  Format: SCAS <destination> or SCASB or SCASW**

Compare byte in AL or word in AX with byte or word at destination addressed by ES:DI and set flags accordingly. If direction flag is 0, add 1 for bytes or 2 for words to DI. If direction flag is 1, subtract 1 for bytes or 2 for words from DI.

**SHL (Shift Logical Left)  Format: SHL <destination>,1 or SHL <destination>,CL**

Shift bits in destination to the left one bit position or number of positions specified in CL. Shift leftmost bit of destination into carry flag. Fill vacated positions to the right with 0s.

**SHR (Shift Logical Right)  Format: SHR <destination>,1 or SHR <destination>,CL**

Shift bits in destination to the right one bit position or number of positions specified in CL. Shift rightmost bit of destination into carry flag. Fill vacated positions to the left with 0s.

**STC (Set Carry Flag)  Format: STC**

Set carry flag to 1.

**STD (Set Direction Flag)  Format: STD**

Set direction flag to 1 to cause DI and/or SI to be decremented in string operations.

**STI (Set Interrupt Flag)  Format: STI**

Set interrupt flag to 1 to enable processor to accept external interrupts.

**STOS/STOSB/STOSW (Store String)  Format: STOS <destination> or STOSB or STOSW**

Store copy of AL if byte or AX if word at destination addressed by ES:DI. If DF = 0, increment DI by 1 for byte or 2 for word. If DF = 1, decrement DI by 1 for byte or 2 for word.

**SUB (Subtract)  Format: SUB <destination>, <source>**
Subtract byte or word at source from destination.

**TEST (Test)  Format: TEST <destination>,<source>**
Perform logical AND on each bit of destination with corresponding bit of source without changing either and set flags accordingly.

**WAIT (Wait)  Format: WAIT**
Instruct processor to do nothing until it receives a signal that the coprocessor has finished with a test performed at the same time.

**XCHG (Exchange)  Format: XCHG <destination>,<source>**
Exchange contents of destination and source.

**XLAT (Translate)  Format: XLAT [<source>]**
Replace byte in AL with byte at address specified by DS:BX+AL. Source may be name of symbol addressed by DS:BX

**XOR (Exclusive OR)  Format: XOR <destination>,<source>**
Modify each bit in destination according to corresponding bit in source. If corresponding bits are alike, result is 0; if different, result is 1.

# 80186, 80286, AND 80386 INSTRUCTIONS

# B

In general, the 80186,80286, and 80386 processors will execute all instructions used by 8086 and 8088 processors. In addition, they can execute instructions not available to the 8086 and 8088 machines.

The following instructions were implemented with the 80186 and also are available on the 80286 and 80386 processors.

**BOUND (Bound)   Format: BOUND <destination>,<source>**

Check if destination is within range specified by source and, if not, execute INT 5. Source must be a doubleword in memory,with the offset of the first element of an array in the first word and the offset of the last array element in the second word. Destination contains an offset to be checked.

**ENTER (Enter)   Format: ENTER <framesize>,<level>**

Set up stack frame. Frame size is a 16-bit constant giving the number of bytes to be reserved to reserve on the stack for local variables. Level is an eight-bit constant specifying the nesting level of the procedure. For BASIC, C, and Fortran, level should always be 0. For Pascal and other languages that enable procedures to access local variables of calling procedures, level can be greater than 0.

**IMUL (Signed Multiply)   Format: IMUL <destination>,<source> or IMUL <destreg16>,<mem16>,<immediate>**

(a) Multiply destination word register by immediate source value and place product in destination. (b) Multiply 16-bit second operand register by 16-bit immediate third operand and place product in 16-bit destination register. Carry and overflow flags are set if product is longer than 16 bits.

**INS/INSB/INSW (Input String from Port)   Format: [REP] INS [ES:] destination,DX or INSB or INSW**

Input byte or word from port specified in DX and place it at destination specified by ES:DI. Increment DI by 1 for byte or 2 for word if DF = 0. Decrement DI by 1 for byte or 2 for word if DF = 1. If REP prefix is used,

CX must contain number of bytes or words to input. Decrement CX by 1 and repeat until CX= 0.

**LEAVE (Leave)  Format: LEAVE**

Reverse effect of last ENTER instruction by restoring BP and SP to their values before the last CALL.

**OUTS/OUTSB/OUTSW (Output String from Port)  Format: [REP] OUTS [DS:] source, DX or OUTSB or OUTSW**

Output byte or word from source specified in DS:SI to port at destination specified by DX. Increment SI by 1 for byte or 2 for word if DF = 0. Decrement SI by 1 for byte or 2 for word if DF = 1. If REP prefix is used, CX must contain number of bytes or words to input. Decrement CX by 1 and repeat until CX = 0.

**POPA (Pop All)  Format: POPA**

Pop all registers in this sequence: DI, SI, BP, SP, BX, DX, CX, AX.

**PUSHA (Push All)  Format: PUSHA**

Push all registers in this sequence: AX, CX, DX, BX, SP, BP, SI, DI.

**PUSH immediate   Format: PUSH <immediate>**

Push immediate value on stack.

**PUSH SP   Format: PUSH SP**

For the 8086/8088, push word in SP after the PUSH operation; for the 80186, 80286, and 80386, push word in SP before the PUSH operation.

**Shift and Rotate instructions, immediate Format: Sxx <destination>,<immediate> or Rxx <destination>,<immediate>**

Shift or rotate destination left or right number of bits specified by immediate. Starting with the 80186, immediate can be greater than 1.

## INSTRUCTIONS FOR 80386 ONLY

**Note:**   Many instruction for the 8088, 8086, 80186, and 80286 processors have been enhanced to permit operations in extended registers on 32-bit numbers. Offset addresses can likewise be 32-bit values. Any general registers can be used as pointers for indirect memory operands. In addition, many new instructions have been created to carry out special operations as described in the following section.

**BOUND (Bound)  Format: BOUND <destination>,<source>**

Check if destination is within range specified by source and, if not, execute INT 5. Source must be a 64-bit area in memory, with the offset of the first element of an array in the first doubleword and the offset of the last array element in the second doubleword. Destination is a 32-bit register that contains an offset to be checked.

**BSF (Bit Scan Forward)  Format: BSF <destination>,<source>**

Scan source register starting with 0 bit and working left and store in destination register the bit position of last (rightmost) bit set. Both source and destination can be only 16- or 32-bit registers.

**BSR (Bit Scan Reverse)  Format: BSR <destination>,<source>**

Scan source register starting with leftmost bit and working right and store in destination register the bit position of first (leftmost) bit set. Both source and destination must be 16- or 32-bit registers.

**BT (Bit Test)  Format: BT <target>,<position>**

Examine bit number specified by position in target and copy it in carry flag. Target can be a register or memory location. Bit can be an immediate value or a register containing the bit position.

**BTC (Bit Test and Complement)  Format: BTC <target>,<position>**

Identical to BT except that, after being copied in the carry flag, the specified bit is complemented.

**BTR (Bit Test and Reset)  Format: BTR <target>,<position>**

Identical to BT except that, after being copied in the carry flag, the specified bit is cleared to 0.

**BTS (Bit Test and Set)  Format: BTS <target>,<position>**

Identical to BT except that, after being copied in the carry flag, the specified bit is set to 1.

**CDQ (Convert Doubleword to Quadword)  Format: CDQ**

Extend 32-bit signed value in EAX to 64-bit signed value in EDX:EAX.

**CMPSD (Compare String Doubleword)  Format: [REPE/REPNE] CMPSD**

Compare doubleword from string pointed to by ES:DI with one from string pointed to by DS:SI. If DF=0, add 4 to DI and SI; otherwise, subtract 4 from DI and SI. If REPE or REPNE prefix is used, CX must contain count of doublewords; subtract 1 from CX and continue so long as comparison is equal (REPE) or not equal (REPNE).

**CWDE (Convert Word to Doubleword Extended)  Format: CWDE**

Convert 16-bit signed value in AX to 32-bit signed value in EAX.

**IMUL (Signed Multiply)  Format: IMUL <destination>,<source>**

Multiply any 16- or 32-bit destination register by same-sized source register or memory location and place product at destination.

**INSD (Input String from Port)  Format: [REP] INSD**

Input doubleword from port specified by DX and place at address specified by ES:DI. If DF=0, increment DI by 4; else, decrement DI by 4. If REP prefix is used, CX must contain count of doublewords; if so, decrement CX by 1.

**IRETD (Interrupt Return Double)  Format: IRETD**

Pop 32-bit instruction pointer upon return from interrupt.

**JMP and Jcondition SHORT   Format: Jcondition SHORT <target>**

When target is within -128 to 127 bytes, cause JMP or conditional jump to generate 2-byte instruction when 80386 processor is enabled; otherwise, near or far jump generates 3- to 7-byte instruction.

**LFS (Load Far Pointer to FS)   Format: LFS <destination>,<source>**

Load first word of memory location at source into FS segment register and second word into destination register. Source should contain a segment-offset address.

**LGS (Load Far Pointer to GS)   Format: LGS <destination>,<source>**

Load first word of memory location at source into GS segment register and second word into destination register. Source should contain a segment-offset address.

**LODSD (Load String Doubleword   Format: LODSD**

Load doubleword into EAX from source string pointed to be DS:SI. If DF=0, add 4 to SI; otherwise, subtract 4 from SI. Do not use with REP prefix.

**LSS (Load Far Pointer to SS)   Format: LSS <destination>,<source>**

Load first word of memory location at source into SS segment register and second word into destination register. Source should contain a segment-offset address.

**MOV (Move)   Format: <destination>,<source>**

Copy source operand into destination. On 80386, can be used for moving 32-bit operands with extended registers and to move data between general-purpose and special-purpose registers.

**MOVSD (Move String Doubleword)   Format: [REP] MOVSD**

Move doubleword from source string specified by DS:SI to destination string specified by ES:DI. If DF = 0, add 4 to SI and DI; otherwise, subtract 4 from each. If REP prefix is used, CX must contain count of doublewords; if so, decrement CX by 1.

**MOVSX (Move and Extend Signed Value)   Format: MOV <destination>,<source>**

Move signed value from source in a register or memory into a destination register of larger data size and extend the sign.

**MOVZX (Move and Extend Unsigned Value)   Format: MOV <destination>, <source>**

Move unsigned value from source in a register or memory into a destination register of larger data size and extend zeros into high-order bits.

**OUTSD (Output Doubleword to Port)   Format: [REP] OUTSD**

Output doubleword from string specified by DS:SI to port specified in DX. If DF = 0, add 4 to SI; otherwise, subtract 4 from SI. If REP prefix is used, CX must contain count of doublewords; if so, decrement CX by 1.

**POPAD (Pop All Doublewords)  Format: POPAD**

Pop all 32-bit registers in this sequence: EDI, ESI, EBP, ESP, EBX, EDX, ECX, EAX.

**POPFD (Pop Flag Doubleword)  Format: POPFD**

Pop 32-bit Eflag register.

**PUSHAD (Push All Doublewords)  Format: PUSHAD**

Push all 32-bit registers in this sequence: EAX, ECX, EDX, EBX, ESP, EBP, ESI, EDI.

**PUSHFD (Push Flag Doubleword)  Format: PUSHFD**

Push 32-bit Eflag register.

**SCASD (Scan String for Doubleword)   Format: [REPE | REPNE] SCASD**

Scan destination string specified by ES:DI for doubleword in EAX. If DF=0, add 4 to DI; otherwise, subtract 4 from DI. If REPE or REPNE prefix is used, CX must contain count of doublewords; CX is decremented by 1 so long as the doublewords are equal (REPE) or not equal (REPNE).

**SETcondition   Format: SETcondition <byte>**

Test flags and set specified register memory byte to 1 if condition is true or 0 if it is false. Condition is same as op code for conditional-jump instructions (GE, NL, etc.)

**SHLD (Shift Left Doubleword)   Format: SHLD <dest>,<source>,<bits>**

Shift 16- or 32-bit dest register left the number of bits specified by third operand. Fill in vacated positions with shifted bits from source. Dest and source must be same size. Bits may be immediate value or CL register.

**SHRD (Shift Right Doubleword)   Format: SHRD <dest>,<source>,<bits>**

Shift 16- or 32-bit dest register right the number of bits specified by third operand. Fill in vacated position with shifted bits from source. Dest and source must be same size. Bits may be immediate value or CL register.

**STOSD (Store String Doubleword)   Format: [REP] STOSD**

Store doubleword in EAX at destination string specified by ES:DI. If DF=0, add 4 to DI; otherwise, subtract 4 from DI. If REP prefix is used, CX must contain count of doublewords; CX is decremented by 1. Use any general purpose 32-bit registers for indirect-memory addressing.

**XLATB (Translate)  Format: XLATB**

Identical to XLAT for 8088 except that no operand is permitted.

# DOS REFERENCE

Microsoft DOS is a disk operating system for the 8086/8088 families of microcomputers. Through it you create, maintain, update, and delete files on disk and communicate with other input/output devices. This appendix covers those features closely related to assembler language programming. Full description of DOS is available through the Microsoft DOS User's Reference Manual and other documents.

## DRIVES, FILENAMES, AND DIRECTORIES

Disk drives are designated by letter. Typically, drive A holds DOS and programs and drive B holds data on a floppy disk system. Drive C and D, if present, are hard disks. A colon (:) follows the drive letter.

The name of a file consists of a filename of one to eight characters and an optional extension consisting of a period (.) followed by one to three characters. The following characters can be used in filenames and extensions:

A-Z a-z 0-9 $ & % ' ( ) - @ ^ { } ! # ~ `

Files are kept in directories on disk. The directory keeps track of the location of each file, the number of bytes it occupies, and the date it was created and updated. An empty *root directory* is created when the disk is formatted. A root directory can hold a limited number of files (114 on some disks), so that additional directories may be created to group files into logical categories. There is no limit to the number of files that can be placed into other directories (called *subdirectories*). Subdirectories can be further divided into other subdirectories. Each subdirectory is indicated by placing its name between two backslashes (\). For example,

```
B:\PROG\ASSEM\FILE7.ASM
```

could refer to a file named FILE7.ASM in subdirectory ASSEM of directory PROG on drive B. A combination of a drive and one or more subdirectories with a filename is called a *path*.

One directory can be designated as the *working directory* so that the subdirectory names between backslashes can be omitted.

## WILDCARDS

Special characters may be used when referring to filenames. They are called *wildcards*, indicating that any character is acceptable in one or more positions specified. The question mark (?) appearing in a filename or extension means that any character could appear in that position. The command

```
B> DIR PROG?.ASM
```

would list directory entries for files named PROG1.ASM, PROG2.ASM, and PROGX.ASM if they were present on drive B.

The asterisk (*) in a filename or extension means that any character can occupy that position or any of the remaining positions in the filename or extension where the asterisk appears. The command

```
B> DIR *.ASM
```

would list directories for all files having an extension of ASM.

## DOS COMMANDS

You communicate with DOS through commands. *Internal commands* are routines stored within the COMMAND.COM module, which is placed in memory when the system is booted up. *External commands* are names of routines stored as separate files. You execute the command by typing its name and additional required or optional parameters.

There are more than 50 DOS commands. We summarize here those most useful to the process of writing, assembling, linking, executing, and storing programs in assembler language.

### Internal Commands

**CHDIR (Change Directory)   Syntax: CHDIR [<pathname>]**
**Synonym: CD**
**Explanation:** Change directory to a different path and display working directory. CHDIR without a <pathname> displays the current working directory.
**Examples:**

```
CHDIR B:\PROG\ASSEM          ;changes directory to path
                             ;shown
CHDIR B:                     ;displays working directory
                             ;on drive B
CD                           ;displays current working
                             ;directory
```

**CLS (Clear Screen)   Syntax: CLS**
**Explanation:** Clear terminal screen.

**COPY** Syntax: COPY [<drive:>] <pathname> [<drive:>] [<pathname>] [/v] [/a] [/b]

COPY <pathname> + <pathname> ... <pathname>

**Explanation:** *First syntax*: copy one or more files to the same or another disk. First file named is copied to second drive or to different name on same drive. /v option verifies sectors copied. a/ and /b specify ASCII or binary files. *Second syntax*: combine files on either side of plus sign (+) and copy to new drive or new name.

**Examples:**
```
COPY A:*.* B:              ;copy all files from drive A
                           ;to drive B
COPY PROG7.ASM TEST        ;copy PROG7.ASM to file
                           ;named TEST on same disk
```

**DATE** Syntax: [<mm> - <dd> - <yy>]

**Explanation:** Enter or change date to be stored in DOS. DATE with no parameter displays date currently stored and issues prompt for new date. DATE with parameter changes date. Valid values:

<mm> = 1-12    <dd> = 1-31    <yy> = 80-99 or 1980-2099

**Examples:**
```
DATE                       ;request date; press <ENTER>
                           ;not to change
DATE 01-01-92              ;set date to January 1, 1992
```

**DIR (Directory)** Syntax: DIR [<drive:>] [<pathname>] [/p] [/w]

**Explanation:** List the files in a directory. DIR without parameters lists directories on default drive. Wildcards may be used. The /p switch pauses listing when screen is filled; to resume, press any key. The /w switch displays only the filenames, five per line.

**Examples:**
```
DIR                        ;list all files on default
                           ;drive
DIR B:PROG*.ASM            ;list all files on drive B
                           ;with name starting with PROG
                           ;and extension ASM
```

**ERASE** Syntax: ERASE [<drive:>] <pathname> or DEL [<drive:>] <pathname>

**Synonym: DEL (Delete)**

**Explanation:** Erase (delete) one or more files with the designated file specification. If the pathname is *.*, the prompt "Are you sure?" appears.

**Examples:**
```
ERASE PROGX.*              ;erase all files named PROGX
                           ;from default drive.
DEL B:*.*                  ;delete all files from drive B
```

**MKDIR (Make Directory)   Syntax: MKDIR [<drive:>] <pathname>**
**Synonym: MD**
**Explanation:** Make a new subdirectory or multilevel subdirectories when you are in the root directory.
**Examples:**

```
      MKDIR B:\SUBS            ;make subdirectory SUBS on
                               ;drive B
      MD \SUBS\ASSEM           ;make subdirectory ASSEM
                               ;under SUBS on default drive
```

**PATH   Syntax: PATH [[<drive:>] [<pathname>]; [<drive:>]**
   **[<pathname>]...]**
**Explanation:** Set a command search path to be followed for external commands after searching the working directory. PATH with no parameters prints the current path. PATH ; sets the NUL path so that only the working directory is searched for external commands.
**Examples:**

```
      PATH                     ;causes printing of current
                               ;path
      PATH ;                   ;cancels previous PATH
                               ;parameters
      PATH \COMMAND\EXT        ;search path \command\ext for
                               ;external commands
```

**REN (Rename)   Syntax: REN [<drive:>]<pathname> <pathname>**
**Explanation:** Give a different name to a file. Wildcards may be used in either option. No <drive> can be specified for second <pathname>.
**Examples:**

```
      REN *.TXT *.DOC          ;change all TXT extensions to
                               ;DOC
      REN B:BOOK4 CHAP4        ;change name of BOOK4 to
                               ;CHAP4 on drive B
```

**RMDIR (Remove Directory)   Syntax: RMDIR <pathname>**
**Synonym: RD**
**Explanation:** Remove a directory from a multilevel directory structure if all files in it have been erased.
**Example:**

```
      RMDIR \PROG\ASSEM        ;remove the named directory
```

**SET   Syntax: SET [<string=string>]**
**Explanation:** Set value of one string in the environment equal to another string for use in later programs. SET with no parameters displays the current environment settings. SET with first <string> only clears the associated string name.

**Examples:**

```
SET INCLUDE=\PROG\INCLUDE;set INCLUDE environment
                         ;string to search path
                         ;\PROG\INCLUDE for INCLUDE
                         ;files
SET MASM=/A/L/C          ;set MASM environment
                         ;variable to make options /A,
                         ;/L, and /C automatically in
                         ;effect
```

**TIME   Syntax: TIME [<hours>:<minutes>]**

**Explanation:** Display and set the time. TIME with parameters sets time based on 24-hour clock. TIME without parameters displays time in form hh:mm:ss.cc and prompts to enter new time. Press <ENTER> to leave time unchanged. Allowable values are:

<hours> = 00–24    <minutes> = 00–59

**Examples:**

```
TIME                     ;request time and optionally
                         ;change it
TIME 14:30               ;set time to 2:30 p.m.
```

**TYPE   Syntax: TYPE [<drive:>] <filename> [>PRN]**

**Explanation:** Display contents of specified file on the screen or printer without modifying it. Display of non-ASCII files can be unpredictable. >PRN option routes display to printer.

**Examples:**

```
TYPE B:PROGA.ASM         ;display PROGA.ASM from drive
                         ;B
TYPE PROGX.LST >PRN      ;display PROGX.LST from
                         ;default drive on screen and
                         ;printer
```

**VER (Version)   Syntax: VER**

**Explanation:** Display version number of DOS operating system.

## External Commands

**CHKDSK (Check Disk)   Syntax: CHKDSK [<drive:>] [<pathname>[ [/f] [/v]**

**Explanation:** Scan disk specified to check for errors. The /f option causes errors to be fixed. The /v option displays messages which CHKDSK is running.

**Examples:**

```
CHKDSK B: /f             ;check drive B: and fix errors
CHKDSK B:\PROG\ASSEM     ;check disk at pathname shown
```

## DISKCOMP (Disk Compare)   Syntax: DISKCOMP [<drive:>] [<drive>] [/1] [/8]

**Explanation:** Compare contents of disk on first drive to those on disk in second drive. If only one drive is named, the default drive is compared with it. If tracks are not the same, DISKCOMP names the track and side number where the mismatch occurred. The /1 switch compares only the first side of the disk. The /8 switch compares only the first eight sectors of each track.
**Examples:**

```
DISKCOMP A: B:          ;compare contents of drives A
                        ;and B
DISKCOMP A:/1           ;compare first sector of each
                        ;track on
                        ;drive A with default drive
```

## DISKCOPY   Syntax: DISKCOPY [<drive:>] [<drive:>]

**Explanation:** Copy contents of disk in first named drive to disk in second named drive. If both drives are the same, you are prompted to insert source disk and target disk at proper times. Copying takes place track by track, so that disks are not reorganized.
**Example:**

```
DISKCOPY A: B:          ;copy disk in drive A to one
                        ;in drive B
```

## EXE2BIN   Syntax: EXE2BIN [<drive:>] <pathname> [<drive:>] [<pathname>]

**Explanation:** Convert EXE file to COM format. If second <pathname> is omitted, output file is given same filename as EXE file and extension of BIN. The EXE file must have no stack segment.
**Example:**

```
EXE2BIN PROG1.EXE PROG1.COM ;convert PROG1 from EXE to
                            ;COM form
```

## FORMAT   Syntax: FORMAT <drive:> [/1] [/4] [/8] [/n:<xx>] [/t:<yy>] [/v] [/s]

**Explanation:** Format the disk in the specified drive to handle DOS files. This command makes a new disk usable and destroys all old files and reinitializes an old disk. The /1 switch formats only one side of a disk. The /4 switch formats a double-sided disk in a high-capacity drive. The /8 switch formats the disk with eight sectors per track. The /b switch formats the side with eight sectors per track and allocates space for the system hidden files. The /n:<xx> option specifies the number of sectors per track to place on a floppy disk. The /t:<yy> option specifies the number of tracks to place on a floppy disk. The /v switch causes a prompt for a volume label for the disk. The /s switch, which must appear last in the command line, causes the system files IO.SYS, MSDOS.SYS, and COMMAND.COM to be copied to the newly formatted disk.

**Examples:**

```
FORMAT B:                          ;format drive B
FORMAT A:/s                        ;format drive A and copy
                                   ;system files
```

**MODE**   Syntax: **MODE LPT<n> :[<char>][,[<lines>][,P]]**

**Explanation:** Set operation mode for parallel printer. <n> = 1, 2, or 3 to specify the printer port. <char> = 80 or 132 characters per line. <lines> = 6 or 8 lines per inch for vertical spacing. P causes MODE to try continuously to send output to the printer if a time-out error occurs. MODE can also be used with communications devices and the display monitor.

**Example:**

```
MODE LPT1:132,6                    ;set printer 1 to 132
                                   ;characters per line
                                   ;(compressed print) and 6
                                   ;lines per inch
```

# ASCII CODES

# D

| DECIMAL | HEX | CHARACTER | DECIMAL | HEX | CHARACTER |
|---------|-----|-----------|---------|-----|-----------|
| 0 | 0 | (null) | 32 | 20 | (space) |
| 1 | 1 | | 33 | 21 | ! |
| 2 | 2 | | 34 | 22 | " |
| 3 | 3 | | 35 | 23 | # |
| 4 | 4 | | 36 | 24 | $ |
| 5 | 5 | | 37 | 25 | % |
| 6 | 6 | | 38 | 26 | & |
| 7 | 7 | (beep) | 39 | 27 | ' |
| 8 | 8 | (backspace) | 40 | 28 | ( |
| 9 | 9 | (tab) | 41 | 29 | ) |
| 10 | A | (line feed) | 42 | 2A | * |
| 11 | B | | 43 | 2B | + |
| 12 | C | (form feed) | 44 | 2C | , |
| 13 | D | (carriage return) | 45 | 2D | - |
| 14 | E | (stop underline) | 46 | 2E | . |
| 15 | F | (start underline) | 47 | 2F | / |
| 16 | 10 | | 48 | 30 | 0 |
| 17 | 11 | | 49 | 31 | 1 |
| 18 | 12 | | 50 | 32 | 2 |
| 19 | 13 | | 51 | 33 | 3 |
| 20 | 14 | | 52 | 34 | 4 |
| 21 | 15 | | 53 | 35 | 5 |
| 22 | 16 | | 54 | 36 | 6 |
| 23 | 17 | | 55 | 37 | 7 |
| 24 | 18 | | 56 | 38 | 8 |
| 25 | 19 | | 57 | 39 | 9 |
| 26 | 1A | | 58 | 3A | : |
| 27 | 1B | | 59 | 3B | ; |

| 28 | 1C |   | 60 | 3C | < |
|----|----|---|----|----|---|
| 29 | 1D |   | 61 | 3D | = |
| 30 | 1E |   | 62 | 3E | > |
| 31 | 1F |   | 63 | 3F | ? |

Note: Some printers display graphics for some codes between 00 and 31 (00h and 1Fh).

| DECIMAL | HEX | CHARACTER | DECIMAL | HEX | CHARACTER |
|---------|-----|-----------|---------|-----|-----------|
| 64 | 40 | @ | 96 | 60 | ` |
| 65 | 41 | A | 97 | 61 | a |
| 66 | 42 | B | 98 | 62 | b |
| 67 | 43 | C | 99 | 63 | c |
| 68 | 44 | D | 100 | 64 | d |
| 69 | 45 | E | 101 | 65 | e |
| 70 | 46 | F | 102 | 66 | f |
| 71 | 47 | G | 103 | 67 | g |
| 72 | 48 | H | 104 | 68 | h |
| 73 | 49 | I | 105 | 69 | i |
| 74 | 4A | J | 106 | 6A | j |
| 76 | 4C | L | 108 | 6C | l |
| 77 | 4D | M | 109 | 6D | m |
| 78 | 4E | N | 110 | 6E | n |
| 79 | 4F | O | 111 | 6F | o |
| 80 | 50 | P | 112 | 70 | p |
| 81 | 51 | Q | 113 | 71 | q |
| 82 | 52 | R | 114 | 72 | r |
| 83 | 53 | S | 115 | 73 | s |
| 84 | 54 | T | 116 | 74 | t |
| 85 | 55 | U | 117 | 75 | u |
| 86 | 56 | V | 118 | 76 | v |
| 87 | 57 | W | 119 | 77 | w |
| 88 | 58 | X | 120 | 78 | x |
| 89 | 59 | Y | 121 | 79 | y |
| 90 | 5A | Z | 122 | 7A | z |
| 91 | 5B | [ | 123 | 7B | { |
| 92 | 5C | \ | 124 | 7C | | |
| 93 | 5D | ] | 125 | 7D | } |
| 94 | 5E | ^ | 126 | 7E | ~ |
| 95 | 5F | – | 127 | 7F | |

| Decimal | Hex | Character | Decimal | Hex | Character |
|---------|-----|-----------|---------|-----|-----------|
| 128 | 80 | ç | 160 | A0 | á |
| 129 | 81 | ü | 161 | A1 | í |
| 130 | 82 | é | 162 | A2 | ó |
| 131 | 83 | â | 163 | A3 | ú |
| 132 | 84 | ä | 164 | A4 | ñ |
| 133 | 85 | à | 165 | A5 | Ñ |
| 134 | 86 | å | 166 | A6 | ª |
| 135 | 87 | ç | 167 | A7 | º |
| 136 | 88 | ê | 168 | A8 | ¿ |
| 137 | 89 | ë | 169 | A9 | ⌐ |
| 138 | 8A | è | 170 | AA | ¬ |
| 139 | 8B | ï | 171 | AB | ½ |
| 140 | 8C | î | 172 | AC | ¼ |
| 141 | 8D | ì | 173 | AD | ¡ |
| 142 | 8E | Ä | 174 | AE | « |
| 143 | 8F | Å | 175 | AF | » |

| <u>Decimal</u> | <u>Hex</u> | <u>Character</u> | <u>Decimal</u> | <u>Hex</u> | <u>Character</u> |
|---|---|---|---|---|---|
| 144 | 90 | É | 176 | B0 | ▓ |
| 145 | 91 | æ | 177 | B1 | ▒ |
| 146 | 92 | Æ | 178 | B2 | ▓ |
| 147 | 93 | ô | 179 | B3 | │ |
| 148 | 94 | ö | 180 | B4 | ┤ |
| 149 | 95 | ò | 181 | B5 | ╡ |
| 150 | 96 | û | 182 | B6 | ╢ |
| 151 | 97 | ù | 183 | B7 | ╖ |
| 152 | 98 | ÿ | 184 | B8 | ╕ |
| 153 | 99 | Ö | 185 | B9 | ╣ |
| 154 | 9A | Ü | 186 | BA | ║ |
| 155 | 9B | ¢ | 187 | BB | ╗ |
| 156 | 9C | £ | 188 | BC | ╝ |
| 157 | 9D | ¥ | 189 | BD | ╜ |
| 158 | 9E | ₧ | 190 | BE | ╛ |
| 159 | 9F | ƒ | 191 | BF | ┐ |

| Decimal | Hex | Character | Decimal | Hex | Character |
|---------|-----|-----------|---------|-----|-----------|
| 192 | C0 | └ | 224 | E0 | α |
| 193 | C1 | ⊥ | 225 | E1 | ß |
| 194 | C2 | ┬ | 226 | E2 | Γ |
| 195 | C3 | ├ | 227 | E3 | π |
| 196 | C4 | ─ | 228 | E4 | Σ |
| 197 | C5 | ┼ | 229 | E5 | σ |
| 198 | C6 | ╞ | 230 | E6 | μ |
| 199 | C7 | ╟ | 231 | E7 | τ |
| 200 | C8 | ╚ | 232 | E8 | Φ |
| 201 | C9 | ╔ | 233 | E9 | Θ |
| 202 | CA | ╩ | 234 | EA | Ω |
| 203 | CB | ╦ | 235 | EB | δ |
| 204 | CC | ╠ | 236 | EC | ∞ |
| 205 | CD | ═ | 237 | ED | ø |
| 206 | CE | ╬ | 238 | EE | ε |
| 207 | CF | ╧ | 239 | EF | ∩ |

| Decimal | Hex | Character | Decimal | Hex | Character |
|---------|-----|-----------|---------|-----|-----------|
| 208 | D0 | ⊥ | 240 | F0 | ≡ |
| 209 | D1 | ⊤ | 241 | F1 | ± |
| 210 | D2 | π | 242 | F2 | ≥ |
| 211 | D3 | ⊔ | 243 | F3 | ≤ |
| 212 | D4 | ⊢ | 244 | F4 | ⌠ |
| 213 | D5 | ╒ | 245 | F5 | ⌡ |
| 214 | D6 | ╥ | 246 | F6 | ÷ |
| 215 | D7 | ╫ | 247 | F7 | ≈ |
| 216 | D8 | ╪ | 248 | F8 | ° |
| 217 | D9 | ┘ | 249 | F9 | · |
| 218 | DA | ┌ | 250 | FA | · |
| 219 | DB | █ | 251 | FB | √ |
| 220 | DC | ▄ | 252 | FC | ⁿ |
| 221 | DD | ▌ | 253 | FD | ² |
| 222 | DE | ▐ | 254 | FE | ■ |
| 223 | DF | ▀ | 255 | FF | |

# DEBUG REFERENCE

Microsoft DEBUG is a utility program that allows you to load, examine, test, modify, and write executable object files. You can execute a single instruction at a time or stop execution at any specified address. You can display and modify the contents of any register or storage location. You can assemble source statements that you type and unassemble machine instructions back into source statements. All numbers and addresses are hexadecimal.

DEBUG is normally found on the system disk holding DOS or MASM. To start it, place the system disk in drive A and the program disk in drive B and enter one of the following commands:

```
A> B:                      ;to make B the default drive
B> A:DEBUG or B> A:DEBUG [<filename> [<arglist>]]
```

With the first option, DEBUG loads the same address into CS, DS, ES, and SS registers and puts 100h into IP and FFEEh into SP. This is the format for a COM file.

With the second option, DEBUG loads the <filename> specified. The optional <arglist> contains parameters and switches that can be placed on the command line if <filename> were executed by DOS.

Each DEBUG command consists of a single letter, upper- or lowercase, followed by one or more parameters. The DEBUG prompt is a hyphen.

## DEBUG COMMAND SUMMARY

| Function | Command and Format |
|---|---|
| Assemble | A [<address>] |
| Compare | C <range> <address> |
| Dump | D [<range>] |
| Enter | E <address> [<list>] |
| Fill | F <range> <list> |
| Go | G [=<address> [<address>...]] |

| Hex | H <value> <value> |
|---|---|
| Input | I <value> |
| Load | L [<address>[<drive:><record><record>]] |
| Move | M <range> <address> |
| Name | N <filename> [<filename>] |
| Output | O <value> <byte> |
| Quit | Q |
| Register | R [<register-name>] |
| Search | S <range> <list> |
| Trace | T [=<address>] [<value>] |
| Unassemble | U [<range>] |
| Write | W [<address> [<drive:><record><record>]] |

## PARAMETER DEFINITIONS

| Parameter | Definition |
|---|---|
| <address> | Two parts consisting of either an alphabetic segment register or a four-digit segment address followed by a colon (:) and an offset value. The segment definition may be omitted, and the default segment is DS for all commands but G, L, T, U, and W, which use CS. |
| <byte> | A two-digit hex value to be placed in or read from an address or register. |
| <drive:> | A one-digit hex value to indicate a disk drive: 0 = drive A  1 = drive B  2 = drive C  3 = drive D |
| <list> | A series of <byte> or <string> values that must be the last parameter on the command line. |
| <range> | Two <address>es or one <address>, the letter L, and a <value>. The L <value> indicates the number of bytes starting at <address>. Omit segment reference from second <address> if two are used. |
| <record> | A one- to three-digit hex value designating the logical record number on disk and the number of disk records to be read or written. |
| <string> | Any number of characters enclosed in single or double quote marks. |
| <value> | One to four hex digits to specify a port number or the number of times a command is to be repeated. |
| [ ] | Optional parameters. |

## COMMAND DESCRIPTIONS

### Assemble (A)   Syntax: A [<address>]
**Explanation:** Assemble 8086/8088 mnemonics directly into memory starting at <address>. All numbers are hex. No labels may be used, but indirect addressing and segment overrides are allowed. DB and DW directives are allowed. Stop assembly by pressing <ENTER> alone.
**Example:**
```
        A 100                    ;assemble starting at CS:100
```

### Compare (C)   Syntax: C <range> <address>
**Explanation:** Compare memory within <range> with memory of same size starting at <address>. Display differences in this format:
```
        <address1> <byte1> <byte2> <address2>
```
**Examples:**
```
        C CS:200 240 CS:3F0     ;compare CS:200-240 with
                                ;CS:3F0-430
        C 300L20 400            ;compare DS:300-31F with
                                ;DS:400-41F
```

### Dump (D)   Syntax: D [<range>]
**Explanation**: Display contents of specified portion or memory. Each line shows the address of a 16-byte boundary in segment-offset form, followed by 16 bytes in hex form and then in character form. D without <range> displays eight lines starting after the last address displayed by the previous D command.
**Examples:**
```
        D CS:100                ;display 128 bytes starting
                                ;at CS:100
        D 200 2FF               ;display bytes DS:200-2FF
```

### Enter (E)   Syntax: E <address> [<list>]
**Explanation:** Enter byte values into memory at the specified <address>. If option <list> appears, values are entered automatically. If <list> is not present, DEBUG display the <address> and its current contents and awaits your input. You may:
1.   Replace the value with whatever hex digits you type.
2.   Press <SPACE> to advance to the next byte.
3.   Type a hyphen (-) to return to the preceding byte.
4.   Press <ENTER> to terminate the Enter command.
**Examples:**
```
        E DS:300 'this is a string.' ;enter string at DS:300
        E 100 <ENTER>
        1037:100 41.EB 42.<SPACE> 43.6E <ENTER>
                                     ;change 100 to EB and 102
                                     ;to 6E
```

**Fill (F)  Syntax: F <range> <list>**
**Explanation:** Fills bytes within <range> with values in <list>. If length of <range> is greater than length of <list>, values are repeated; if length of <range> is shorter, extra values in <list> are ignored.
**Example:**

```
F DS:0450 0464 20                    ;fill spaces (20h) in
                                     ;DS:0450-0464
```

**Go (G)  Syntax: G [=<address> [<address>...]]**
**Explanation:** Executes program presently in memory. G without <address>es executes program the same as outside DEBUG. The optional parameter = <address> is the starting point for execution; if it is omitted, execution starts at the address currently in IP. The next optional <address> is the breakpoint where program execution stops and the registers, flags, and next instruction are displayed. Up to 10 breakpoints may be specified.
**Examples:**

```
G                                    ;execute entire program
G 288                                ;execute from current IP
                                     ;to CS:288
```

**Hex (H)  Syntax: H <value> <value>**
**Explanation:** Perform hex arithmetic on two values specified and display results on one line, first the sum and then the difference.
**Examples:**

```
H 14 9
001D 000B                            ;14 + 9 = 1D ;14 - 9 = B
```

**Input (I)  Syntax: I <value>**
**Explanation:** Input and display a byte from port specified by <value>. <Value> may be up to four hex digits.
**Example:**

```
I 3B8                                ;input from port 3B8
```

**Load (L)  Syntax: L [<address> [<drive:> <record> <record>]]**
**Explanation:** Load a file from disk into memory. File must have been named in command line when DEBUG was loaded or by N command. L with no paramenters loads a COM file at CS:100 and sets BX:CX to the number of bytes loaded. L with <address> loads a COM file at the specified <address>. An EXE file is always loaded at the address specified in the file header. L with all parameters loads a file into <address> from <drive:> starting with the sector specified in the first <record> and loading as many sectors as specified in the second <record>. Values for <drive:>:

```
0=A    1=B    2=C    3=D
```

**Examples:**

```
N PROG4.EXE                          ;name of file to be loaded
L                                    ;load PROG4.EXE
```

```
       L CS:100 1 12 5C              ;load 92 records (5Ch)
                                     ;from drive B
                                     ;starting with record 18
                                     ;(12h)
```

## Move (M)   Syntax: M <range) <address>
**Explanation:** Move contents of memory block at <range> to block of same size starting at <address>. To avoid overwriting, for moves from lower <range> to higher <address>, data is moved starting with the higher addresses of <range> and working toward lower addresses. For moves from higher <range> to lower <address>, data is moved starting with lower addresses of <range> and working toward higher addresses.
**Examples:**

```
       M CS:100 120 CS:400          ;move CS:120 to CS:420 first
                                    ;and work downward
       M CS:400 450 CS:300          ;move CS:400 to CS:300 first
                                    ;and work upward
```

## Name (N)   Syntax: N <filename> [<filename>...]
**Explanation:** Assign <filename> to file to be loaded from or written to disk. Each <filename> after the first (if any) specifies names that might have been shown on a command line if <filename> were executed outside DEBUG. Always execute a name command before a load or a write command.
**Examples:**

```
       N B:PROG4.EXE                ;give name PROG4.EXE on drive B
       L                            ;load file
       N B:FILEX.DAT                ;give name of data file
       G                            ;execute B:PROG4 using
                                    ;B:FILEX.DAT
```

## Output (O)   Syntax: O <value> <byte>
**Explanation:** Send <byte> to output port specified by <value>. <Value> may be up to four hex digits.
**Example:**

```
       O 2E8 3F                     ;send hex 3F to port 2E8
```

## Quit (Q)   Syntax: Q
**Explanation:** Terminate DEBUG and exit to DOS. No parameters are required, and file is not saved.
**Example:**

```
       Q
```

## Register (R)   Syntax: R [<register-name>]
**Explanation:** Display the contents of one or more processor registers. If no <register-name> is specified, the contents of all registers and flags are displayed. If <register-name> is specified, the contents of that register are displayed and then a colon (:). You may press <ENTER> to leave the contents unchanged or type a <value> to change them. Only the following <register-

name>s are valid: AX, BX, CX, DX, SP, BP, SI, DI, DS, ES, SS, CS, IP, PC, and F. The flag (F) register is displayed showing each flag as a two-character alphabetic code. Change any flag by typing its opposite two-character code.

**Examples:**

```
R                       ;display all registers and flags
R AX
0000                    ;AX contains 0000
:20C5                   ;AX now contains 20C5
```

### Search (S)   Syntax: S <range> <list>

**Explanation:** Search <range> specified for bytes contained in <list>. The <list> may contain one or more bytes, separated by spaces or commas. Only the first address of the <list> is displayed if <list> contains more than one byte. All addresses within <range> are displayed where <list> occurs if <list> contains only one byte.

**Examples:**

```
S CS:100 200 EB         ;search CS:100-200 for EB
0137:135                ;EB found at 0137:135
0137:1B9                ;and 0137:1B9
S 0:0 FFF 0D 0A         ;search 0:0-FFF for 0D 0A
0000:0742               ;0D 0A found first at 0:742
```

### Trace (T)   Syntax: T [=<address>] [<value>

**Explanation:** Execute one instruction, display contents of all registers and flags, and display next decoded instruction. If the optional =<address> is present, tracing starts at that <address>. The optional <value> specifies how many instructions to trace.

**Examples:**

```
T                       ;trace only instruction
                        ;pointed to by IP
T =01BF 14              ;trace 20 (14h) instructions
                        ;starting at CS:01BF
```

### Unassemble (U)   Syntax: U [<range>]

**Explanation:** Disassemble bytes within <range> and display corresponding source statements with addresses and original bytes. The display resembles an assembler listing file (without comments). U without <range> disassembles 32 (20h) bytes starting at the address following the last previous U command. If <range> is a single <address>, then 32 (20h) bytes beginning at <address> are disassembled.

**Examples:**

```
U                       ;disassemble 32 (20h) bytes
                        ;from address where last U
                        ;ended
U CS:100 108            ;disassemble 9 bytes between
                        ;CS:100-108
```

**Write (W)   Syntax: W [<address> [ <drive:> <record> <record>]]**
**Explanation:** Write the file in memory to a disk file. If W has no parameters, BX:CX must contain number of bytes to be written, the file must have been named through DEBUG command line or N command, and the file is written from CS:100. If the optional <address> is given, the file is written from <address>. If full parameters are given, the file is written starting at <address> starting on <drive:> at logical record number specified by first <record> and continuing until the number of sectors specified by second <record> have been written. WARNING: Writing to absolute sectors bypasses DOS routines and can overwrite existing files. Values for <drive:>:

    0=A    1=B    2=C    3=D

**Examples:**

```
        W                       ;write named file from CS:100
                                ;or address to which loaded.
                                ;If new file, BX:CX must
                                ;contain length.
        W CS:100 1 2B 37        ;write file from CS:100 to
                                ;drive B, sector 2B,
                                ;continuing for 55 (37h)
                                ;sectors.
```

# ANSWERS TO EXERCISES

## CHAPTER 1

1.

| DECIMAL VALUES | BINARY PLACE VALUES | | | | | | | |
|---|---|---|---|---|---|---|---|---|
| | 128 | 64 | 32 | 16 | 8 | 4 | 2 | 1 |
| 31 | 0 | 0 | 0 | 1 | 1 | 1 | 1 | 1 |
| 57 | 0 | 0 | 1 | 1 | 1 | 0 | 0 | 1 |
| 84 | 0 | 1 | 0 | 1 | 0 | 1 | 0 | 0 |
| 106 | 0 | 1 | 1 | 0 | 1 | 0 | 1 | 0 |
| 127 | 0 | 1 | 1 | 1 | 1 | 1 | 1 | 1 |
| 155 | 1 | 0 | 0 | 1 | 1 | 0 | 1 | 1 |
| 189 | 1 | 0 | 1 | 1 | 1 | 1 | 0 | 1 |
| 240 | 1 | 1 | 1 | 1 | 0 | 0 | 0 | 0 |

2.

| DECIMAL VALUES | BINARY PLACE VALUES | | | | | | | |
|---|---|---|---|---|---|---|---|---|
| | 128 | 64 | 32 | 16 | 8 | 4 | 2 | 1 |
| 48 | 0 | 0 | 1 | 1 | 0 | 0 | 0 | 0 |
| 96 | 0 | 1 | 1 | 0 | 0 | 0 | 0 | 0 |
| 125 | 0 | 1 | 1 | 1 | 1 | 1 | 0 | 1 |
| −1 | 1 | 1 | 1 | 1 | 1 | 1 | 1 | 1 |
| −19 | 1 | 1 | 1 | 0 | 1 | 1 | 0 | 1 |
| −64 | 1 | 1 | 0 | 0 | 0 | 0 | 0 | 0 |
| −100 | 1 | 0 | 0 | 1 | 1 | 1 | 0 | 0 |
| −128 | 1 | 0 | 0 | 0 | 0 | 0 | 0 | 0 |

3.

| SIGNED BINARY INTEGER | DECIMAL VALUE |
|---|---|
| 01010101 | 85 |
| 10101010 | −86 |
| 00010011 | 19 |
| 11110000 | −16 |
| 10000001 | −127 |

4.

```
  00001111  15   00001010  10   00110011     51
 +00001100 +12  +00101010 +42  +11001101 +(-51)
  00011011  27   00110100  52   00000000      0


  11110000 -16   11001100    -52
 +00111100 +60  +11101011 +(-21)
  00101100  44   10110111    -73
```

5.  
```
  00101010  42  01100110   102  01111111     127
 +01000100 +68 +01000000   +64 +11111100   + (-4)
  01101110 110 *10100110   166  01111011     123


  01111111 127  10010101   -107
 +01010101 +85 +10111111  + (-65)
 *11010100 212 *01010100   -172
```

*indicates overflow

6.

|  | HEX PLACE VALUES | | | |
|---|---|---|---|---|
| DECIMAL VALUES | 4096 | 256 | 16 | 1 |
| 33 | 0 | 0 | 2 | 1 |
| 59 | 0 | 0 | 3 | B |
| 86 | 0 | 0 | 5 | 6 |
| 108 | 0 | 0 | 6 | C |
| 255 | 0 | 0 | F | F |
| 512 | 0 | 2 | 0 | 0 |
| 4095 | 0 | F | F | F |
| 5000 | 1 | 3 | 8 | 8 |

7.

|  | HEX PLACE VALUES | | | |
|---|---|---|---|---|
| DECIMAL VALUES | 4096 | 256 | 16 | 1 |
| 64 | 0 | 0 | 4 | 0 |
| 135 | 0 | 0 | 8 | 7 |
| 256 | 0 | 1 | 0 | 0 |
| 293 | 0 | 1 | 2 | 5 |
| 519 | 0 | 2 | 0 | 7 |
| 1195 | 0 | 4 | A | B |
| 3245 | 0 | C | A | D |
| 48889 | B | E | E | F |

8.  
```
  1234   5793   47AD   9999   FF29   BEAD
 +1345  +4321  +9904  +0BAD  +FFED  +DEAF
  1579   9AB4   E0B1   A546   1FF16  19D5C
```

9. 
```
Alton R. Kindred 41 6C 74 6F 6E 20 52 2E 20 4B 69 6E 64 72 65
     64
MS-DOS          4D 53 2D 44 4F 53
$1,234.56       24 31 2C 32 33 34 2E 35 36
IBM PC          49 42 4D 20 50 43
DEBUG           44 45 42 55 47
```

10. 
```
RAX <ENTER> 4328
RCX <ENTER> 0005 or 5
RES <ENTER> 4800
RSI <ENTER> 0060 or 60
RDX <ENTER> FFFF
```

11. U 7600:0100

12. E 7600:0100 <ENTER> 41 6C 74 6F 6E 20 52 2E 20 4B 69 6E 64 72
    65 64
    D 7600:0100

# CHAPTER 2

1. Program    Input Extension    Output Extension
   EDLIN         None            .ASM
   MASM          .ASM            .OBJ, .LST, .CRF
   LINK          .OBJ            .EXE, .MAP
   EXE2BIN       .EXE            .COM

2. code       segment
              assume cs:code
              org 100
   proga      proc near
              ...
   proga      endp
   code       ends
              end proga

3. stack      segment stack
              db 16 dup ('STACK    ')
   stack      ends

4. data       segment
   myname     DB 13,10,'Alton R. Kindred$'
   address    DB 13,10,'211 48th Street N.W.$'
   citystzip  DB 13,10,'Bradenton, FL 34209$'
   data       ends

5. A> EDLIN testfile
   1I
   1. this is the first line.
   2. This is line 2.
   3. Here is the original line 3.
   4. This is the next-to-last line.
   5. This is the last line.
   3I
   3. This is the inserted line 3.
   4. This is the inserted line 4.
   1L
   1. This is the first line.
   2. This is line 2.
   3. This is the inserted line 3.

```
4. This is the inserted line 4.
5. Here is the original line 3.
6. This is the next-to-last line.
7. This is the last line.
```

6. ```
   1,2,8C
   1,2D
   1L
   1. This is the inserted line 3.
   2. This is the inserted  line 4.
   3. Here is the original line 3.
   4. This is the next-to-last line.
   5. This is the last line.
   6. This is the first line
   7. This is line 2.
   ```

7. ```
   A> EDLIN B:EX7.ASM
   1I
   1. code        segment
   2.             assume cs:code
   3.             org 100
   4. ex7         proc near
   5.             mov ax,5
   6.             mov bl,300
   7.             int 20h
   8. <CTRL-Z>
   E
   A>MASM B:EX7.ASM,B:EX7.OBJ,B:EX7.LST;
   A>TYPE B:EX7.LST
   Change mov bl,300 to mov bx,300.
   ```

# CHAPTER 3

1. ```
   mov ah,1                        ;get character with echo
   int 21h
   mov ah,8                        ;get character without echo
   int 21h
   ```

2. <u>DATA:</u>
   ```
   prompt    db 13,10,'Enter up to 20 characters: $'
   buffer    db 21,?,21 dup (?)
   ```
   <u>CODE:</u>
   ```
           mov ah,9               ;display prompt
           mov dx,prompt
           int 21h
           mov dx,offset buffer   ;accept string into buffer
           mov ah,10
   ```
   ```

```
                int 21h
                mov dl,'A'                    ;move 'A' to DL
                mov ah,2                      ;display character in DL
                int 21h
```

4. <u>DATA:</u>
   down3   ` db 10,10,10,13,'$'`
   <u>CODE:</u>

```
                mov dx,offset down3          ;put address of control
                                             ;string in DX
                mov ah,9                     ;display string
                int 21h
```

5. <u>DATA:</u>
   prompt   ` db 'What is your name? $'`
   buffer   ` db 16,?,16 dup (?)`
   <u>CODE:</u>

```
                mov dx,offset prompt         ;get address of prompt in
                                             ;DX
                mov ah,9                     ;display prompt
                int 21h
                mov dx,offset buffer         ;put address of buffer in
                                             ;DX
                mov ah,10                    ;get response
                int 21h
```

6.

```
                mov dh,4                     ;set row 4
                mov dl,40                    ;set column 40
                mov ah,2                     ;set cursor
                int 10h
```

7.

```
                mov ch,12                    ;upper row of window
                mov cl,0                     ;upper left column of
                                             ;window
                mov dh,24                    ;lower row of window
                mov dl,79                    ;lower right column of
                                             ;window
                mov al,3                     ;number of lines to scroll
                mov bh,7                     ;white-on-black attribute
                mov ah,7                     ;scroll down
                int 10h                      ;scroll lower half down 3
                                             ;lines
```

8. <u>DATA:</u>
   hyphens   ` db '-----$'`
   <u>CODE:</u>

```
                mov dx,offset hyphens        ;get address of string
                                             ;into DX
                mov ah,9                     ;display the string
                int 21h
```

# CHAPTER 4

1. ```
Set number to 5
WHILE number <= 100
     Print number
     Add 5 to number
WEND
```

2.

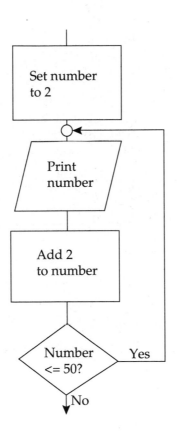
```

3.

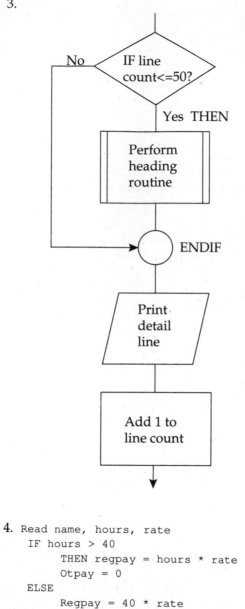

4. 
```
Read name, hours, rate
  IF hours > 40
      THEN regpay = hours * rate
      Otpay = 0
  ELSE
      Regpay = 40 * rate
      Otpay = (hours - 40) * rate * 1.5
  ENDIF
  Gross = regpay + otpay
```

5. <u>DATA:</u>
```
myname    db 13,10,'Alton R. Kindred$'
```
<u>CODE:</u>
```
          mov ax,0                    ;set counter in AX to 0
```

```
while:      cmp ax,5                ;WHILE counter < 5
            jge wend
            mov dx,offset myname    ; display name
            push AX                 ; save AX
            mov ah,9
            int 21h
            pop AX                  ; restore AX
            add ax,1                ; add 1 to counter
            jmp while
wend:                               ;WEND
```

6.
```
            mov bh,0                ;read cursor position
            mov ah,3
            int 10h
            mov dl,0                ;set to column 0
            add dh,1                ;set to next row
            int 10h                 ;move cursor
            mov cx,80               ;set counter to 80
repeat:                             ;REPEAT
            mov dl,'-'              ; move hyphen to DL
            mov ah,2                ; display hyphen
            int 21h
            loop repeat             ; subtract 1 from counter
until:                              ; UNTIL counter = 0
```

7. <u>DATA</u>:
```
prompt      db 13,10,'Set caps lock ON, then press any keys.'
            db 13,10,'Press ENTER to stop.'
crlf        db 13,10,'$'
```
<u>CODE:</u>
```
            mov dx,offset prompt    ;display prompt
            mov ah,9
            int 21h
            mov ah,8                ;get character without echo
            int 21h
while:      cmp al,13               ;WHILE character <> 13
                                    ; (ENTER)
            je wend
if01:       cmp al,'A'              ; IF character => 'A'
            jb endif01
and01:      cmp al,'Z'              ; AND character <='Z'
            ja endif01
then01:     mov dl,al               ; THEN move character to DL
            mov ah,2                ; and display it
            int 21h
endif01:                            ; ENDIF
            mov ah,8                ; get another
            int21h jmp while
wend:                               ;WEND
```

## CHAPTER 5

1.
```
                add ax,bx            ;add AX and BX
if01:           jc else01            ;IF no carry (unsigned
                                     ;overflow)
then01:         (other instructions) ; THEN do something
                jmp endif01
else01:                              ;ELSE
                (overflow routine)   ; do overflow routine
endif01:                             ;ENDIF
```

2.
```
                add al,byte1         ;add byte1 to AL
if01:           jo else01            ;IF no signed overflow
then01:         (other instructions) ; THEN do something
                jmp endif01
else01:                              ;ELSE
                (overflow routine)   ; do overflow routine
endif01:                             ;ENDIF
```

3.
```
                sub bx,3             ;subtract 3 from BX
```

4.
```
                dec bx               ;decrement BX 3 times
                dec bx
                dec bx
```

5.
```
                mov al,55            ;move 55 to AL
                mov bl,17            ;move 17 to BL
                mul bl               ;multiply AL by BL
                mov ax,55            ;move 55 to AX
                mov bx,17            ;move 17 to BX
                mul bx               ;multiply AX by BX
```

6.
```
                mov ax,65000         ;move 65000 to AX
                mov dx,0             ;move 0 to  DX
                mov bx,3             ;move 3 to BX
                div bx               ;divide DX-AX by BX
```

As written, divide overflow would not occur, since quotient will fit into AX and remainder in DX. An attempt to divide AX by BL would cause divide overflow, since the quotient is too large to fit into AL.

7.
```
                mov ax,5000h         ;move 5000h into AX
                mov dx,6h            ;move 6 to DX; dividend =
                                     ;65000h
                mov bx,3h            ;move 3h to BX
                div bx               ;divide DX-AX by BX
```

The dividend must be loaded into DX-AX in two parts. 65000h = 413696 decimal. Dividing by 3 gives a quotient of 21AAAh, or 137898 decimal, and will not fit into AX. This does produce divide overflow.

```
8.          and al,11101111b      ;set bit 4 to zero

9.          or ah,00001000b       ;set bit 3 to 1

10.         test bh,00100000b     ;test bit 5
            jnz endif             ;jump if not zero

11.         xor dx,11111111b      ;reverse bits in DX
   or       not dx                ;reverse bits in DX

12.         mov cl,8              ;set counter to 8
            rol ax,cl            ;rotate 8 bits of AH and AL
13.         mov cl,8              ;set counter to 8
            shr dx,cl            ;shift DH to DL and clear
                                 ;DH
14.         mov ax,12            ;AX=000Ch
            add al,37h           ;AX=0043h
            mov dl,al            ;DL=43h or 'C'
            mov ah,2             ;display byte in DL
            int 21h
```

# CHAPTER 6

```
1. stack      segment stack
              db 128 dup (0)
   stack      ends

2. 0080 = SP   when stack in Exercise 1 is loaded
   007E = SP   after first push
   007C = SP   after second push if no pop

3. sub1       proc near
              (subroutine statements)
   sub1       endp

4. sub1       proc near
              push ax
              push cx
              push dx
              (other statements)
              pop dx
              pop cx
```

```
                        pop ax
                        ret
            sub1        endp


   5. code         segment
                   public sub2
         sub2      proc far
                   (other statements)
                   ret
         sub2      endp
         code      ends
                   end


   6.              extrn suba:near,subb:near


   7. code         segment
                   public space5
         space5    proc near
                   mov dx,offset cs:string ;get address of control
                                           ;string
                        mov ah,9           ;display the string
                        int 21h
                        ret
         string    db 13,10,10,10,10,10,'$'
         space5    endp
         code      ends
                   end
         A> B:
         B> A:MASM SPACE5,,SPACE5;
         B> A:LINK MAINPROG + SPACE5,;


   8. B> A:LIB SUB.LIB + SPACE5,SUB.LST;
      B> A:LINK MAINPROG,,,SUB.LIB


   9. code         segment
                   public multx
         multx     proc near
                   mov ax,bx
                   mul cx
                   ret
         multx     endp
         code      ends
                   ends
```

10. <u>MAIN PROGRAM:</u>
```
                   extrn diffstk:far
                   ...
                   push word1
```

```
                 push word2
                 call diffstk
                 ...
SUBROUTINE:
code        segment
            public diffstk
diffstk     proc far
            push bp                      ;save BP
            mov bp,sp                    ;get BP address
            mov ax,[bp+8]                ;put first word into AX
            sub ax,[bp+6]                ;subtract second word
                                         ;from AX

            pop bp                       ;restore BP
            ret 4                        ;return and clear extra 4
                                         ;bytes

diffstk     endp
code        ends
            end
```

# CHAPTER 7

```
1.          mov ax,word1
            mov bx,word2
            mov word2,ax
            mov word1,bx


2.          mov cx,5                     ;set counter to 5
            mov si,offset array1         ;set address of array1
            mov di,offset array2         ;set address of array2
    repeat:                              ;REPEAT
            mov ax,[si]                  ; move first word of
                                         ; array1 to AX
            mov [di],ax                  ; move AX to first word
                                         ; of array2
            add si,2                     ; add2 to array1 address
            add di,2                     ; add 2 to array2 address
            loop repeat                  ; subtract 1 from counter
    until:                               ;UNTIL counter = 0
3.          mov bx,offset array1         ;put array1 address in
                                         ;base register
            mov di,offset array2         ;put array2 address in
                                         ;index register
            mov cx,10                    ;set counter to 10
            mov ax,2                     ;set array1 value (N) to 2
    repeat:                              ;REPEAT
            mov [bx],ax                  ; store array1 value
```

```
                    mov dx,ax              ; compute array2 value
                                           ; (N*2-1)

                    add dx,dx
                    dec dx
                    mov [di],dx            ; store array2 value
                    add bx,2               ; adjust array1 address
                    add di,2               ; adjust array2 address
                    add ax,2               ; add 2 to N
                    loop repeat            ; subtract 1 from counter
          until:                           ;UNTIL counter = 0

    4.              mov bx,offset array    ;set array row address
                    mov ax,10              ;set initial value for row
                    mov cx,5               ;set row counter to 5
          repeat1:                         ;REPEAT
                    mov di,0               ; set first column address
                    push cx                ; save row counter
                    mov cx,5               ; set column counter to 5
          repeat2:                         ; REPEAT
                    add ax,1               ; add 1 to value for row
                    mov[bx+di],ax          ; set value into row and
                                           ; column
                    add di,2               ; add 2 to column address
                    loop repeat2           ; subtract 1 from column
                                           ; counter
          until2:                          ; UNTIL column counter = 0
                    add ax,5               ; set initial value for
                                           ; next row
                    add bx,10              ; add 10 to row address
                    pop cx                 ; restore row counter
                    loop repeat1           ; subtract 1 from row
                                           ; counter
          until1:                          ;UNTIL column counter = 0

    5.              mov bx,offset array    ;set array address to
                                           ;first value
                    mov si,2               ;set index to second value
                    mov cx,19              ;set compare counter to 19
          repeat:                          ;REPEAT
                    mov ax,[bx]            ; move first value of
                                           ; pair to AX
          if01:     cmp ax,[bx][si]        ; IF first value > second
                                           ; value
                    jng endif01
          then01:   mov dx,[bx][si]        ; THEN move second value
                                           ; to DX
                    mov [bx],dx
                    mov [bx][si],ax
          endif01:                         ; ENDIF
```

```
                add bx,2                ; add 2 to address of
                                        ; first value
                loop repeat             ; subtract 1 from compare
                                        ; counter
until:                                  ;UNTIL compare counter = 0
```

6. <u>DATA:</u>

```
bytarray    db 100 dup (?)
count       db 0
average     db ?
```
<u>CODE:</u>
```
                mov count,0             ;set nonzero count to 0
                mov cx,100              ;set array counter to 100
                mov ax,0                ;set nonzero total to 0
                mov si,offset bytarray  ;set array address
repeat:                                 ;REPEAT
if01:           cmp [si],0              ; IF array value <> 0
                je endif01
then01:         inc count               ; THEN add 1 to nonzero
                                        ; count

              , add ax,[si]             ; add value to nonzero
                                        ; total
endif01:                                ; ENDIF
                inc si                  ; add 1 to array address
                loop repeat             ; subtract 1 from array
                                        ; counter
until:                                  ;UNTIL array counter = 0
                mov bx,count            ;move nonzero count to BX
                xor dx,dx               ;clear DX part of dividend
                div bx                  ;divide nonzero total by
                                        ;nonzero count
                mov average,ax          ;store quotient
```

7. <u>DATA:</u>

```
array       dw 100 dup(?)
large       dw ?
small       dw ?
```
<u>CODE:</u>
```
                mov large,-65535        ;set large to very small
                                        ;value
                mov small,65535         ;set small to very large
                                        ;value
                mov si,offset array     ;set address of array
                mov cx,100              ;set array counter to 100
repeat:                                 ;REPEAT
                mov ax,[si]             ; move array element to AX
if01:           cmp ax,large            ; IF AX > large
                jng endif01
then01:         mov large,ax            ;    THEN move AX to large
```

```
         endif01:                       ; ENDIF
         if02:       cmp ax,small       ; IF AX < small
                     jnl endif02
         then02:     mov small,ax       ;    THEN move AX to small
         endif02:                       ; ENDIF
                     add si,2           ; add 2 to array address
                     loop repeat        ; subtract 1 from array
                                        ; counter
         until:                         ;UNTIL array counter = 0
```

# CHAPTER 8

```
    1.              lea di,n1          ;put address of first
                                       ;number in DI
                    lea si,n2          ;put address of second
                                       ;number in SI
                    lea bx,n1          ;put address of sum in BX
                    mov cx,10          ;put number of words in CX
                    call multiadd      ;add the two numbers

    2.              lea di,n1          ;put address of first
                                       ;number in DI
                    lea si,n2          ;put address of second
  num-
                                       ;ber in SI
                    lea bx,n1          ;put address of
                                       ;difference in BX
                    mov cx,4           ;put number of words in CX
                    call multisub      ;subtract the two numbers
                    lea si,x1+10       ;point to sixth word of X1
                    lea di,x2+10       ;point to sixth word of X2
                    mov cx,6           ;put number of words in CX
                    call multicmp      ;compare the two numbers
         if01:      jne else 01        ;IF numbers are equal
         then01:    (instructions if equal)  ; THEN do equal routine
                    jmp endif01
         else01:                       ;ELSE
         if02:      jng else02         ; IF X1 is larger
         then02:    (X1 larger instructions)  ;    THEN do this routine
                    jump endif02
         else02:    (X2 larger instructions)  ; ELSE do this routine
         endif02:                      ; ENDIF
         endif01:                      ;ENDIF
```

4. 

| OPERATION | PARTIAL PRODUCT | FINAL PRODUCT |
|-----------|-----------------|---------------|
| 30972 * 1 | 30972 | 30972 |
| 30972 * 2 | 61944 | 650412 |

```
30972 * 3          92916              9942012
30972 * 4         123888            133830012
30972 * 5         154860           1682430012
```

5.              lea si,number+8          ;point to fifth word of
                                         ;number

                lea di,string           ;point to leftmost byte
                                         ;of string

                call hex5dec             ;convert number to string
                lea si,string+17         ;point to last 8 bytes of
                                         ;string

                mov cx,8                 ;set counter to 8
     repeat:                             ;REPEAT
                mov dl,[si]              ; move byte to DL
                call dspchr              ; display byte
                inc si                   ; add 1 to byte address
                loop cx                  ; subtract 1 from counter
     until:                              ;UNTIL counter = 0


6.              lea si,number+10         ;point to MSW of number
                mov cx,6                 ;set word counter to 6
     repeat:                             ;REPEAT

                mov dx,[si]
                push cx                  ; save word counter
                mov cx,4                 ; set counter for 4 digits
                call dsphex              ; display word in hex
                sub si,2                 ; point to next MSW of
     number

                pop cx                   ; restore word counter
                loop repeat              ; subtract 1 from word
                                         ; counter
     until:                              ;UNTIL word counter = 0


7.              mov al,128               ;move 128 (80h) to AL
                mov ah,0                 ;AX = 0080
                ...
                mov al,128               ;move 128 (80h) to AL
                cbw                      ;AX = FF80


8. <u>DATA:</u>
   n1           db 7,6,5,4,3
   n2           db 5,4,3,2,1
   sum          db 6 dup (?)
   <u>CODE:</u>

                lea si,n1+4              ;put LSB address of N1
                                         ;into SI

                lea di,n2+4              ;put LSB address of N2
                                         ;into DI

```
              lea bx,sum+5            ;put LSB address of sum
                                      ;into BX
              mov cx,5                ;set byte counter to 5
              clc                     ;clear carry flag
    repeat:                           ;REPEAT
              mov al,[si]             ; get byte of first number
              adc al,[di]             ; add byte with carry if
                                      ; any
              aaa                     ; adjust sum to ASCII
              mov [bx],al             ; store byte in sum
              dec si                  ; decrement addresses
              dec di
              dec bx
              loop repeat             ; subtract 1 from byte
                                      ; counter
    until:                            ;UNTIL byte counter = 0
              mov [bx],0              ;zero MSB byte of sum
              adc [bx],0              ;add carry if any to MSB
                                      ;of sum
```

```
 9.  mov ah,8         ;move 8 BCD to AH              AX = 08??
     mov al,5         ;move 5 BCD to AL              AX = 0805
     mov bl,7         ;move 7 BCD to BL              AX = 0805
     aad              ;adjust AX                     AX = 0055
     div bl           ;divide (quot.=12;rem.=01      AX = 010C
     aam              ;adjust quotient to BCD        AX = 0102
```

10. B>A:LINK PROG8 + MULTIADD + MULTINDC,,PROG8;

11. B>A:LIB SUBR.LIB + MULTIADD + MULTINDC,SUBR.LST;
    B>A:LINK PROG8,,PROG8,SUBR.LIB

# CHAPTER 9

```
 1.          std                     ;set direction flag for
                                     ;right to left
             mov ax,0FFFFh           ;move FFFFh to AX
             lea di,words+98         ;set destination address
             mov cx,50               ;set word count to 50
             rep stosw               ;move AX to 50 words

 2.          cld                     ;clear direction flag
             lea si,buffer+2         ;set source address
             mov cl,buffer+1         ;set byte count in CL
             mov ch,0                ;set byte count in CX
    while:   jcxz wend               ;WHILE CX <> 0
             lodsb                   ; move byte to AL and
```

```
                    mov dl,al              ; adjust addresses
                    call dspchr            ; put byte in DL
                    jmp while              ; display byte

          wend:                            ;WEND
```

3.
```
                    lods byte ptr ds:si
```

4.
```
                    cld                    ;clear direction flag
                    mov ax,0               ;move zeros to AX
                    lea di,words           ;set address of leftmost
                                           ;word
                    mov cx,100             ;set word count to 100
                    repnz scasw            ;scan words until zero
                    sub di,2               ;set DI back to zero word
```

5.
```
                    cld                    ;clear direction flag
                    lea si,first           ;set address of source
                                           ;array
                    lea di,second          ;set address of
                                           ;destination array
                    mov cx,25              ;set byte count to 25
                    rep movsb              ;move the 25 bytes
```

6.
```
                    rep movs second,first
```

7.
```
                    cld                    ;clear direction flag
                    lea si, first          ;set source address
                    lea di, second         ;set destination address
                    mov cx,25              ;set byte count to 25
          repeat:                          ;REPEAT
                    lodsb                  ; put byte in AL and
                                           ; adjust SI
                    stosb                  ; store byte from AL and
                                           ; adjust DI
                    loop repeat            ; subtract 1 from byte
                                           ; count
          until:                           ;UNTIL byte count = 0
```

8.
```
                    cld                    ;clear direction flag
                    lea si,input           ;set address of first
                                           ;array
                    lea di,output          ;set address of second
                                           ;array
                    mov cx,25              ;set count for 25 bytes
                    repe cmpsb             ;compare until different
                    dec si                 ;back up 1 byte in first
                                           ;array
```

```
                dec di                          ;back up 1 byte in second
                                                ;array
                inc cx                          ;back up counter
                mov dl,[si]                     ;display byte from first
                                                ;array
                call dspchr
                mov dl,20h                      ;display space
                call dspchr
                mov dl,[es:di]                  ;display byte from second
                                                ;array
                call dspchr
                mov dl,20h                      ;display space
                call dspchr
                mov dx,25                       ;move 25 to DX
                sub dx,cx                       ;subtract counter from 25
                call dspdec                     ;display position in
                                                ;decimal
```

# CHAPTER 10

1. DATA:
```
prompt     db 13,10,'Enter filename: $'
buffer     db 20,?,20 dup (?)
```
CODE:
```
                lea dx, prompt                  ;display prompt
                call dspline
                lea dx,buffer                   ;get filename
                call inpline
                mov al,buffer+1                 ;get string length
                cbw                             ;extend length to word
                mov di,ax                       ;put length in DI
                mov buffer+2[di],0              ;put zero at end of string
```

2. DATA:
```
filename   db 'b:testfile',0
errormsg   db 13,10,'Error on file creation $'
```
CODE:
```
                lea dx,filename                 ;get address of filename
                mov cx,0                        ;set normal attribute
                mov ah,3Ch                      ;create file
                int 21h
if01:           jc else01                       ;IF no error
then01:         (process file)                  ; THEN process file
                jmp endif01
else01:                                         ;ELSE
                lea dx,errormsg                 ; display error message
                call dspline
endif01:                                        ;ENDIF
```

3. <u>DATA:</u>
```
filename   db 'b:testfile',0
errormsg   db 13,10,'Error on file open $'
handle     dw ?
```
<u>CODE:</u>
```
           lea dx,filename        ;get address of filename
           mov al,0               ;access code for reading
           mov ah,3Dh             ;read the file
           int 21h
if01:      jc else01              ;IF no error on open
then01:    mov handle,ax          ; THEN save handle
           jmp endif01
else01:                           ;ELSE
           lea dx,errormsg        ; display error message
           call dspline
endif01:                          ;ENDIF
```

4. <u>DATA:</u>
```
filebuff   db 256 dup (?)
errormsg   db 13,10,'Error in reading file ?'
```
<u>CODE:</u>
```
           mov bx,handle          ;put handle in BX
           lea dx,filebuff        ;put buffer address in DX
           mov cx,256             ;set byte count to 256
           mov ah,3Fh             ;read the file
           int 21h
if01:      jc else01              ;IF no read error
then01:    (process if read OK)   ; THEN process record
           jmp endif01
else01:                           ;ELSE
           lea dx,errormsg        ; display error message
           call dspline
endif01:                          ;ENDIF
```

5. <u>DATA:</u>
```
oldname    db 'b:testfile',0
newname    db 'b:newfile',0
errormsg   db 'Error on rename $'
```
<u>CODE:</u>
```
           lea dx,oldfile         ;get address of old file
           lea di,newfile         ;get address of new file
           mov ax,ds              ;put data segment address
                                  ;in ES
           mov es,ax
           mov ah,56h             ;rename the file
           int 21h
if01:      jc else01              ;IF no error
then01:    (continue processing)  ; THEN continue
                                  ; processing
```

```
                    jmp endif01
        else01:                                 ;ELSE
                    lea dx,errormsg             ; display error message
                    call dspline
        endif01:                                ;ENDIF
```

6. <u>DATA:</u>
```
   filename  db 'b:newfile',0
```
   <u>CODE:</u>
```
                    lea dx,filename             ;put filename into DX
                    mov ah,41h                  ;delete the file
                    int 21h
```

7. <u>DATA:</u>
```
   message   db 13,10,'B: Bytes Available $'
   bytes     dw 5 dup (0)
   string    db 25 dup (?)
```
   <u>CODE:</u>
```
                    mov dl,2                    ;specify drive B
                    mov ah,36h                  ;get free disk space
                    int 21h
                    mul bx                      ;multiply AX by BX
                    mul cx                      ;then multiply AX by CX
                    mov bytes+6,ax              ;move product to 2 words
                                                ;in storage
                    mov bytes+8,dx
                    lea si,word+8               ;set address to most
                                                ;significant word
                    lea di,string              ;set address of leftmost
                                                ;byte of string
                    call hex5dec                ;convert words to
                                                ;character string
                    lea dx,message              ;display message
                    call dspline
                    lea si,string+19            ;set address of last six
                                                ;bytes
                    mov cx,6                    ;set counter to 6
        repeat:                                 ;REPEAT
                    mov dl,[si]                 ; move byte to DL
                    call dspchr                 ; display it
                    inc si                      ; add 1 to source address
                    loop repeat                 ; subtract 1 from counter
        until:                                  ;UNTIL counter = 0
```

8. birthday  date <01,08,1922>

9. address   struc
```
   myname    db 'Kindred,Alton R.      '
   street    db '211 48th Street N.W.'
```

```
           city       db 'Bradenton
           state      db 'FL'
           zip        dw '34209'
```

10. ```
    dummy      record field1:3,field2:4,field3:2,field4:1
```

| FIELD | BIT POSITIONS | WORD |
|-------|---------------|------|
| unused | 7-2 | 1 |
| field1 | 1-0 | 1 |
| and | 7 | 2 |
| field2 | 6-3 | 2 |
| field3 | 2-1 | 2 |
| field4 | 0 | 2 |

11. ```
    recorda    dummy <2,9,3,0>
```

12. ```
    wfield1    equ width field1        ;wfield1 = 3
```

13. ```
               or ax,mask field2       ;mask = 0000000001111000
```

# CHAPTER 11

1. ```
   stackseg   macro number
   stack      segment stack
              db number dup ('STACK    ')
   stack      ends
              endm
```

2. ```
   myname     macro
              db 'Alton R. Kindred',13,10
              db '211 48th Street N.W.',13,10
              db 'Bradenton, FL 34209',13,10,'$'
              endm
```

3. ```
   upcase     macro
              local if99,and99,then99,endif99
   if99:      cmp al,'a'
              jb endif99
   and99:     cmp al,'z'
              ja endif99
   then99:    and al,11111101b
   endif99:
              endm
```

4. ```
   wd500      macro
   value      = 100
              rept 5
              dw (value)
```

```
value       = value + 100
            endm
            endm
```

5. 
```
defarray  macro type,size,value
array&type d&type size dup (value)
          endm
```

6. 
```
          irp nbr,<1,2,3,4,5,6,7,8,9,10>
          dw (nbr*nbr*nbr)
          endm
```

7. 
```
swapwds   macro word1,word2
          ifdifi <word1>,<word2>
          push word1
          push word2
          pop word1
          pop word2
          endm
```

8. 
```
pack      macro
          and ax,0F0Fh
          mov cl,4
          shl al,cl
          mov cl,4
          shr ax,cl
          endm
```

# CHAPTER 12

1. 
```
B>A:MASM /B63K /D /L /C /V /X PROGX,,,;
```

2. 
```
SET INCLUDE=B:\SOURCE
```

3. 
```
          dosseg
          .model small
          .data
string1   db 'This string has a cursor return and line feed.
          ',13,10,'$'
string2   db 'This is an ordinary string. $ '
          stack 256
          .code
ex3       proc
          mov ax,@data
          mov ds,ax
          lea dx,string1
          mov ah,9
```

```
              int 21h
              lea dx,string2
              mov ah,9
              int 21h
              mov ax,4C00h
              int 21h
   ex3        endp
              end ex3
```

4. <u>STATEMENT</u>     <u>DEFAULT NAME</u>

| STATEMENT | DEFAULT NAME |
|---|---|
| .CODE | _TEXT |
| .DATA | _DATA |
| .DATA? | _BSS |
| .STACK | STACK |
| .FARDATA | FAR_DATA |
| .FARDATA? | FAR_BSS |

5. <u>MODEL</u>     <u>@CODESIZE</u>   <u>@DATASIZE</u>

| MODEL | @CODESIZE | @DATASIZE |
|---|---|---|
| Small | 0 | 0 |
| Medium | 1 | 0 |
| Compact | 0 | 1 |
| Large | 1 | 1 |
| Huge | 1 | 2 |

6. .STACK, .CONST, .DATA, .DATA? are automatically placed in DGROUP.

7.
```
   code        segment para, public, 'code'
   code        ends
```

8.
```
              .sall
              .lall
              crlf
              sall
```

9.
```
   a          label
   b          this byte
   c          equ a
   d          db(?)
```

10. If A = -5 and B = 3:

   a.  A + B = -2
   b.  A MOD B = -2
   c.  NOT B = -4
   d.  A AND B = 3
   e.  A XOR B = -8

   f.  A SHL 2 = -20
   g.  B SHR 2 = 0
   h.  A GT B = 0 (False)
   i.  6 EQ B SHL 1 = 1 (True)

11.
```
              mov segaddr,seg prompt
              mov offstaddr,offset prompt
```

12. <u>DATA:</u>
```
word1       dw 3456h
```
<u>CODE:</u>
```
            mov al,high word1
            mov bl,low word1
```

13. `array dw 25 dup (0)`
   a. `.type array = 00100011b`
   b. `type array = 2`
   c. `length array = 25`
   d. `size array = 50`

## CHAPTER 13

1.
```
            push bp
            mov bp,sp
            sub sp,10
```

2.
```
            mov cx,[bp+8]
            mov [bp-2],cx
            mov cx,[bp+6]
```

3.
```
            mov si,[bp+8]
            mov cx,[si]
            mov [bp-2],cx
            mov si,[bp-6]
            mov cx,[si]
```

4.
```
            lds si,[bp+14]
            mov ax,[si]
            mov [bp-2],ax
            les si,[bp+10]
            mov ax,es:[si]
            mov [bp-4],ax
            les si,[bp+6]
            mov ax,es:[si]
            mov bp-6,ax
```

5. 
```
var x, y, z: integer;
procedure subx(x, y, z: integer); extern;
subx(x, y, z);
```

6. 
```
MYSUB = &HF000
FOR I = 1 TO 48
  READ HEX$
  POKE &HEFFF = I, VAL ("$H" + HEX$)
NEXT I
```

7. 
```
INTERFACE TO SUBROUTINE ASSEMSUB [ALIAS: 'ASSEMSUB' (N1, N2)]
INTEGER*2 N1, N2 [NEAR, REFERENCE]
END
```

8. 
```
int short wd;
extern dspbin16 (short n);
```

```
       main ()
       {
       wd = 32517
       dspbin16 (wd);
       }
```

9. 
```
       ;------------------------------------------------------------
       ;                       _DSPBIN16 Subroutine
       ;------------------------------------------------------------
       ---
       ; This routine is designed to be called by a C program to
       ; display a 16-bit word passed by value. It requires a far
       ; call. At entry: BP-6 contains value of word.
       ;
       code       segment
                  assume cs:code
                  public _dspbin16
       _dspbin16 proc far
                  push bp                    ;push bp
                  mov bp,sp
                  push ax
                  push bx
                  push cx
                  push dx
                  mov bx,[bp-6]              ;get word into bx
                  mov cx,16                  ;set counter for 16 bits
       repeat01:                            ;REPEAT
                  rol bx,1                   ; move bit to carry
                  mov dl,30h                 ; move printable 0 to dl
                  adc dl,0                   ; add bit from carry
                  mov ah,2                   ; display the bit
                  int 21h
                  loop repeat01              ; subtract 1 from counter
       until04:                             ;UNTIL counter = 0
                  pop dx                     ;restore registers
                  pop cx
                  pop bx
                  pop ax
                  pop bp
                  ret                        ;return
       _dspbin16 endp
       code       ends
                  end
```

# CHAPTER 14

1. 
```
                  mov ax,0B000h             ;set monochrome address
                  mov es,ax
```

```
                mov   ah,70h              ;set black on white
                mov   al,' '              ;make character a space
                mov   di,0                ;set destination offset in
                                          ;DI
                mov   cx,2000             ;set counter for 2000 words
                rep   stosw               ;move 2000 words
```

2.
```
                mov   ah,6                ;set function to scroll up
                mov   al,0                ;scroll entire screen
                mov   bh,70h              ;set black on white
                mov   ch,0                ;upper left = column 0
                mov   cl,0                ;upper left = row 0
                mov   dh,79               ;lower right = column 79
                mov   dl,24               ;lower right = row 24
                int   10h
```

3. DATA:
```
  myname        db 'Alton R. Kindred'
  lmyname       $- myname
```
   CODE:
```
                mov   ax,0B800h           ;set color video address
   in ES
                mov   es,ax
                lea   di,2*4096+(12*80+0)*2;offset = page 2, line 12,
                                           ;column 0
                lea   si,myname           ;set source address
                mov   cx,lmyname          ;set length in CX
  repeat01:                               ;REPEAT
                mov   al,[si]             ; move source byte to AL
                mov   ah,6Eh              ; set attribute = yellow
                                          ; on brown
                stosw                     ; move byte and attribute
                                          ; to destination
                inc   si                  ; add 1 to source address
                loop  repeat01            ; subtract 1 from CX
  until01:                                ;UNTIL CX = 0
```

4. Base color video memory address   = B800h
   Page 3 x 1000h                     = 3000h
   Line 4 x 80 x 2 = 640              =  280h
   Column 20 x 2 = 40                 =   28h
   Total offset                       = 32A8h
   Address                            = B800:32A8h or BB00:2A8h

5.
```
                mov   ah,0                ;set mode
                mov   al,6                ;640 x 200 graphics
                int   10h
```

```
                mov ah,0Ch              ;write graphics pixel
                mov al,1                ;set pixel value
                mov bh,0                ;page = 0
                mov cx,310              ;center column - 10
                mov dx,100              ;center row
        repeat01:                       ;REPEAT
                int 10h                 ; write pixel
                inc cx                  ; increment column
                cmp cx,330
                jbe repeat01
        until01:                        ;UNTIL column = center + 10
```

6.
```
                mov ax,40h              ;set ES to 40h
                mov es,ax
                mov al,es:[10h]         ;get equipment flag 1
                mov video_memory,0B000h ;set monochrome buffer
                                        ;address
        if01:   test al,30h             ;IF bits 5-4 <> 1
                jne endif01
        then01: mov video_memory,0B000h ; THEN set color buffer
                                        ; address
        endif01:                        ;ENDIF
                mov ax,es:[63h]         ;get index register port
                                        ;address
                mov reg_port,ax
```

7.
```
                mov ax,0B000h           ;get monochrome address
                                        ;into ES
                mov es,ax
                mov ah,87h              ;set attribute to blink
                mov al,' '              ;set character to blank
                mov cx,80               ;set counter to 80
                mov di,(24*80+0)*2      ;set offset to line 24,
                                        ;column 0
                rep stosw               ;store 80 bytes with
                                        ;attributes
```

8.
```
                mov al,10               ;select register 10
                mov dx,3B4h             ;in port 3B5h
                out dx,al
                mov al,00               ;top scan line = 0
                mov dx,3B5h             ;write to register 10,port
                                        ;3B5h
                out dx,al
                mov al,11               ;select register 11
                mov dx,3B4h             ;in port 3B5h
                out dx,al
                mov al,07h              ;bottom scan line = 7
```

```
           mov dx,3B5h                ;write to register 11,
                                      ;port 3B5h
           out dx,al

  9.       mov al,1Ah                 ;set on bits 4,3,and 1
           mov dx,3D8h                ;of port 3D8h
           out dx,al
```

# MASM DIRECTIVES AND OTHER RESERVED NAMES

**Note:** A reserved name is a name having a special, predefined meaning to the assembler. All machine instruction mnemonics listed in Appendices A and B, register names, and words listed here in Appendix G are reserved names. Any use of one of these names as a symbol will cause the assembler to indicate an error.

## DIRECTIVES

**.186**  Enable assembly of instructions for 8086, 8087, and 80186 processors.

**.286**  Enable assembly of instructions for 8086 and 80287 processors and for nonprivileged instructions of the 80286 processor.

**.286P**  Enable assembly of earlier processors and also privileged instructions of the 80286.

**.287**  Enable assembly of instructions for 8087 and 80287 processors.

**.386**  Enable assembly of 8086 and 80387 instructions and nonprivileged instructions of the 80286 and 80386 processors.

**.386P**  Enable assembly of all instructions in .386, plus privileged instructions of the 80386.

**.387**  Enable assembly of instruction for 8087 and 80287 coprocessors and additional instructions and addressing modes for the 80387.

**.8086**  Enable assembly of instructions for 8086, 8088, and 8087 processors; disable assembly for special 80186, 80286, and 80386 instructions.

**.8087**  Enable assembly of instructions for 8087 coprocessor; disable assembly of instructions unique to the 80287 and 80387 coprocessors.

**ALIGN**  Pad object file so that next variable starts on even- numbered byte. May be used in form ALIGN *n*, where *n* must be a power of 2, to align on an address evenly divisible by *n*.

**.ALPHA** Specify that segments will be placed in object file in alphabetic order.

**ASSUME** Specify for each segment the address that should be in the segment register when the program is run.

**.CODE** Define start of code segment (simplified form) and end of any segment previously defined.

**COMM** Define communal variable that may be named in several modules but will be physically present in only one address.

**COMMENT** Tell assembler to ignore all text between the first specified delimiter and including the line containing the next appearance of the delimiter.

**.CONST** Define start of a constant-data segment and end of any open segment previously defined in source code.

**.CREF** Generate label, variable, and symbol cross-references from this point.

**.DATA** Define start of initialized near-data segment (simplied form) and end of any open segment previously defined.

**.DATA?** Define start of uninitialized near-data segment (simplified form) and end of any open segment previously defined.

**DB** Define byte or bytes and, optionally, specify initial contents.

**DD** Define one or more doublewords (four bytes) and, optionally, specify initial contents.

**DF** Define farword (six bytes). Normally used only with the 80386 processor.

**DOSSEG** Place segments in order according to DOS segment-order convention used by Microsoft high-level language compilers.

**DQ** Define one or more quadwords (eight bytes).

**DT** Define one or more tenwords (10 bytes holding 18 decimal digits).

**DW** Define one or more words (two bytes) and, optionally, specify initial contents.

**ELSE** Mark conditional block of statements to be assembled if condition specified by IF is not true.

**END** Close last open segment in source file and mark end of source file. In form END [startaddress], startaddress must be label of first instruction to be executed, usually the first instruction in the code segment. Only one startaddress may be given if there are several modules.

**ENDIF** Mark end of any conditional-assembly block.

**ENDM** Define end of a macro or repeat block.

**ENDP** Define end of a procedure.

**ENDS**  Define end of a segment or a structure.

**EQU**  Make named symbol equal to specified number, expression, or string. A string equate can be reassigned at assembly time, but a numeric value cannot be reassigned.

**= (equal sign)** Assign numeric constant to the named symbol. Value can be reassigned at assembly time.

**.ERR**  Force an error where the directive occurs in the source file.

**.ERR1**  Force an error during the first pass of the assembler.

**.ERR2**  Force an error during the second pass of the assembler.

**.ERRB**  Force an error if specified argument was not passed to a macro.

**.ERRDEF**  Force an error if specified name is defined.

**.ERRDIF**  Force an error if two specified macro arguments are different.

**.ERRE**  Test an expression and force an error if result is false (zero).

**.ERRIDN**  Force an error if two specified macro arguments are identical.

**.ERRNB**  Force an error if specified argument was passed to a macro.

**.ERRNDEF**  Force an error if specified name is not defined.

**.ERRNZ**  Test an expression and force an error if result is nonzero.

**EVEN**  Pad object file to align next variable on next even-numbered byte.

**EXITM**  Exit macro expansion before all statements in the macro have been assembled.

**EXTRN**  Specify symbol used in the current module but defined in another.

**.FARDATA**  Define start of initialized fardata segment and end of any open segment previously defined in the source code.

**.FARDATA?**  Define start of unitialized fardata segment and end of any open segment previously defined in the source code.

**GROUP**  Collect specified segments so as to have same starting address.

**IF**  Test value of expression and grant assembly if result is nonzero.

**IF1**  Grant assembly only on first pass of assembler.

**IF2**  Grant assembly only on second pass of assembler.

**IFB**  Grant assembly if specified argument was not passed to a macro.

**IFDEF**  Grant assembly if specified name was defined.

**IFDIF**  Grant assembly if specified macro arguments are different.

**IFE**  Test value of expression and grant assembly if result is false (zero).

**IFIDN**  Grant assembly if specified macro arguments are identical.

**IFNB**  Grant assembly if specified argument was passed to a macro.

**IFNDEF** Grant assembly if specified name was not defined.

**INCLUDE** Insert source code from specified file into source file at the point where the INCLUDE directive appears.

**INCLUDELIB** Pass message through MASM to LINK to name library file to be searched for routines to be linked to object module.

**IRP** Create repeat blocks for which number of repetitions and value of parameters for each repetition are specified in a list of arguments.

**IRPC** Create repeat blocks in which number of repetitions and value of arguments for each repetition are specified in a string.

**LABEL** Define code label at specific address, or define variable of a given size.

**.LALL** List all statements in macro expansions.

**.LFCOND** List false-conditional blocks in assembly listings.

**.LIST** List statements in program listing.

**LOCAL** Define symbol available only within the defined macro.

**MACRO** Define beginning of macro definition.

**.MODEL** Initialize memory model as SMALL, MEDIUM, COMPACT, LARGE, or HUGE. Must precede any other segment directive in source code.

**.MSFLOAT** Disable all coprocessor instructions and specify that initialized real-number variables be encoded in Microsoft binary format.

**NAME** (MASM prior to version 5.0.) Specify name of source module. No effect on version 5.

**ORG** Set specific address in location counter.

**%OUT** Direct assembler to display text on the standard output device.

**PAGE** Designate number of lines per page and characters per line of program listing. Without an argument, PAGE skips program listing to a new page. Followed by a plus sign, PAGE starts a new section number and resets page number to one.

**PROC** Specify start of a procedure. Must be NEAR or FAR.

**PUBLIC** Specify symbol defined in this module but used in another.

**PURGE** Delete one or more currently defined macros from memory.

**.RADIX** Set default radix for integer constants in the source file to be binary, octal, decimal, hexadecimal, or numbers of some other base.

**RECORD** Declare a record type for eight- or 16-bit record that contains one or more bit fields.

**REPT** Create specified number of repeat blocks. Block is ended with ENDM.

**.SALL**  Suppress listing of all macro expansions.

**SEGMENT**  Define the beginning of a segment.

**.SEQ**  Specify that segments will be placed in object code in the sequence they are written in the source code.

**.SFCOND**  Suppress listing of false-conditional blocks.

**.STACK**  Define stack segment of size given by operand (simplified form) and end of any segment previously defined.

**STRUC**  Mark the beginning of a type declaration for a structure.

**SUBTTL**  Specify subtitle for each page of assembler listings.

**.TFCOND**  Toggle current status of listing of false-conditional blocks.

**TITLE**  Specify title to be used on each page of assembly listings.

**.XALL**  List only statements in macro expansion that generate code.

**.XCREF**  Suppress generation of label, variable, and symbol cross-references after this point.

**.XLIST**  Suppress listing of object program.

## OTHER RESERVED NAMES

**& (ampersand) substitute operator**  Replace a parameter with its corresponding actual argument value when the parameter immediately precedes or follows other characters or appears in a quoted string.

**<> (angle brackets) literal-text operator**  Direct MASM to treat the enclosed list as a single string rather than as separate arguments.

**\* (asterisk) arithmetic operator**  Multiply expression1 by expression2.

**[] (brackets) index operator**  Specify that the enclosed base or index register is to be added to other operands to create an effective address.

**: (colon) segment override operator**  Force address of a variable or label to be computed relative to the specific segment preceding the colon.

**$ (dollar sign) operator**  Represent current location counter value.

**! (exclamation point) literal character operator**  Force the assembler to treat the following character literally rather than as a symbol.

**- (minus sign) arithmetic operator**  (a) Negative (unary); (b) subtract expression.

**% (percent sign) expression operator**  Direct assembler to compute the following argument as an expression and replace the text with the result.

**+ (plus sign) arithmetic operator**  (a) Positive (unary); (b) add expression.

**? (question mark) initializer** Specify that the value of a variable is undefined.

**; (semicolon) comment operator** Indicate that the following text is a comment for documentation only and is to be ignored by the assembler.

**;; (double semicolons) macro comment operator** Start a comment to appear in a macro definition but not in the expanded statements.

**/ (slash) arithmetic operator** Divide expression2 by expression1.

**AND—logical operator** Perform bitwise AND at assembly time.

**AT address—segment combine type** Cause all addresses defined in the segment to be relative to address specified.

**BYTE—(a) segment align type** Start segment on next available byte address. **(b) data type specifier** Specify that data operand contains one byte.

**'CODE'—segment class type** Associate segments having different names as belonging to CODE class and containing program code. Must be enclosed in single quotes.

**COMMON—segment combine type** Create overlapping segments having the same name by starting them all at the same address.

**'DATA'—segment class type** Associate segments with different names as belonging to DATA class.

**DWORD—(a) segment align type** Start segment on next available doubleword address (address evenly divisible by four). Normally used in 32-bit segments with the 80386. **(b) data type specifier** Specify that data operand contains four bytes.

**EQ—relational operator** True if expression1 is equal to expression2.

**FAR—distance type specifier** Specify that a label reference is both the segment and offset address of the label.

**FWORD—data type specifier** Specify that data operand contains six bytes.

**GE—relational operator** True if expression1 is greater than or equal to expression2.

**GT—relational operator** True if expression1 is greater than expression2.

**HIGH—type operator** Return high-order eight bits of an expression that evaluates to a constant.

**LE—relational operator** True if expression1 is less than or equal to expression2.

**LENGTH—type operator** Return number of data elements in a variable defined with the DUP operator.

**LOW—type operator** Return low-order eight bits of an expression that evaluates to a constant.

**LT—relational operator** True if expression1 is less than expression2.

**MASK—record operator** Return a bit mask containing 1s for the bit positions in a record occupied by the given record field.

**MEMORY—segment combine type** Join all segments having the same name to form a single, contiguous segment. (Identical to PUBLIC but not recognized by LINK.)

**MOD—arithmetic operator** Return remainder of expression1 divided by expression2.

**NE—relational operator** True if expression1 is not equal to expression2.

**NEAR—distance type specifier** Specify that a label reference is only the offset of the label.

**NOT—logical operator** Perform bitwise complement at assembly time.

**OFFSET—type operator** Return the offset address of an expression.

**OR—logical operator** Perform bitwise inclusive OR at assembly time.

**PAGE—segment align type** Start segment on next available page address (address evenly divisible by 256).

**PARA—segment align type** Start segment on next available paragraph address (address evenly divisible by 16). Default setting for processors, except 80386.

**PROC—distance type specifier** Specify that the label default type is near with full segment definitions; with simplified segment definitions, the default type is near for small and compact models, and far for medium, large, and huge models.

**PTR—type operator** Use with data type specifier to specify the data type an operand has.

**PUBLIC—segment combine type** Combine all segments having the same name into a single, contiguous segment.

**QWORD—data type specifier** Specify that data operand contains eight bytes.

**SEG—type operator** Return the segment address of any label, variable, segment name, group name, or other memory operand, but not with a constant expression.

**SHL—shift operator** Shift expression left specified number of bits at assembly time.

**SHORT—type operator** Set type of specified label to SHORT whenever distance of jump is less than 128 bytes.

**SHR—shift operator** Shift expression right specified number of bits at assembly time.

**SIZE—type operator** Return total number of bytes allocated for a variable defined with the DUP operator.

**STACK—segment combine type** Combine all segments having same name into single segment relative to SS segment register; initialize SP to length of segment.

**'STACK'—segment class type** Associate segments with different names as belonging to STACK class.

**TBYTE—data type specifier** Specify that data operand contains 10 bytes.

**THIS—type operator** Use with EQU or = (equal sign) directive to create an operand with offset and segment values are equal to the current location counter and type specified by data type operator for memory operands or NEAR, FAR, or PROC for labels.

**TYPE—type operator** Return code representing number of bytes in variable, structure, structure variable, label, or constant.

**.TYPE—type operator** Return a byte that defines the mode and scope of an expression.

**USE16/USE32—(80386 only) segment use type** Specify segment operand and address size of segment as 16 or 32 bits.

**WIDTH—record operator** Return width in bits of a record or record field.

**WORD—(a) segment align type** Start segment at next available word address (even-numbered address). (b)**data type specifier** Specify that data operand contains two bytes.

**XOR—logical operator** Perform bitwise exclusive OR at assembly time.

# EDLIN REFERENCE

# H

EDLIN is a line editor program supplied with DOS. It divides all text into lines, and each line can have up to 253 characters. Consecutive line numbers appear on the screen, but are not actually saved with the text file on disk.

You can use EDLIN to create new files; save them on disk; update existing files; delete, edit, insert, and display lines in files; and search for, delete, or replace text within one or more lines.

You issue commands to EDLIN. Each command consists of one letter (upper- or lowercase). Some commands have one or more options.

## EDLIN COMMAND OPTIONS

**line**   Indicates a line number that you type. Separate line numbers or other options by a comma or space. Line number may be written in any of three ways:

**<ENTER>**   A command without a line number uses a default value for each command.

**line**   Any number less than 65534. You can refer to line numbers relative to the current line: -1 refers to the line before the current line; +10 refers to the 10th line after the current one.

**period (.)**   The last line edited, i.e., the current line number.

**pound sign (#)**   The line after the  last line number used.

**?**   Used only with replace and search commands to tell EDLIN to ask you if the correct string has been found.

**string**   Used only with replace and search commands to represent text to be found. Each string must be ended with a <CTRL-Z> or <ENTER>. Only spaces that are part of the string should be included within the string.

**count**   Used with the copy command to specify the number of times a range of lines is to be copied.

## EDLIN COMMANDS

Each command consists of a single letter,which may be upper- or lowercase. Operands enclosed in brackets [ ] are optional. The format, explanation, and some samples of each command follow. Spaces before or after commands are optional.

### Append (A)   Format: [n] A

**Explanation:** Read *n* lines from disk and add to end of text. Meaningful only if file is too large to be read into memory at one time. After editing the original portion in memory, use write (W) command to free up memory for additional lines. If *n* is omitted, lines will be appended until memory is 3/4 full.

**Examples:**

```
100a                        ;append 100 lines
a                           ;append lines until memory
                            ;3/4 full
```

### Copy (C)   Format: [line1],[line2],line3[,count]C

**Explanation:** Copy a range of lines from line1 to line2 and place them ahead of line3 for the number of times indicated by count. If line1 or line2 is omitted, the current line number is assumed. If count is omitted, 1 is assumed. Lines following line3 are renumbered. Line numbers must not overlap.

**Examples:**

```
2,5,10c                     ;copy lines 2 through 5 ahead
                            ;of line 10.
,20,50,3c                   ;copy current line through
                            ;line 20 ahead of line 50
                            ;three times.
,,100,5c                    ;copy current line ahead of
                            ;line 100 five times.
```

### Delete (D)   Format: [line1][,line2]D

**Explanation:** Delete all lines in range line1 through line2. If both line1 and line2 are omitted, current line is deleted. Lines following the deleted lines are renumbered.

**Examples:**

```
1,5d                        ;delete lines 1 through 5.
                            ;Line 6 becomes line 1 and so
                            ;forth.
d                           ;delete current line only.
```

### Edit (E)   Format: line

**Explanation:** Display the specified line, and reprint the line number immediately below it. Use any of the editing commands (see Editing Commands) to edit the line. Press <ENTER> before making any change to accept the line as it is. Press <ENTER>in the middle of the line to delete the rest of the line.

**Examples:**

```
12                          ;display line 12 for editing.
<ENTER> only                ;display line after current
                            ;line for editing.
```

**End (E)  Format: E**
**Explanation:** Save text to disk under name given when EDLIN was loaded; end EDLIN and return to DOS. Rename original file with extension of .BAK as a backup file.
**Example:**

```
e                                ;save text and exit EDLIN.
```

**Insert (I)  Format: [line]I**
**Explanation:** Insert text before specified line and renumber following lines. When <ENTER> is pressed, next line number is displayed. Press <CTRL-Z> to leave Insert mode. If line is omitted, text is inserted before the current line.
**Examples:**

```
8i                               ;insert text at line 8.
#i                               ;insert at cnd of file.
i                                ;insert text before current
                                 ;line.
```

**List (L)  Format: [line1][,line2]L**
**Explanation:** Display on screen all lines from line1 through linc2. If line1 is omitted, display will start 11 lines before the current line and end with line2. If line2 is omitted, 23 lines will be displayed, starting with line1. If both line1 and line2 are omitted, 23 lines will be displayed, starting 11 lines before the current line.
**Examples:**

```
1,10L                            ;list lines 1 through 10.
,25L                             ;list from 11 lines before
                                 ;current line
                                 ;through line 25.
25L                              ;list 23 lines starting with
                                 ;line 25.
L                                ;list 23 lines starting 11
                                 ;lines before
                                 ;current line.
```

**Move (M)  Format: [line1],line2,line3M**
**Explanation:** Move all lines in range line1 through line2 to line before line3 and renumber all lines accordingly. If line1 or line2 is omitted, current line is used. Line numbers must not overlap.
**Examples:**

```
10,15,50m                        ;move lines 10 through 15
                                 ;ahead of line 50.
,+20,100m                        ;move current line plus
                                 ;20 lines ahead of line 100.
```

**Page (P)  Format: [line1][,line2]P**
**Explanation:** Page through the file 23 lines at a time or list specified blocks of lines. If line1 is omitted, paging starts at currents line + 1. If line2 is omitted, 23 lines are listed. The last line displayed becomes the new current line.

**Examples:**

```
1,200p                          ;page lines 1 through 200
                                ;showing 23
                                ;lines at a time.
52,70p                          ;display lines 52 through
                                ;70.
48p                             ;display 23 lines starting
                                ;at line 48.
,150p                           ;display from current line
                                ;+ 1 through line 150
                                ;showing 23 lines at a time.
```

### Quit (Q)   Format: Q

**Explanation:** Quit EDLIN without saving current text. EDLIN will issue prompt Abort edit (Y/N)?. Respond Y to quit or N to continue.

**Example:**

```
q
```

### Replace (R)   Format: [line1][,line2][?]Rstring1<Control-Z>string2

**Explanation:** Replace all occurrences of string1 with string2 within range line1 through line2. The string may be in the middle of another word or string. EDLIN displays each line that changes. If string1 is omitted on first replace, the command ends; otherwise, the previous value for string1 is used. If string2 is omitted following <CTRL-Z>, EDLIN replaces string1 with blanks; but if string2 is omitted following <ENTER> the previous value for string2 is used. If line1 is omitted, the search starts one line after the current line. If line2 is omitted, the default is the last line after end of file. The question mark (?) causes EDLIN to display the prompt O.K.? each time string1is found. A response of Y causes the replacement; any other response leaves string1 as it was.

**Examples:**

```
1,200r DOS<Control-Z>MS-DOS ;replace all occurrences
                            ;of DOS with MS-DOS within
                            ;lines 1 through 200.
r very<Control-Z><ENTER>    ;blank out all occurrences
                            ;of very between current
                            ;line and end of file.
r<ENTER>                    ;previous string1 becomes
                            ;previous string2 between
                            ;current line and end of
                            ;file.
```

### Search (S)   Format: [line1][,line2][?]Sstring<ENTER>

**Explanation:** Search range from line1 through line2 for string of text. The string may be in the middle of another string or word. If no question mark is typed, the line on which the string is found is displayed, becomes the current line, and the search ends. If the question mark is typed, EDLIN displays the first line with the matching string and the prompt O.K.? If you answer Y or

<ENTER>, that line becomes the current line and the search ends. With any other response, the search continues until another match is found or all lines have been searched. If line1 is omitted, the search starts with the line after the current line. If line2 is omitted, the search continues to end of file.

**Examples:**

```
5,10sand                    ;search lines 5 through 10
                            ;for and.
1,?sxyz                     ;search line 1 through end of
                            ;file for xyz. Display O.K.?
                            ;prompt if match.
```

**Transfer (T)   Format: [line]Tpathname**

**Explanation:** Transfer (insert) the contents of the disk file named pathname into file currently being edited at the specified line number. If line is omitted, the current line is used. The following lines are renumbered.

**Examples:**

```
50tb:sub1.asm               ;insert sub1.asm from drive b
                            ;before line 50.
tb:prog7.asm                ;insert prog7.asm from drive
                            ;b before current line.
```

**Write (W)   Format: [<n>]W**

**Explanation:** Write *n* lines to disk beginning with line1. This command applies only if the file being edited is too large to fit into memory. When EDLIN is started, only enough lines are read in to fill 3/4 of memory. To edit the rest of the file, you must write the edited lines to disk and load additional unedited lines by using the append command. If *n* is not specified, lines are written until memory is only 3/4 full. Remaining lines are renumbered, starting with line 1.

**Examples:**

```
500w                        ;write 500 lines to disk
                            ;starting with line 1.
w                           ;write lines to disk until
                            ;memory is only 3/4 full
```

## EDITING COMMANDS OR KEY

The *template* is a special area in memory where DOS commands and EDLIN lines of text may be placed. When an EDLIN line number is typed for editing, that line is placed in the template and displayed on the screen. The line number is repeated on the following line on the screen, and one or more of the following keys may be used to edit the line. MS-DOS provides names for special keys to carry out special editing functions with EDLIN text. In the listing below, the keys are those used on the keyboard for the Tandy 1000 TX. These function keys may be different on other keyboards.

| DOS Name | Editing Function | Tandy Key |
|---|---|---|
| <NEWLINE> | Enter the line. Make the new line the new template. | <ENTER> or <F5> |
| <INSERT> | Enter/exit insert mode. | <INSERT> |
| <SKIP1> | Delete character from template. | <DELETE> |
| <COPY1> | Copy one character from template to edited line . | <F1>or right arrow |
| <COPYALL> | Copy all remaining characters in template to edited line. | <F3> |
| <COPYUP> | Copy all characters up to specified character from template to edited line. | <F2>*char* |
| <SKIPUP> | Skip over and do not copy any characters in template up to specified character. | <F4>*char* |
| <VOID> | Void the current input and leave template unchanged. | <ESC> |
| <CTRL-Z> | Put end of file character in template. | <F6> or <CTRL-Z> |

## USING EDLIN TO ENTER A PROGRAM

To boot up DOS, place the system diskette into drive A and a formatted data diskette into drive B. Turn on the power, or, if already on, press <CTRL><ALT><DELETE>all  at the same time. Respond to prompts for DATE and TIME. At the A> prompt, place system diskette containing EDLIN into drive A.

To start EDLIN, type:

```
A>EDLIN B:progname.ASM
```

where *progname* is the name of your program. If progname is a new file, EDLIN will respond with:

```
New file
*
```

If progname already exists on disk,EDLIN will load it into storage so that you can add, modify, or delete the source statements.

The prompt for EDLIN is an asterisk (*), and the underscore indicates the cursor position. EDLIN accepts commands consisting of a single letter, which may be entered in either upper- or lowercase. The command may be preceded or followed by line numbers or other operands. Each source statement is assigned a line number automatically. The most recently entered or edited line number is the *current line,* and shows an asterisk (*) following the line number.

**Insert Command**   Use the I (insert) command to enter lines of text, one at a time. EDLIN displays the line number, followed by a colon. Enter a line and press <ENTER>. EDLIN will present the next line number and a prompt.

You can continue typing additional statements as EDLIN assigns new line numbers. Use the tab key to move to the tab positions preset by EDLIN. You can use the arrow keys or the insert or delete keys to edit anything on the line on which you are working. When you press <ENTER>, the current line is terminated and a new line number is displayed.  You can return to the EDLIN command level by typing the CTRL key and the letter Z at the same time <CTRL-Z>.

To insert one or more lines into existing text, precede the I command with the line number to be replaced. For example, to insert a new line 6 into the text, type:

```
*6I
```

EDLIN continues to provide new lines until you press <CTRL-Z>. If at line 8 you press <CTRL-Z>, then the original line 6 is now line 8, and the current line is line 7, the last one entered.

**List Command**   The L (list) command displays one or more lines on the screen. L without any other operand starts 11 lines before the current line and lists everything up to 11 lines beyond the current line. A line or a range of lines to be listed must precede the L command. 8L lists line 8 only. 1,5L will list the first five lines.

**Delete Command**   The D (delete) command erases one or more lines. Lines following those deleted are renumbered, so that line numbers are always consecutive. 4D deletes line 4. 5,10D deletes lines 5 through 10, and the previous line 11 now becomes line 5.

**Edit Command**   Typing any line number without a command allows that line to be edited. The full line is displayed, and the line number is repeated just below it. You may then retype the line as you wish. There are special editing codes and procedures that may be used. Refer to the section Editing Commands for further information.

**Copy and Move Commands**   You may copy or move lines to other places in the text using the C or M commands. The command 5,10,15C copies lines 5 through 10 starting at line 15 and continuing through line 20. The original lines 15–20 are renumbered to lines 21–25. The copy command does not destroy the original lines that are copied.

The M (move) command copies the designated lines into the last  line number specified and erases the original lines that were copied. The lines are renumbered according to the direction of the move. The command 20,30,100M will move lines 20–30 to line 100 (through 110).

**Leaving EDLIN**   There are two ways to leave EDLIN. The Q (quit) command returns to DOS without saving your text file on disk. The E (end) command saves the edited file on disk, renames the original input file (if any) as filename.BAK, and returns to DOS. You should always use E to exit EDLIN if you wish to save changes you have made during editing.

| Instruction | ZF | SF | CF | OF | AF | PF | DF | IF | TF |
|---|---|---|---|---|---|---|---|---|---|
| ADC, ADD, CMP, CMPS, NEG, SBB, SCAS, SUB | * | * | * | * | * | * | – | – | – |
| CALL, CBW, CWD, ESC, HLT, IN, JMP, conditional jumps, LAHF, LDS, LEA, LES, LOCK, LODS, LOOP, LOOPE,LOOPNE, MOV, MOVS, NOP, NOT, OUT, POP, PUSH, PUSHF, REP, REPE, REPNE, RET, STOS, WAIT, XCHG, XLAT | – | – | – | – | – | – | – | – | – |
| DEC and INC | * | * | – | * | * | * | – | – | – |
| AND, OR, TEST, XOR | * | * | 0 | 0 | ? | * | – | – | – |
| SAL, SAR, SHL, SHR | * | * | * | * | ? | * | – | – | – |
| RCL, RCR, ROL, ROR | – | – | * | * | – | – | – | – | – |
| DIV and IDIV | ? | ? | ? | ? | ? | ? | – | – | – |
| MUL and IMUL | ? | ? | * | * | ? | ? | – | – | – |
| AAA and AAS | ? | ? | * | ? | * | ? | – | – | – |
| AAD and AAM | * | * | ? | ? | ? | * | – | – | – |
| DAA and DAS | * | * | * | ? | * | * | – | – | – |
| INT and INTO | – | – | – | – | – | – | – | 0 | 0 |
| IRET and POPF | restore all 9 flags from stack | | | | | | | | |
| SAHF | restores ZF, SF, CF, AF, PF from AH | | | | | | | | |
| CLC, CMC, STC | – | – | * | – | – | – | – | – | – |
| CLD, STD | – | – | – | – | – | – | * | – | – |
| CLI, STI | – | – | – | – | – | – | – | * | – |

Legend: *flag is set according to result of instruction
- flag is not changed
? flag is randomly changed
0 flag is cleared

## Flag Names:

ZF = zero flag, set when result is 0.
SF = sign flag, set when leftmost bit of result is 1 (negative).
CF = carry flag, set when unsigned result is too large.

OF = overflow flag, set when signed result is too large.
AF = auxiliary carry flag, set when bit 3 carries to bit 4.
PF = parity flag.
DF = direction flag for string processing; 0= up, 1 = down.
IF = interrupt flag; 0 = enabled, 1 = disabled.
TF = trap flag; to enable interrupt 1 after each instruction.

## Flag Register Bit Positions:

```
15 14 13 12 11 10  9  8  7  6  5  4  3  2  1  0
 -  -  -  - OF DF IF TF SF ZF  - AF  - PF  - CF
```

# GLOSSARY

**Address**  The location of the leftmost byte of a segment, instruction, or data element in main storage.

**Address modification**  A method of altering the effective address of one or more operands between successive iterations of a loop by changing the contents of a base or index register.

**Align type**  A parameter in a SEGMENT directive that tells the assembler and linker how to select the starting address for the segment. The starting address may be a multiple of 1, 2, 4, 16, or 256.

**AND**  A logical operation in which a bit is set to 1 only if both corresponding bits in two operands are 1s.

**Applications software**  Programs designed to meet the specific needs of the user. Contrast with **System software.**

**Arithmetic-logic unit (ALU)**  The part of the central processing unit that carries out arithmetic operations, shifting of data within registers, and logical instructions affecting individual bits.

**Array**  A series of data elements of the same type each having the same number of bytes.

**ASCII**  The American Standard Code for Information Interchange, in which each group of eight bits represents a letter, digit, special information, or graphics character. Used mainly with microcomputers. Contrast with **EBCDIC.**

**ASCIIZ**  A file name in ASCII code ended with a byte of binary zeros.

**Assembler**  A computer program that translates statements written in assembler language into the machine language of a specific computer. Contrast with **Compiler.**

**Assembler language**  A low-level language in which each source statement normally is translated into a single machine instruction. It permits decimal numbers and names to be used instead of hexadecimal numbers and addresses.

**Assembly process**  Those steps necessary to write a program in assembler language and assemble, link, test, and execute it.

**Assembly time**  The period of time during which the assembler is translating the source statements into the machine language object code.

**AT**  A segment combine type that indicates that a segment address shall be at a specified memory location.

**Attributes**  The colors, intensity, and other characteristics of each character of the display screen. Each data byte on the screen has a corresponding attribute byte.

**Auxiliary carry flag (AF)**  A bit in the flag register set to 1 (ON) whenever there is a carry from bit 3 to bit 4 in a general register.

**Base register**  Either the BP or BX register on the 8088 processor, used to form part of the address of an operand.

**BCD (binary-coded decimal) data**  A form of representing numbers in which each decimal digit is represented in four bits. *See* Packed BCD data; Unpacked BCD data.

**Binary numbers**  A number system based on only the digits 0 and 1.

**BIOS (Basic Input/Output System)**  A group of routines accessed through interrupts that perform input and output functions for the keyboard, display screen, and other devices.

**Bit**  A shortened name for binary digit, which can be only 0 or 1.

**Body**  In macro definitions, the conditional assembly statements, data definitions, and machine instructions that determine the source statements to be generated when the macro is invoked.

**Boolean logic**  A system of symbolic logic based on the digits 0 and 1.

**Boot up**  To read the resident portion of the operating system from disk into main memory to begin or resume normal operations.

**Buffer**  An area of main memory in which data is placed coming from an input device or going to an output device.

**Byte**  One storage location capable of holding eight data bits.

**CALL**  An instruction which saves the address of the following instruction and then jumps to a subroutine.

**Called module**  A procedure or subroutine designed to do a specific task and return to the calling module. It usually receives data, or the addresses of data, to be processed. It ends with a RET (return) instruction.

**Calling module**  A procedure that contains a CALL instruction to invoke another procedure or subroutine to perform some useful task.

**Carry flag (CF)**  A bit in the flag register set to 1 (ON) whenever there is a carry out of the leftmost bit of a general register.

**Central processing unit (CPU)**  The heart of a computer system, containing the control unit and the arithmetic-logic unit, that directs the execution of instructions.

**Class type**  An assembler directive indicating how segments are to be grouped when loaded into memory. Segments having the same class type enclosed is single quotation marks are loaded contiguously.

**Code segment**  A portion of a program containing the instructions to be executed. The CS register contains the address where the code segment begins in main memory.

**Coding**  Writing the source statements of a computer program.

**COM program**  An executable load module in which the code, data, and stack are all in a single 64K segment. Contrast with **EXE program.**

**Combine type**  An optional assembler directive that states how segments with the same name will be combined.

**Command line**  A command to DOS that names a program to be executed along with optional parameters to be used by the program.

**COMMON**  A segment combine type that causes segments with the same name and the COMMON combine type to overlap beginning at the same memory location.

**Communication area**  An area of main memory reserved to hold information needed by BIOS about the specific hardware configuration of the system.

**Compiler**  A program that translates source statements in FORTRAN, BASIC, or other high-level languages into machine language. Contrast with **Assembler.**

**Compound condition**  A decision based on more than one comparison or set of relationships.

**Concatenation**  The joining together of two or more words or characters.

**Conditional assembly**  Statements within macro definitions that cause certain source statements to be generated or not, depending upon conditions encountered at assembly time.

**Conditional jump**  A machine instruction that causes control to be transferred to some instruction other than the next one in sequence based upon the setting of the flag register. Contrast with **Unconditional jump.**

**Control unit**  That portion of the central processing unit that decodes and executes machine instructions and directs the channel to carry out input/output instructions.

**Cross-reference listing**  An optional output of the assembler showing each name used in the program, together with its length, location, statement in which defined, and statements that refer to it.

**Cursor**  A small indicator, usually a rectangle, indicating the position where data is to be displayed on the screen.

**DASD (direct access storage device)**  A name normally applied to a disk drive.

**Data**  The basic figures or facts that are processed by a computer program into meaningful information.

**Data definition**   An assembler directive that gives the type, length, and value of constants or the length of storage areas required within a program.

**Data element**   A category of data, such as date, name, or amount due.

**Data segment**   An area of main storage containing data to be processed by a computer program. The DS register contains the lowest address of the data segment.

**DEBUG**   A DOS utility program useful for examining and testing load modules.

**Decimal digit**   One of the numerals 0–9.

**Desk checking**   A method of visually and mentally reviewing a source program for correctness before submitting it to the assembler.

**Destination field**   A data element that receives data moved or modified from some other location.

**Device**   A piece of equipment or hardware that is part of a computer system. Contrast with **Medium.**

**Diagnostics**   Messages printed by the assembler indicating errors in source programs and their possible causes.

**Direction flag (DF)**   A bit in the flag register indicating the direction in which string-handling instructions are to modify addresses in index registers:  0 designates ascending order; 1 designates descending order.

**Directive**   A statement telling the assembler to take some action at assembly time. Contrast with **Instruction.**

**Directory**   A logical subdivision of a disk. There may be one root directory and any number of subdirectories, which may be further divided into other subdirectories.

**Displacement**   A distance, expressed in bytes, from a base address.

**Display adapter**   A hardware device that acts as an interface between a character and attribute in main memory and the way that character appears on the display screen.

**Display screen**   The principal output device for a microcomputer. Also called video, screen, monitor, or visual display screen.

**Documentation**   Supporting papers that provide specifications and characteristics about systems and programs.

**DOS (disk operating system)**   *See* Operating system.

**Doubleword**   A 32-bit binary number.

**Duplication factor**   In a data definition, a number preceding the word DUP indicating the number of times that the data described is to be repeated.

**EBCDIC**   Extended Binary Coded Decimal Interchange Code. A method of representing digits, letters, or special characters with an arrangement of eight bits, used mainly on larger IBM computers. Contrast with **ASCII.**

**EDLIN**   A text editor, often provided on the same disk as an operating system or an assembler.

**Effective address**   The sum of the value in a segment register, a base register and/or an index register if used, and an offset in a machine instruction; the actual location of an operand.

**Environment variables**   Variables named in a DOS SET command that set options to be used when executing various programs.

**EQU (equate)**   A directive that causes one name to have the same value as another number or name.

**EXE program**   An executable load module organized so that the code, data, and stack occupy separate segments. This is the normal output of the linker. Contrast with **COM program.**

**Executable program**   *See* Load module.

**Execution time**   That period of time during which a computer program is run, or executed. Contrast with **Assembly time.**

**Extension**   One to three letters or digits that may be appended to a file name to classify it in some way. *See also* File name.

**External address**   An address needed by a program of some area or instruction that is not defined within the program.

**EXTRN (external)**   An assembler directive identifying procedures or data elements referenced in one program but defined in another.

**Far procedure**   A procedure whose address must be represented with both a segment address and an offset. Any number of far procedures may be linked together to form a program. Contrast with **Near procedure.**

**Field**   A division of a structure or record that holds one data element.

**File handle**   A number assigned by DOS to a file when it is created or opened.

**File name**   One to eight letters or digits giving a name to a disk file. *See also* Extension.

**Flag**   An indicator, usually a bit, that is set to 0 to mean OFF or FALSE, or to 1 to mean ON or TRUE.

**General register**   One of the registers AX, BX, CX, or DX, capable of performing binary arithmetic and logical operations and of shifting or rotating bits to the left or right.

**Graphics mode**   A method of dividing the display screen into a large number of rows and columns to permit many different shapes and figures to be represented. Contrast with **Text mode.**

**Group**   A collection of segments that must fit within a 64K segment of main memory.

**Handle**   *See* File handle.

**Hardware**   A general name for the equipment and devices of a computer system.

**Hexadecimal numbers**   A number system based on a set of 16 digits, represented as 0–9 and A–F, widely used to represent combinations of four bits.

**IF-THEN structure**   *See* One-way selection.

**IF-THEN-ELSE structure**   *See* Two-way selection.

**Immediate operand**   An operand consisting of an actual value instead of a register or main memory location.

**INCLUDE**   A directive to the assembler to insert at that point a file of source statements from disk and assemble them along with other source statements making up a program.

**Index register**   Either the SI or the DI register, which may contain a value to be used as part of an address along with a segment register, a base register, and a constant to form an effective address.

**Initialization**   Operations necessary to begin operations or to prepare for repetitive functions, such as clearing totals and setting initial values.

**Instruction**   An assembler statement giving an operation (op) code and one or more operands, translated by the assembler into machine language.

**Instruction pointer (IP)**   A register containing a value to be added to the code segment address in the CS register to point to the next instruction to be executed as the program progresses.

**Instruction set**   That group of instructions that any processor is designed to execute.

**Interrupt (INT)**   An instruction that causes the address of the next instruction to be saved, a segment and offset address to be fetched from the lower part of main memory, and a routine at that address to be executed.

**Interrupt flag (IF)**   A bit in the flag register that, when set to 1 or ON, permits interrupts to be handled; when set to 0 or OFF, interrupts are ignored.

**Invoke**   To use or call a macro, subroutine, or subprogram.

**I/O port**   *See* Port.

**K (kilobyte)**   A unit of 1,024 bytes, used to measure the capacity of main memory or of storage devices.

**Key**   A data element that uniquely identifies a record within a file.

**Label**   A name of an instruction in the code segment of a program.

**Library**   A disk file holding a collection of similar procedures or data. Examples include macro library, object file library.

**Linker**   A program in the operating system that can join two or more modules together and adjust addresses as necessary to permit communication among modules.

**Link map** A record produced by the linker showing the length and starting location of each module linked together to form a program.

**Load** To move the a program or file from disk into main memory. Contrast with **Save.**

**Load module** The output of the linker, consisting of one or more object modules with all addresses adjusted and ready for execution.

**Local data space** A portion of the stack used by a subroutine to hold data temporarily.

**LOCAL directive** In a macro definition, a statement requiring the assembler to replace named symbol with a unique name each time the macro is called. The name appears in the form ??nnnn, where nnnn can be from 0000h–FFFFh.

**Location counter** An accumulator used by the assembler to keep track of the address of each instruction and data definition in a program.

**Logical instructions** A set of machine instructions capable of modifying the content of individual bits within registers or memory locations.

**Loop** Another name for repetition structure or iteration structure. A series of instructions executed repeatedly until some condition causes termination.

**Machine language** A program in executable form. Op codes, addresses, and data are represented in binary form.

**Macro definition** A formal statement of instructions to be generated whenever a macro is used, or invoked.

**Macro instruction** A statement in assembler language that causes one or more other statements to be generated.

**Main memory** An area of numbered locations into which all data or instructions must be placed for processing by a computer.

**Map** *See* Link map.

**Mask** A code for processing data in which 1 indicates the position of a bit or byte to be processed and 0 indicates the position to be ignored.

**MASM** An assembler written by Microsoft.

**Medium** A type of material on which data is recorded, such as paper, magnetic tape or disk, or visual display screen. Contrast with **Device.**

**MEMORY** A segment combine type that causes all segments with the same name to be joined into a single contiguous segment.

**Memory dump** A display or printout of main memory and the content of certain registers and indicators in the computer.

**Memory model** One of six choices of default data and code sizes to make assembler object code compatible with object code of high-level languages.

**Mixed-language programming** The ability to write procedures in different languages, compile or assemble them into machine language, and link them into single load modules.

**.MODEL**  A directive allowing one of the six types of memory model, TINY, SMALL, MEDIUM, COMPACT, LARGE, or HUGE, to be selected for a program.

**Monochrome**  A type of display screen having one background color and one foreground color.

**Near procedure**  A procedure whose address requires only an offset. It must use the same segment address as the procedure that calls it.

**Nested IF statements**  A program logical structure in which either or both of the THEN or ELSE options in an IF structure contains one or more additional IF structures to determine what actions are to be taken.

**NOP (No-op)**  A machine instruction that does nothing but proceed to the next instruction in sequence.

**Number base**  *See* Radix.

**Numeric bits**  The four rightmost (low-order) bits of a byte. Contrast with **Zone bits.**

**Object code**  Machine language instructions and data constants created by a language translator such as an assembler or compiler.

**Object module**  The machine language output of a complete program or procedure from an assembler or compiler.

**Offset**  The distance in bytes between the address in a segment register and the address of a data element or instruction in main memory.

**One-way selection**  A type of conditional statement that causes one or more instructions to be executed if a condition is true but merely bypassed if the condition is false. Contrast with **Two-way selection.**

**Ones complement**  A binary number resulting from changing all the zeros to ones and all the ones to zeros in a register or memory location.

**Operand**  A register, memory location, or immediate value that is operated on by an instruction.

**Operation (op) code**  A reserved word, often an abbreviation, defining the action to be taken by an instruction.

**Operating system**  A collection of programs providing operations common to most applications, such as loading programs, performing input/output operations, maintaining libraries, and sorting records.

**OR**  A machine instruction in which a bit is set to 1 if either of the corresponding bits in two operands is a 1.

**ORG (origin)**  An assembler directive that permits the location counter to be set to some specified value.

**Overflow flag (OF)**  A bit in the flag register that is set to 1 whenever addition or subtraction of signed integers produces a result too large to be stored in the destination.

**Overlapping fields**   Two fields of data containing one or more bytes in common.

**Packed BCD data**   An arrangement of data in which two decimal digits are represented in one byte, each in a four-bit code. Contrast with **Unpacked BCD data.**

**PAGE**   A directive designating the line length and width of the program listing and also allowing a page break to take place.

**Page**   An area in main memory reserved to hold the characters and attributes to be displayed on the screen. Color/graphics adapters allow multiple pages.

**Palette**   A selection of colors available for use with color/graphics adapters.

**Parameter**   A name or number representing a value to be passed to a macro or a subroutine.

**Parity flag (PF)**   A bit in the flag register that is set to 1 when the number of 1 bits in a result is even and set to 0 when the number of 1 bits is odd.

**Path**   A combination of disk drive code, one or more directories, and a file name that tells DOS where to find a specific file on disk.

**Pixel (picture element)**   A small division of the display screen where one dot can be placed into a row and column position. Used in color/graphics displays. Various adapters allow as many as 640 rows and 480 columns of pixels.

**Place value**   The magnitude associated with a digit depending upon its position within a number. It is a power of the radix of the number system.

**Port**   A special type of memory holding data needed by communications, printer and disk control, timer, and other system features.

**Posttest loop**   A program logical structure in which certain statements are performed at least once before a condition is tested to see if they should be repeated. Contrast with **Pretest loop.**

**Pretest loop**   A program logical structure in which a test is made prior to performing the statements in a loop to see if they should be continued or terminated. Contrast with **Posttest loop.**

**PROC**   A directive indicating the start of a procedure. The ENDP directive must end the procedure.

**Procedure**   A division of the code segment of a program. Each program must have one main procedure and zero or more subprocedures.

**Processor**   *See* Central processing unit.

**Program flowchart**   A graphic representation of program logic using a limited set of symbols and connecting lines.

**Program segment prefix (PSP)**   A 256-byte area established by DOS preceding a load module that is loaded into main memory for execution.

**Pseudo-op**   *See* Directive.

**Pseudocode**   The use of ordinary English words, along with a few key words and indentation, to represent program logic.

**PUBLIC**   (1) A directive specifying that a procedure or data element may be referred to by another procedure. (2) A segment combine type causing all segments having the same name to be joined into a single contiguous segment.

**Radix**   The number of digits used in a number system. Also called the number base. The radix for binary numbers is 2, for decimal numbers 10, and for hex numbers 16.

**RAM (random access memory)**   Main memory of a computer into which data can be both placed and retrieved.

**Read**   To move data from an input device to main memory. Contrast with **Write.**

**RECORD**   A directive declaring the type for an eight- or 16-bit record containing one or more bit fields.

**Recursion**   The ability of a macro or subroutine to call itself to repeat tasks until some condition is met.

**Register**   A device in the central processing unit that may contain a 16- bit word to be used in arithmetic and logical operations or for addressing.

**Relative address**   The location of some byte or field in relation to some other location that is named, usually expressed as plus or minus a certain number of bytes.

**Repeat directives**   Three directives, REPT, IRP, and IRPC, that designate the start of a block of repeated statements that must be ended with the ENDM directive.

**REPEAT-UNTIL structure**   *See* Posttest loop.

**RET (return)**   An instruction used at the end of a subroutine to cause an orderly return to the calling procedure.

**ROM (read-only memory)**   A type of memory in which instructions and data can normally be placed only once and then read into RAM as needed.

**Root directory**   The first level of the directory structure of a magnetic disk. There may be any number of additional subdirectories.

**Run time**   That period of time during which a program is being executed. Also called Execution time. Contrast with **Assembly time.**

**Save**   To move a program or file from main memory to a disk file. Contrast with **Load.**

**Scan**   To search a string of words or bytes for a specific character or value.

**Scroll**   To move the lines on the display screen up or down to provide space for additional lines.

**Secondary storage**   Devices such as disk drives or magnetic tape units capable of storing data apart from the processor or main memory.

**Segment**   A division of a program, normally limited to 64K bytes, that holds data, code, or the stack.

**Segment/offset addressing**   A system of addressing memory by which the contents of a segment register is multiplied by 16 (10h) and added to an offset value.

**Segment register**   A register containing the address of the first byte of a segment.

**Selection structure**   *See* One-way selection and Two-way selection.

**Sequence structure**   A program logical structure in which instructions are executed one after another with no deviation.

**Sign**   A code indicating whether a number is positive or negative, normally the leftmost bit of a binary number.

**Sign flag (SF)**   A bit in the flag register that contains a copy of the leftmost bit of an operand after a comparison or certain arithmetic operations. A 0 bit indicates the result is positive, and a 1 bit indicates negative.

**Simplified segments**   A group of directives implemented with MASM version 5.00 reducing the number of statements needed to define segments.

**Software**   A general name for computer programs and supporting documentation.

**Source field**   A data element that is to be moved to another location called the destination or to perform some operation on the destination. Contrast with **Destination field.**

**Source statements**   Statements written by the programmer in some language that are to be translated into machine language by a compiler or assembler.

**Stack**   An area of main memory reserved for saving the contents of registers and memory locations during execution of a program.

**STACK**   A segment combine type causing all segments having the same name to be joined into a single contiguous segment with all addresses relative to the SS segment register. SP is initialized to the length of the stack.

**Stack pointer (SP)**   A register containing a value to be added to the address in the SS register to point to the top of the stack where the most recent word has been pushed.

**Stack segment**   A division of a program giving the name and size of the stack. The lowest address of the stack is placed in the SS register by DOS when the program is loaded.

**String**   A series of related bytes or words.

**STRUC (structure)**   A directive designating the start of a structure type, which is a collection of separate data elements, or fields, that can be accessed individually or as a group.

**Structured programming**   An organized method of developing and writing computer programs by constructing a hierarchy of procedures, each of which utilizes sequence, repetition, or selection structures.

**Subroutine**   A procedure to perform some specific task assembled with or linked to a procedure that calls it.

**Symbol**  The name assigned to a data element or instruction.

**System software**  *See* Operating system. Contrast with **Applications software.**

**Table**  An orderly arrangement of data consisting of a key, or identifier, for each entry, together with data elements giving attributes or characteristics of that entry.

**Text editor**  A program that permits creation of source programs and documents such as letters and reports.

**Text mode**  An arrangement of the display screen that normally allows 25 lines of 80 letters, numbers, or special symbols to be presented. Contrast with **Graphics mode.**

**Trap flag (TF)**  A bit in the flag register that when set to 1 allows DEBUG to halt a program after each instruction is executed.

**Truth tables**  An organization of alternate conditions, usually TRUE and FALSE or 0 and 1, to indicate the result of various compound conditions.

**Two-way selection**  A logical program structure in which one set of actions is taken if a condition is true and an alternate set if false. Contrast with **One-way selection.**

**Twos complement**  A binary number formed by changing all zeros in the original number to ones and all ones to zeros, and then adding one to the result. It represents the negative of the original number.

**Unconditional jump**  A transfer of control to some instruction other than the next one in sequence, without considering whether any condition is true or false. Contrast with **Conditional jump.**

**Unpacked BCD data**  An arrangement of data by which a decimal number is represented in the rightmost four bits of a byte, with the leftmost four bits being zeros. Contrast with **Packed BCD data.**

**Value**  The quantity or amount assigned to a constant or to a variable at any given time.

**Variable**  The name of an area in main storage whose value changes at different times during execution of a program.

**WHILE-WEND structure**  *See* Pretest loop.

**Word**  A 16-bit binary number.

**Word processor**  A program that assists in producing, editing, and printing text. Useful in preparing source programs.

**Wraparound**  A term applied to an operation where bits rotated out of one end of a register are moved back into the other end.

**Write**  To move data from main memory to an output device. Contrast with **Read**.

**XOR (exclusive OR)**  A machine instruction in which a bit is set to 1 only if the corresponding bits in two operands are unlike.

**Zero flag (ZF)** A bit in the flag register that is set to 1 when the result of a comparison or arithmetic is zero and set to 0 for nonzero results.

**Zone bits** The leftmost (high-order) four bits of a byte. Contrast with **Numeric bits.**

# INDEX

A 0
B 1
C 2
D 3
E 4
F 5
G 6
H 7
I 8
J 9